THE CONCRETE DRAGON

THE
CONCRETE
DRAGON

CHINA'S URBAN REVOLUTION
AND WHAT IT MEANS FOR THE WORLD

Thomas J. Campanella

PRINCETON ARCHITECTURAL PRESS

NEW YORK

For Tunney Lee

Published by
Princeton Architectural Press
37 East Seventh Street
New York, New York 10003

For a free catalog of books, call 1.800.722.6657.
Visit our web site at www.papress.com.

Project Editor: Clare Jacobson
Copy Editor: Dorothy Ball
Designer: Paul Wagner

Special thanks to: Nettie Aljian, Sara Bader,
Nicola Bednarek, Janet Behning, Becca Casbon,
Penny (Yuen Pik) Chu, Russell Fernandez,
Pete Fitzpatrick, Wendy Fuller, Jan Haux,
Aileen Kwun, Nancy Eklund Later, Linda Lee,
Laurie Manfra, Katharine Myers,
Lauren Nelson Packard, Jennifer Thompson,
Arnoud Verhaeghe, Joseph Weston, and
Deb Wood of Princeton Architectural Press
—Kevin C. Lippert, publisher

The Library of Congress has catalogued the
hardcover edition as follows:
Campanella, Thomas J.
The concrete dragon : China's urban revolution and
what it means for the world / Thomas J. Campanella.
— 1st ed.
    334 p. : ill., maps ; 24 cm.
Includes bibliographical references and index.
1. Urbanization—China. 2. Cities and towns—China.
3. Cities and towns—China—Growth.
4. Rural-urban migration—China. 5. Architecture
and society—China. 6. Social change—China.
I. Title.
HT384.C6C36 2008
307.760951—dc22
                                        2007029870

ISBN 978-1-61689-043-8
ISBN 978-1-56898-948-8 (digital)

CONTENTS

INTRODUCTION
The Urbanism of Ambition   12

CHAPTER ONE
Thunder from the South   26

CHAPTER TWO
Reclaiming Shanghai   56

CHAPTER THREE
The Politics of the Past   92

CHAPTER FOUR
Capital Improvements   120

CHAPTER FIVE
City of *Chai*   144

CHAPTER SIX
The Country and the City   172

CHAPTER SEVEN
Suburbanization and the Mechanics of Sprawl   188

CHAPTER EIGHT
Driving the Capitalist Road   216

CHAPTER NINE
Theme Parks and the Landscape of Consumption   240

EPILOGUE
China Reinvents the City   280

NOTES   303

INDEX   327

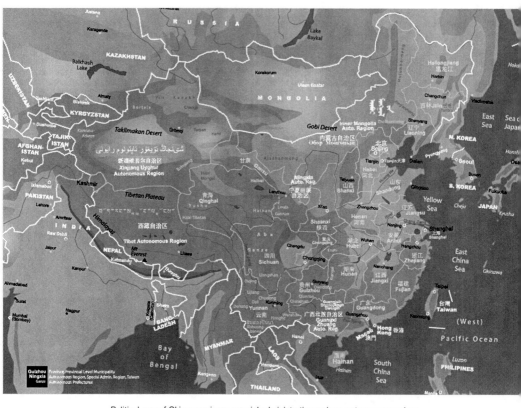

Political map of China: provinces, special administrative regions, autonomous regions, and autonomous prefectures. COURTESY OF JOHOMAPS.COM

ACKNOWLEDGMENTS

Many individuals helped bring this book about. First and foremost is Tunney F. Lee, professor emeritus in the School of Architecture and Planning at the Massachusetts Institute of Technology. In the early 1990s I had the good fortune of working with Tunney and his late wife, Irene, on a number of research projects at the Chinese University of Hong Kong, where Tunney had just launched a new department of architecture. Born in Taishan in the Pearl River Delta and raised in Boston's Chinatown, Tunney studied architecture at the University of Michigan and took a job with Buckminster Fuller's office in Raleigh, North Carolina, in 1954. He later worked for I. M. Pei and Marcel Breuer, and he helped build Resurrection City on the Washington Mall in 1968 before joining MIT'S Department of City and Regional Planning three years later. Tunney was among the first American architects to visit the People's Republic of China, and in 1980 he was part of the first official delegation of U.S. planners to visit the country—a group that also included Kevin Lynch, David Godschalk, Carol Thomas, Tridib Banerjee, and Donald Appleyard. One of the fruits of that trip was the MIT–Tsinghua University Beijing Urban Design studio, launched in 1985 and the first and longest-running teaching collaboration between a Chinese and an American university. It was the third such studio, in 1992, that first brought me to China.

Tunney has always been a source of sane and measured analysis of cities, and has more than once reeled in my hyperbole. When I first met Tunney in 1993, I told him I would like to one day write a book about Chinese urbanism. He responded with an irritating little parable about an American academic who "discovers" China: Upon his first visit, the scholar is ready to write a book; after visiting a second time, he decides to settle for an article. By the third visit, our erstwhile academic realizes he knows virtually nothing about China, and had better keep his mouth shut. I can't say I heeded Tunney's advice, but it did take a decade and many China trips to get that book out.

I must also thank Gary Hack and Jan Wampler, who codirected the 1992 studio, and my Tsinghua University *lao shi* (master teachers), Zhu Zixuan and Wu Liangyong. Mike Joroff, who directed MIT'S East Asia Architecture and Planning Program for many years, was also instrumental in facilitating my early travel to Hong Kong and the People's Republic. My good friend and mentor Jeff Cody has been a perennial source of wisdom and insight about Chinese urbanism, and also provided extensive comments on an early draft of this book. Daniel Abramson, another alumnus of the MIT Beijing studio, also deserves special thanks for assistance over the years, as do Wallace P. H. Chang, Anthony G. O. Yeh, Larry Vale, Andrew Li, and Shrinath Tandur. Several of my colleagues at the University of North Carolina–Chapel Hill helped bring this book to fruition, especially Yan Song, Meenu Tewari, Emil Malizia, Robin Visser, Dave Godschalk, Gang Yue, Peter Coclanis, Kevin Hewison, Udo Reisinger, and Christine Boyle. I also benefited from the counsel of many of my colleagues at Nanjing University's School of Architecture, especially Zhao Chen, Ding Wowo, Ji Guohua, Zhang Lei, and Zhang Qiang. For their input, guidance, and support I also thank Thomas Hahn, Bob Epting, Bill McDonough, Jerold Kayden, Ralph Gakenheimer, Wang Jun, Peter Rowe, Zhang Ming, Max Page, Mark Schuster, Fang Ke and Zhang Yan, Ronald Knapp, Annabel Leung, Nelson Chen, Michael Tomlan, Dennis Frenchman, Paul Wang, Tao Ho, Qing Shen, Zhan Guo, and Anne Patrone. Photographer Jiang Shigao generously allowed me to reproduce two of his extraordinary photographs of Shenzhen in the 1980s. My editor at Princeton Architectural Press, Clare Jacobson, helped shepherd this book to press with both charm and discipline. Finally, a large number of friends and family helped make the labor behind this book worthwhile. I thank especially Alfreda Stadlin, Michele Berger and Tim Keim, Wu Nong, Paul Kapp, Jean Riesman, Vishaan Chakrabarti, Uwe Brandes, Anthony Townsend, Roy Strickland, Wing-sze Cheung, and Jamie Morano. And above all I thank my parents, Mario and Rose Campanella, for their innumerable gifts over the years; my brother and fellow urbanist, Richard Campanella; and the sunbeam of my life, Wu Wei, without whom this book—and its author—would be sad work indeed.

This book was enriched, directly and indirectly, by funding from the Kelly-Webb Trust, the Paul Sun Endowment Fund, the Albert Kunstadter

Family Foundation, the Rockefeller Brothers Fund, and a Fulbright Fellowship from the Institute for International Education. Grants from the Carolina Asia Center, the University Research Council, and the College of Arts and Sciences at UNC also helped support field work and preparation of the finished manuscript. For all this, I am most grateful.

Following spread: Migrant worker on demolition site, Nanjing, Gulou District, 2006; the demolished buildings were part of the last old neighborhood in the center city. PHOTOGRAPH BY AUTHOR

"Into the ruthless centrifuge of change."

–Carl Schorske

The Urbanism of Ambition

走向城市化的雄心

In the first few months of 2007, a remarkable story began spreading around China, largely via internet bulletin boards, bloggers, and cell phone instant messaging. It involved a plucky restaurateur named Wu Ping, whose Chongqing house had been condemned for a commercial mixed-use development. The woman refused all offers of compensation from the real estate developer and steadfastly defended her property even as the neighboring structures were pulled down one by one. By mid-March, her house stood alone at the center of a vast crater of mud and rubble. As the construction pit deepened, the structure slowly rose in prominence until it loomed defiantly over the entire site. Though forced to vacate the property, Wu Ping took her case to the media; dressed in a blazing red coat, she stood in front of news crews and cameramen waving her lease and demanding that the government make good on a groundbreaking new law, enacted only days before on March 16, 2007, that strengthened private property rights in China. Wu Ping's husband added to the drama by planting an oversized Chinese flag on the roof of the house and draping a banner across the front that read "A citizen's legal property is not to be encroached upon!"[1]

The case touched a national nerve, one rubbed raw by three decades of often cataclysmic development in China's major cities. Wu Ping's courageous act of defiance voiced the pent-up rage of millions of Chinese whose homes have been sacrificed in the nation's wholesale rush toward a gleaming urban future. The woman—and her house—became widely known as "the most stubborn nail in history" (*shi shang zui niu de ding zi hu*). The singular, unforgettable image of the "nail house" alone in the middle of an excavated pit is the very picture of resistance and immediately calls to mind that brave young man who stood down a

Wu Ping's "stubborn nail," Chongqing, 2007. GETTY IMAGES

tank on Chang'an Boulevard in June 1989. I relate this story because it touches on so many essential themes related to city making and urban redevelopment in China's post-Mao era—an age of unprecedented economic growth and societal transformation that has shaken both China and the world.

To write about China's urban revolution is to traffic in superlatives. Over the last twenty years, the People's Republic has undergone the greatest period of urban growth and transformation in history. Since the 1980s, China has built more skyscrapers; more office buildings; more shopping malls and hotels; more housing estates and gated communities; more highways, bridges, subways, and tunnels; more public parks, playgrounds, squares, and plazas; more golf courses and resorts and theme parks than any other nation on earth—indeed, than probably all other nations combined.

The number and size of cities alone is staggering. There were fewer than 200 cities in China in the late 1970s; today there are nearly 700. Many of these are simply reclassified towns and counties, but even the smallest among them are immense by American standards. Forty-six Chinese cities passed the one-million mark since 1992, making for a national total of 102 cities with more than a million residents. In the United States we have all of nine such cities. There are scores of Chinese cities most Americans have never heard of that rank with our largest. Guiyang and Jinan, for example, are roughly the same size as Phoenix and Philadelphia, and Hefei and Wuxi—middling cities in China—each exceeds Los Angeles in population. What makes this all the more extraordinary is that only about 38 percent of the Chinese population is currently urban, as opposed to 80 percent in the United States. An equivalent urban population in China—80 percent of the total—would mean more than one billion city dwellers.

In other words, China's urban revolution is just getting under way. Bigness and supersized sprawl may have once been American specialties, but that monopoly has been usurped. China is now home to the world's biggest airport and largest shopping mall, as well as some of the planet's tallest buildings and longest bridges; it boasts the world's largest automobile showrooms and the biggest gated community; it has built the most expansive golf course on earth and the biggest bowling alley, and even the world's largest skateboard park. The controversial Three Gorges Dam on the Yangtze River makes Boston's Big Dig look like child's play—a mega project that displaced more than one million people and destroyed nearly a dozen cities.[2]

China has indeed redefined the meaning of Joseph Schumpeter's much-quoted phrase "creative destruction," razing more urban fabric in its twenty-year building binge than any nation in peacetime—and easily surpassing the losses, human and physical, of urban renewal in America. In Shanghai alone, redevelopment projects in the 1990s displaced more people than thirty years of urban renewal in the United States.[3] Not even mountains can stand in the way of China's urban ambition. In 1997, a Lanzhou entrepreneur named Zhu Qihua launched a campaign to remove 900-foot Big Green Mountain, located on the outskirts of town, so that winds could flush clean the city's heavily polluted air. As one city resident, cheered by Zhu's bold scheme, put it, "If removing that mountain can do the trick, then get rid of the mountain. Get rid of them all." In the summit's stead would be built a 500-acre industrial park.[4]

Indeed, in terms of speed and scale and sheer audacity, China's urban revolution is off the charts of Western or even global experience. China is in the midst of a wholesale reinvention of the city as we know it, forcing urbanists worldwide to recalibrate their most basic tools and assumptions and develop a whole new vocabulary for describing and critiquing urban phenomena. In China precedents and practices may be borrowed willy-nilly from other cultures, but they undergo a process of transmutation that renders them both familiar and thoroughly Chinese at the same time. The only place remotely comparable to China today is Dubai, which, thanks to our addiction to oil, has been growing by leaps and bounds in recent years. But Dubai is a tiny city-state of just over a million people. China is a hundred Dubais, with a thousand times its ambition.

The numbers speak for themselves. In 2003 alone, China put up 28 billion square feet of new housing—one eighth of the housing stock of the United States.[5] In the year 2004 alone, some $400 billion was spent on construction projects in the People's Republic, nearly the total gross domestic product (GDP) of sub-Saharan Africa that year.[6] There were virtually no modern high-rise office towers in Shanghai in 1980; today it has more than twice as many as New York City.[7] According to the Shanghai statistics bureau, some 925 million square feet of new building floor space was added to the city between 1990 and 2004, equivalent to 334 Empire State Buildings. By the end of the 1990s, Shanghai had more than 23,000 construction sites scattered across the city. Nationwide, China's construction industry employs a workforce equal to the population of California.[8] Nearly half the world's steel and cement is devoured by China, a level of demand that sends shock waves through the global build-ing-supply chain.[9] Much of the world's heavy construction equipment is in China, and the tower crane is such a ubiquitous presence on the skyline that people call it China's national bird (a particular irony, given the esteemed place of cranes—the feathered sort—in classical Chinese painting).

China had a mere 180 miles of modern motorway in the 1980s; today its National Trunk Highway System spans nearly 30,000 miles and is sec-ond in length only to America's interstate system. By 2020, China will likely have 53,000 miles of national-level highway, surpassing the United States as the most freeway-laced nation on earth.[10] Even Mt. Everest is being scaled by the hydra of Chinese asphalt. In June 2007, plans were announced for a 67-mile, $20 million highway winding up from the foot of the mountain to a base camp at 17,000 feet. The finished road will be part of the 2008 Olympic torch relay (itself the longest in Olympic history, encompassing five continents and 85,000 miles), but is also designed to make it easier for "tourists and moun-taineers" to consume the once-remote peak.[11] Other roads have been ham-mered through some of the most dense and populous urban neighborhoods in the world, forcing the relocation of tens of thousands of families. Again, the American urban experience is quickly exceeded here. In Shanghai, the con-struction of a single section of the Inner Ring Road, through the Luwan and Huangpu districts—a mere two-mile run—displaced an estimated 12,000 people—many more than were displaced along the entire route of the much-lamented Cross Bronx Expressway in New York, the first major American highway built through dense urban terrain.[12] How unsettling to see the most egregious, much-studied monuments of Western planning practice suddenly rendered insignificant! Robert Moses at his megalomaniacal max is tame in comparison to China. In his entire master-builder career, Moses constructed some 415 miles of highway in the New York metropolitan region; Shanghai offi-cials built well over three times that amount in the 1990s alone.[13]

Given all these new roads, its hardly surprising that China is the most rapidly motorizing society in the world today. The People's Republic was long a nation of bicycles, but now the two-wheelers are in decline: the number of bicyclists in China's cities dropped 26 percent between 2001 and 2006, and they are now even banned outright on many city streets. The domestic motor vehicle market, on the other hand, is booming, and second in size now only to that of the United States. Industry analysts forecast that China may well be the world's largest producer and consumer of cars by 2020, with total car ownership exceeding even that of the United States.[14] The number of cars in Shanghai jumped from a mere 212,000 to 1.2 million between 1990 and 2003; and Beijing swept past the million-car mark in the spring of 2002, when more than 1,000 new cars were being added to the city's streets and highways each day.[15] Today there are more automobile brands in China than in the United States, and while the total number of cars is still small in comparison, keep in mind that there were virtually no private automobiles in the People's Republic as late as the 1970s.

The motorization trend has profound implications for the form and structure of China's cities. It is helping drive a complex process of land conversion on the urban fringe that yields a uniquely Chinese kind of urban sprawl. Sprawl in China is very different from its American cousin, but no less land hungry. Between about 1980 and 2004, nearly 44,000 square miles of agricultural land were lost to development in China—equivalent to the combined area of all of Massachusetts, Connecticut, Rhode Island, Vermont, New Hampshire, and half of Maine.[16] Due to such losses, the People's Republic is no longer self-sufficient in agricultural production; for the first time in its history, China has become a net importer of food.[17] The situation is more than a little reminiscent of *The Good Earth*, in which the land Wang Lung worked all his life—that nurtured and enriched his family—is pawned off by his profligate sons. The extent of Chinese sprawl is readily evident from space, much the way the Great Wall was long rumored to be.

LANDSAT images of China's coastal cities from the early 1980s and today reveal an outward expansion of urban matter reminiscent of a colossal stellar explosion. While the Chinese suburban landscape is very different from that of the United States, it is no less catalytic in enabling a car-dependent lifestyle of commuting and big-box consumerism. Most housing on the urban fringe consists of mid- and high-rise condominium estates—much denser than anything in suburban America. Yet their outlying location and the lack of public transportation has encouraged high rates of automobile ownership among residents. Mixed among these housing estates are also tracts of single-family homes virtually identical in spirit—and often in architectural appointment—to "McMansion"-style gated communities in the United States. Other artifacts of American sprawl and "strip" culture have also appeared, albeit tailored to local (or at least Chinese) needs and tastes. These include drive-through fast-food restaurants like KFC and McDonald's; big-box retail giants such as Lotus and Wal-Mart, IKEA, Costco, and an Anglo-Chinese Home Depot knockoff called B&Q; shopping malls with expansive parking lots out front; colossal supermarkets; even budget motel chains and that vintage icon of American suburbia, the drive-in cinema.

What makes these and other facets of the new Chinese landscape so extraordinary is their sharp contrast with what came before. Scarcely a generation has passed between the Cultural Revolution and the present, yet what epochal change those three decades have wrought! The shopping malls and subdivisions, the cars and color TVs, the theme parks and golf courses— all unthinkable a short time ago. The dull blue-gray world of Mao suits and rationed goods is long gone; China today is a 24/7 frenzy of consumerism and construction. The birthplace of the Chinese Communist Party is now part of an exclusive shopping district in Shanghai, only steps from a Starbucks and upscale martini bars. Golf is a required course for business students at Xiamen University; and even the celebrated commune in Shanxi Province that cadres were implored to study in the 1960s—"In agriculture, learn from Dazhai!"— has struck out on the capitalist road, turning its famous name into a lucrative (and copyrighted) brand.

The saga of transition from Maoist scarcity to full-blown consumerism was driven home for me in 1999 by a television advertisement, of all things, for an upscale housing estate in the Pearl River Delta. I was at a restaurant in Zhongshan with Wallace Chang, as guests of a team of local planning officials for whom we were doing some consulting work. The television was playing silently in our private dining room, and a program came on that I took at first to be a historical drama about the hardships of life during the Cultural Revolution. The film was shot in black and white, and showed a young peasant working the fields and struggling to feed his family. The same man was then depicted as a foreman in a village factory, bicycling off now in the morning with an attaché case. Finally, the film turned full color, and the former peasant was now a well-groomed executive stepping confidently out of a suburban villa (at the advertised development, of course), waving goodbye to an adoring family before heading to the office in his late-model BMW. Here was, in effect, the creation story of post-Mao China, a rags-to-riches fable celebrating the economic miracle unleashed by Deng Xiaoping in the early 1980s.

The primary motive force behind China's urban revolution is, of course, the explosive growth of the Chinese economy over the last three decades. Not only did Deng Xiaoping's market reforms stimulate free enterprise at home— unleashing "a tidal wave of long suppressed entrepreneurial energy and ambition," as Li Conghua has written—but his "open-door" campaign brought a flood tide of money from foreign investors hungry for a piece of the Chinese pie.[18] Foreign direct investment flowed first to China via a series of special economic zones established for that purpose, initially from Hong Kong and the Chinese diaspora communities across Southeast Asia. But before long, investors from the United States, Japan, Canada, the United Kingdom, Australia, and Europe were also pouring millions into joint-venture projects in the People's Republic. China's economic engine stirred to life in the early 1980s, and then launched into the longest period of sustained economic growth in modern times. Between 1980 and 1990 the Chinese economy grew faster than even the vaunted "East Asian Tigers" (Hong Kong, Singapore, Taiwan, and South Korea) during their exuberant early years in the 1970s and 1980s. By 1994, the People's Republic accounted for fully 40 percent of the world's GDP growth; today its GDP represents 13 percent of global output, making it second in productivity only to the United States. China's economy has been expanding an average 9 percent per annum since the start of the reform era, a rate three times the growth of the American economy over the much-ballyhooed dot-com boom of the late 1990s.

Nor is it showing any signs of slowing: China overtook the United Kingdom in 2005 to become the third-largest economy in the world, and it may well soon eclipse Germany. In 2006, China's GDP increased by nearly 11 percent, the fastest growth rate in more than a decade. And as economist Pam Woodall has pointed out, China's growth is "real"—the result of real productivity growth rather than the funny-money gains of overvalued stock or inflated real estate. (As Woodall puts it, "rising house prices do not represent an increase in wealth for a country as a whole. They merely redistribute wealth to home-owners from non-home-owners who may hope to buy in the future.")[19] China is also now history's greatest exporter and churns out most of the world's televisions, stereos, DVD players, microwave ovens, vacuum cleaners, computer equipment, cameras, photocopiers, laser printers, telephones, tools, home furnishings, shoes, motors, and toys. Of course, just how long China can sustain this breakneck pace of growth is anyone's guess, and a subject of intense debate among economists. Unchecked environmental degradation, rising unemployment, a growing dependence on foreign oil and other resources, and a swollen property market are just some of the many issues that threaten to derail the growth locomotive. None, however, is more menacing to China's internal stability and continued growth than the widening gap between haves and have-nots, both within cities and between regions.

Capitalism in the People's Republic is in a brutally efficient early stage, largely unfettered by unions, workmen's compensation laws, well-enforced environmental regulations, and other inconveniences to capital accumulation. The economic juggernaut has crushed many a soul. While an estimated 300 million Chinese have been lifted out of poverty by economic growth in the last quarter century, such blessings have not been spread evenly throughout the nation. China's coastal cities and provinces have been the chief beneficiaries of the surging economy, a coastal swath not unlike the Boston-to-Washington, or "BosWash," corridor along the Atlantic seaboard. Official residents of Shenzhen, Guangzhou, Fuzhou, Shanghai, Beijing, Tianjin, Dalian, and other cities enjoy an average income significantly higher than the national average.

In their midst, however, is a vast "floating population" (liudong renkou) of migrant workers who receive few of the perks and privileges of full urban citizenship. The disequilibrium between booming coastal cities and poor inland provinces has prompted as many as 225 million peasants—roughly the population of the United States—to flock to China's cities in recent years in search of jobs and a better life. In 1998 alone, twenty-seven million rural migrants made their way to China's major metropolitan centers. That equals the sum total of all European emigration to the United States between 1820 and 1920. Even the "Great Migration" of African Americans from the rural South to northern cities after the Second World War—a demographic shift that helped shape contemporary American culture—pales in comparison to internal Chinese migration in recent years. Migrant workers in Beijing alone outnumber all the African Americans who migrated to the urban north between 1940 and 1970.[20]

How ironic that China's urban revolution is so deeply indebted to the countryside. Chinese cities are built by farmers. Men from impoverished rural villages put up the posh malls and glittering skyscrapers and six-lane expressways, while their sisters and daughters work the mills and assembly lines that have made China the workshop of the world. But even though they turn the

碧桂園實景拍攝

Artist's rendering, Country Garden housing estate, Guangdong Province, 1999.

COURTESY COUNTRY GARDEN

gears of China's economic engine, migrant workers are an unappreciated lot. They have little or no access to health care, educational opportunities, or good housing; they are blamed for nearly every social ill and literally live on the margins of society.

Far at the other end of fate's spectrum is the self-made millionaire, the folk hero of the new China. This one-time land of Red Guards and little red books is churning out more new millionaires than any country in the world. In a nation where a bicycle will set you back all of $15, a millionaire has the spending power of a billionaire in the United States. The legendary exhortation often attributed to Deng Xiaoping—"to get rich is glorious"—has rehabilitated wealth and affluence in China. Capitalists were once excoriated as "running dogs" of Western imperialism; now they are heaped with encomiums and can even join the Communist Party. On May Day 2005, several such self-made millionaires were feted as "model workers" by the Chinese Communist

Party (so was Houston Rockets star Yao Ming, who first thought such awards were for "ordinary people who worked tirelessly...without asking for anything in return," but then allowed that perhaps he was "a special kind of migrant worker").[21]

Like the Hearsts, Vanderbilts, and Rockefellers before them, China's merchant elite has a penchant for arriviste extravagance. Beijing property mogul Zhang Yuchen, who made a fortune in the 1990s building single-family suburban homes, celebrated his arrival by replicating the Château de Maisons-Laffitte on a windswept site north of the Chinese capital. The nouveau chateau was crafted using François Mansart's original drawings from 1650 and constructed with the same Chantilly stone, this time shipped halfway across the globe. Unfortunately, some 800 peasants raising wheat on the land had to be forcibly evicted to make way for the trophy house—a particular irony given Zhang's membership in the Communist Party.[22]

Other magnates have built simulacra of Beverly Hills mansions or even the architectural landmarks of American democracy. On the outskirts of Hangzhou, Chinese tourism tycoon Huang Qiaoling built a $10 million full-scale replica of the White House, complete with a portrait gallery of American presidents, an Oval Office, and a Blue Room. Outside is a miniature Washington Monument, along with a one-third scale version of Mount Rushmore (quarters for his employees are neatly tucked behind). What inspired Huang's building spree was a glossy New Year calendar of American landmarks that his peasant parents received when he was a child.[23] In 2002 Huang was surprised with a visit from none other than George W. Bush, who was himself delighted to see a knockoff of the White House in China. Another tycoon, Li Qinfu, took the Washington trope a step further by erecting a mini U.S. Capitol in the Shanghai suburbs, the headquarters of his textile and manufacturing conglomerate. The building is topped with a three-ton statue of Li himself, a former Red Guard, and now one of China's richest men.[24]

China's roaring economy has also enriched professionals in the building, design, and development fields—from quantity surveyors and construction managers to real estate brokers, architects, engineers, and urban planners. Architects have been especially nimble in riding the zeitgeist of the building boom, and many have become fabulously rich in the process. Young architects still in their twenties often have several built projects in their portfolios, and

Zhang Yuchen in front of his replica Maisons-Laffitte on the outskirts of Beijing, 2004.

PHOTOGRAPH BY MARK RALSTON / NEW YORK TIMES

not just a summer house for mom and dad. Architecture students in Shenzhen in the 1980s helped build that overnight city, working on real commissions alongside their studio assignments. By the 1990s Chinese architects had five times the volume of work of their American colleagues, who outnumbered them nonetheless by a factor of ten.[25] This relative scarcity has made Chinese architects the most influential in the world, if influence be measured by bricks and mortar. The great demand for skilled designers led to a surge in the number of architecture students in the last decade. Today, architecture ranks with computer science and economics as one of the most competitive fields of study in China; admission to a top-flight architecture program, say at Tsinghua or Nanjing universities, is statistically equivalent to getting into Harvard or Yale, and architects in China enjoy considerably higher occupational prestige than do their counterparts in the United States.

To architects overseas, China is nothing short of the Holy Grail. Foreign design and planning firms fall all over themselves for a piece of the action, and for good reason: the great Chinese building boom has made the skills and expertise of design professionals in demand as never before. There are architects and planners from Virginia to California whose previous contact with the Chinese world was limited to the local take-out, who now have half a dozen projects on the boards in Shenzhen, Beijing, and Shanghai. This is not the first time foreign professionals have helped shaped China's future, of course; Americans and Europeans left a rich legacy of architecture and urban design in China in the first half of the twentieth century. But that early work was often related to missionary or philanthropic endeavors, or commissioned by foreign companies busily exploiting China. Today, foreign architects build in China at China's pleasure, and save for a handful of global superstars—Koolhaas, Foster, Herzog & de Meuron, and the like—they may well soon find themselves displaced by twenty-something Chinese kids.

There is a bewitching consonance between the American urban experience and the transfiguration of China's cities today. China's drive, energy, and ambition—its hunger to be powerful and prosperous, to be a player on the global stage—is more than a little reminiscent of America in its youth. Henry James's descriptions of lower Manhattan in 1904—of the "multitudinous sky-scrapers standing up to the view, from the water, like extravagant pins in a cushion already overplanted"—could well describe Shanghai's Pudong District today.[26] We gazed in wonder at promise-filled miniature metropoles like Norman Bel Geddes's Futurama exhibit at the 1939 New York World's Fair, just as Chinese today pore over spectacular models of the Shanghai- or Beijing-to-be. We were China once, and Europe was us. In spirit at least, China is like the United States of a century ago—punch-drunk with possibility, pumped and reckless and on the move. Americans invented the modern metropolis, and the world looked to us with wonder. It was on the blustery shores of Lake Michigan that the modern office tower was born, in the wake of the Great Chicago Fire, and in New York that the skyscraper city achieved its finest early form. We wrote poems once to our bridges and roads. We dreamed, like Moses King or Hugh Ferriss, of cities studded with impossible towers and airborne streets. Given wheels by Henry Ford, we scattered across the landscape and created a new kind of semicity in places like Los Angeles, Dallas, Atlanta, and Phoenix.

Of course, much of this ended badly. We got urban renewal and lost our past; we got the Cross Bronx Expressway and lost our homes. But the West End and the South Bronx did not die in vain. We are older and wiser now, more responsible, aware of the problems of building for automobiles rather than human beings—or of simply building too big. A new emphasis on sustainability impels us to rethink the way we make architecture and assemble cities. In short, our values have changed. But with wisdom has also come timidity. We are a suburban nation in tweedy middle age, cautious and conservative, no longer smitten with audacity. Our architecture and urbanism is retrospective, measured, and sane. We build new towns that look old, shop at Restoration Hardware and bury—like the Central Artery—the very icons of modernity we once celebrated. In America today, the notion of penning verse to a piece of infrastructure is a little laughable. Just as it once crossed the Atlantic, the urbanism of ambition has crossed the Pacific; Hart Crane has gone to China.

CHAPTER ONE

Thunder from the South

南方春雷

The south China city of Shenzhen has an official theme song, one that captures the spirit of the place as fully as Frank Sinatra's paean to the Big Apple, "New York, New York." It has an unlikely title—"Story of Springtime" (Chun Tian De Gu Shi). Written by Jiang Kairu and composer Wang Yougui, the piece was originally recorded by a popular People's Liberation Army vocalist named Dong Wenhua, who belts out the lyrics against a mighty choral backdrop reminiscent of Maoist anthems from the Cultural Revolution: "In the spring of 1979 / An old man drew a circle / On the southern coast of China / And city after city rose up like fairy tales / And mountains and mountains of gold / Gathered like a miracle."[1] "Story of Springtime" played over and over in south China in the 1990s, on the radio and TV and in pubs and bars; it even became a popular song for visiting foreigners to learn for their obligatory turns at the karaoke microphone. And though it sounds much like a Communist anthem, "Story of Springtime" celebrates a revolution of a very different sort—the miraculous economic growth unleashed by Deng Xiaoping that, in a few short years, made good at last Napoleon's hoary dictum—"When China wakes, the world will tremble." And tremble it has, to the incessant drumbeat of pile drivers and jack-hammers. In effect, "Story of Springtime" became the overture to a spectacular production—the greatest building boom in history. This production stirred to life in south China, and Shenzhen was ground zero.

It was actually on December 13, 1978—two years, three months, and four days after the death of Mao Zedong—that Deng Xiaoping drew that circle around south China, after which "city after city rose up like fairy tales." That day the Chinese premier delivered a speech to the closing session of the Chinese Communist Party's Central Work Conference, which had dragged on

Deng Xiaoping billboard, Shenzhen, 1999. PHOTO BY AUTHOR

now for more than a month. In it he outlined, among other things, a program of policy reform calling for the decentralization of economic activity to provincial and local authorities and—more radically—to rural and village collectives and work-unit enterprises, even to individual laborers and farmers.[2] A "responsibility system" should be adopted to reward productivity and create incentive for effort and innovation; rather than receive the usual "iron ricebowl" handouts from the state, Deng thought people should be encouraged to "vie with one another to become advanced...working hard and aiming high." He realized such competition would put some ahead of others, creating inequality. But Deng also understood that this itself would act as a powerful incentive: "Allowing some regions and enterprises and some workers and peasants to earn more and become better off before others, in accordance with their hard work and greater contributions to society," he argued, "will inevitably be an impressive example to their 'neighbors,' and people in other regions and units will want to learn from the them. This will help the whole national economy to advance wave upon wave."[3]

The speech, and the weeks of debate and discussion leading up to it, effectively put China on a trajectory of economic renewal and rebirth. As Jiang Zemin later described it, the speech was a "declaration for charting a new course," one that forged a "new theory of building socialism with Chinese characteristics."[4] The phrase stuck, and came to denote the unique blend of socialism and free-market capitalism that enabled China to transform its economy without "shock therapy" and the kind of socioeconomic chaos that followed the fall of the Soviet Union. At the Third Plenum of the 11th Party Congress, which convened a few days after the Work Conference, Deng's proposed reforms were reviewed and approved. Bureaucracy aside, these meetings were of momentous historical significance and have been described as "the forty-one days that changed the fate of China."[5] They launched a new era of Chinese engagement with the global community, setting in motion an era of development that would soon make China the fastest-growing economy on earth.

Deng Xiaoping thus opened China's door to the world, but not the front door, with red carpet and concierge; it was really the nation's back door that he left unlatched. Though the economic reforms came from Beijing, the nation's capital, they were effectively field-tested far from the center of power, in China's southernmost, semitropical Guangdong Province—specifically that part centered about the Pearl River and its water-laced delta. This was done much

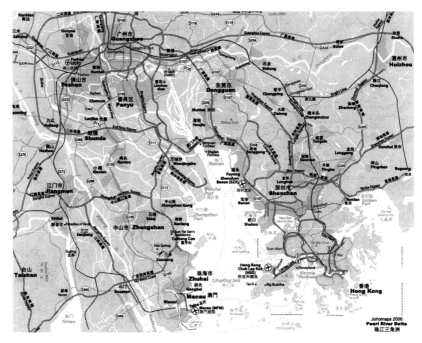

Map of the Pearl River Delta. COURTESY OF JOHOMAPS.COM

the way a promising but potentially deadly new source of energy might be first tested safely distant from the laboratory and its staff. But there were other factors, related to both geography and history, that made Guangdong ideal for a vanguard role in China's liberalization drive. Guangdong—a vast province equal in size to many nations—is culturally different from the rest of China, almost a Cantonese-speaking subnation whose language, customs, and kinship networks have more in common with Hong Kong and Southeast Asia than most of the People's Republic.

Historically, the remoteness of the province, its sheer physical distance from the various seats of imperial authority over the centuries—Chang'an, Hangzhou, Nanjing, Beijing—had bred a fierce spirit of independence in the Guangdong people. Far from the imperial cats, the mice could safely play; or as an old south China adage puts it, "the mountains are tall and the emperor is far away." It was in Guangdong, after all, that the Chinese forcefully resisted British opium trafficking, leading to the First Opium War in 1840. This in turn helped seed the Taiping Rebellion, which also stirred to life in Guangdong a decade later, largely among the ethnic Hakka people led by Huadu native Hong

Xiuquan. Hong came to believe that he was the younger brother of Jesus Christ, destined to found a utopian "heavenly kingdom" in China. In fact, the venture ended badly, with some twenty million people killed by the time Hong's army was defeated near Shanghai (by a Yankee adventurer named Frederick Townsend Ward).[6] It was around then, back in the Pearl River Delta town Cuiheng, that Sun Yat-sen was born; he would later lead a successful revolution against the Qing Dynasty and establish the Chinese Republic in 1911.

Guangdong has also long looked outward to the larger world, its people among the earliest in China to trade with "foreign barbarians" from the West—an activity that was, again, tolerated by imperial authorities because distance and geography insulated the throne from the alien interlopers. Guangdong's minglings with the outside world began as early as the Han Dynasty (206 BC–AD 220), when Arab traders journeyed to the region in search of spices prized for preserving food.[7] Physical access was easy; the Pearl River Delta's dendritic drainage system provided a network of navigable waterways from the South China Sea deep into the region's hinterland. By the end of the Tang Dynasty (AD 618–907), trade routes connecting the Pearl River Delta with Southeast Asia and the Middle East were well in place.[8]

The first Europeans on the scene were the Portuguese, who secured permission to establish a settlement at Macau in 1557—a toehold they would maintain until 1999. By 1699, the British had set up a trading base at Guangzhou (anglicized as Canton), the provincial capital. From the 1760s until the First Opium War, Guangzhou was the only Chinese port open to foreign traders. Then in 1841, the Union Jack was raised on the sparsely populated island of Hong Kong just off China's southern coast. Famously dismissed as a "barren rock," Hong Kong grew steadily and was soon siphoning away trade and commerce from Guangzhou. The economic geography of the Pearl River Delta gradually tilted in Hong Kong's favor, eventually making this distant outpost Britannia's most lucrative colonial possession. The ultimate entrepôt, Hong Kong flourished as a broker of trade and commerce with the Chinese mainland. It was both the world's window into China and China's portal to the world—a legacy that was foremost in Deng Xiaoping's mind when he mapped out a strategy for China's economic liberalization.

Centuries of engagement with the outside world thus gave the Cantonese a flair for trade and commerce and a reputation as "worldly men of affairs, shrewd bargainers, knowledgeable in technology, frank in criticism, oriented to defending their own interests."[9] This spirit remained alive through the Communist era and even the Cultural Revolution. An annual trade exhibition—the Canton Fair—was launched in Guangzhou in 1957 and is still going strong. Known today as the Chinese Export Commodities Fair, it was for years the only officially sanctioned opportunity for foreign trade with the People's Republic.

The Cantonese have often been compared to the Jews of Europe; skilled traders and merchants, they are also a diasporic people. Famine, floods, and civil unrest in the region have forced millions to find new lives elsewhere over the years—throughout Southeast Asia, in Hong Kong, and in the United States, Canada, Australia, and the United Kingdom. A large percentage of Chinese Americans trace their roots to Guangdong Province, which is one reason the Chinese cuisine most familiar to Americans is Cantonese. Many of these migrants maintained close ties to kith and kin in the old country, sending home money and stories of life abroad. This yielded a vast kinship network connecting Guangdong to the prosperous Chinese diaspora around the world—another factor that gave the region an enormous competitive advantage in the reform era, making it the best launch pad for China's economic reform and "opening up" (gaige kaifeng) to the greater world. "The homeland of an international network of overseas Chinese," writes Mihai Craciun, "the Pearl River Delta could provide the foreign capital needed to fuel open-door economic reform while the region's mercantile background could serve as the foundation of a new socialist market economy."[10] Thus did Beijing officialdom, from over the mountains and far away, allow Guangdong "to walk one step ahead" of China, and strike a path toward reform.[11]

The economic giant that now stirred to life soon made its mark upon the landscape. Given the vast urbanization that the post-Mao economic reforms set into motion, it is odd that the earliest and most visible physical transformations did not occur in cities, but in the countryside around Shenzhen and Guangzhou and nearby towns throughout the Pearl River Delta—Dongguan, Jiangmen, Foshan, Nansha, Zhongshan, and others. This was largely the result of an early reform-era economic experiment known as the "Household Responsibility System," introduced to boost agricultural production and increase peasant income. Farm families were allotted land and required to meet a certain production quota, but after this they were allowed to sell what they could on the open market. This incentive system dramatically increased the efficiency and yield of agricultural production, culminating in a great bumper harvest in 1984. As supplies of meat and produce increased, commodity prices fell, and food became more plentiful than it had been in decades. Farmers prospered, especially those whose land was close to big city markets. Peasants, paradoxically, were thus among the first in Guangdong to get rich, and they soon acquired the coveted trio of household appliances—refrigerator, washing machine, and television set.

The farmers also built new homes, roomy two- and three-story peasant villas often proudly emblazoned with their year of construction. Such new development was so extensive on the outskirts of Guangzhou that entire rural farming villages went through a process of in situ urbanization within a few short years, gaining many of the amenities, institutions, and even cultural practices usually associated with city life.[12] By 2000, farmers in Shenzhen were reaping a per capita annual income of nearly 10,000 yuan, about four times the national per capita annual income of rural families.[13] The household responsibility system was followed by policy encouraging the development of "township and village enterprises." The ensuing grassroots entrepreneurialism had, by the early 1990s, become one of the main drivers of economic growth in China and the engine of a regional development phenomenon that would turn the rice fields and banana groves of the Pearl River Delta into the workshop of the world.

It was only after the successful implementation of rural and village-level reforms that similar policies were developed for China's cities. In the summer of 1980, legislation based on an initiative Deng Xiaoping made the previous year—"Provisional Regulations on Promoting Economic Cooperation"—authorized "special economic zones" in several Chinese cities. The first four zones, or "SEZS," as they came to be known in English, were in southern China: three in Guangdong Province and one in Fujian Province just to the north. Shenzhen, the first, was then still a small agricultural city just over the border from Hong Kong's New Territories. There was also Zhuhai, a small city across the border from Macau; Shantou, farther north along the coast in Guangdong; and the old Fujian port city Xiamen, once known as Amoy. Four years later the special economic zones were joined by Hainan Island (later granted full provincial status in 1988) and fourteen "coastal open cities," including (from south to north) Beihai in Guangxi Province; Zhangjiang and Guangzhou in Guangdong Province; Fuzhou in Fujian Province; Wenzhou and Ningbo in Zhejiang

Shennan Boulevard in Shenzhen, looking west, 1982. PHOTOGRAPH BY JIANG SHIGAO

Province; Shanghai (a provincial-level city); Nantong and Lianyungang in Jiangsu Province; Qingdao and Yantai in Shandong Province; Tianjin (also a provincial-level city); Qinhuangdao in Hebei Province; and Dalian in Liaoning Province, not far from the North Korean border.[14] Nearly all of these cities were former "treaty ports" conceded to Britain, Japan, and an alliance of Western powers in a series of "unequal treaties" following the Opium Wars (Shanghai, Fuzhou, Xiamen, Guangzhou, and Ningbo were the first, established by the Treaty of Nanking in 1842). The chief purpose of the treaty ports was to make it easier for outsiders to extract China's wealth, hence their coastal location. By definition oriented to the outside world, the treaty ports soon shifted China's economic locus to the sea.[15]

Though forced open by the West, the treaty ports also worked in reverse; that is, they came to play a seminal role in China's modernization, especially in the 1920s and 1930s (and nowhere more powerfully than in Shanghai). Leveraging this historical function, Deng Xiaoping turned the treaty ports inside out; the old outposts of foreign exploitation would now be agents of Chinese renewal, fuel injectors of foreign capital that would prime China's economic engines. The act was rich with symbolism: China had fully transcended the humiliations of the past; trade and commerce would now take place on its terms.

But the open cities and special economic zones were much more than retrofitted treaty ports. Because Mao had isolated the People's Republic from most of the globe—eventually even from its onetime Socialist mentor, the Soviet Union—China had fallen far behind the developed world. By the 1970s it lacked even basic technologies and expertise. The special economic zones and open cities were intended to remedy this, to serve as portals through which capital, ideas, and technology from overseas could be filtered and selectively admitted. As Ezra Vogel has put it, the SEZS were meant to be "laboratories for the contained unleashing of capitalism," experimental zones where determinations could be made about "which Western practices were most suitable for China." The cream of the world would be skimmed here and passed on to the rest of the nation, while anything deemed morally corruptive would be rejected. Like Guangdong itself, the initial set of SEZS were sufficiently removed from the seat of power in Beijing to make such experimentation safe; if a cultural "virus" got in, so to speak, the zones could be effectively sealed off and quarantined.[16]

Of course, this was of little interest to most foreign investors; what lured them in droves was the host of inducements available only in the economic zones—reduced land-use fees, capital gains and income tax concessions, turnkey factory sites, simplified customs and immigration procedures, and a generally streamlined bureaucracy. Labor was plentiful and cheap, and nearby Hong Kong and Macau offered easy access to global markets, technology, and information. Foreign investors who had been cautiously circling China ever since Richard Nixon's epochal visit in 1972 now had a place to land. Capital began flowing into China, merely trickling at first, then up to $4 billion in annual actual investments in 1991, and surging to $41 billion by 2000. Guangdong never lost its early lead; between 1986 and 1999 the province accounted for fully 28 percent of all foreign direct investment in China.[17]

All of the new economic incubators were successful, but none more so than Shenzhen. Of the four original SEZS, Shenzhen enjoyed competitive advantages that made it the darling of the reform era. Not only was Shenzhen physically larger than any of the other zones, but its proximity to Hong Kong was lightning in a jar; it had at its fingertips a wealth of world-class technology, managerial expertise, market capital, and kinship networks that would help it become a mainland version of the freewheeling capitalist entrepôt. This was of course the very reason Deng had tapped the former fishing village for such weighty duty—and also the very same reason Mao largely spurned the area during the Cultural Revolution, making Shenzhen part of a "political defense frontier," the very antithesis of an open economic zone. During the Cultural Revolution, Red Guard youth even staged demonstrations along the Shenzhen River to incite their capitalist brethren and carry the spark of revolution to Hong Kong.[18]

As China's door opened wider, the once-tight border became increasingly permeable. More and more people began moving between Hong Kong and Shenzhen. In the 1970s only a handful of Hong Kong residents crossed each year into Shenzhen. By the late 1980s more than ten million people a year were making the trip, the vast majority of whom were Hong Kong residents visiting mainland family in ancestral villages, particularly during the Qingming Festival and Lunar New Year holiday. The border crossers were agents of modernization; they carried to their poor China relatives television sets, stereos, kitchen appliances, Cantopop cassettes. Along with the material goods came also new tastes, new values, and new ideas. With these incursions and a steady influx of foreign capital, the once-quiet border village (known best for seafood and lychee fruit) became a raging boomtown. In its first five years as a special economic zone, Shenzhen's industrial output rose from sixty million yuan to more than 2.5 billion yuan, while its total GDP jumped from 270 million yuan in 1980 to 79.6 billion yuan in 1995.[19] Per capita GDP also rose dramatically, from 606 yuan in 1979 to 23,381 yuan in 1995, making Shenzhen one of China's most affluent cities.

Population soared as well. The old town of Shenzhen was home to 27,366 people in 1978. Even counting the adjacent rural districts that would later become part of the SEZ and extended metropolitan area, Shenzhen still had a population of only 68,166—making it roughly the size of Chapel Hill, North Carolina, today. Seven years later the population of the greater Shenzhen metropolitan area broke the one-million mark; it clocked in at four million by the mid-1990s and seven million by 2000.[20] In April 2006 Shenzhen's population was reported to be 8.27 million, putting it ahead of New York City. Shenzhen effectively grew from a Chapel Hill to the Big Apple in less than a generation—a pace of growth we haven't seen in North America since Chicago in the nineteenth century. Shenzhen's spatial growth has been just as astonishing.

The special economic zone, officially designated a city in the 1990s, today occupies some 772 square miles of land, more than 600 times the size it was in the 1980s.[21]

The transition from fishing village to metropolis also meant a cataclysm of construction: between 1982 and 1996 Shenzhen erected more than 600 major buildings, dramatically altering the local landscape in the process.[22] It was the People's Liberation Army, ironically, that helped do much of this first-round construction. In the early 1980s the Army Engineer Corps was still helping rebuild Tangshan in north China after an earthquake leveled the city in 1976 (at the time this was the largest urban construction effort in China). As that work wound down, some 20,000 Corps officers and soldiers were transferred to Shenzhen to assist with public works in the nascent SEZ. These men and women formed the core of Shenzhen's civil engineering staff, and with demobilization in 1983 many took jobs as foremen and project managers in the more than a hundred construction companies operating in the SEZ at the time.[23]

One of the buildings that former Corps personnel helped erect was the International Foreign Trade Center, Shenzhen's first skyscraper and, when it was completed in 1985, the tallest building in China. The tower was topped by an architectural curiosity first seen in Seattle at the 1964 World's Fair—a revolving rooftop restaurant. By the 1970s, the rotating restaurant had become the sine qua non symbol of urban progress and prosperity in the United States—a "must-have weapon in the civic arsenal of every latter-day Babbitt," as Tom Vanderbilt put it.[24] Now the rotating restaurant was embraced in China, and for much the same reason; well into the 1990s, a skyscraper topped with a revolving restaurant was essential for every mayor on the make, a perch from which the unfolding metamorphosis on the streets below might be shown proudly to VIPs and foreign guests. In the early reform era, foreign trends and practices often made their way to China via Hong Kong, and this is precisely what happened with the revolving-restaurant craze. Shenzhen's Foreign Trade Center was modeled after an earlier structure in Hong Kong—Gordon Wu's sixty-six-story Hopewell Centre, completed in 1980 and for a time the queen of the Hong Kong skyline. The building type rapidly replicated throughout China over the next decade or so—first to Shenzhen, then Guangzhou (Garden Hotel), Beijing (Beijing International Hotel), and elsewhere. Even more famous than its revolving cap was the speed at which the Foreign Trade Center was erected: one floor every three days, soon christened "Shenzhen tempo." It is only appropriate that another Shenzhen tower, the sixty-seven-story Land King (Diwang) Tower, would shatter the record. Workers on Land King completed a floor every two and a half days in the mid-1990s, thanks in part to an additive that made the concrete cure faster.

★ ★ ★

By the early 1990s, the Trade Center's rotating aerie provided a stunning introduction to the vast work-in-progress that was Shenzhen. I will never forget peering out the restaurant's windows on a steamy afternoon in June 1992, one of the first stops on my first visit to the People's Republic. I was one of a group of rather cocksure MIT and Harvard urban planning students on our way to Beijing, and local officials had taken us to lunch. By the time we sat down to eat, most of us had been awed into silence; we had stolen a furtive glimpse into the birth chamber of a new age. As the restaurant moved steadily through its orbit, it revealed scenes worthy of a Ridley Scott film. Bright red upturned earth was being dug and hauled and piled at hundreds of construction sites. Larval buildings rose all around us, each wrapped in a cocoon-like husk of bamboo scaffolding (the hand-tied sticks are still used to erect even the most modern buildings in south China). In the middle distance, clusters of new buildings were etched against a pastoral scene of oxen and rice paddies—perhaps unchanged for hundreds of years. Farther away on the horizon, mountains bore bright quarry scars where hillsides were literally being blown apart to provide fill for lowland building sites. The explosions reverberated across the landscape all day, and often well into the night.

Only several months before we came to Shenzhen, a more illustrious visitor had surveyed the city from the same aerie—Deng Xiaoping. His visit to the rotating restaurant was one of the storied stops on a trip that changed Chinese history. From the Trade Center lookout on January 19, 1992, Deng effectively gave his blessing to Shenzhen, refreshing the city's commitment to leading China into a free-market future. It was two weeks before the start of the Lunar New Year Festival. An auspicious eighty-eight years old (in Chinese, "eight" is homophonous with the word for wealth or prosperity) and officially retired, Deng then held no formal position or title; the trip could well have been an old man's last holiday sojourn. But, of course, he was still the most powerful man

Topping-out ceremony, International Foreign Trade Center, Shenzhen, September 4, 1984.

PHOTOGRAPH BY JIANG SHIGAO

in China, the nation's de facto paramount leader. A mumbled word from the Little Helmsman could make markets rise or fall, sending shockwaves around the globe. And now Deng had a lot to say. His month-long trip, to Shenzhen and several other cities in south China, was no idle junket but a cool political move, one meant to rehabilitate his standing in China, solidify his power base, and make sure that his economic reforms—and his legacy—were not thwarted by events and actors beyond his control.

Deng Xiaoping had already survived several purgings in his extraordinary career, but his handling of the Tiananmen Square protests—and the subsequent bloodbath—nearly finished him politically. Leftist hardliners, none too pleased with the radical changes he had made over the years, seized on Tiananmen as proof that the old man was no longer fit to lead. Not satisfied with his resignation as premier in the weeks after June 4, 1989, Deng's political enemies moved to roll back his reform agenda, which they felt encouraged social unrest and a new willingness among the Chinese people to voice their dissatisfaction with the Communist leadership.

How ironic that this man, responsible for a massacre of students and workers at Tiananmen just three years earlier, would now be defending his legacy from an even more reactionary cohort that blamed him for having helped—however inadvertently—bring about the protests. More ironic still is that Deng would go to the Chinese people for support. Not surprisingly, he went where people had most benefited from his reforms—south China, especially Shenzhen. By the early 1990s, Shenzhen was more a sensation than a city, already one of the most prosperous cities in China. Shenzhen was the flagship of China's post-Mao economic revolution, poster child of Deng's vision of an affluent, modern, competitive, globally engaged People's Republic. This was well understood by the city's residents, to whom Deng Xiaoping was no disenfranchised octogenarian but a patron saint, a god of wealth whose golden sheen could never be tarnished.

The return of this city-god, at the start of the Year of the Monkey, was auspicious indeed. It was doubly so for reasons that reach deep into China's imperial past. When word got out of Deng's intended sojourn, it was immediately compared to the celebrated tours—known as *nanxun*, or "southern inspection journeys,"—undertaken over the course of a century by the Emperors Kangxi and Qianlong of the Qing Dynasty. The first of Kangxi's six southern tours began in the fall of 1684, and his imperial grandson Qianlong continued the tradition by undertaking six journeys of his own, the last of which was in 1784.[25] The inspection tours were nominally administrative, enabling the emperors to oversee key hydraulic works, but they also clearly had a political purpose and were meant to strengthen the emperors' power throughout the realm. The emperors' subjects thought the *nanxun* brought fortune and the blessings of heaven. All along the imperial route, cities and towns were decked out in splendor in anticipation of the Son of Heaven. The scenes were captured in magnificent scroll paintings produced for each tour.[26] With a little imagination, the scrolls might well convey the spirit and atmosphere of Deng Xiaoping's arrival in Shenzhen on his latter-day *nanxun*.

As a political strategy, Deng Xiaoping's *nanxun* worked like a charm. Deng's enemies miscalculated how highly regarded the man was among the people, in southern China especially. Here was a man who had already lifted hundreds of millions out of poverty—more than any nation or leader had done before. To the Chinese people, Deng was a hero whose standing was undiminished even by the catastrophe of Tiananmen. It soon became clear that reversing Deng's economic reform agenda was not an option, especially considering that he also enjoyed the allegiance of the People's Liberation Army. The hardliners began to backpedal. A news blackout on Deng's travels was lifted, and word quickly spread of the new *nanxun*. On March 26, while the National People's Congress was meeting in Beijing, a Shenzhen newspaper ran a flattering front-page feature on Deng's sojourn, entitled "An Eastern Wind Brings Spring—Reports on Comrade Deng Xiaoping in Shenzhen City." The article was reprinted widely, and the state television station, CCTV, broadcast excerpts to a nationwide audience. Nearly everything Deng said on the trip, including homey anecdotes and off-the-cuff comments, was eventually published in a series of special "red banner" documents (*hong tou wenjie*) and added to the already large body of "Deng Xiaoping thought."[27]

All told, the Little Helmsman's legacy was not only preserved, it was kicked into overdrive. China's economy had been growing steadily since the early 1980s at a pace three times the world average. But the *nanxun* sparked a new surge of economic activity throughout the Pearl River Delta and propelled China into one of the greatest periods of sustained economic growth the world has ever seen. China's gross domestic product jumped an astonishing 14 percent in 1992 and enjoyed double-digit growth for several years to come. Deng Xiaoping's *nanxun* was a threshold moment in the shaping of contemporary China.[28]

Explosive growth in Shenzhen drew people from far and wide. Ambitious strivers from all over the People's Republic flocked to the "overnight city" in search of jobs and career opportunities available nowhere else in the People's Republic. Shenzhen became the New York of China: if you can make it there, you might well make it anywhere. Like the typical New Yorker, most Shenzhen denizens were from someplace else. Migrant laborers, especially, rushed to the upstart city, and today make up more than 80 percent of Shenzhen's population, more than in any other major Chinese city. The special economic zone drew so many economic migrants that the government decided to physically cordon it off from the rest of Shenzhen and neighboring Bao'an County.

The new barrier bifurcated the geography of the region, literally and figuratively, and in the end proved counterproductive; as costs escalated within the fence, factories simply set up just beyond, where land was cheaper and laws more lax. "The Shenzhen area became divided into two worlds," writes Peter Hessler, "which were described by residents as *guannei* and *guanwai*—'within the gates' and 'beyond the gates'"—phrases used long ago to describe the Great Wall. Outside the gates, life was more dangerous and difficult, the landscape a "sprawl of cheaply constructed factories and worker dormitories" where wages were lower and industrial accidents far more frequent.[29]

As more and more newcomers flooded into Shenzhen, native people became minorities in their own home. But many locals also became rich as a result of Shenzhen's rapid metamorphosis. Because the city grew so quickly, entire villages in the surrounding countryside were soon engulfed by Shenzhen's expanding footprint. Nevertheless, the villages were still sitting on land officially designated as "rural." While the government could easily condemn the farmland that once sustained such communities, the villages themselves— with all their houses, shops, markets, schools, and other improvements—were much more costly to condemn, as villagers had to be compensated fairly for all improvements. As a result, Shenzhen grew around and about these nucleated villages, leaving them marooned in a fast-rising urban sea. Their rural livelihoods gone, the villagers embarked on a process of urbanization themselves. They tore down the old one-story farmhouses and built taller and taller tenements, which they rented out at rates far below those in the city proper.

By 2000 there were some 240 so-called urban villages (*cheng zhong cun*) in Shenzhen, encompassing more than sixteen square miles of the city and accommodating a population of more than two million people.[30] Village urbanization has not only enriched village residents but has also been a major source of affordable housing for the migrant labor force—in Shenzhen and many other cities. Any effort to get rid of these villages—and there have been numerous attempts by municipalities in recent years—will also have to make up for the lost low-cost housing. Shenzhen's urban villages are not without problems, and have been much criticized as unsafe, overcrowded warrens where building and health codes are routinely disregarded. They have also become havens for crime and prostitution, and in this respect are more than a little reminiscent of Hong Kong's infamous Kowloon Walled City, one of the densest slums in the world by the time it was demolished in 1993 and "the closest thing," one critic argued, "to a truly self-regulating, self-sufficient, self-determining modern city that has ever been built."[31]

The controlled anarchy of the urban villages contrasts vividly with the order and discipline that has characterized Shenzhen's development in recent years. As China's vanguard experiment in urban modernization, Shenzhen quickly became a kind of laboratory where a number of bold initiatives in land management and urban planning were first launched. It was in Shenzhen that the formation of a residential property market was first tested in China, and there that the first extensive commodity housing was built, largely by experienced private developers from Hong Kong. By 1995, these builders were supplying nearly half the total housing stock in Shenzhen.[32]

Shenzhen was also the beneficiary of extensive urban planning, and was developed according to a comprehensive master plan for infrastructure and utilities.[33] Urban planning activity actually began a year before the special economic zone was created, in the Shekou Industrial Zone, but was later carried out by the planning department of the quasi-governmental Shenzhen SEZ Construction Company. This agency created both a land-use master plan and more detailed layout plans for districts charted for development in the master plan. The aim of urban planning at Shenzhen was as simple as it was visionary: to create a "perfect environment for investment." From the start, however, planning Shenzhen was more a game of catch-up than course setting. The planning process, by nature sluggish and cumbersome, simply could not keep pace with the maelstrom of development; state-of-the-art plans, reflecting the input of the most skilled planning professionals in the country, were obsolete within months.

Moreover, master plans had no legal teeth at the time; "any proposal for development not conforming to the master plan," writes Anthony G. O. Yeh, had to be dealt with "mainly by persuasion." In other words, lack of enforcement mechanisms meant that there was nothing to assure that development would progress as planned. A variety of forces quickly altered whatever vision was put to paper. In the early 1980s, for example, a Hong Kong real estate company took an interest in developing Shenzhen's Futian District and relayed that interest to authorities in Beijing; Beijing in turn forced the Shenzhen planning department to adjust its population cap for Futian to accommodate the new project.[34] But more than any other influence it was simply the rapid growth of the city that forced plans to be "constantly modified, adjusted and substantiated," making the act of planning in Shenzhen analogous to sweeping leaves in a hurricane.[35] Impotent in the face of a raging marketplace, planners were largely relegated to a nursemaid role. As Mihai Craciun has put it, "the confrontation between market and planning consistently canceled any obvious continuity between today's realities and tomorrow's goals: it humiliated vision."[36]

Complicating the planning process was another signal innovation of the special economic zones—a land tenure system that separated land-use rights from land ownership. Prior to reform, all land in China was "administratively allocated" to users by the central government free of charge. Now foreign investors could lease the right to use a parcel of land for a specified period of time (usually between forty and seventy years). They held no title to the property in a fee-simple sense—in China all land is still owned by the state—but were granted comforting new legal assurances that the land would not be arbitrarily taken away. Shenzhen was the site of the first property auction in the People's Republic when, on December 1, 1987, use rights to a parcel of land were sold for residential development.[37]

Thus safely tested in the SEZ "laboratory," the new land tenure system became national policy in 1988.[38] Only five lots were sold in 1987; within a decade the national number of land transactions was up to 105,473.[39] All this "opened a new era of lawful urban land transactions" in China, writes Anthony Yeh, creating a virtual real estate market in which land-use rights, rather than fee-simple property, could be bought and sold. The system allowed Beijing to have its cake and eat it, too; it would profit from the leases, yet never relinquish proprietary interest in the land itself. The sale of land rights also enables cities "to capture revenue from land which, in turn, can be used to develop infrastructure to enhance land value"[40] elsewhere. This self-seeding system, where land development breeds more land development, is known as *yi di yang di* and is one of the principal drivers of urban sprawl (explored in Chapter 7, "Suburbanization and the Mechanics of Sprawl"). Put more accurately, China has a dual land market, with both administratively allocated land meted out under the old system and land leased to developers in exchange for a fee and taxed by local municipalities.[41]

★　★　★

As the Shenzhen miracle spread throughout the Pearl River Delta, a new pattern of regional urban development began to take shape. Instead of concentrating in existing urban pockets, development sprawled across the once-rural landscape, largely following an expanding regional network of roads and highways. Unlike later limited-access expressways with specific points of egress, most of these early roads stimulated a continuous band of development, "corridor urbanization," along their routes. Just as the railroads were a kind of "metropolitan corridor" in nineteenth-century America, extending city ways into the hinterland, the delta highways carried a variety of urban spatial forms and socioeconomic practices deep into the countryside.[42]

Corridal development, oriented to the asphalt arterials, also created a kind of "town-village blending" (*chengxiang yitihua*) that blurred traditional boundaries between hinterland communities.[43] Once a new road was completed, or simply widened or otherwise upgraded, land all along its flanks developed rapidly into a hodgepodge of roadside retail and commercial uses—a sinofied version of the American highway "strip." The motorways acted like freshets of water flowing across a once-dry field, causing urban seeds to sprout along the way. Throughout the Pearl River Delta, ancient villages can be seen peering from behind the new roadside development. The contrast between the two spaces is striking: the densely packed, centuries-old gray brick dwellings of the village, with an entrance often still marked by a colorful ceremonial arch (*pailou*), now cringing behind a rampart of neon-lit, white-tiled buildings of the new commercial strip.

Of course, the Pearl River Delta is not the only region that has seen its economic geography reshuffled by roads. When the 171-mile Huning Expressway was completed between Nanjing and Shanghai in 1996, the long-dormant city Changzhou regained overnight the economic potency it once had as a way station on the Grand Canal. The expressway plugged Changzhou into a regional system of flows much the way the canal had done more than a thousand years earlier. Within months, just off the expressway ramp, office towers, apartment complexes, and hotels sprouted.[44] Not far away, in suburban Shanghai, studies have shown that towns blessed with a highway interchange reap measurable economic benefits, while those bypassed by the infrastructure often go downhill—a contemporary Chinese version of a pattern seen in the United States in both the railroad age and the interstate-highway era.[45]

Because the Pearl River Delta was the earliest regional economy to boom in the post-Mao period, road-driven urbanization there has been particularly extensive, and it can be easily detected in satellite images of the area. Perhaps the most dramatic example is the development unleashed by the completion of the Pearl River Delta's most important single stretch of road—the Guangzhou-Shenzhen Expressway. One of the first modern, high-speed, limited-access motorways in China, the expressway has been a catalyst for extensive development in the eastern half of the Pearl River Delta since its opening in July 1994. The road was built by Hong Kong engineer and property baron Gordon Wu, who recognized that the future of both Hong Kong and the greater delta region depended on an efficient conduit from the mainland border and Shenzhen north to Guangzhou. The Guangzhou-Shenzhen Expressway is today the jugular of China's most economically vital region, a mainline arterial analogous in many respects to Interstate 95 along the Boston-to-Washington (BosWash) corridor in the northeastern United States. Indeed Gordon Wu modeled the Guangzhou-Shenzhen Expressway on part of I-95—the New Jersey Turnpike.

Just as the New Jersey Turnpike set into motion the mechanics of suburban sprawl that would reconfigure New Jersey's pastoral landscape, the Guangzhou-Shenzhen Expressway stimulated extensive, low-density industrial, commercial, and residential development in towns and cities all along its route. Wu expected this and positioned himself to capture some of the economic benefits. He retained options to develop each of the expressway's many interchanges, where he planned to build ingenious multilevel shopping malls tucked under the on- and off-ramps of the interchanges themselves. The malls were also meant to seed development nearby—forming the nuclei of vast new suburban settlements along the route. Though the interchange-malls were never constructed, the Guangzhou-Shenzhen Expressway did stimulate extensive development along its flanks. This is immediately evident in aerial and satellite imagery of the eastern delta, in which Wu's seminal road and all the building it unleashed sprawls like a mighty dragon across the landscape.

The Guangzhou-Shenzhen Expressway was only the first strand of an arterial tapestry Wu hoped to weave out of the greater Pearl River Delta. This meant building a circumferential highway around the delta itself by connecting the Guangzhou-Shenzhen Expressway to a second road that would carry traffic back south from Guangzhou along the west side of the delta, eventually into the Zhuhai SEZ at the border with Macau. In the north, the two routes would be fused together by a twenty-four–mile ring-road halo around Guangzhou (completed in 2002). To the south, across the gaping mouth of the Pearl River itself, Wu proposed that a causeway be constructed, thus forming the east-west bar of a great letter "A" inscribed upon the delta. The road across the sea would run from Zhuhai and Macau across open water to Hong Kong's Lantau Island, itself the site of Hong Kong International Airport and a hub of extensive highway and rail links (not to mention Hong Kong Disneyland). The Chinese penchant for numerology quickly suggested a name—"one bridge, three connections" (Hong Kong, Zhuhai, and Macau). As with the Guangzhou-Shenzhen Expressway, Wu's grand design was inspired by landmarks of American engineering—the Chesapeake Bay Bridge-Tunnel and the even longer Lake Pontchartrain Causeway in Louisiana. As he pointed out in an interview, if the Bridge-Tunnel were pulled taut and superimposed on the Pearl River Delta, it would fit almost perfectly between Zhuhai and Hong Kong.

By 1997 Wu had already helped build a smaller road bridge between Nansha and the Humen district of Dongguan, one of the delta's leading boomtowns. The ten-mile causeway sports a main span 888 meters (2,913 feet) in length. The Humen Pearl River Bridge is still the largest bridge on the Pearl River and one of the longest suspension bridges in the People's Republic. The transdelta causeway, on the other hand, has been the subject of controversy and debate for years; for all its merits, it is still nowhere near being built. In 2000, Wu was appointed chairman of Hong Kong's powerful Port and Maritime Board, giving him a bully pulpit from which to promote the project. He was aided by a study at the Chinese University of Hong Kong that estimated the bridge could boost the entire Pearl Delta economy by some US$14 billion—much to Hong Kong's benefit.[46] In 2003 a team of researchers led by regional economist Michael J. Enright published an influential study of Hong Kong's position in the Pearl River economic constellation. The report showed that the western delta was developing at a slower pace than the east side, largely due to the latter's "better linkages to Hong Kong." For example, in 2001 Shenzhen and Dongguan had seven times the combined exports of Zhuhai and Zhongshan. The Enright team determined that Wu's bridge was begging to be built, and that its long-term value to the region would dwarf all estimated costs.[47]

By this time, two equally ambitious sea-crossing bridges had been undertaken at the mouth of the Yangtze Delta, both promising clear benefits to the Pearl River Delta's chief rival—the greater Shanghai region. The Donghai (Eastern Sea) Bridge, completed in December 2005, connects Shanghai to its offshore deep-water port at Yangshan; at 20.2 miles it is currently the longest sea-crossing highway in the world (the Lake Pontchartrain Causeway is longer, but it crosses fresh water). A second transocean linkage was under construction nearby, across Hangzhou Bay, connecting the Zhejiang

超车道 主车道 主车道 路 肩
Passing Lane Main Lane Main Lane Shoulder

Guangzhou-Shenzhen Expressway, 1999. PHOTOGRAPH BY AUTHOR

provincial cities of Cixi (part of Ningbo) and Jiaxing for a total run of 22.4 miles—a crossing originally envisioned nearly a century ago by Sun Yat-sen. When completed, the Hangzhou Bay Bridge will be the world's longest trans-oceanic road crossing. The project has presented immense engineering challenges due to Hangzhou Bay's powerful tides and vulnerability to typhoons. With six lanes in two directions and a midpoint traveler's oasis, the crossing will reduce the distance between Ningbo and Shanghai by seventy-five miles. Like so many major projects in China, the Hangzhou Bay Bridge is expected to open in time for the Olympic Summer Games in 2008.[48]

While less demanding in terms of engineering, the Pearl River Bridge presents a greater political challenge due to the many jurisdictions involved—two special administrative regions (Hong Kong and Macau), two special economic zones (Shenzhen and Zhuhai), the Guangdong provincial government, and, above all, China's national government. The administration of such an infrastructure would require a higher degree of cooperation, coordination, and transparency among the various parties than currently exists. The exact jurisdictional balance depends largely on the route of the bridge itself. Four different alignments have been explored and debated over the last decade, including Gordon Wu's original Y-shaped south alignment linking Lantau to Zhuhai and Macau; a more diplomatic "double Y" configuration that connects also to Shenzhen; a northern alignment dashed between Zhongshan and Shenzhen, and a twin-bridge scheme, proposed by MIT professor Tunney Lee. This alignment would have separate parallel crossings between Zhongshan and Shenzhen and Zhuhai and Hong Kong—a scheme that can be implemented in stages and has the added benefit of redundancy in the event of a catastrophic failure.[49] All of these options trigger a panoply of funding and environmental issues. For one, the west side of Lantau Island—where the causeway would make landfall in several of the schemes—is home to the 800-year-old fishing village Tai O and serves as breeding grounds for an endangered species of white dolphin.

Even if the Pearl River crossing is ever realized, it is unlikely that Gordon Wu will build it. Hopewell Holdings nearly went bankrupt after the Asian economic meltdown in 1997, and it has struggled to gain its balance ever since, even taking on local school construction projects to keep afloat. Wu was able to build only a small portion of the vast highway system he envisioned for the Pearl River Delta. But in subsequent years, many of Wu's intended roads have been built by provincial and municipal authorities in the region, and so has part of an even grander scheme he conceived to put Guangdong Province within reach of rich regions beyond its borders. Though the Pearl River Delta is blessed with fertile land and easy access to the sea, it is separated from the rest of China by a belt of mountains to the north. Wu reasoned that if a highway could be punched through this barrier, the booming Pearl River Delta could tap a much larger hinterland; the highway would be, in effect, an asphalt river draining a vast economic watershed.

This is just what he had in mind. The Chinese land mass is drained by three great river systems: the Yellow River (Huang He) through the north China plains; the Yangtze (Chang Jiang) through the heart of the nation, emptying near Shanghai; and, to the south, the West River (Xi Jiang)—of which the Pearl River (Zhu Jiang) is part. But not all of China has been equally blessed by these life-giving waters. The vast country south of the Yangtze, north of Guangdong, and east of the Yunnan Plateau, for example, is unserved by any major sea-bound rivers. Wu thought this shortcoming of geography could be rectified with a strategic deployment of infrastructure: a superhighway running north from Guangzhou to Hengyang, the southernmost navigable point on the

Xiang River and the transportation hub of Hunan Province (the Xiang flows into Dongting Lake, which is in turn connected to the Yangtze River by canal). From there the highway would beat a path due north, terminating at the city of Yueyang on the eastern shore of Dongting Lake, a stone's throw from the Yangtze itself. The road, to be called the Guangzhou-Yueyang Expressway, would be China's missing "fourth river"—a six-lane, 600-mile-long asphalt tributary hacked through a mountain range and spanning the administrative boundaries of scores of townships and municipalities.

The plan was as outrageous as it was ingenious. Not only would the road provide access to resource-rich lands all along its route, but by tapping into the Yangtze River it would enable Guangdong Province—and, of course, Hong Kong—to capture a share of the riches flowing toward Shanghai. This interregional raid was in fact drawn from the playbook of another American landmark—New York's Erie Canal. Long before the age of asphalt, the Erie Canal reconfigured the economic geography of the United States. The water highway, stretching 363 miles across central New York, linked the Great Lakes to the Hudson River and, thus, to the port city and the river's mouth. The Erie Canal not only tapped the rich hinterlands of upstate New York, but also put New York City a barge-ride away from the great agricultural and natural-resource wealth of the upper Midwest. The canal's opening in 1825 put New England's agricultural economy on the skids and helped moved New York ahead of Boston and Philadelphia, its chief rivals, making it the most important economic center on the eastern seaboard.

Wu was convinced the Guangzhou-Yueyang Expressway would do for Guangdong and the Pearl River Delta what the Erie Canal did for New York, bringing large areas of Jiangxi, Hunan, Guangxi, and even Sichuan Province into its economic orbit—a region with a combined population of some 300 million people. When Gordon Wu first proposed this road in 1982, it was dismissed as a fantasy that could never be built without a mandate from heaven. But like so many of Wu's highway visions, it eventually became reality. Guangdong authorities adopted Wu's route and eventually constructed an expressway to the northern boundary of the province. Hunan Province picked up the baton and built their section of the highway to Hengyang, a project funded in part by the World Bank. Today, the entire route from the Guangzhou ring road to the Xiang River at Hengyang and on to the Hunan provincial capital, Changsha, is part of the National Trunk Highway System.

A seemingly endless convoy of container trucks plies the asphalt arteries of the Pearl River Delta today, the blood cells of China's most important
regional economy. The greater Pearl River Delta has, in the last two decades,
evolved from a largely rural landscape of farms and rice fields into one of the
most rapidly urbanizing places on earth—a polycentric regional conurbation
of immense scale that is already one of the world's leading "megacites," home
to a population that will likely top thirty million by 2020. As Manuel Castells
has argued, megacities are the primary spatial forms of the new global economy, nodes that concentrate "directional, productive, and managerial upper
functions all over the planet."[50] One of the distinctive features of megacity
urban form, according to Castells, is their externalized connection to a global
space of flows, and simultaneous "discontinuity" with patterns and flows that
once prevailed locally. In his analysis, the greater Pearl River Delta region—
what Castells has termed the "South China Metropolis"—will likely emerge as
"one of the preeminent industrial, business, and cultural centers of the twenty-
first century."[51]

Just as Deng Xiaoping had envisioned, proximity to Hong Kong's managerial and technical expertise and capital enabled the region to jump to life. As
Castells points out, in the ten-year period between 1985 and 1995, "Hong Kong
industrialists induced one of the largest-scale processes of industrialization in
human history in the small towns of the Pearl River Delta. By the end of 1994,
Hong Kong investors, often using family and ancestral-village connections,
had established in the Pearl River Delta 10,000 joint ventures and 20,000
processing factories, in which were working about six million workers."[52]

In terms of spatial structure, Castells has argued that this South China
Metropolis is wholly unlike the "traditional Megalopolis" described by Jean
Gottmann in his studies of the BosWash corridor of the eastern United States,
which consists of functionally autonomous "successive urban/suburban units";
it is rather a "new spatial form" in which a range of regional units operate with
a high degree of both interdependency and global connectivity. What distinguishes this new kind of city, Castells observes, are the "internal linkages of
the area and the indispensable connection of the whole system to the global
economy via multiple communication links." It is the ultimate space of flows.
Castells was prescient in anticipating, more than a decade ago, that the South
China Metropolis might well become "the most representative urban face of
the twenty-first century."[53]

But regional development theory is hardly needed to see this in action; a trip to the local Wal-Mart will do. Today, the Pearl River Delta is the workshop of the world. Millions of people in the United States, many who might never have even heard of Guangdong Province, know well the fruits of this extraordinary industrial cornucopia. Americans may bristle at all the manufacturing jobs lost to China in recent decades, but we relish the new affordability of so many consumer goods made there. Most of the stuff that stocks the shelves of Target, Costco, Wal-Mart, Toys"R"Us, Home Depot, and other big American retailers comes from China, and the lion's share is made in factories in the Pearl River Delta. The Chinese economic miracle, driven largely by Guangdong Province, is why we can buy an air conditioner for $79.95 when a similar unit ten years ago cost three times that, or why a powerful desktop computer can be purchased for under $500. A large percentage of the decorative goods that flood American stores around the holidays are manufactured in the Pearl River Delta, never more visibly than at Christmas. In 1999, some ten million artificial Christmas trees and 128 million wired light sets were imported to the United States from China, enough to turn all of Staten Island into a plastic forest and string lights from the earth to the moon.[54]

There is hardly any manufacturing sector that China, specifically Guangdong, does not dominate. As Michael Enright and Edith Scott found, the Pearl River Delta currently produces "roughly a third of the world's footwear, a third of the world's consumer electronics, a third of the world's microwave ovens, half of the world's toys, two thirds of the world's watches, and sizeable shares of world production in garments, plastic products, other home appliances, mobile and cordless phones." If import quotas are lifted, delta garment manufacturers could take up as much as a third of the global production share in the textile industry, while furniture production in Dongguan alone has been "almost single-handedly responsible for a reduction in employment in the U.S. furniture industry by about a third."[55] North Carolina, once a major producer of furniture in the United States, has been hammered hard by all this. The city of High Point, about an hour west of Chapel Hill, is still famous for its biannual furniture fair. But today much of the furniture sold there is actually manufactured half a world away in the Pearl River Delta. Remarkably, it is cheaper to ship Appalachian hardwoods to China and back again as tables, chairs, and sofas than to turn the raw material into furniture locally.

Like Dongguan, delta towns and cities have each developed their own manufacturing specialties, and successful local industries often become the very identity of such places. Xiaolan is known for locks, Shaxi is the Casual Garment City, and Dafen, a village near Shenzhen, from which much of the world's knockoff art comes, advertises itself as the Oil Painting Village. Shenzhen, Dongguan, and Huizhou are home to vast computer and electronics plants. One of the largest is the manufacturing complex in Shenzhen's Longhua District for Taiwanese-owned Foxconn, manufacturer of Apple's Macbook and iPhone and a supplier of components for seemingly every brand of computer and cell phone in the world. The plant, which came under much criticism in the Western press for substandard working conditions, is rumored to employ more than 200,000 people on site (imagine all of Reno, Nevada, working for a single employer). Foshan manufactures most of China's "sanitary ceramics," such as sinks, lavatories, and toilet bowls. Jiangmen is a center for textiles and garments. Chencun is known for turf grass and ornamental fish, Panyu for toys and sporting goods, and little Guzhen is China's Lighting Capital. A town in the northwest section of Zhongshan City, Guzhen is home to some 2,000 lighting factories, most of which are small- or medium-sized family operations that began as township and village enterprises in the early reform era. By the 1990s the growing agglomeration of manufacturers in the area displaced Zhejiang Province as China's number one lighting producer.

Today, Guzhen's products dominate the domestic market and exports—to over 100 countries—bring in $300 million annually. Most of the lights for sale in American home-improvement stores come from Guzhen. Lighting is Guzhen's very raison d'être and it dominates town life—hardly surprising given that the industry generates 70 percent of local GDP and employs half the population. Just off Lighting Square is Guzhen's main drag, Lighting Street, lined with more than a thousand showrooms. Every year the town hosts the China International Lighting Fair, one of the largest in the world; and at the event in 1999 town officials announced plans to erect a mighty symbol of Guzhen's native industry—the world's biggest lamp. The idea came from none other than the chairman of the Guzhen Communist Party, Wu Renfu, who felt that the town "needed a tangible icon that spoke of Guzhen as much as the Eiffel Tower spoke of Paris," one that might also "serve as a totem for the people…a reminder of the source of their livelihoods and prosperity." Thus were hatched plans for Lamp King Tower (*Deng Wang*), the height of which was

古镇灯王博物馆效果图二

Artist's rendering of Guzhen's Lamp King Tower. COURTESY CUI CHAOWEN, TOWN OF GUZHEN

ratcheted up each year as the town's exports swelled. From a relatively modest 125 feet it grew, in turn, to 453 feet, 682 feet, and 702 feet, before finally topping out at a colossal 833 feet—nearly three times the height of the Statue of Liberty.

In October 2004 a seventy-foot model of the big lamp was unveiled, and a year later ground was broken on the thing itself. Chairman Wu realized that Guzhen's icon should be "universally recognizable as a lamp." Thus the colossal luminaire is not a rarefied Chinese antique or trendy torchiere, but "the world's only architecture shaped like a huge western classical oil lamp," as promotional material describes it. The $38 million structure will contain 430,560 square feet of area on forty-eight floors, with an immense glass chimney on which an array of images will be projected at night from inside. An observation deck will be incorporated into the chimney, and the "base" of the lamp will contain shops, restaurants, and a museum to document "humanity's quest for light against darkness." Town officials hope that the Lamp King Tower will put Guzhen on the tourist map, drawing visitors from nearby Shenzhen and Hong Kong. Like the Hangzhou Bay Bridge, the Lamp King Tower is scheduled to be illuminated in time for the 2008 Summer Olympic Games.[56]

★   ★   ★

The vast new wealth generated by these new industrial giants—former agricultural centers like Zhongshan, Panyu, Nanhai, Foshan, and Shunde—is also evident in extraordinary civic architectural works, infrastructural improvements, and other "image projects" undertaken by city officials. Vast public squares and plazas, well-appointed libraries and city halls, museums, exhibition centers, and concert halls have sprouted in once-poor cities around the delta in recent years. Dongguan is perhaps the best example; it has been a spectacular success story in the reform era, every bit as lauded in post-Mao China as was Dazhai by Mao during the Cultural Revolution. A once-sleepy town halfway between Shenzhen and Guangzhou, Dongguan is now one of the most affluent cities in the People's Republic, its new status best symbolized by its South China Mall, currently the largest shopping mall in the world (see Chapter 9, "Theme Parks and the Landscape of Consumption"). Dongguan is one of the manufacturing engines of the Pearl River Delta, with an annual growth rate of 23 percent and exports trailing only those of much-larger Shanghai and Shenzhen. Those fortunate enough to be legal residents (as opposed to the many migrant workers laboring in its factories) enjoy some of the highest incomes of any city in China, which helps explain why Dongguan enjoys the highest per capita automobile ownership in the nation. Dongguan's wealth and ambition can be readily observed in the built environment: hundreds of high-rise residential housing towers encircle the horizon. The city's spectacular new administrative complex features a 230-acre plaza anchored by a high-rise city hall and surrounded by a stunning collection of public buildings—a theater, museums, a conference center, and library. Not far away a high-tech new town—Songshan Lake Pioneer Park—will expand the city's skilled workforce by more than 300,000 people.[57]

Of course, the Pearl River Delta is not the only boom region in China; several hundred miles to the north, the deltaic landscape of another great river—the Yangtze—has itself been the site of extraordinary economic growth and, at Shanghai especially, of even greater efforts to reinvent urban terrain.

CHAPTER TWO

Reclaiming Shanghai

上海的重新定位

If you fly to Shanghai via Google Earth, you will be set down in a vast space at the center of town known as People's Park (Renmin Guangchang). Here, on a former British racetrack turned into a public park after 1949, four major civic buildings have been erected in recent decades. They sit proudly in the park and glow at night like chalices on a grand metropolitan altar. The first two erected were City Hall and the Shanghai Art Museum. Jean-Marie Charpentier's Grand Theatre, easily the most spectacular, followed. But none of the buildings is more expressive of the zeitgeist of China's urban revolution than the Shanghai Urban Planning Exposition Center (Shanghai Chengshi Guihua Zhanshiguan). With five floors of exhibits dedicated to nearly every aspect of city planning and design, it is a temple of urban futurism, like nothing seen in the United States since the Futurama exhibit a lifetime ago.

Entering the lobby of the Expo Center, a visitor is greeted by a monumental gilded sculpture of the city's iconic buildings, a kind of architectural golden calf that slowly rotates on a pedestal, flooded worshipfully with lights. The piece is a kaleidoscopic assemblage of Shanghai's urban architectural history, compressing a century's worth of buildings into a single work of art. A flock of seagulls encircles all the buildings, as if to consecrate this union of past and future. Skyscrapers of recent vintage—the Pearl of the Orient TV Tower, the Jin Mao Tower, and the World Financial Center—dominate the group, while gathered at their feet are a number of landmark structures from Shanghai's neocolonial past, most conspicuously the former headquarters of the Hongkong and Shanghai Banking Corporation, the clock-towered Customs House, and Victor Sassoon's venerable Peace Hotel. These are relics

A gathering of symbols; lobby sculpture, Shanghai Urban Planning Exposition Center, 2007.
PHOTOGRAPH BY AUTHOR

of Shanghai's century-long tenure as the principal treaty port on the China coast—a well-oiled resource extraction machine designed to keep China stoned and drooling while foreigners spirited away much of her wealth. But here, the hoary landmarks of Western imperialism look small and insignificant, huddled humbly at the feet of New China's architectural giants. The onetime masters are mendicants now, their very survival contingent and provisional. Whether it was meant to be or not, the gilded sculpture is a symbol of triumph over the past and its humiliations. Shanghai may have long been an imperial outpost dominated by foreigners, but it is now the flagship of Chinese ambition.

Shanghai's urban landscape has long been contested terrain, at least since British imperialists set their sights on the place in the mid-nineteenth century. In 1843, after a contentious and lopsided year-long process of treatymaking between China and Britain, five ports were officially opened to foreign traders along the coast, conceded in reprisal for China's ill-fated attempt, several years earlier, to end the opium trade—an act that led to the First Opium War. Prior to the 1842 Treaty of Nanking, British and other foreigners seeking access to Chinese tea, silk, porcelain, jade, and other valuables were largely confined to Guangzhou, where all business was channeled through strictly monitored Chinese brokerage houses, or *godowns*, known as the Thirteen Factories. Trade with the "foreign barbarians" was prohibited within the city proper, and movement of the aliens in general was highly circumscribed. But the antiquated Canton System, as it became known, quickly fell apart with the advent of the opium trade. Opium was addictive to both merchant and user. British traders were desperate for a commodity valuable enough in China to balance steep demand for Chinese tea and silk back home. While Indian cotton answered this need for a time, opium quickly displaced it. In the brutal logic of the marketplace, opium was the perfect commodity—plentiful, easy to ship, and very profitable, with addictive properties guaranteed to stoke demand: instead of becoming saturated, the market for the narcotic steadily increased as more and more people became dependent.

While the British may have masterminded the opium trade—what John King Fairbank called "one of the longest-continued international crimes of modern times"—it involved a truly multicultural cast of characters.[1] These included esteemed British trading houses; Scots merchant firms such as Dent and Jardine, Matheson & Company; Parsi and Iraqi Jewish opium dealers in India, the greatest of which was the House of Sassoon; fleet-of-foot American shippers; and a network of Chinese smugglers and corrupt Qing officials who grew fat allowing the drug into their midst. Opium was so profitable to the British Crown that it not only tolerated its trade, despite the manifold iniquities therein, but even committed its military forces to assure that the opium trade flourished.[2]

Thus it was addiction to a potent narcotic—and the profits it yielded—that led to the forced opening of the Chinese coast, and to the rise of what would become the first modern cities in China. The first five treaty ports—"shrewdly chosen," writes Fairbank, "as points of entrance into the avenues of Chinese maritime trade which already existed"—included the ancient trading centers of Xiamen (Amoy), Fuzhou (Foochow), Ningbo (Ningpo), and Guangzhou (Canton), as well as a relative upstart named Shanghai.[3] Set on rich alluvial lands at a bend in the Huangpu River, fifteen miles south of its confluence with the Yangtze River (Chang Jiang), Shanghai had been a small trading center and market town for several centuries, vital but far less important than nearby Hangzhou, Suzhou, Yangzhou, or Quanzhou. But Shanghai grew rapidly after it was formally opened as a treaty port in November 1843, and soon it outranked all regional rivals in terms of population and economic power— a nineteenth-century, quasi-colonial version of Shenzhen.[4] By 1900—barely two generations after it opened as a treaty port—Shanghai was already ranked with Paris, London, and New York as one of the world's great metropolitan centers. The city's population, about 500,000 in 1843, topped one million by 1880 and reached four million in 1935.[5]

Shanghai also became the subject of myth and fable in the Western imagination, in turn celebrated as the "Paris of the East" and excoriated as a bastion of immorality—the "Whore of Asia." Visitors could easily validate either version, and invariably found Shanghai both exotic and oddly familiar—an Eastern city whose architecture and urbanism was similar in many respects to that of New York or Paris. Also familiar to Western visitors, especially those from England and the United States, was the structure of governance in Shanghai. Like so many other aspects of the city, this was unlike anything in China at the time. Before it became a treaty port, Shanghai was little more than a large rural village in terms of governance and administration. Like most Chinese urban communities at the time, writes Kerrie MacPherson, Shanghai "had no 'municipal' government; no central self-governing body required to register its needs or to oversee its activities, and therefore no body that was obliged to take account of the effects of rapid change, let alone to prepare for swift communal adjustments or to plan for the future."[6]

Large areas of the future city were still tidal flats—a malarial "wilderness of marshes," as MacPherson has put it. The incomers found this untenable and undertook a variety of improvements to remake Shanghai in the image of a Western city. Improvements were at first limited to those parts of the city specifically granted by the treaty—the so-called French Concession and the adjacent International Settlement, formed from the combined British and American settlements. In these areas the foreigners enjoyed the extraordinary privilege of extraterritoriality—full exemption from local laws and legal jurisdiction, which gave them the administrative autonomy necessary for creating their very own Shanghai.[7] Though built on Chinese soil and existing at the sufferance of the Chinese, the international settlements took on "something of the quality of a sovereign state, directly answerable to no higher power."[8] Missionaries aside, most foreigners saw Shanghai as little more than an engine of fortune, a "merchants' Utopia," as one historian put it, and "probably the last of the world's great cities that could be regarded, in the tradition of Genoa and Venice and the great Hansa towns, as a republic living and dominated by the trader."[9]

This of course required administrative stability and the steady rule of law. Toward that end the foreigners formed Shanghai's first permanent elected municipal government, the Shanghai Municipal Council, in 1854. Under the auspices of the council, the foreign community could tax itself to raise revenue for a multitude of progressive public works. Although these were often carried out in collaboration with Chinese officials, the council itself, elected by a tiny minority of property owners, was made up exclusively of foreigners.[10] Over the next thirty years Shanghai's foreign community constructed and maintained roads, improved the river for navigation, and developed a sewer system and China's first modern waterworks. They also opened hospitals, initiated public health programs, and built some of the first institutions of higher learning in Asia.[11] Even soccer came to China via Shanghai, introduced by American educator F. L. Hawks Pott at St. John's University.[12] By the close of the nineteenth century, Shanghai was Asia's most modern metropolis, with gas lighting and electric trams, several daily newspapers, and telegraph and telephone service linked to the world by trans-Pacific cable.[13]

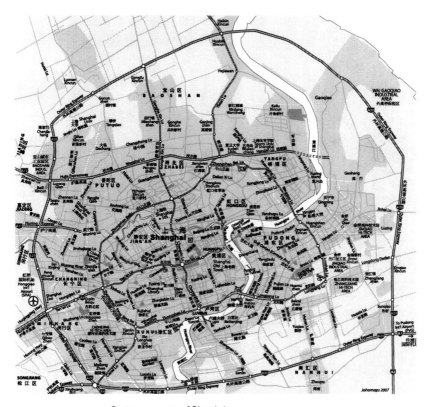

Contemporary map of Shanghai. COURTESY OF JOHOMAPS.COM

The most lauded symbol of all this was the bund, a waterfront boulevard flanked by a wall of imposing neoclassical buildings—banks and trading houses, the customs house, hotels and clubs, and other architectural
appurtenances of mercantile imperialism. The bund (not a German word, but
derived from the Persian term for an earthen dam or dyke) had begun as a tow-
path on the east bank of the Huangpu River; now it was the "Wall Street of
China."[14] Its urbanism was imported wholesale from the West, with buildings designed almost exclusively by foreign architects. Only one early bund
structure, the Bank of China, was the work of a Chinese architect, Luke Him
Sau (Lu Qianshou); but he, too, was employed at the time by the Hong Kong
British firm Palmer and Turner.[15] The bund's panorama of brick and stone was
thus the sine qua non symbol of Western power and privilege in both Shanghai
and China; it was flatteringly photographed from the wharves across the

View of the bund, ca. 1938. COURTESY INSTITUT D'ASIE ORIENTALE

river at Pudong much the way the skyscrapers of lower Manhattan are admired from Brooklyn Heights.

To the Chinese, on the other hand, the bund was little more than a symbol of their nation's weakness and subjugation. But the bund and the impositional city it represented were also useful to China. The settlements had served as a neutral political zone and sanctuary for Chinese in times of civil strife, most notably during the decade-long Taiping Rebellion, when an estimated one million refugees flocked to Shanghai's foreign settlements.[16] Moreover, the municipal improvements in the international settlements—and even their governance structure—later served as an example for Chinese-led modernization efforts.

Though sidelined from the actual administration of the international settlements, the Chinese of Shanghai were not idle bystanders in the reinvention of their city; however undervalued, they played a signal role in the city's transformation into a modern metropolis (not to mention, of course, contributing most of the labor necessary to build its vast public works). With the overthrow of the Qing government and subsequent founding of the Chinese Republic—and especially after the May Fourth Movement of 1919—the Shanghainese became increasingly discontented with being second-class citizens in their own land. Now a new generation of reformers came to the fore, eager to modernize China and bring about what Michael Tsin has called "a new political rationality." Doing so necessarily meant learning from Western science and technical expertise, which of course precipitated a moral dilemma, one that only sharpened as Chinese nationalism and antiforeign sentiment grew stronger.[17]

Many of China's young reformers had studied architecture, engineering, city planning, and municipal administration in the United States and Europe, often on scholarships provided by the American share of the Boxer Indemnity Fund.[18] They returned home with a passion to make China a progressive, prosperous nation and advocated a wide range of public works meant to promote "hygienic modernity" (weisheng).[19] Invariably the reformers came to see Chinese cities as alarmingly antiquated, with overcrowded housing, poor sanitary conditions, congested streets, and virtually no modern infrastructure. The ancient walls that still encircled many Chinese cities, now seen as obsolete relics standing in the way of progress, were a particular target of their reformist zeal. Throughout the 1920s and 1930s, Chinese planners repeatedly called for the demolition of these city walls, often to clear the way for modern motorways.[20]

In Shanghai, old walls fell to make way for modern infrastructure and literally enabled the Chinese to cut loose from the past and reclaim their city. In 1912, the newly appointed governor of Shanghai, former revolutionary general Chen Qimei, inaugurated a series of reforms in the old Chinese city, the most visible of which was the demolition of its enceinte.[21] The northern half of Shanghai's wall was gone by 1913, replaced by Ming Guo Road, and the southern half—nearly two miles long—was taken down a year later. Zhong Hua Road was laid out in its place.[22]

Though the walls were ostensibly removed to make way for motor vehicles, doing so was also a highly symbolic act; by eliminating the ancient barricade, Chinese Shanghai was now set free to expand beyond the confines of the old city—often ironically labeled "Chinatown" on old Shanghai maps—and lay claim to the larger city. Not content with such incremental gains, some reformers advocated more dramatic action—dismantling not just old walls but the foreign settlements themselves. Doing so obviously had visceral appeal. Though the treaty ports were conduits of ideas and technologies that helped make China modern, they were also the nation's great shame and represented a colossal loss of face for a proud, ancient culture that saw itself comfortably at the center of the universe—literally, the Middle Kingdom. Nowhere was such cultural humiliation more acute than in Shanghai, which was essentially an occupied territory. As one Kuomintang official put it, the settlements in Shanghai were effectively an "independent country within the borders of China, which is not under Chinese, but under foreign control."[23]

Such an affront to national sovereignty was increasingly intolerable to the idealistic young Chinese nationalists of the 1920s. Resistance became even stronger in 1925 after imperial police violently suppressed peaceful demonstrations in Shanghai and Guangzhou. Racism, too, added much salt to the wounds of history. "The attitude of the average Shanghai resident towards the inhabitants of the country in which he lives," commented one diplomat, "is a constant and increasing source of resentment to the Chinese."[24]

But however tempting it might be, evicting the foreigners wholesale from Shanghai would end up hurting China even more. Shanghai's reformers therefore sought a more diplomatic course of action, if only to avoid alienating the foreign-dominated business community and thus committing economic suicide.[25] Nevertheless, increasingly stern actions were carried out by the Chinese to contain the foreigners and check the expansion of the international settlement. The construction of new roads beyond the settlements, for example, was stopped cold by Chinese authorities, who correctly saw such activity as the first step toward increasing the foreign footprint. "In recent years," wrote one local official in 1926, "the population within the Settlement has been constantly increasing. The foreigners have therefore demanded the extension of the Settlement. From their point of view this seems to be a reasonable demand, but during the last 20 years the national conscientiousness of the Chinese has been rapidly growing, so they have never obtained the consent of the Chinese for the purposed extensions. I may say frankly that they will never obtain such consent in the future."[26]

The foreign concessions would also be contained by surrounding them with "an impenetrable barrier of a new Chinese settlement," a new kind of enclosing wall that would effectively make the international settlements an island "isolated from the mainland from which it received its vital forces."[27] If the foreigners wanted more room, they would have to work with local authorities to help improve the dilapidated, overcrowded Chinese districts beyond their privileged sanctuaries—"to improve thoroughly the municipal affairs in the territories adjacent to the concessions so that the difference between concessions and non-concessions may be wiped out, and both foreigners and Chinese may co-operate in the most friendly way for the creation of a new and greater Shanghai."[28]

The hale spirit of Chinese nationalism and the May Fourth Movement spawned even bolder attempts to reclaim Shanghai and reinvent the city on China's terms. The most ambitious of these was put forth, appropriately enough, by Sun Yat-sen, founder of the Chinese Republic and its first president. Sun's "Great Port of Pudong" plan, outlined in 1919, was intended to replace Shanghai's ossifying port with a whole new facility across the Huangpu River in Pudong, a largely rural place a world away from cosmopolitan Shanghai. Sun proposed filling in a long stretch of the Huangpu River between Puxi and Pudong and channeling its waters into a great canal (*xin kai hu*) stretched across the Pudong peninsula. Along the canal's lower reaches a new, Chinese bund would rise. A boulevard, shopping district, and civic center would be built at Pudong Point and on thirty square miles of adjacent filled land.[29]

Sun was a physician and a forceful politician, but he readily admitted a lack of technical competency when it came to city planning. His Great Port scheme, however visionary, was impractical and would have been prohibitively expensive to implement (a bit like proposing to divert the East River through Queens and moving midtown Manhattan over to Long Island City) but the symbolism of the plan rang clear as a bell. Here was a Shanghai reclaimed and reinvented by the Chinese, free of the stain of history and the humiliations of the past. Deprived of its life-sustaining river port, the foreign bund would literally be left high and dry, the international settlements engulfed by a new Chinese city. Obviously, this prospect did not thrill Shanghai's expatriate community. As one historian dispassionately put it, "Cut-off from their access to the sea, the source of their prosperity, and contained geographically, the settlements faced declining prospects. A swift retreat would seem prudent or alternatively, to accept the fact that the future of Shanghai would be in the hands of the Chinese and negotiate accordingly."[30]

Within a few years, Sun Yat-sen's proposal gave way to more realistic, though no less visionary, Chinese plans to reclaim Shanghai. In July 1927 a new City Government of Greater Shanghai was created, its mayor now directly accountable not to the foreign-dominated Shanghai Municipal Council, but to the newly established Nationalist government in Nanjing. Shanghai was declared a "special administrative city" (*te bie shi*) that now had to answer only to China's central government—foreshadowing by decades the special economic zones and coastal open cities created by Deng Xiaoping.

These administrative innovations were accompanied by equally bold plans for Shanghai's built environment. In 1929 a City Planning Commission was formed, charged "with the goal of creating a comprehensive plan that would provide for the necessary physical expansion of the City."[31] The Commission was headed by Sheng Yi, a hydraulic engineer trained in Shanghai and Dresden who had previously been Shanghai's Commissioner of Public Works. The commission's architectural advisor was Dong Dayou, a graduate of the University of Minnesota and Columbia University who would go on to become one of China's most influential architects. In all, the commission consisted of eleven members, heads of local municipal bureaus as well as several consultants from overseas, including the Americans Asa Phillips, an engineer and city planner, and hydrologist Carl E. Grunsky, who had helped engineer the transformation of California's Imperial Valley early in his career.

With this arsenal of expertise, the City Planning Commission and mayor Huang Fu laid out a bold new scheme for reclaiming Shanghai, later named the "Greater Shanghai Plan." It called for a new administration center in the city's Jiangwan District, north of Suzhou Creek and the foreign settlements. Jiangwan offered a number of advantages. It was relatively undeveloped at the time, with room for future growth. It was served by a major rail line and was close to Wusong, a Yangtze River port town. There, a complex of new basins, piers, and wharves would be developed to replace Shanghai's aging ship-handling infrastructure, thus making Jiangwan the new center of economic activity in the city. In real and symbolic terms, the Greater Shanghai Plan was—like Sun's earlier scheme—intended to shift the focal point of Shanghai away from the international settlements, and form the nucleus of a reclaimed Chinese metropolis.[32]

The centerpiece of the Greater Shanghai Plan was its Civic Centre, designs for which were solicited in a public competition. Ambitions for the new center were prodigious from the start; it was to neutralize symbolically the international settlements and replace them with a new Chinese-built city center, thus serving as a "great monument to the new China and an example to the entire country."[33] The winning scheme was authored by architects Zhao Shen and Sun Ximing, though Dong Dayou subsequently modified and enlarged it at the request of the judges.[34]

In its final iteration, the plan called for a cruciform Civic Centre, laid out much like the footprint of a great cathedral. A pair of axial boulevards, each about 200 feet wide, met in a broad square anchored in the center by a pagoda. To the north was the main administrative complex, capped by the City Hall, or Mayor's Building. From there a pair of boulevards radiated northward on either side of the Sun Yat-sen Memorial Hall and Auditorium. Malls to the east and west of the pagoda square, each with parallel lawns and a central reflecting pool, were flanked by various government bureaus; the longer mall to the south featured a library, museum, art gallery, concert hall, and a five-arched ceremonial gate, or *pailou,* at the entrance. Each of the malls was capped by a semicircular road, beyond which the city was laid out in a simple rectilinear grid of blocks. Homes for affluent businessmen and officials were situated about parks on either side of the central axis, and these were surrounded in turn by neighborhoods for workers. A new commercial district was located near the new harbor at Wusong, while an athletic complex would be built just west of the Civic Centre and an airfield to the east, close to the Huangpu River.[35] The Civic Centre buildings themselves utilized the so-called Chinese Renaissance style and were designed by Dong Dayou and Zhao Shen. Both men had worked for an American pioneer of this style, Henry K. Murphy, a Connecticut Yankee whose China portfolio included several college campuses and plans for the new Chinese capital in Nanjing.[36]

In terms of urban design, the Civic Centre is derivative of the neoclassical City Beautiful tradition that dominated American planning pedagogy and practice in the years after the 1893 Columbian Exposition in Chicago. Indeed, both Zhao and Dong had studied at American architecture schools— Pennsylvania, Minnesota, and Columbia—where Beaux Arts and City Beautiful traditions were particularly strong. The City Beautiful approach to urban design can be traced, in spirit at least, to the axial makeover of Rome undertaken by Pope Sixtus V during the late Renaissance. It emphasized architectural unity and aesthetic grandeur and was particularly useful in radiating a measure of authoritarian control. American proponents of the style—thinking more of Pierre Charles L'Enfant, designer of Washington DC, than some obscure pope—preferred to imagine the City Beautiful calling forth exalted ideals of democracy and civic virtue. But even their patron saint, Daniel Burnham, used City Beautiful formalism toward imperial ends when he was commissioned by the U.S. War Department in 1905 to reshape Manila into

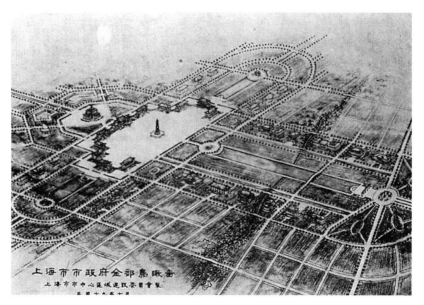

Civic Centre, Greater Shanghai Plan, 1930.
FROM FU CHAO-CHING, *ZHONGGUO GUDIAN SHIYANG XIN JIANZHU* (1993)

something that bespoke the power and supremacy of the American government. Edwin Lutyens and Herbert Baker did much the same thing on a much grander scale a decade later at New Delhi, their scheme for the new Indian capital a last-ditch attempt to prop up the dying British Raj with an awesome spectacle of architectural order and monumentality.

The Greater Shanghai Civic Centre employed kindred urbanism to telegraph a very different message—one of a semicolonized society breaking free of its shackles, reasserting itself and staking its claim on both city and nation. And for a while it looked as if it all might happen. Several key structures were built according to the plan between 1931 and 1937. The most exuberant was the Mayor's Building, with a glazed-tile gable roof and an interior decorated with polychromatic columns, coffers, and beams. The Shanghai Municipal Library and Municipal Museum, both also by Dong Dayou and Zhao Shen, were added two years later. These were followed by a hospital, stadium complex, and swimming pool, and a building for the China Air Transport Association.[37]

That even these few buildings were completed is astonishing given the political turmoil that was engulfing the city. Shanghai in the 1930s was in a constant state of terror. There was savage fighting between Nationalists

Inauguration ceremony of the Mayor's Building, Civic Centre, October 10, 1933.
COURTESY INSTITUT D'ASIE ORIENTALE

and Communists; and bombings by the Japanese in the spring of 1932 drove tens of thousands of Chinese refugees into the international settlements.[38] Eventually all construction at the Civic Centre came to a halt. The Japanese occupied the incomplete buildings from January through May 1932, inflicting extensive damage and making off with nearly all the building materials on site. On October 10, 1933, an inauguration ceremony held for the new Mayor's Building was attended by thousands of Chinese and foreigners, but fate intervened nonetheless. When the Japanese entered Shanghai again in the summer of 1937, there were bloody clashes with Chinese troops in Jiangwan. The new Greater Shanghai Municipal Government fled to the safety of the international settlement, leaving the battered Civic Centre buildings to the invaders when Shanghai fell on November 9, 1937. Japanese troops encamped at the Civic Centre for the duration of the subsequent occupation.[39]

Jiangwan would never again be the focus of Shanghai's dreams. The Civic Centre buildings were used instead to house a hodgepodge of cultural and educational institutions in the ensuing years. Once prominent landmarks surrounded by open space, they are now largely lost in a dense thicket of urban matter. The library and art museum are, respectively, a table tennis training

Former library building, Civic Centre, Jiangwan District, Shanghai, 2007. PHOTOGRAPH BY AUTHOR

academy and a hospital outbuilding, while the Mayor's Building has retained a semblance of dignity as the centerpiece of the Shanghai University of Sport, whose campus occupies much of the original Civic Centre cruciform. Faint traces of the Beaux Arts plan can also be picked out in high-resolution aerial satellite photographs.[40]

A stone's throw to the northeast of the old Civic Centre lies New Jiangwan City, a sprawling new town. Covering some 2,335 acres of land adjacent to the Huangpu River, much of which was a former military airport, New Jiangwan City is half again as big as the Civic Centre and will eventually support a population of some 80,000 residents. The new town is intended to "represent the spirit of Shanghai in the new era," and has been billed a "green ecological city" (*lu se sheng tai*) for well-educated professionals—"knowledge workers with an international outlook" (*guo ji zhi hui cheng*).[41] The most celebrated feature of New Jiangwan City is a delightfully ironic counterpoint to the gravitas of the historical drama once enacted nearby. This is the New Jiangwan City SMP Skate Park, the largest in the world. Aiming to become "the hub for extreme sports in Asia," the $26 million skate park, designed by Simon Oxenham of Australia, is already something of a pilgrimage site for global skater youth. To this rising generation, city planning in Jiangwan calls to mind not the stillborn metropolis of the Nationalist era and all that it symbolized, but doing ollies and tailslides in a 130,000-square-foot city of "concrete bowls, banks, hips and rails." ("I like the mega-pipe here especially," one visiting skater commented; "It takes real guts and skill to do tricks on that."[42])

★ ★ ★

But the old dream of a reclaimed Shanghai has, in the meantime, shifted back across the Huangpu to Pudong, to the very same ground that Sun Yat-sen envisioned for his Great Port scheme in the 1920s. The idea of creating a new city center at Pudong was taken up again by Shanghai authorities in the 1980s. As early as 1984, city officials first proposed Pudong as part of an overall economic development strategy for Shanghai, and the 1988 Comprehensive Plan of Shanghai focused on the "expansion and redevelopment of the east bank of the Huangpu River," along with building the bridge and tunnel connections necessary to transform Pudong into a modern metropolis.[43] In April 1990 the State Council endorsed the city's plans for the area, anointing the Pudong New Area as a national-level special development zone. A series of "preferential policies" were outlined to make Pudong an even more attractive place for foreign investment and business enterprise than the special economic zones. The vast Pudong area, now christened the "Head of the Dragon" by Deng Xiaoping, was divided into several priority development zones, including the Jinqiao Export-Processing Zone; the Waigaoqiao Free Trade Zone and deep-water port on the Yangtze River; the Zhangjiang High-tech Park; and, most importantly, the Lujiazui Financial and Trade Zone. If Pudong was to be the dragon's head, Lujiazui would be its eye.[44]

Long a place of agriculture and scattered industry, Pudong was now the blank slate on which the future of Shanghai would be written. It was not, of course, all that blank to begin with; there were more than a million people living in Pudong's several towns and rural villages. Added to that population now were thousands of redevelopment refugees from across the river, as Pudong was also to be a "decanting site for urban renewal of the highly dense old areas of Puxi."[45] As the centerpiece and cerebellum of the new metropolis—its "golden zone"—the ten-square-mile Lujiazui District became the focus of a high-profile design and planning process, well-publicized through a series of "international consultations" involving some of the leading architects and urban designers in the world.

French professionals would play an especially influential role in the planning process. Shanghai city officials entered a partnership in 1985 with the quasi-public French urban planning agency Institut d'Aménagement et d'Urbanisme de la Région Île-de-France, or IAURIF (Development and Town-Planning Institute of the Paris Region). Little of tangible value was born at first from this odd union, but with Pudong's official baptism in 1990, IAURIF officials found themselves ideally placed to influence planning activities related to the new city. There is in fact a certain historical precedent to this French connection; in the treaty-port era, Shanghai's Chinese leaders often looked to the French Concession as a model of municipal management, preferring "the stronger predilections for centralized authority" that characterized its governance over the more liberal democratic ways that prevailed in the Anglo-American international settlement.[46] Already, local planners had, in 1990, prepared a development plan for Lujiazui, calling for some forty million square feet of floor space and emphasizing the importance of using "gleaming skyscrapers with striking downtown skylines" to create a symbol of the new Shanghai.[47]

But Shanghai's then-mayor, Zhu Rongji, had reservations about this "in-house" planning effort and urged consulting foreign experts to encourage innovation and experimentation. He also understood the public relations value of creating a big stir with Pudong. If the new city could be made the focus of a well-publicized international design effort, it would attract media attention, which in turn would help bring in foreign capital and thus assure authorities in Beijing that their investment would bear fruit.[48] In April 1991 Zhu Rongji visited Paris to formalize Sino-French collaboration and pave the way for a high-profile "international consultation" for the development of Lujiazui District.[49] That fall, the Groupe Français d'appui au développement de Shanghai-Pudong (French Back-up Group for the Development of Shanghai-Pudong) was formed, led by Joseph Belmont, one of the key figures behind the celebrated Parisian Grands Projets, including the Grande Arche at La Défense and I. M. Pei's Louvre Pyramid.[50]

As Kris Olds has pointed out, the decision to go with a "consultancy" rather than an open competition was largely due to "the Chinese preference to remain in control of the development process." Consulting experts enabled Shanghai officials to pick and choose from among the submitted designs, rather than commit themselves to a single "winning" design. After the Paris meeting, Belmont identified a group of eight architects and planners who might participate in the consultancy, including Renzo Piano and Massimiliano Fuksas from Italy; Richard Rogers and Norman Foster from the United Kingdom; Toyo Ito and Kazuo Shinohara from Japan; and Dominique Perrault and Jean Nouvel from France. From this initial list, Shanghai officials selected four participants—Ito, Fuksas, Perrault, and Rogers. The four made a brief visit to Shanghai in May 1992 and returned several months later to present their design proposals.[51]

Even as this was happening, wrecking crews were leveling villages in Pudong and making way for the first round of construction. The first major building in Lujiazui—the symbolic stake in the ground—was an immense television and radio broadcasting tower known as the Pearl of the Orient (Dong Fang Zhi Zhu), designed by a team of architects and engineers from the Shanghai East China Institute of Architectural Design.[52] Groundbreaking for the tower took place in 1991, and construction was well under way by the time the Lujiazui consultants toured the city—a reminder, perhaps, that their paper visions were going to face some stiff competition from grounded reality. When I visited Shanghai in June 1992, the workers were only up to the first orb of the tower, yet the structure already dominated the skyline. By the time the tower reached its full height—1,535 feet—it was hovering like a colossal apparition above the city. Though not the most graceful building in the world (it is visually top-heavy and its tripod base, seen from some angles, appears knock-kneed and off-balanced), there is no denying the tower's awesome presence on the skyline, or its role as beacon for both resident and visitor. Because it is visible from nearly all parts of the city, the tower is a constant reckoning device that helps one navigate the city. The Pearl's proximity to the river greatly magnifies its visual impact, and it sits directly across the water from the bund's busy junction with Nanjing Road, Shanghai's equivalent of both Broadway and Fifth Avenue. The Pearl of the Orient had no serious rivals until the mid-1990s, and even though it now shares the sky with a number of equally lofty buildings, it remains Shanghai's most visible landmark and one of the city's top tourist attractions.

Although the Pearl was but one of several such broadcasting towers built in Chinese cities in the 1990s, it alone has become a universally recognized

Demolition, Pudong, Lujiazui District, 1999. PHOTOGRAPH BY AUTHOR

Souvenir models of the Pearl TV Tower, Pudong, 2007. Note pairing with Eiffel Tower (left).
PHOTOGRAPH BY AUTHOR

landmark—largely due to its anchor role in China's most celebrated skyline. Unlike the Beijing TV Tower or Nanjing's Jiangsu TV Tower, the Pearl quickly became a symbol of both its city and China's urban ambitions at large. The structure is generally regarded as Shanghai's Eiffel Tower, and this symbolism is made clear for even the dullest visitor by a souvenir featuring a mini-Pearl TV Tower set proudly alongside a same-scale Eiffel Tower (the latter, of course, is significantly shorter). Within China, the Pearl's symbolic prestige stimulated a variety of knockoffs and emulations. There is a Pearl of the West, the Sichuan radio and TV tower in Chengdu; and miniature versions of the Shanghai tower appeared on the rooftops of office towers throughout China in the late 1990s.[53] But however iconic, the Pearl's status as a symbol of the future is also ironic: the structure, reminiscent of big Soviet radio towers from the Cold War era, represents an old technology, centralized broadcast media, making the structure in tune more with the 1960s than the 1990s. Indeed, the first big data pipes connecting China to the global internet—the paragon of decentralized communication—were completed within months of the tower's opening in 1995.

Mini-Pearl TV Tower (left) as rooftop superstructure, Bank of Communications Tower, Qingdao, 2006.
PHOTOGRAPH BY AUTHOR

The TV Tower was not the only thing well under way by 1992. Already much of Shanghai's urban landscape had been reconfigured to make way for the rise of Pudong. The Huangpu River, though long the city's source of sustenance, also separates Pudong from the rest of the city. Making the new area a viable part of greater Shanghai meant bridging the river, figuratively and literally; the two "halves" of Shanghai—Puxi, (literally "west of the Huangpu") and Pudong ("east of the Huangpu")—would have to be stitched into a single, unified whole. To carry this off, Shanghai planners laid out two great highway hoops, or ring roads, encircling the entire city, crossing the river both north and south of the bund and drawing together Puxi and Pudong. As an official Pudong atlas put it at the time, the highways would create "a new pattern of city" in Shanghai, with the Huangpu now merely running through the center rather than defining its edge.[54]

Construction on the Inner Ring Road was well under way in 1992, part of a massive urban expressway program that would extend the city's total road length 40 percent by 2000, to a total of 4,244 miles. The ring road, most of it elevated, was built through some of the most populous urban terrain in the world, where residential densities were several times those of even the most crowded sections of Manhattan.[55] Building the loop through Puxi required demolishing many more buildings—and displacing many more people—than the largest urban expressway projects undertaken in the United States during the 1960s. Under construction, the highway resembled a great concrete leviathan in larval form, encased in a birth-husk of steel scaffolding. In the devastated neighborhoods along the way local residents went about their business seemingly oblivious to the monster in their midst, or at least resigned to fate's unkind ways. Similar projects in the United States in the 1970s drew public outrage and led to protests and demonstrations, but resistance of this kind has only recently begun to manifest itself in Chinese cities—most notably in Shenzhen, where middle-class homeowners have organized to defend their property investments against encroachments.[56]

The two bridges taking the Inner Ring Road across the Huangpu—especially the great coiled access ramp for the Nanpu Bridge in Puxi—also required the removal of hundreds of families. The decision to go with bridges for the symbolic first linkage to Pudong is itself revealing. Feasibility studies had actually shown that a tunnel would be less expensive to build and more efficient, requiring minimal condemnation and demolition. But tunnels are not photogenic; they strike no heroic silhouette against the sky, despite whatever ingenious engineering might have gone into their construction. A bridge, on the other hand, is a proud and soaring thing that makes for great publicity shots and tourist brochures. It is a rare mayor or city official who can turn down such eye candy, especially when competing for the good will and fiscal blessings of Beijing officialdom.

The first of the vanguard bridges was the Nanpu, a 2,776-foot cable-stay toll bridge just south of the bund that opened in December 1991, two years ahead of schedule. Designed by the Shanghai Municipal Engineering Design Institute, it was modeled on—indeed, is virtually identical to—the Alex Fraser (Annacis) Bridge in Vancouver, whose 1,526-foot main span made it the longest cable-stayed bridge in the world when it was completed in 1986.[57] The Nanpu was followed two years later by a even longer sibling, the Yangpu Bridge, carrying the north section of the Inner Ring Road across the Huangpu. Both bridges, funded in part by loans from the Asian Development Bank, became landmarks in China overnight. A lavish, oversized folio entitled *Bridges of the Century* was published in 1994 to celebrate the completion of the crossings. With chapters entitled "Songs of the Bridgebuilders," "Love for the Bridges,"

Coiled access ramps, Nanpu Bridge between Puxi and Pudong. PHOTOGRAPH BY PAUL CHESLEY, NATIONAL GEOGRAPHIC / GETTY IMAGES

and "A Century-Long Dream of Bridging the Huangpu Comes True," the book epitomizes the "infrastructure pride" seen throughout China in recent decades. More recent Shanghai bridges include the Xupu, completed in 1996; the 1,800-foot Lupu, opened in 2003 and currently the world's longest arch bridge; and a double-decked span, the Minpu Bridge, begun in 2005 and set to open in time for the 2008 Olympic games in Beijing.[58]

Symbolism thus satisfied with this surfeit of bridges, city officials were now free to burrow underground. A series of tunnels was built to lace up the two halves of Shanghai, a more cost-effective—if less glamorous—means of handling traffic and unifying the metropolis. But the new bridges and tunnels were quickly filled to capacity: between 1990 and 2003, the number of cars and trucks crossing to Pudong rose from 6.6 million to 16.3 million.[59] Tunnels now carry the Outer Ring Road and several other arteries between Puxi and Pudong, and as many as six new tunnels may be in place by 2020, to cope with an expected quadrupling of vehicles in the city by that time.[60] Shanghai will then have some twenty vehicular linkages across the Huangpu River. This may not render Puxi and Pudong a seamless whole, but will certainly make the

Huangpu River one of the most crossed, spanned, and tunneled urban water-ways in the world.[61]

★   ★   ★

The international consultancy launched in the wake of Zhu Rongji's Parisian junket produced a range of innovative urban design proposals for Lujiazui.[62] But as Shanghai's planning officials intended all along, no one plan was cho-sen as a "winner"; instead, the several schemes were gleaned (some would say cannibalized) for good ideas that were incorporated into the Chinese plan. In the end, the international consultancy simply provided Shanghai's in-house planners a kit of parts to use at will—an approach that often results in a cobbled-together scheme lacking an essential *parti*, or idea. Indeed, the final design for Lujiazui was criticized for lacking any of the innovative features that distinguished the independent proposals, and it looked suspiciously similar to the scheme prepared by the Shanghai Urban Planning and Design Institute in the late 1980s. But now of course the world knew about Pudong; the much-publicized quasi-competition attracted a considerable amount of international media attention, exactly as intended. The Pudong consultancy put Shanghai back on the global architecture and urban design map and set the stage for what would soon become a flood tide of lucrative commissions for design and planning professionals around the world.[63] Ironically (though hardly a sur-prise), one of the few recommendations that was actually adopted came not from the invited consultants but from the French organizers themselves. Belmont and others emphasized the importance of creating a signature sky-line at Pudong, one that might become a symbol of both Shanghai and China itself, which could be accomplished using a "tri-tower landmark"—three very tall buildings in close proximity to one another.[64]

The French also helped shape Century Avenue, the central axis or armature that is Lujiazui's principal spatial organizing device. The boulevard begins at the Pearl TV Tower and terminates in a large public park three miles east, run-ning through several districts—Lujiazui, Zhuyuan, and Huamu. Like so many features of China's new urban landscape, Century Avenue is immense in scale, with an eight-lane carriageway and generous margins for sidewalks. It was originally designed by the Shanghai Urban Planning and Design Institute as a grand boulevard rather than a mere traffic conduit. Zhu Rongji took a personal interest in Century Avenue when he was mayor of Shanghai, and after becoming premier in 1998, he continued to oversee its design and planning. That year Jean-Marie Charpentier was commissioned to advise on the landscaping of the road, and perhaps give it a bit of Parisian élan. Charpentier argued instead that Century Avenue should be something entirely new and not "just another Avenue des Champs-Élysées." He focused on using trees, artwork, and street furniture to reduce the immense scale of the artery (at 328 feet, it is nearly 100 feet wider than the Champs-Élysées).

Thousands of camphor and gingko trees were planted in regimented rows all along the route: four deep on the north side, two deep on the south. Themed botanical gardens planted with another 80,000 trees and shrubs were tucked along the flanks of Central Avenue. Monumental sculptures were set out at intervals, the largest of which is a giant speared disk titled *Light of the East*. As with the first Huangpu bridges, Century Avenue was celebrated as a hallmark of progress. A poem was even written in praise—Gui Xing Hua's "Hymn to Century Avenue" ("Shi Ji Da Dao Fang Ge").[65] Century Park, at the terminus of Century Avenue, is a kind of spatial yin to the priapic yang of the TV tower— a 346-acre "modern landscape with Chinese garden characteristics" designed by faculty at a local university in collaboration with a team of British landscape architects. Like so much of Lujiazui, the park is vast and windswept and best admired from up high in a nearby office tower. On the ground, park visitors are reminded that local law prohibits "patients with mental or infectious disease or improperly dressed persons from entering the Park."[66] Most days the lawns and gardens are virtually empty.

Conspicuously absent in the early planning of Pudong were Americans: not a single one figured amongst Belmont's chosen group of celebrity designers. But the Yankees have had their revenge, both in spirit and in fact. Despite being weaned by French urbanists, Lujiazui has come off looking more like a jacked version of Dallas than any city in France. Hong Kong architect Tao Ho warned years ago that Pudong's planners were making a big mistake embracing "tall buildings and the car-oriented mentality of the West" as the benchmarks of progressive urbanism, and his words were prophetic.[67] Lujiazui indeed suffers from the same shortcomings that make so many American edge cities and office parks unpleasant places to be—an overemphasis on motor-vehicle infrastructure, huge parcel sizes, and large plazas and deep setbacks that create a poorly defined street wall and an almost suburban level of density.

Exclusionary zoning makes matters worse still, banishing the kaleidoscopic array of uses that brings such vitality and life to the Chinese streetscape. The result is a pedestrian-unfriendly realm where those unfortunate enough to be on foot are buffeted by ricocheting winds and dwarfed by skyscrapers and sweeping vistas. Even the sidewalks in Lujiazui—148 feet wide in some places—seem to have been designed as parade routes rather than places to walk. What appears so definitively urban from afar—as a skyline—is on foot not only dull but spatially unpleasant and even intimidating. In the end, Lujiazui is little more than a preening clutch of monuments lunging for the sky. This is the urbanism of naked ambition, if it is urbanism at all. Here was an opportunity to build a model city, and what has come about instead is photogenic monumentality—a stage-set city intended to impress from a distance, from the bund, from the air, from the pages of a glossy magazine. Lujiazui is indeed a good place for architectural photography; its austere vistas are most of the time unencumbered by messy pedestrians, bicyclists, or street vendors with their stacks of steaming buns.

It has also been a popular location for futuristic movies, featured in a number of blockbuster films in recent years. Michael Winterbottom shot much his sci-fi thriller *Code 46* (2003) in Lujiazui, as did the Japanese producers of *Godzilla: Final Wars* (2004). In this epic, the legendary green monster is dispatched at the foot of the Pearl TV Tower by, appropriately enough (given Pudong's "Head of the Dragon" status), a fire-breathing dragon. The Pearl also takes a beating in the film, thus launching what may well become a tradition in the creative arts: the virtual destruction of Pudong. Shanghai would be in good company in this regard; New York, after all, has been imaginatively destroyed countless times in literature and cinema.[68] The 2006 film *Ultraviolet* was also filmed in Lujiazui, but it was outshone that year by an even more glamorous production—*Mission: Impossible III*, in which Tom Cruise can be seen bungee jumping from the Bank of China Tower.

Lujiazui's extreme verticality itself has a strong American pedigree; the tallest of Pudong's monuments—indeed the tallest buildings in China—have all been designed by U.S. architectural firms. The phoenix-like reconstruction of Chicago in the decade following of the Great Fire of 1871 brought about a number of architectural innovations, first among them the modern, steel-frame office building. The embryonic skyscrapers of William Le Baron Jenney, Louis Sullivan, Daniel Burnham, John Wellborn Root, and other Chicago School

The signature skyline of China's urban revolution, 2007. PHOTOGRAPH BY AUTHOR

architects used a seemingly gossamer skeleton of steel members to transfer the building load to the foundation. The structures were often clad with a facade of masonry or terracotta and decorated with forms drawn from architecture's masonry past (or, in Sullivan's case, from nature). But no longer were the stones themselves bearing, Atlas-like, the full weight of the mass above. Until then, building higher than ten or fifteen stories was a fool's errand; whatever was gained in floor area up top would be lost below to the increasingly massive walls (Burnham and Root's original Monadnock Building, the last and loftiest of the old line, has walls six feet thick at the base).

Iron-frame construction had been used to good effect beginning in the 1850s, but iron is quickly weakened by fire. Steel-frame construction could make a fire-resistant building that would truly scrape the sky. The passenger elevator, first used in New York just before the Civil War, made the tall office building readily accessible; and another technology of the era, the telephone, enabled its use as a corporate command center, from which remote manufacturing or retail operations could be managed by wire. Jenney's Home Insurance Building, completed in 1885, was the first of a number of steel-framed office buildings that by century's end had turned Chicago into the world's first skyscraper city. Given this history, it is perhaps appropriate that a Chicago architect crowned Shanghai's skyline with what was, for a decade, China's tallest building. Asia may have displaced the United States as the biggest consumer of vertiginous architecture, but Americans are still the masters of the form.

Designed by Chicago native Adrian Smith, then of Skidmore, Owings & Merrill's Chicago office, the Jin Mao Tower—the second leg of Belmont's "tri-tower landmark"—rises 1,380 feet above Pudong. The building's 70,000 tons of steel bear aloft what was in 1999 the highest hotel in the world—the Grand Hyatt Shanghai (which also boasts the world's tallest atrium as well as a laundry chute so high that buffers were needed to slow the falling duds). Built at a cost of $540 million, Jin Mao broke a number of records even while it was still under construction; never before had concrete been pumped so high in China, nor had more pilings been driven so deep. The building was also China's most intelligent, with the processing power of a spaceship and wire enough to span the Pacific. Only months after its completion in 1999, Jin Mao was already competing with the Pearl TV Tower next door to be the symbol of the city. In its first few years, Jin Mao rose like a clean silver bolt above Lujiazui's frenzy of mass and form; today, the building's once shimmering skin of glass and stainless steel has been prematurely dulled by the relentless onslaught of acid rain and airborne particulates.

A series of setbacks taper the building into thirteen segments, each diminishing in height by a factor of eight until the top floor is reached, eighty-eight stories above the street. The preponderance of eights, an invocation of auspicious numerology, was doubly significant because plans for the building were announced on Deng Xiaoping's eighty-eighth birthday in that providential *nanxun* year of 1992. But the real purpose of the segmented facade was to create a form evocative of a Chinese pagoda, the deep symbolic resonance of which answered Smith's quest for a building "that in some way evoked the culture and memory of China, that was unmistakably Chinese." To Smith, recalling this ancient building type was a no-brainer; as the architect put it in a 2000 interview, "The pagoda struck me as a fitting reference point from which to begin thinking about the design of a Chinese skyscraper."[69]

Visually, the pagoda-like setbacks lend momentum to Jin Mao's shaft, thrusting its mass skyward and creating an impression of lightness. Not everyone agreed that a religious architectural form, plucked from the Chinese past, was an appropriate carriage for modern commercial functions. But though early pagodas were indeed religious, many were later used for secular purposes. By the time of the Ming Dynasty, pagodas "were often built for *feng shui* reasons," relates architectural historian Ho Puay-peng, "to block an evil force, or to supplement ground form and create, in effect, a hill where geomancers determined one was needed." Pagodas were also associated with success on the imperial examinations because they were thought to "help draw into alignment the literary constellations." These "star-gathering pagodas," Ho relates, were considered highly auspicious for young scholars hoping to join the imperial service.[70]

On the other hand, does such genuflection to China's past have real and substantive meaning today, especially coming from a foreigner? Eager to pay homage to a culture they barely understand, designers often rummage through the China closet, grabbing willy-nilly at form and image. But Smith's use of the past is subtle and nuanced and cleverly adapts a historical form to a modern program. Perhaps more importantly, the pagoda-like imagery is very popular on the street. Nearly all the people I interviewed in and around Lujiazui for an *Architectural Record* article told me that Jin Mao was a symbol of Shanghai and a point of pride for the Chinese. Several praised its beauty and "unique

Jin Mao Tower (right) and the World Financial Center.
COURTESY KOHN PEDERSEN FOX, CRYSTAL RENDERING

shape." A teenager in a village nearby told me that it was "not just another box like all the other buildings." Jin Mao was "different" because it combined modern technology and materials with a traditional style; "it's like a pagoda," she said with a smile. All told, not bad work for a Chicagoan. The Jin Mao complex actually comprises two buildings: the eighty-eight-story tower and a squat, six-story podium hunkered beneath it. With a roofline resembling an open book, the smaller structure is an effective counterweight to the tower, giving the pair a satisfying equilibrium. The ensemble is often referred to as a "pencil and open book"—a reference not intended by the designers but amplified by both the association of pagodas with learning as well as an axiom favored by Deng Xiaoping: "knowledge is power."[71]

Big buildings in Asia are quickly superseded, and few expected that Jin Mao's reign as China's tallest building would last long. (Smith, for that matter, went on to design the 3,000-foot Burj Dubai, which will be far and away the world's tallest building when completed in 2009.) That Jin Mao held the

China title for as long as it did was due less to loft than luck—its chief rival and inevitable superior, the Shanghai World Financial Center, languished for years due to financial uncertainties, engineering problems, design controversies, and security concerns prompted by the terrorist attacks of September 11, 2001. The project, launched in August 1997, was grounded a few months later by the Asian economic meltdown, and it did not get going again until the fall of 2005. But now, even as I write, Jin Mao's next-door neighbor is racing toward the sky. The World Financial Center will top out at 101 stories, more than 1,600 feet above the Huangpu River—taller even (by a hair) than the Pearl TV Tower. I often checked in on the progress of this tower remotely, via a webcam operated by the German School of Shanghai from a building near the bund. Wearing a twiggy crown of construction cranes, the Center would be just a little bit taller each week, Jin Mao, adjacent, looking a bit more deflated in turn.

The World Financial Center was designed by another American from the Midwest, Minnesota native William E. Pedersen of Kohn Pedersen Fox Associates (KPF), for the Mori Corporation, the Japanese property developers who built Roppongi Hills in Tokyo and a number of other major complexes. That a Japanese corporation is building and will own the tallest skyscraper in China has not gone over well with all, as memories of Japanese aggression and atrocities committed in Shanghai, and especially in nearby Nanjing, have not abated with the passing decades. This issue came to a head, literally, over the design of the topmost section of the World Financial Center. Pedersen's original scheme called for a great oculus cut out of the chisel-like top of the building. The hole was described as a "moon gate," a decorative element in traditional Chinese garden design, though its real purpose was to reduce lateral loads on the building caused by high wind. But to many people (including Shanghai's mayor) the big circle looked suspiciously like the Rising Sun. Such imagery did little to endear the building to the locals, who saw it as a devious Japanese plot to invade Shanghai again, this time by sky.

Pedersen's initial solution, a skyway bridging the hole, was dismissed, so eventually the oculus was reformatted into a trapezoid. The result is not only compositionally weaker, but the building now bears an uncanny resemblance to a giant bottle opener. Also lost, regrettably, was a funicular that would have run on a track encircling the opening—a variation, perhaps, on the revolving-restaurant theme. The World Financial Center, like nearly all major projects underway in China today, is set to open in time for the 2008

Summer Olympiad in Beijing. It will also complete a much larger composition, Belmont's "tri-point landmark."

*   *   *

If Pudong is the ground zero of a reclaimed Shanghai, a rather different choreography is unfolding on the city's outskirts. There, transplanted urban geographies from the West give form and spirit to a series of nine new residential towns on the urban fringe. Situated in a vast ring around the city, the nine towns will eventually house a population of more than 500,000 people. Hand-picked foreign architects have designed the towns, each meant to evoke the urbanism of a different Western nation, including Italy, Spain, England, the United States, Sweden, the Netherlands, Australia, New Zealand, and Germany. Known as "One City, Nine Towns," the project began as a pipe dream of former Shanghai Communist Party Secretary Huang Ju, who conceived of the themed towns as a way to celebrate Shanghai's history as a global city. It is somewhat ironic that a city once subjugated by Western imperialism should choose to build simulacra of Western cities as part of a regional growth strategy, especially since many of the towns selected for redevelopment are themselves many times older than Shanghai itself. But this can also be interpreted as a claim-laying of sorts, a triumph over history and its humiliations. Such an act could only be undertaken by a society supremely confident in itself and its future, if also somewhat confused about its emergent identity.

Best-known of the nine towns is German-themed Anting, where Weimar-styled *Fachwerkhause*—half-timbered houses—lie a short distance from Shanghai International Automobile City, home to the manufacturing works churning out China's popular Volkswagen cars and also the site of China's first Formula One racetrack. Both Anting New Town and International Automobile City were planned by German urbanist Albert Speer Jr., whose work in Beijing is discussed in Chapter 4, "Capital Improvements." North of Shanghai is a Swedish-flavored new town at Luodian, close to Volvo's China headquarters. Luodian itself dates to the Ming Dynasty, and the Swedes hired to plan its neo-Nordic reincarnation based their scheme on Sweden's oldest town: Sigtuna, north of Stockholm, founded in 980. The developers later decided to interpret the Nordic theme more loosely. Along with the medieval architecture of Sigtuna and the Nobel Science and Technology Garden, they tossed in a building modeled on the Althingi, Iceland's house of parliament, and—for good measure—a replica of the famous Little Mermaid in Copenhagen Harbor.[72]

Farther to the south is Fengcheng, the Spanish-themed town, which began as a coastal stronghold in the late fourteenth century. Relics from Fengcheng's early history, including defensive walls, are now accompanied by a number of Catalan references, such as a replica of the Ramblas, a Gaudí-inspired cultural center, and a Catholic church—Shanghai's second. Gaoqiao, the Dutch-themed town, is an old fishing village at the confluence of the Huangpu and Yangtze rivers, founded during the European Middle Ages; its new manifestation will evoke suburban Amersfoort, with canals inspired by Amsterdam and a variety of other elements meant "to formulate a visually Dutch town," as a competition brief put it.[73] Ironically, an even older settlement, Fengjing, with a history extending back 1,500 years, was chosen for the suburban villas of the American town. Pujiang, the Italian-themed town, was laid out on a Roman grid by Gregotti Associati International of Milan, with a palazzo and a system of neo-Venetian canals. For some reason, the developers chose to also include a sampling of American elements, surely making Pujiang the only Italian-American theme town in Asia. The Australian town, Buzhen, located on Chongming Island in the Yangtze River, is planned to be a model of ecologically sensitive development (it lies just upstream of Dongtang, site of the planned ecological city discussed later in this book).

Most compelling of all is Songjiang, the English town southwest of the city center. As several local universities will eventually be relocated there, it is expected the town will be home for numerous faculty and staff. One place they may reside is Thames Town, completed in the fall of 2006, the first residential community at Songjiang. Laid out about a medieval town square by Paul Rice of the British firm Atkins, Thames Town's cobbled lanes, Tudor homes, Georgian townhouses, and Victorian warehouses squeeze "500 years of British architectural development into a five-year construction project."[74] At the center of town is a church copied from one in Clifton, Bristol. There, couples may experience "exotic marriage customs in which you exchange vows in front of a pastor."[75] They may afterward enjoy a pint at the requisite English pub, which also serves as a brilliant example of the hazards of imitation. Chinese architects touring England to find prototypes for Thames Town's buildings evidently snapped a photograph of a picturesque seaside pub and chip shop at Lyme Regis, Dorset, which was then used to create a nearly identical set of buildings at Thames

City model, Shanghai Urban Planning Exposition Center, 2007. PHOTOGRAPH BY AUTHOR

Town. News of this eventually reached the pub's owner, Gail Caddy, who was understandably indignant that her establishment had been replicated without permission on the other side of the globe. "We are the only fish and chip shop next to a pub on a river mouth in England," Caddy complained to the *Telegraph*, "and they have given it the same front and back, in an identical position but on the mouth of the Yangtse." The developers were unfazed, pointing out that such copying violated no Chinese law, and that the neighboring municipality of Minhang had just built itself a replica of the White House.[76]

It is a challenge indeed to absorb both Pudong and the orbiting Nine Towns in one take; doing so requires Olympian perspective. And for this it is best to head back to the Shanghai Urban Planning Exposition Center. Sprawling across the building's third floor, in the Master Plan Hall, is a highly detailed, 6,400-square-foot model of metropolitan Shanghai in which nearly every city street, block, and building has been dutifully represented in miniaturized form.[77] The Huangpu River here is the width of a small creek; the Jin Mao Tower is about the height of a Hoover upright. The breathtaking scale of Shanghai is suddenly, finally, manageable here (though even this mini-Shanghai is itself a record breaker, the largest urban planning model in the world). The epicenter of the model is formed by Lujiazui's rising clutch of sky-scrapers—the hub about which the rest of the minimetropolis appears to orbit. Across the river, dwarfed now to the size of tissue boxes, are the neoclassical buildings of the bund. Farther out, the Nine Towns orbit in the city's Van Allen Belt, amidst a dizzying sprawl of office towers and housing estates. The model explains well Shanghai's grand urban ambition, but to feel the real pulse of the emerging city requires a stroll along the Huangpu riverfront at night.

Looking out across the water from the bund, with one's back turned upon the architecture of the past, one sees an awesome spectacle unfold. The view is analogous to that lauded by foreigners a century ago, of the bund itself viewed from Pudong. If China once gazed in wonder at the monuments of foreign capitalism along the bund, now the West gazes, with an odd mix of fear and fascination, at the rising metropolis on the other side, already the signature skyline of the Chinese urban revolution. There Lujiazui's gathered towers are washed with floodlights or radiate with moving images like immense television screens, while laser beams pulse and dance across the sky as if to telegraph a message to the heavens: Make way for the Chinese century.

CHAPTER THREE

The Politics of the Past

城規條例的變遷

Shanghai is, of course, not alone in its ambition to lead China into a glorious urban future. However spectacular it may be, however vibrant its culture and nightlife, Shanghai will always have a watchful uncle up north—Beijing—with no small will of its own and a single colossal advantage: it is China's capital. Unlike its merely economic brethren, a capital city is a symbol of a nation's values, ideologies, and aspirations. A capital must invariably project an image of power, prestige, and authority to domestic nationals as well as a global audience. Capital city architecture and urbanism are doubly tasked with serving practical needs as well as those related to representation and symbolic diplomacy. When one nation reaches out to another in peace, it sends envoys to the foreign capital. In time of war, seizing a capital city strikes a severe blow to a nation's standing and self-esteem. Even if its ports and economy are still functioning, the occupation or destruction of a nation's symbolic center may well lead to capitulation—in spirit, if not in fact. Indeed, "symbols are the choicest targets," writes Anthony Pitch, "for those who would make war or instill terror." This is precisely what British troops had in mind when they invaded Washington DC during the War of 1812, strategically limiting their vandalism to structures of paramount symbolic importance to the upstart republic—the Capitol and White House.¹ If it means to stay around, a new regime will often attempt to tap the latent symbolic power in the architecture and urbanism of a seized capital. Doing so legitimizes the authority of the new regime while making a clear statement about supremacy and succession.

Beijing was retooled and retrofitted for capital service by several dynastic regimes over the centuries. And when Mao Zedong proclaimed the founding

Chairman Mao reviews plans for the new capital city, ca. 1950.

FROM LONG XIN MIN ET AL., EDS., *TREMENDOUS CHANGES IN THE ANCIENT CAPITAL* (BEIJING: BEIJING PUBLISHING HOUSE, 1999)

of the People's Republic of China on October 1, 1949, he did so from a place steeped in significance—the balcony of Tiananmen, the Gate of Heavenly Peace. The city Mao looked out upon on that day was virtually unchanged in form and structure since the Ming Dynasty—an almost perfectly preserved example of imperial Chinese urbanism, or as Wu Liangyong has put it, "the ultimate crystallization of classical Chinese city planning and design."[2] After the collapse of the Mongol Yuan Dynasty, China was again ruled by native Chinese. The third Ming emperor, Zhu Di, having made the decision to relocate the Chinese capital from Nanjing to Beijing, set about creating on the ruins of the Mongol Dadu, Beijing's predecessor, a new city that would function as a vessel for the rituals, rites, and ceremonies essential to imperial rule—what Jeffrey Meyer has called the "vast imperial liturgy."[3]

In the traditional Chinese worldview, the emperor was a moral exemplar and universal father figure, as well as the exalted Son of Heaven (Tian Zi). He occupied a position at the very center of the universe, a kind of pivot of the cosmos mediating between the earthly and celestial realms. This power was not given outright, but was conditional upon a "heavenly mandate" predicated on the sovereign's able discharge of imperial duties and rituals. As Meyer writes, "the harmony in what we call the natural world, the cycles of the seasons, the proper amount of sun and rain, heat and cold, and thus the success of the yearly harvest, depended upon the virtue of his administration." An incompetent or corrupt emperor could bring ruin upon the realm, while "the influence of good emperors could be felt everywhere in the realm and even attracted well-disposed barbarians to their sway."[4]

Like earlier imperial seats, Beijing was no mean city of men but an *axis mundi*—a conduit "through which the power of Heaven was focused and channelled."[5] Its layout was based, writes Meyer, on "a cosmic pattern derived from the positions and motion of the heavenly bodies which, if realized on earth, [would] ensure the strength and continuity of the capital and the empire."[6] The Chinese imperial city was, in effect, a transcription of heavenly order in urban form. Many of its key elements had astral counterparts. Beijing's central axis replicated the celestial meridian, while the Forbidden City—its full name is "Purple Forbidden City" (Zijin Cheng)—referred to a royal constellation near the polestar known as the "Purple Hidden Enclosure." Other star groupings were evoked in the names of city gates, while the placid centrality of the

polestar, apparently motionless in the night sky while all others circle worshipfully about, was a symbol of the emperor himself.[7]

Highly specific design guidelines—an exalted urban design code, in
effect—assured the city's fitness as a grand altar for the imperial liturgy. These
principles were already more than a thousand years old by the time of the Ming
Dynasty and had been used earlier to plan Dadu during the Yuan Dynasty.
Design guidelines for Chinese royal cities were first set forth in the *Kaogong Ji*
(Record of Trades)—part of a Confucian text from the Eastern Zhou Dynasty
(770–476 BC) known as the *Zhou Li* (Rituals of Zhou).[8] While the plan of
Dadu closely followed the *Kaogong Ji*, Beijing was an even more exquisite manifestation of its key principles, which included orientation to the cardinal compass points; symmetrical rectilinear layout with a palace complex at the center;
a north-south cardinal axis or "ritual way"; a gridiron of streets and blocks;
and a defensive wall with gates positioned along each side.[9] In essential, dia-
grammatic form the imperial city plan, an enclosed square pierced with a central axis, calls to mind one of the most important Chinese characters—*zhong*
(中), used in the name of China (Zhong Guo,中国) and the Chinese language
(zhong wen,中文).

Chinese imperial urban design made no provision for a grand architec-
tural climax at the very center of the otherwise centripetal capital city. From
the south, Beijing's central axis passed through the front gate of the outer city
(Yongdingmen) and that of the inner city (Zhengyangmen, also known as
Qianmen). It entered the Imperial City through the Gate of Heavenly Peace
(Tiananmen), and the Forbidden City through the Meridian Gate (Wumen).
Once inside, the axis passed through a variety of courts, halls, and pavilions,
each of which was dedicated to specific imperial functions. The most important ceremonies took place in the Hall of Perfect Harmony (Zhonghe Dian) and
the Hall of Supreme Harmony (Tiahe Dian), in which the emperor's throne was
located. But nowhere along this grand procession was the observer confronted
with the kind of architectural pièce de résistance that such centripetality might
suggest. After all, the pivot of the Chinese imperial cosmos "was not a place,"
writes Meyer, "but a person, the Son of Heaven."[10] So it is only fitting that,
within the Forbidden City, Beijing's grand processional ended not with a monumental edifice, but a relatively modest residential sanctum sanctorum known
as the Inner Court (Nei Ting).

This tranquil compound, the actual home of the emperor and his family, was no different in basic form and function from the lowly *siheyuan* (courtyard houses) that carpeted the city beyond the palace walls. A certain nested logic thus governed this metropolis of courtyard and enclosure, like a *matryoshka* doll in the form of a city: Beijing was a courtyard complex in the larger landscape; the Imperial City was a courtyard complex within Beijing; the Forbidden City within the Imperial City; and the Inner Court within the Forbidden City.[11] One can even map this in the other direction and imagine all China as a space enclosed by the Great Wall, much of which itself was built or reconstructed during the Ming Dynasty. What distinguished imperial Beijing, then, was not exalted individual temples or palaces, but the totality of its composition. It was a singular work of urban design with a universal structural logic evident in its grandest and lowest parts. The late city planner Edmund Bacon, who spent a year working in China during the Great Depression, described Beijing as "possibly the greatest single work of man on the face of the earth." It was no exaggeration.[12]

★   ★   ★

Mao Zedong and the Chinese Communists saw things rather differently; to them imperial Beijing was a relic of China's feudal past. A new Chinese nation was about to be born, and the detritus of lost empires would be tolerated now only if it could serve the new political order. On October 1, 1949, Mao mounted Tiananmen, the old imperial gate, and from its balcony proclaimed the founding of the People's Republic of China. "No other gesture," writes art historian Wu Hung, "could more effectively prove the newness of the Communist leadership and no other act could more convincingly seal the title of People's Republic."[13] By this act, Mao supplanted the past, yet did so in a manner deferential to its latent symbolic power. The Communists did not raze Tiananmen, after all; they repurposed it and made it their own. The moment of national birth was rendered for the ages, and with appropriate gravitas, by the painter Dong Xiwen in his *Founding of the Nation* (1953). Dong used liberal artistic license to amplify the historic moment. He turned what was an overcast day into one of bright blue skies and racing clouds, and elevated Mao "at least half a head taller," writes Wu, than any of the other men or women on the dais. What in reality was a small, crowded balcony became an exalted platform with a

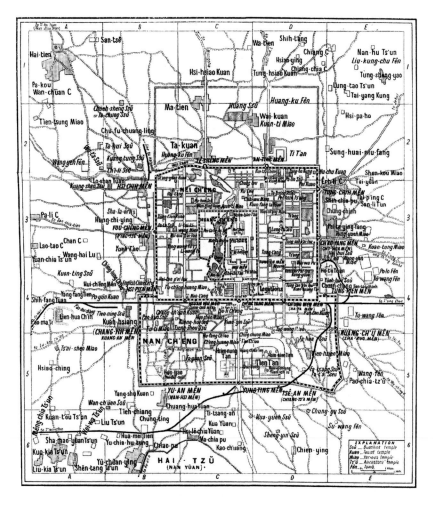

"Peking and Its Environs," ca. 1912. The Old City lies within the walls (heavy dashed line);
the later "outer city" is the flatter, wider rectangle at bottom.

FROM *MADROLLE'S GUIDE BOOKS: NORTHERN CHINA, THE VALLEY OF THE BLUE RIVER, KOREA*

(HACHETTE & COMPANY, 1912); COURTESY UNIVERSITY OF TEXAS LIBRARIES

panoramic view of Tiananmen Square and the skyline of Beijing—all quite fitting for the founding of a nation. To accentuate the expansive scene, the painter even raised the horizon and used multiple points of perspective. He also eliminated one of the red-lacquered columns to the right of Mao—a literal removal of the architectural past to make way for a new Chinese empire.[14] It foreshadowed much bigger things to come.

Mao's antipathy toward the imperial urban past was endorsed by foreign experts sent to help the Chinese plan an appropriately socialist capital city. The Americans, who played a key role in shaping the Nationalist capital at Nanjing, were now out of the picture. General Joseph Stilwell's admiration for the tenacious Communists, whose troops were more disciplined and better trained than Chiang Kai-shek's, only got him fired by President Roosevelt. His replacement was a plain-talking, stridently anti-Communist Nebraskan— General Albert C. Wedemeyer—who met with Mao and Zhou Enlai on several occasions, but "politely refused" their offer of Communist troops to help push the Japanese out of China.[15] As civil war broke out, the United States sided with Chiang and the Nationalists, who were soon sent packing to Taiwan; America thus "lost China," as it was often put at the time. Needful of aid and expertise, China had little choice but turn to its ideological counterpart, the Soviet Union, which was only too happy to help remake this most populous new nation in its own image. In February 1950, China and the Soviet Union signed a "Treaty of Friendship, Alliance and Mutual Assistance." Young Chinese began to study Russian and train in the Soviet Union, which created a generation of bureaucrats with a taste for vodka and youthful memories of Moscow. The Soviet Union became China's "big elder brother" (lao da ge), and the nation was exhorted to "Learn everything from the Soviets," including how to retrofit Beijing in the name of Karl Marx.[16]

The first team of Soviet planning experts arrived in Beijing in September 1949, invited by the newly formed Municipal Town Planning Commission. This was followed by visits in March 1953 and April 1955. The Soviet influence was explicit and substantial: Soviet experts presided over or supervised nearly all major planning activity in the city, introducing a range of planning principles drawn largely from the 1935 General Plan of Moscow.[17] First, the socialist city should be limited in size; growth should be closely monitored to prevent the city from becoming a parasite on the region. It should also be a city of smokestacks, with an emphasis on industrial production, heavy

"The Soviet Union Is Our Example," propaganda poster, 1951.
COURTESY INTERNATIONAL INSTITUTE OF SOCIAL HISTORY, AMSTERDAM

manufacturing, construction, and transport, rather than on the "exploitative" secondary and tertiary sector activities such as retailing and finance, considered hallmarks of decadent Western capitalism. Moreover, plants and factories should be distributed throughout the city, not shunted off to some industrial ghetto. This would reduce commuting time and traffic, but also assure that Beijing did not turn into (or return to) a "high-level consumptive city" of vast ministries, universities, and cultural institutions staffed by educated elites.[18]

Big factories in the city proper would help form the urban industrial proletariat essential to the socialist model of society. Self-contained, largely self-sufficient live-work compounds were established, again closely following Soviet models. This is the origin of the work-unit compound, or *danwei*, that would become the basic unit of Chinese urbanism in the Mao era (discussed in greater detail in Chapter 7, "Suburbanization and the Mechanics of Sprawl"). As they evolved, the work-unit compounds met more and more daily life needs, from housing and schooling to work and medical care. As a result, public spaces in the socialist city were relatively empty, and streets and boulevards were free of the diurnal commuter throngs typical of capitalist cities. No matter; the

Soviets advised Beijing to build an extensive road network nonetheless, based on the Moscow model of ring roads and vast avenues radiating outward from the center.

Diagrammatically, the radial-concentric road pattern reinforced another essential Soviet planning idea, one nowhere more important than in the layout of a national capital: to create a clearly defined administrative center, a symbolic nucleus of the capital city, with great squares for mass rallies and monumental buildings that would "reflect the glory of the socialist state."[19] This and other Soviet planning advice was accepted wholesale by the Chinese, with profound and lasting implications for Beijing. Most fateful was the decision to make the Old City the administrative center of the new capital, a strategy pushed by the Soviets in a series of planning sessions in the fall of 1949 and embodied in the earliest drafts of the city's master plan. As Victor Sit tells it, "The Russians...insisted that time and cost considerations dictated the use of whatever vacant space already existed and recommended the demolition of old and dilapidated structures in and around the southern part of the Imperial City to make way for building the national administrative headquarters."[20]

This was more or less what Mao also intended. After all, he had proclaimed the birth of the nation from Tiananmen; here too should the new government be seated. Recycling capitals in this manner has deep roots in Chinese history. Imperial cities became more or less permanent by the end of the second millennium. Successive conquering dynastic rulers and warlords may have altered or amended a city's plan, but they honored its site and essential form. Doing so helped legitimize the new regime and position them as filial stewards of a greater, common past. Even Mao partook of this tradition. In spite of his abhorrence of China's feudal past—a loathing that eventually led to a purge of all things old during the Cultural Revolution—Mao himself looked to harness the symbolic power of the old imperial center by making it the seat of the People's Republic.

This was the core principle of the first of two planning proposals born out of the Soviet planning collaborations of 1949–1951. The scheme, credited to Zhu Zhaoxue and Zhao Dongri, called for building the new administrative center right in the heart of Beijing's Old City. It made almost no mention of the historic city and its significance. It didn't need to. "The idea underpinning this proposal," writes Wu Liangyong, "was that making way for a new world required destroying the old."[21] The second proposal was altogether different.

Coauthored by architects Liang Sicheng and Chen Zhanxiang, the scheme looked to spare the Old City by placing the governmental complex in a new administrative center just outside, where it would have plenty of room to grow.

The Liang-Chen Plan, as it was known, has an almost mythic quality among urbanists today, and for good reason: the plan could well have saved Beijing from itself, if only it had been adopted. Its principal author, Liang Sicheng, is a towering figure in the history of Chinese architecture, a man whose life mirrored the triumph and tragedy of China in the twentieth century. Liang was born in 1901 into a distinguished and progressive family; his father, Liang Qichao, was one of China's leading intellectuals (his writings on history and culture inspired the May Fourth Movement).[22] Sicheng, who studied art in high school, developed an interest in architecture after meeting the young woman he would eventually marry, Lin Huiyin. Lin accompanied Liang to the United States where he was to pursue studies on a Boxer Indemnity Fellowship. The couple spent a blissful summer at Cornell before enrolling at the University of Pennsylvania in the fall of 1924. Lin, who was barred from the male-only architecture program, studied in the School of Fine Arts instead but was later asked to teach architectural design. Liang excelled in his studies under the tutelage of Paul P. Cret. Cret, educated at the École des Beaux-Arts in Paris, was one of the leading proponents of Beaux Arts classicism in the United States, then the prevailing style for civic and institutional buildings. Cret and a second teacher, Alfred Gumaer, sparked Liang's interest in the architectural history of China, of which very little was known in the West at the time. It was Liang's father, however, who placed into his hands a remarkable document, discovered in a Nanjing library in 1919, that would ignite his son's passion for China's architectural past. This was a Song Dynasty building manual known as the *Ying Zao Fa Shi*, written by an official in the imperial Department of Works in AD 1103, to estimate quantities of materials used in the construction of palace buildings.[23]

The archaic language and obscure terminology at first baffled Liang. Moreover, details regarding the size and configuration of timber bracket sets, columns, and other structural elements were usually written in code, to protect the trade secrets of various craftsmen.[24] But after decoding a similar manual from the Qing Dynasty and field checking against surviving Song-era buildings, Liang and Lin eventually deciphered the *Ying Zao Fa Shi*. Working in a small office in Tiananmen under the auspices of the Institute for Research in

Chinese Architecture, Liang annotated an important section on structural carpentry and illustrated it with exquisite drawings; this document, numerous articles, and two manuscripts on traditional buildings in Chinese and English established Liang as the preeminent authority on China's architectural history. He also helped establish the modern field of architectural studies in China, founding departments at Northeast and Tsinghua universities and mentoring the first generation of China-trained architects and urbanists, including Zhang Jinqiu, Zhang Bo, and Wu Liangyong.[25]

Liang's knowledge of Chinese architectural culture and passion for history brought him accolades and honorary degrees; it also eventually earned him the enmity of the Communist Party. Liang had high hopes at first for Mao's new regime. Shortly before Beijing was liberated in February 1949, the architect was contacted by an advance unit of the People's Liberation Army that had infiltrated the area near Tsinghua University, where Liang was then teaching. As Wilma Fairbank put it in her 1994 biography of Liang and Lin, "An officer brought Sicheng a map of the city and explained that Professor Liang was asked to designate areas where precious buildings and cultural relics must be preserved if artillery should be called into action."[26] Earlier, during the Second World War, Liang and one of his students, Wu Liangyong, had produced a study of historic sites with the Chinese Commission for the Preservation of Cultural Objects in War Areas. It was this work, which evidently came to the attention of Zhou Enlai, that brought about the officer's request.[27]

That a revolutionary army should be so concerned with antiquities obviously impressed Liang. And, indeed, once the new government was in place a sense of order and purpose did come to the capital: streets were cleaned and accumulated debris removed; inflation was halted and a new spirit of national pride swelled forth. Liang, who had earlier represented China on the design team for the United Nations' headquarters in New York, was appointed vice director of the Municipal Town Planning Commission. But the honeymoon was short. Liang's vision of the new capital was antithetical to nearly everything the Soviets were pushing and that Mao himself demanded. Liang was outraged at the prospect of turning Beijing into a city of smokestack industry. He believed that the Forbidden City should be preserved as a national monument, and, most importantly, that the seat of the new national government should be built on a spacious new site outside the city center, not forced into the fragile and congested Old City.

Liang and Chen argued that it would be "impossible to find land with the proper location and sufficient size for such construction within the city wall."[28] Erecting a proper complex for the new government would require an "arrangement and sequence" of buildings that could never be realized "sandwiched between...the ancient buildings in the old city."[29] There, new construction would be "subject to extreme and unreasonable limitations, which might itself lead to chaos and decentralization."[30] In addition, the greatly enlarged population would cause an unbearable level of residential density in the Old City, while vast new ministry buildings erected along principal arteries would "immediately raise the flow and complexity of traffic, sharpen the chaos of the cars coming to and fro and...lead to more traffic accidents."[31]

Liang made an equally compelling case for conservation. Beijing—"this solemn and beautiful city"—expressed "excellent characteristics of our native national tradition."[32] He argued that "we must consider Beijing's original style of layout and physical form when planning new construction," and strive to "protect the essence of Beijing."[33] For this urban landscape possessed "characteristics...rare and unmatched even throughout the world."[34] "Beijing is an ancient capital and a famous historic city," Liang wrote. "Many old buildings have become commemorative cultural relics today. Not only are their physical bodies beautiful and worth protecting, but the orderly disposition of their larger environmental setting makes this famous city even more magnificent." The integrity of the whole should not be destroyed by mixing in "unharmonious things."[35] The fate of the city was in their hands. Deciding where and how to build the new government complex would have immense implications for the future of the metropolis. "If we make errors in principle," cautioned Liang, "a series of irremediable mistakes will surely occur."[36]

To help sway the Soviet advisors, Liang cited examples from the Soviet Union, in which their own planner-comrades had rebuilt and "reoccupied historically valued cities taken by the German invaders in 1943."[37] Liang quoted the esteemed Soviet architect and historian Nikolai N. Voronin, whose work emphasized the "special problems...faced in reconstructing famous historical cities such as Novgorod, Kaliningrad and Smolenska." Voronin stressed that in planning a city, "the living history of its people and their architectural traditions" must always be honored.[38] Citing the case of Novgorod—an ancient Slavic city in northwestern Russia—Voronin described how the city's redevelopment was planned by architect Alexey Schusev, whose appreciation for history led him to create a modern metropolis "in accordance with the system of its ancient urban plan." Modern improvements were added, of course, but not to the detriment of old landmarks, which were themselves surrounded by "gardens serving as a foil for people to view and admire the ancient buildings."[39] "We should learn from Schusev's principle of reconstructing Novrogod to design our Beijing," urged Liang. "We should never harm our beautiful Beijing with hundreds of new architectural forms…[but rather] select the most beautiful architecture of dynasties past and create space surrounding them for trees and grasses, and turn them into gardens for the people."[40]

None of this swayed either Mao or the Soviet advisers. A conservative proposal made to revolutionaries, the Liang-Chen Plan was doomed from the start. To Mao and the Party elite, Liang seemed more interested in preserving the past than assuring the success of the socialist utopia. Mao led a revolution into Beijing after all, which demanded that the new supplant the old, not settle for a next-best place alongside it. Creating a new capital district west of the Old City may have been good urban planning, but it offered none of the triumphant symbolism achieved by retooling the architectural remains of the ancien régime to serve a new political order. Liang was maligned and misinterpreted. He was accused of wanting to turn Beijing into a "museum city," when in fact he had no objection to using historic buildings for low-impact cultural or administrative functions.[41]

Worse, his proposal was haunted by a similar plan dating from the Japanese occupation of 1937 to 1945. In anticipation of their permanent colonial rule in the region, Japanese officials drafted a simple gridiron plan for a new administrative city about five kilometers west of Beijing, slightly farther out than Liang would later place his center.[42] The Japanese site was apparently considered in the Soviet-led planning sessions, for in the very first sentence of Liang's own proposal he dismisses it as unsuitable as a capital district: "the new urban area in the western suburbs, carved out in the reign of the Japanese puppet regime, is too far away from the downtown area." He did, however, suggest the area might be useful to accommodate future growth.[43] In any case, the memory of Japan's plan for the western suburbs "was enough," writes Wu Liangyong, "to discredit Liang's scheme to a certain degree."[44]

The Liang-Chen Plan was rejected, and within a year Mao "personally decided," writes Wu Hung, "to locate the government in the old city."[45] Mao ridiculed Liang as a sentimental antiquarian and censured his plan as "an attempt to negate Tiananmen, the country's political centre cherished by the revolutionary people."[46] Of course, the Liang-Chen Plan was not perfect, but like many missed opportunities in history, it has been hallowed and glorified by remorse. There were aspects of the proposal that were of dubious viability at the time. Economic realities, for example, would have made the ground-up construction of a new capital district impossible, especially after the outbreak of the Korean War in 1950.[47] In retrospect, however, these and other challenges seem to pale in comparison with the litany of planning nightmares—ever mounting in complexity and scale—that have plagued Beijing in the decades since Mao's fateful decision. As Wu Hung writes, "The consequences of Mao's decision cannot be exaggerated: all the subsequent destruction and construction of Beijing were fundamentally determined at this moment.... In short, Beijing's fate was sealed by locating the government in the old city."[48]

The Old City was soon in a frenzy of demolition and construction. Chang'an Avenue, a mere forty-nine feet wide in 1949, underwent a series of expansions that eventually produced a grand thoroughfare more than 260 feet in width. Chang'an was the new prime meridian of Beijing, supplementing the old north-south axis of the imperial city. In the past, the *axis mundi* of the Celestial Empire ran through the emperor's throne in the heart of the Forbidden City; now Chairman Mao commanded both the old axis and the new one that passed in front of his portrait hanging on the facade of Tiananmen. Widening Chang'an meant the destruction of numerous historic gates, ceremonial archways (*pailou*), and other relics.[49] But an even more spectacular transformation was in store—the making of Tiananmen Square. Prior to Mao's intervention, the square had evolved from a long, narrow space lined since the Ming Dynasty with timber structures known as the "Thousand-step Porches," behind which were ministries and bureaus of the imperial government. The Porches were demolished in the early twentieth century, around the time the Republican government opened the Forbidden City to the public. But the wall behind the Porches remained, and at the time of the founding of the People's Republic in October 1949, it defined the extent of the square.[50] The modern political use of the space had begun in earnest in 1919, with the rallies that launched the May Fourth Movement, but it was only after 1949 that Tiananmen Square came into its own as China's superlative political space.

Public squares were an important element of Chinese urbanism and political culture in the Mao era. As Wu Hung writes, "Every city, town or village had to have a square for public gatherings on important (thus political) occasions—holiday parades and pageants, announcements of the Party's instructions, and struggle rallies against enemies of the people."[51] The mother of all these squares would, of course, have to be in Beijing, at the heart of the nation's capital. By 1959, the old walls around Tiananmen Square had been removed, along with the gatehouse to its south and scores of official buildings and residences. Extensive clearing of this historic fabric eventually yielded a space large enough to match Mao's ego—thirty-eight American football fields' worth of space for mass rallies and meetings.[52]

Flanking Tiananmen Square were two immense new buildings—the Great Hall of the People on the west, and the Museum of Chinese History on the east. These breathtaking structures, every bit equal in scale to the square itself, were part of a "Ten Great Buildings" campaign (Shi Da Jian Zhu) launched at the outset of the Great Leap Forward in 1958. Construction of the Great Buildings was itself conducted like a revolutionary campaign; 1,000 architects and engineers and 10,000 craftsmen and artisans from all over the country took part.[53] All ten Great Buildings were completed in less than a year, an astonishing achievement that galvanized the nation. They opened just as Tiananmen Square was also completed, in time for China's tenth anniversary celebrations on October 1, 1959. Architecturally, the structures drew from a range of styles. The Great Hall and the Museum of Chinese History were neoclassical with Chinese decorative motifs, while the Military Museum emulated the wedding-cake form of the early Soviet Union Exhibition Hall (1957). Most of the Great Buildings, however, employed a so-called National style characterized by big roofs and upswept eaves, a historicist mode that Liang Sicheng helped develop and would later be excoriated for (the Cultural Palace of Nationalities and Beijing Railway Station are examples). The vast scale of the Great Buildings— "gigantic, cement structures such as the city had never seen before"—was just what Liang feared would come to the Old City once it became the symbolic center of the new nation.[54]

★   ★   ★

These projects—the Great Buildings, Tiananmen Square, and Chang'an Avenue—brought dramatic change to Beijing. But it was the razing of Beijing's great defensive walls that destroyed the city's soul. Eliminating the city walls was originally advanced as a solution to inevitable future pressures of traffic congestion and overcrowding, which soon became a reality once the Old City was made the seat of the new government—just as Liang Sicheng had warned. The walls were precisely the kind of "old architecture" that Mao condemned as obsolete and the Soviets warned would "constrict the perspective of development" of Beijing—one of six guiding principles they had built into the 1953 master plan.[55]

Walls are an essential component of classical Chinese urbanism. The very meaning of "city" in Chinese culture is bound up, literally, with the notion of walled enclosure. One implies the other; for, as Sen-Dou Chang has written, "there was no such thing as a proper city without a wall."[56] This symmetry of meaning is well illustrated by the Chinese root character for "city"—cheng (城), which indeed also means "wall." Early city walls were simply made of rammed earth, sometimes covered with reeds to protect them from weathering; later, bricks and stone blocks were used to form a more durable surface.

Though walls had enclosed Chinese settlements since the dawn of time, the greatest period of city wall construction began with the overthrow of the Mongol regime (Yuan Dynasty) in 1368.[57] The Mongols, a nomadic people, were unaccustomed to walled settlements; Yuan records suggest that in the early period of their rule the Mongols even prohibited city walls to discourage insurrection and facilitate colonial administration. Eventually, however, they too adopted this ancient Chinese practice and erected an extensive system of walls at Dadu. The early Ming rulers rebuilt and extended city walls throughout the country. The walls of Nanjing, Beijing, Xi'an, and other cities all date principally to the Ming Dynasty, as does the Great Wall as we know it today. (The Mongols had little use for the Great Wall, for their homeland was on the other side.)[58]

The north wall of Beijing was erected around 1370, forty feet high and fifty wide at the top. It was built across the center of old Dadu, its perfect walled rectangle leveled after being conquered two years earlier. The old east and west walls of Dadu were rebuilt to serve the new city at twice their original width. Fifty years later, after Beijing had been made China's northern capital by the Emperor Yongle, the walls were clad with great clay bricks and fortified with bastions, gate towers, and massive defensive works known as "barbicans." Moats, typically constructed in tandem with the walls, ran in front of the ramparts (the moats were excavated to build up the walls, an ancient example of balancing cut and fill).[59] Finally, around 1553, a new set of walls was built incorporating the suburbs south of the city, near the Altar of Heaven—an "outer city" appended to the "inner city" to the north.[60] Thus encircled by twenty-five miles of walls and moats, Beijing achieved its full urban architectural glory. It was a superlative example of a classical Chinese walled city. As Sen-Dou Chang writes, "Towers were erected at the corners and over the gates. The corner towers were fortified on their outer faces, and were built of brick and loopholed for cannon. The gate towers, designed like three-story pagodas, but of rectangular form, were built largely of wood and had tiled roofs. These towers, which were usually the most striking features of the city's architecture, were intended to serve as living quarters for soldiers on duty at the gate, and as posts for archers in times of war."[61]

The vital role of walls in Chinese urban history did not prevent their frequent destruction—particularly at the hands of would-be modernizers, as we have already seen at Shanghai. Mao Zedong was hardly the first to consider city walls an impediment to urban progress, nor the first to build modern roads in their place. Youthful reformers in the republican era—many of whom, like Liang Sicheng, had studied in the West on Boxer Indemnity Fellowships—came home convinced that ramparts were a curse. In the 1920s and 1930s Chinese planners and engineers urged the demolition of city walls to ease traffic flow and make way for modern streets and motorways. In his 1930 masters thesis at Iowa State—"Design of Streets and the Use of City Walls in the Development of Highway Systems in the Municipalities of China"—Han-Veng Woo concluded that Chinese city walls were medieval structures "valueless in the modern world." Not only had the wall "lost its original significance," but it was "a hindrance to the traffic movement, city growth, or the development of highway and street systems."[62] Nonetheless, Woo showed how Nanjing's meandering walls—the most extensive in the world—could be modernized into an elevated "loop highway," complete with access ramps and separate lanes for local and through traffic.[63]

Elsewhere, walls made way for modern streets. By 1914 new avenues and tramways had replaced the walls of Shanghai's Chinese city. In Changzhou, Jiangsu Province, ramparts were sacrificed to build ten miles of new streets "surfaced with granite slabs seven inches thick, taken from the city walls."[64] The 800-year-old wall enclosing parts of Guangzhou was dismantled on the advice of the American-educated director of the city's Public Works

Xibianmen, ca. 1928.

FROM *PERCKHAMMER, PEKING, DAS GESICHT DER STÄDTE* (ALBERTUS VERLAG, 1928)

Department, and by 1919 more than six miles of the city's ramparts and fifteen gates had been replaced by a broad new boulevard paved with recycled wall bricks—the old literally pressed into the service of the new. The Guangzhou elite was soon on the move, having "taken rapidly to the use of automobiles," according to a report by the American Trade Commissioner in Shanghai (in 1919 there were two motor vehicles in Guangzhou; by 1921 the number was up to 175).[65]

By 1931, U.S. Department of Commerce analysts studying the China market for American automobiles happily reported that more than two dozen Chinese cities had razed their old walls for modern roads, or were planning to do so.[66] The Good Roads Association of China, founded in Shanghai, itself urged that "all the city walls...be demolished to construct loop highways."[67] Chinese walls did eventually fall to roads engineered with American expertise, and even to American motorcars. To the enterprising American auto salesmen in Beijing in the 1930s, the city's mighty ramparts became a medium for proving the mettle of their motorcars. On a visit to China in 1932, the Reverend Hewlett Johnson, Dean of Canterbury, reported observing American car dealers conducting demonstrations by driving their vehicles "up the steep angle leading to the wall surrounding the city of Peking."[68] A more fantastic juxtaposition of symbols—of East and West, past and future—can hardly be imagined.

The destruction (with American help) of Chinese walls for modern motorways was strangely presaged in one of the great hoaxes of the late nineteenth century. In June 1899, newspapers across the United States ran a story about American businessmen bidding for the contract to demolish the Great Wall of China and build a road in its place. The Qing government had conceived the project, it was said, to stimulate foreign investment and modernize its infrastructure. A Chicago firm, responding to the opportunity, was sending a team of engineers to China to conduct initial surveys. The group, allegedly stopped in Denver en route to the coast, were in fact four mischievous Denver reporters who, bored with the lack of news, had concocted the story in a local saloon.

Within days it was front page news from coast to coast. Even the *New York Times* was duped: "WILL CHINA'S WALL COME DOWN" fretted a headline on June 27, 1899; "Several Syndicates Are Said to Be After the Contract." The article reported that "According to Frank Lewis, a Chicago civil engineer… the Chinese Government contemplates the destruction of the ancient Chinese wall." Lewis, representing "a syndicate of Chicago capitalists" (backed by none other than Marshall Field and the Armours) was "en route to China to assist in tearing down the famous structure." The story gained startling new facts along the way; one East Coast daily even quoted a prominent Chinese businessman who confirmed the story as true. The Great Wall hoax itself spawned a second hoax—that the imminent demolition of the beloved wall sparked no less than the Boxer Rebellion, which led to the deaths of thousands of foreign missionaries. That story was later traced to a 1939 article in the *North American Review*, but not before it was featured in countless Sunday sermons, parental lectures, and even Paul Harvey's popular radio program, *The Rest of the Story*. The Great Wall hoax had become, ironically, a morality tale on the evils of fibbing.[69]

The practice of replacing city walls with roads has an even older pedigree in Europe. In Paris and other cities, the earliest boulevards ran alongside or on top of defensive perimeter walls, or in the space they once occupied; the French term *boulevard* in fact derives from *bolwerk*, the Dutch word for bulwark, which is why, originally, boulevards encircled a city while avenues radiated outward from the center.[70] Louis XIV began razing the medieval walls of Paris in 1670, shortly after the start of the Qing Dynasty in Beijing. On the

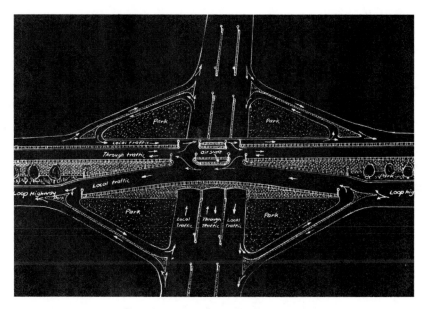

City wall as elevated highway, with access ramps.

FROM HAN-VENG WOO, "DESIGN OF STREETS AND THE USE OF CITY WALLS IN THE DEVELOPMENT OF HIGHWAY SYSTEMS IN

THE MUNICIPALITIES OF CHINA" (UNPUBLISHED MASTERS THESIS, IOWA STATE COLLEGE, 1930)

Right Bank the walls were replaced with a tree-shaded promenade, the Grand
Boulevards which ran from the present-day Place de la Madeleine to the Place
de la République. Vienna's Ringstrasse is an even better-known example of
the walls-to-boulevard metamorphosis. Foreshadowing Mao by a century,
Emperor Franz Josef issued a famous decree in 1857—*"Es ist mein Wille"* (It
Is My Will)—that brought down the city's medieval ramparts. In place of the
wall and glacis, Franz Josef specified that a grand boulevard, the Ringstrasse,
be built, along which a range of civic and institutional buildings and new housing for the city's rising middle class were erected.[71]

The modern deconstruction of Beijing's imperial walls actually began long
before Mao ascended Tiananmen. The Nationalist government removed the
walls of the Imperial City between 1917 and 1927; in other places the massive
barbican enclosures of Chaoyangmen and other gates were destroyed to allow
a circumferential rail line to slip around the city.[72] Liang Sicheng's defense of
the enceinte also had precedent. In 1930, his last year teaching at Northeast
University, Liang struggled to convince Shenyang's mayor to spare the city's

magnificent Drum and Bell towers, scheduled for demolition in a bid to improve traffic conditions. "Demolition is easy, preservation is difficult," Liang wrote. Shenyang's towers fell nonetheless.[73]

This failure was no doubt in Liang's mind when the subject of razing Beijing's walls and gates was first broached in the Soviet-dominated planning consultations of 1949 and 1950. Liang again moved into action. In April 1950 he drafted an argument that weighed the merits of preservation against those of demolition. He tried to convince Mao and the Party that Beijing's walls were not impediments to progress but a treasure of Chinese civilization that could easily be turned into an amenity. "Far from impeding the city's evolution," Liang argued, "the city wall would help rather than hinder the development of Beijing into a modern city if preserved ... its existence will enrich the life of people in Beijing as well as enhance our precious environment in the long run."[74] The broad glacis between wall and moat, then used for a circumferential railroad, could become a greenbelt and linear park, he argued, and the moat itself used for boating, fishing, and skating in winter.

But the real treasure was the rampart itself. Upon the wall, Liang wrote, "beds can be laid, shrubs like clove and rosebush planted, a bit of turf spread, flowers planted and benches installed." There, in summer, people could "stroll about and enjoy the cool air. On balmy autumn days, by climbing to the top of the city wall, gazing into the distance and overlooking the whole city, the vast Western Hills in the northwest and the boundless plains in the southeast, city people can meld with nature, and expand and refresh their minds." The gate towers and watchtowers could even be transformed into galleries and tea rooms for the enjoyment of all. "Such a round-the-city cultural and recreational area and three-dimensional park would be unique in the world. ... Encircling the city, the wall is waiting to serve the people, relax their tired bones and muscles, cultivate their taste and enrich their lives with national cultural relics and natural scenery."[75]

Even with all this, the wall could still serve its original defensive purpose; for as Liang added, it "can serve as a good anti-aircraft gun base if needed for national defense. The ancient fortification can fulfill its historical task once again!" Accommodating increased traffic, another argument against the old walls, could easily be achieved by opening more gates; why destroy the whole system, Liang asked, when only selected thoroughfares needed to pass beyond the walls?[76] Finally, regarding the "feudal relic" issue, Liang charged that such

South wall of Beijing's inner city, looking west toward Chongwenmen and Qianmen, ca. 1928.
Portions here survived Mao's onslaught and were restored recently as Ming City Wall Park.
FROM *PERCKHAMMER, PEKING, DAS GESICHT DER STÄDTE* (ALBERTUS VERLAG, 1928).

an argument was misleading and naïve: "Was not the Imperial Palace the palace of emperors? It is now the People's museum. Was not Tiananmen Square
the forecourt of the Imperial Palace? The birth of the People's Republic of China
was proclaimed to the world by Chairman Mao on Tiananmen. We should
never forget that these relics…are masterpieces created by countless ancient
working people, and although they once served emperors and were used exclusively by the elite, they have now become the common property and are our
national monuments."[77]

As he had done earlier, Liang summoned up an example of enlightened
urban planning from the Soviet Union that should have given the Moscow
advisors pause. He pointed to Smolensk, whose seventeenth-century wall was
not only spared by the Soviets, but meticulously reconstructed after sustain-
ing heavy damage in the Second World War. If Smolensk's modest wall, barely
more than four miles long, was the "Stone Necklace of Russia," shouldn't
that make Beijing's ramparts—nearly seven times longer, more massive, and
older—rather a more precious artifact? Evidently the Soviets only considered

Russian walls worth preserving. Liang suggested Beijing's walls were not only the "Necklace of China," but the "Necklace of the World."[78] This all fell on deaf ears. It was Mao's will that the walls come down, and so they did.

As Liang had sadly predicted, dismantling the walls was slow, hard work and consumed the labor of thousands of men and women. Liang calculated it would take eighty-three years to level Beijing's walls.[79] On this he was wrong: it took less than twenty years, and would have gone much more quickly had the Great Leap Forward and Cultural Revolution not intervened. Wall bricks were used for construction projects ranging from factories to pigsties. Many were carted off to build squatter villages on the edges of the city. Others were used for the construction, beginning in 1965, of the city's first subway line, which ran directly beneath the former location of the inner city's southern wall. The subway was actually conceived as a means of swiftly and secretly moving troops into the city in the event of war, and it did not open to public use for years.

After the Sino-Soviet split and increasing tensions between the two nations in the 1960s, Mao was consumed by fears of a nuclear strike from Moscow. This also led him to construct—again using wall bricks—hundreds of bomb shelters and air-raid tunnels beneath the city. As Jianying Zha has observed, in building these subterranean defenses, Mao simply "replaced the old walls with winding underground walls."[80] The imperial ramparts that the Soviets helped destroy would now, in pieces, help defend China against Soviet expansionism. More visibly, the now-cleared footprint of the old inner-city wall became the first in a series of circumferential highways, or ring roads, that now loop around the capital. The second ring road (Er Huan Lu) is a ghostly negative of the vanished ramparts, its sentry-like gates recalled in the names of overpasses and highway exits.

The destruction of Beijing's walls surely ranks among the greatest acts of urban vandalism in history. The ramparts made the city, and their removal changed forever the essence and character of Beijing. "For those who knew and loved old Beijing," writes journalist Orville Schell, "it was the wall, more than anything else, that gave the city its identity." To Schell and countless others, Beijing was now a city "purged of its past, its sense of itself and, indeed, of its beauty."[81]

In tragic symmetry, the fall of the enceinte paralleled Liang Sicheng's own demise. The Great Proletarian Cultural Revolution, which began in 1966, made Liang's life a living hell. Red Guards, dutifully following Mao's orders to destroy the "Four Olds" (*si jiu*)—old customs, culture, habits, and ideas—declared war on history and the past. Red Guards at Beijing's Number Two Middle School did so literally, posting a "Declaration of War on the Old World" around the school in August 1966.[82] Tsinghua University, where Liang had established the Department of Architecture and taught since 1946, was a particular hotbed of Red Guard rampages. The elegant stone gate from Tsinghua's early years as an American missionary school was smashed and defaced. Red Guards terrorized the campus searching out "counter-revolutionary" professors and staff or anyone accused of being a "rightist" or indulging in the "Four Olds" purged by Mao.

As a prominent intellectual, historian, and scion of a distinguished family, Liang was targeted for especially brutal treatment. He was paraded about campus with a black placard labeling him a "reactionary academic authority," his name crossed out below. Posters hung in the architecture department accused Liang of various thought crimes and political infractions. He was charged with having cultivated ties to Chiang Kai-shek and the Kuomintang, for hadn't he advised them on cultural heritage preservation matters during the war? He was excoriated for participating in the design of the United Nations headquarters in New York. He was even condemned for having greeted with a kiss, in the European manner, the female leader of a delegation of French architects several years earlier. More damning still, Liang was accused of having opposed Chairman Mao on matters related to urban planning.[83] Liang's home was pillaged and his second wife, Lin Zhu, was beaten repeatedly (Lin Huiyin had succumbed to tuberculosis in 1955, and Liang remarried in 1962). His books and papers were burned or sold for scrap. It is a miracle indeed that Liang's most precious work survived, eventually to be published as *The Collected Writings of Liang Sicheng*. Liang, now seriously ill, spent his last few years scribbling pathetic self-criticisms, in the meager hope that he would be "rehabilitated" by the mob that tormented him. Liang Sicheng died a broken man in January 1972.[84]

In the four decades since Beijing's walls were destroyed, the capital has been transformed from a city steeped in history to a "perpetually provisional" place, to paraphrase Henry James—a city constantly torn apart and rebuilt, that has not only rubbed out its past but increasingly now seems to have "no credible possibility of time for history," as James once wrote of Manhattan.[85] Yet even in this contingent and provisional city, the past lives on in haunts and traces—and in a number of virtual reconstructions. The world will never again see the magnificent walled complex that was Beijing before Mao, but it may at least get a glimpse of Ming Beijing, in somewhat diminished form, in the southeast suburbs of the capital.

About thirty miles from Tiananmen, in the town of Xianghe, Hebei Province, there is an extraordinary place called Grand Epoch City (Di Yi Cheng, literally "The First City"), a multilayered leisure landscape that includes a 540-acre hotel, conference and exhibition center, and golf resort as well as a spectacular three-story Buddhist temple. Nearly all of Grand Epoch's facilities are contained within a one-sixth scale replica of Beijing's mighty enceinte and its original barbican gates, bastions, and defensive towers. Even at this scale, this mini-Beijing is hardly small; its three miles of walls make it very nearly the size of a petit-Peking built by the Kangxi emperor at Yuanming Yuan in the eighteenth century (see Chapter 9, "Theme Parks and the Landscape of Consumption"). It is only at this curious theme park that we can finally get a (one-sixth) sense of what imperial Beijing was like in its architectural glory. Like its imperial predecessor, Grand Epoch City is the pivot of an empire—this time a sports and entertainment empire built by former People's Liberation Army soldier and Xianghe native Li Shilin, who made a fortune as an entrepreneur in the early Deng Xiaoping era and owns the popular Guoan Football Club, Beijing's answer to Manchester United.

Grand Epoch City actually began in 1992 as a small hotel built near the Xianghe fields his footballers practiced on. As the facility expanded, Li saw an opportunity to both develop a world-class leisure facility and give China back something taken from it decades before—the old walled city of Beijing. In doing so he consulted experts on Chinese classical city planning and employed scores of traditional craftsmen to produce an authentic replica. Of course, old Beijing's ramparts were six times larger and solid, made of rammed earth and sheathed with massive bricks; those at Grand Epoch City are hollow and contain restaurants, banquet halls, shops, fitness centers, a natatorium, squash courts, a bowling alley, a *Topgun* laser-tag shooting range, an indoor rock-climbing wall, and "the biggest indoor sea-view entertainment center in Asia" (complete with palm trees, sandy beach, and artificial surf), along with 430,556 square feet of exhibition and conference space and 1,000 hotel rooms. Many of the gates are in fact the lobbies of Grand Epoch's five hotels, led by a five-star flagship facility at Zhengyangmen, once the front door of Beijing. The

Yongdingmen reconstituted at one-sixth scale as the main gate of Grand Epoch City, Xianghe, Hebei Province, 2006. PHOTOGRAPH BY AUTHOR

space enclosed by the city walls, rather than a teeming metropolis, is a championship twenty-seven-hole "Golf Garden." The course, with nine holes in the old inner city and eighteen holes in the outer city, was the site of the 2003 Bob Hope Chrysler of China PGA Golf Tournament, and has been ranked as one of Asia's best.[86]

The pro shop for Grand Epoch's golf course is located in a reconstituted Deshengmen, a gate tower originally on the north side of Beijing. Ironically, Deshengmen is one of the few pieces of the real city wall that survived Mao's onslaught, even if it lives on as a glorious traffic island. There are other survivors. Zhengyangmen, the old front door to the city, though long ago deprived of its barbican section and marooned now in a sea of traffic, remains. So do the southeast and southwest corner towers of the old inner city, Dongbianmen and Xibianmen. And a short walk south of Beijing's main rail station lies a 4,000-foot-long fragment of the wall itself, running from the southeast corner tower at Dongbianmen to where Chongwenmen—the Gate of Esteemed Culture—

Ming City Wall Park, 2006. PHOTOGRAPH BY AUTHOR

once stood. A Ming Dynasty artifact and a Mao-era survivor, the Chongwen wall section is doubly a relic. It only survived because a colony of squatter shacks had been erected alongside it in the 1950s by workers on the Beijing Railway Station and the city's first subway line. Bricks cannibalized from adjoining wall sections became part of small shacks and sheds, many of which actually incorporated the city wall into their structure; for dozens of families living along the remnant rampart, the city wall was also the kitchen wall.

In 2002, the hodgepodge structures were bulldozed and several hundred families relocated so that the wall could be restored as the centerpiece of the new Ming City Wall Park. Because so many bricks had been removed over the decades, rebuilding to the original height required a city-wide search for the long-lost building material. Municipal authorities issued a call for their return. One elderly resident, Feng Baohua, took it upon himself to relocate and return as many of the forty-four-pound, 400-year-old blocks as he could find, foraging around demolition sites throughout the city and carting his redeemed loot to the construction site night after night on a tricycle. A retired chemical plant worker, Feng had played on the wall as a child and wanted to help bring back a fragment, however small, of the city's lost heritage.[87]

Feng Baohua's recovered wall bricks, 2002. PHOTOGRAPH BY AUTHOR

Not far from Ming City Wall Park another fragment of the past was resurrected several years ago, this one from the ground up, using all new material. Yongdingmen, demolished in 1957, was the front gate of the outer city and the starting point of the great central meridian—the *axis mundi* of both Beijing and the Chinese universe. Like the Ming City Wall Park, its reconstruction was carried out under the so-called Humanistic Olympics Cultural Relics Protection Program, itself part of a larger capital improvement campaign aimed at readying Beijing for the 2008 Summer Olympic Games. The Relics Protection Program—which also included comprehensive rehabilitation of the Forbidden City, the Altar of the Moon, Temple of Heaven, Altar of the Earth, and Altar of the Sun—was conceived to "restore the historical image of Beijing as an ancient capital," to salvage what little remained of Beijing's long and storied past.[88] Yongdingmen, in particular, was needed to anchor the south end of the central axis, now extended north of the Old City to incorporate the main Olympics site.

CHAPTER FOUR

Capital Improvements

大都市大項目

For nearly a decade now, 2008 has been spun in the popular imagination as China's annus mirabilis—a year of miracles and all things good. The reason, of course, is the Games of the XXIX Olympiad, an event that looms like a glorious beacon on China's national horizon. For two weeks in August 2008, China will be at the center of global attention as it hosts what may well be the most expensive, most watched, and most attended Olympics in history. Most Olympic Games are a city's shining moment. The 1984 and 1996 Summer Games were great achievements for, respectively, Los Angeles and Atlanta. But they were hardly signal events in American history. The 2008 Olympiad, on the other hand, belongs not just to a city, but to a nation; as such, it could only be hosted by the Chinese capital. For the People's Republic and its ruling Communist Party, the political symbolism of the 2008 Games is beyond calculation.

Winning the Games back in 2001 was, for China, proof positive of its arrival on the world stage. No nation in recent years has wanted the Olympics more desperately than China, nor been more needful of the global prestige it promises. The world has stood in awe of Chinese accomplishment in recent decades. It has watched with envy, fear, and admiration as China has built vast new cities, lifted millions of lives out of poverty, and flooded the globe with newly affordable appliances, electronics, furniture, toys, clothing, and a thousand other things—destroying, in the process, entire industries in other countries. The People's Republic has surely arrived. Yet China still hungers for the sanction of the world community, like the parvenu with his mansion and self-made wealth who yet longs for the legitimacy of the country club. Now that the invitation has been extended, China is determined to awe the world and in the process purge the manifold humiliations of the past. The 2008 Olympiad will

The Bird's Nest, 2007. PHOTOGRAPH BY GEORGE LEW

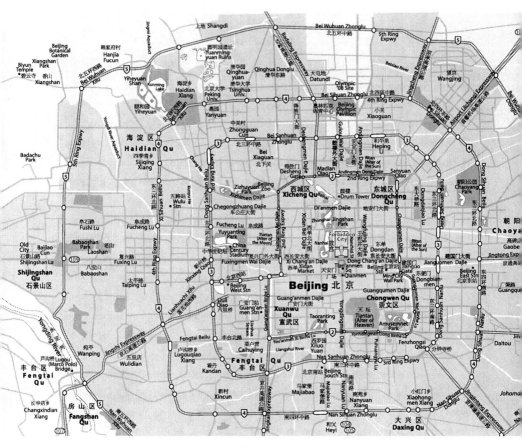

Contemporary map of Beijing. COURTESY OF JOHOMAPS.COM

be China's great coming-out party, its official debut, the capstone event of its three-decade economic miracle.

In breadth and scale, China's Olympic ambition is simply without precedent. In terms of population alone, no Olympiad in history has meant more to more people—1.3 billion people, to be precise. I was in Shanghai with a friend on the night of July 13, 2001, part of an immense throng that had gathered in People's Square before a Jumbotron broadcast of the International Olympic Committee meeting in Moscow. I will never forget the ecstasy unleashed when Juan Antonio Samaranch uttered the word "Beijing." It was a scene of collective release—and this was not even Beijing! Imagine New Yorkers, crowded into Times Square, cheering the announcement that Washington had won the Games! As the city around us erupted in wild celebration, I was left with the nagging sensation that, somehow, the klieg lights of history had just shifted a bit further to the East.

Needless to say, China pulled out all the stops to ready itself—and its capital—for this momentous event. Within weeks of being awarded the 2008 Games the city launched the most ambitious urban construction effort in Olympic history. The total bill for these capital improvements may well top $40 billion, which would make the 2008 Summer Games the most expensive in Olympic history by far. The actual competition venues themselves—nineteen purpose-built facilities and a dozen or so refurbished and expanded existing facilities, most located in the Olympic Green and the Wukesong Culture and Sports Center—are only part of this massive capital improvement. Beijing's regional highway and rail infrastructure has also been extensively upgraded, including two new ring roads, numbers five (known as "Olympic Avenue") and six, with a combined length of nearly 142 miles; eight new subway lines; and a ninety-six-mile light-rail system. Even a new house numbering system and multilanguage street and highway signs have been ordered.[1]

To accommodate the expected 250,000 foreign visitors and more than two million domestic tourists, a major expansion of Beijing Capital International Airport was begun in 2004. Already one of the busiest in Asia, the recent completion of Terminal Three has made Beijing's the largest airport in the world. The new facility was designed by British architect Sir Norman Foster, one of several foreign superstars tasked with helping Beijing revamp its image in advance of 2008. Urbanist Deyan Sudjic, visiting the terminal construction site in the fall of 2005, described it as "a medieval battlefield conceived on the scale of a Japanese epic" where "swarming warrior armies cluster around giant cranes, more than 100 of them, ranged like ancient siege engines across a frontline almost two miles long."[2] Additionally, there are thousands of major commercial and government projects, both in Beijing and throughout China, not directly related to the Games but scheduled nonetheless for completion by the mythic date, August 2008. So many big projects ending with the arrival of the Olympic torch may well cause a hiccup in the global economy, as demand for cement, steel, and other construction materials suddenly falls.

Of course, Beijing is hardly the first metropolis to hitch its dreams to an Olympic star. Cities have long looked to the Games as a kind of wonder-working genie, and international superevents, beginning with the world's fairs and expositions of the nineteenth century, have endowed cities with land-mark buildings and other improvements.[3] The Great Exhibition of 1851— really the first modern world expo—left London with the Crystal Palace; Paris got the Eiffel Tower from the 1889 centennial commemoration of the French Revolution; and San Francisco's Palace of Fine Arts was built for the 1915 Panama-Pacific International Exposition. Flushing Meadows-Corona Park in New York, home of Shea Stadium and the U.S. Open, was the site of world's fairs in both 1939 and 1964. But the Olympics is the mother of all global super-events. None has greater prestige, or draws more attention and more viewers. The Athens Summer Games in 2004 set TV audience records as some four billion people tuned in worldwide to watch at least part of the events. This level of global exposure means incalculable publicity and marketing opportunities for a host city. For decades now, the Games have been used as a catalyst for leveraging a great range of urban improvements, often with the support of the national government.

The first in this regard was Rome, host of the 1960 Olympiad, where highway, airport, and urban landscape improvements were implemented in advance of the event. For the 1964 Summer Olympic Games, Tokyo built two new underground rail lines, expanded its metropolitan highway network, and implemented long-planned improvements of its public housing, sewer infra-structure, and harbor facilities. Munich's Olympic Village was designed to be a community for moderate- and low-income residents after the Games, and host-ing the ill-fated 1972 Games was the impetus for restoring the historic city cen-ter and constructing new roads, hotels, a major shopping center, and a variety of public transport facilities. Montreal, host of the 1976 Summer Olympiad, built a new airport, roads, and a twelve-mile Metro extension to an "Olympic Park."[4] For the host city, then, the Olympic Games is not just a chance to play but, as Brian Chalkley and Stephen Essex write, "a means of achieving international prominence and an instrument for promoting physical and economic regeneration."[5] And though it is an Olympic virgin, Beijing has extensive experience reinventing itself as a setting for politically charged events. It is, after all, China's capital city, and thus a symbolic political space as much as a working metropolis of nearly fifteen million people.

Beijing hosted two major events in the 1990s that anticipated the Olympics. The first was the 11th Asian Games in 1990, shadowed by the tragedy of Tiananmen just a year before. The second and more significant event was the grand celebration of the fiftieth anniversary of the People's Republic of China on October 1, 1999. Preparations for this national birthday bash ranged from the noble to the draconian. The good work was substantial and deserves praise. Landmark buildings such as the Great Hall of the People and the Beijing Railway Station were scrubbed and restored. Automobile emissions controls were established to reduce air pollution, and older, high-polluting vehicles such as the tiny Xiali taxis and *mianbao* (bread loaf) microvans were banned from major routes. Billboards on Chang'an Avenue and around Tiananmen Square were ordered removed. Citywide landscape improvements created acres of new parks and green space; public art was commissioned and 2,000 new park benches installed. More than one million trees were planted, the largest greening operation in the city's history. Mature specimens were used for immediate effect; streets became leafy thoroughfares overnight, as planting typically took place in the evening, when traffic was minimal.[6] Even more extraordinary were improvements aimed at the skies above. For several days prior to October 1, military aircraft seeded the clouds over Beijing, producing torrential rains the night before the big event. National Day dawned crystal clear, dry, and sunny—a perfect day.

That even the weather was disciplined for National Day was not the only example of authoritarian extremism. More Orwellian still was the restoration of China's political center-of-centers, Tiananmen Square. The year 1999 was one of several major anniversaries in China. Well before the nation's fiftieth anniversary in October was the eightieth anniversary of the May Fourth Movement (1919) and, more significant still, the tenth anniversary of the Tiananmen massacre on June 4, 1989. To circumvent any commemorative gatherings that might make it lose face, the Communist Party closed Tiananmen Square for renovations a full year in advance of National Day.

Behind an impenetrable screen of steel construction barriers, Tiananmen Square was itself transformed into yet another kind of walled Chinese space; inside, scores of workers carried out a comprehensive facelift. Broad lawns were installed and the old meter-square concrete pavers were replaced with heavy granite flagging—one of the most durable materials available for urban hardscaping. While the national significance of Tiananmen Square certainly deserves the best materials, some critics saw a sinister side to the choice of granite; the *South China Morning Post*, for instance, branded the new surface as "tank-proof paving."[7] Tiananmen Square's once dull field of concrete block was thus transformed into a dazzling expanse of pink granite trimmed with well-groomed lawn panels—an appropriate metaphor for China's metamorphosis from monochromatic Maoism to the polychromy of affluence and arrival. Many of the old concrete pavers became part of a parking lot at China's first drive-in movie theater.

Other National Day image improvements had a more direct—and negative—impact on the built environment and people's lives. In the year before October 1, 1999, several major avenues were widened as part of the Beijing Environment Improvement Project, ostensibly to ease traffic congestion. The widening of an avenue in Xuanwu District consumed scores of historic *siheyuan*, courtyard houses, including a complex in which Sun Yat-sen had once lectured and the Hundred Days' Reform was launched in 1898 (in part by Liang Sicheng's father). In spite of being declared a historic site—and marked as such with a plaque—the building was turned to rubble in September 1998.[8] Closer to the Forbidden City, Ping'an Avenue was transformed from a narrow, crowded street to an eight-lane thoroughfare. Broadening this road, which parallels Chang'an Avenue, had been discussed as early as 1957 as a means of expediting cross-town traffic through the Old City. Lacking the funds for such a costly upgrade, the city gave developers priceless land flanking Ping'an in exchange for widening and improving the street. The strategy was dubious at best, for all the new development—shopping centers, apartments, offices—would likely make the new road just as congested as the old one.[9] Regardless, an ample corridor of land, home to some 20,000 families, was condemned and handed to the developers.

But the Ping'an project ran into unexpected opposition. To complete this scheme, a large number of historic buildings would have to be destroyed, including the homes of well-connected and politically savvy residents who took their fight to the international press. One of these was Zhao Jingxin, an elderly professor who struggled to save his home of fifty years from demolition. After a long court battle and considerable press coverage, a judge ruled that the old homestead had "no historic value," and could be razed. On the morning of demolition 200 police and government officials showed up to make sure no one interfered with its destruction; reporters were ordered to leave and photography was prohibited. Zhao, an octogenarian, was forced to relocate to an unheated, unfinished flat beyond the fifth ring road, a forty-minute walk to the nearest bus stop.[10] Zhao's campaign failed, but it did result in a number of broad concessions from both the city and the developers. In its final iteration, Ping'an Avenue was reduced in width from 230 feet to as "little" as 92 feet in some places. The route was shifted here and there to avoid landmark buildings, and new construction along its flanks subjected to height limitations. A number of historic structures were indeed spared, including the former home of a daughter of the Emperor Qianlong and the house where Sun Yat-sen died.[11]

In other places, street widenings in advance of National Day were motivated more by politics than transportation planning; they were part of a citywide effort to eliminate environments—and people—considered unsightly or problematic by the central government. Such interventions have a long history in Beijing, and often targeted the so-called peasant enclaves that began forming in the city as the economy surged in the 1980s. By the early 1990s there were a number of enclaves scattered throughout Beijing settled by migrants from Xinjiang, Zhejiang, Anhui, Henan, and Fujian provinces.[12] In October 1995, bustling and populous Zhejiang Village was razed; the government considered it an eyesore and potential source of political unrest only three miles from Tiananmen Square.[13] Before that, thousands of migrants from Zhenjiang and other migrant enclaves were expelled in advance of the 1990 Asian Games, and again in 1992 and 1993 for the benefit of visiting officials in town to evaluate Beijing's candidacy in its failed bid for the 2000 Summer Olympic Games.[14]

In the months prior to National Day, Xinjiang Village in Ganjiakou District fell into the gun sights of officialdom. Located on Beijing's west side, the community was inhabited by a large number of Muslim Uighur (Uygur) immigrants from Xinjiang Province in northwestern China. Xinjiang has been a trouble spot for the Chinese government for decades, the source of a menacing separatist movement. Xinjiang Village was a busy place, popular with both foreign backpacker tourists and students from nearby universities, who enjoyed barbecued lamb, flat-breads, and other Muslim specialties (hashish and heroin were also said to be available). The neighborhood was congested, but hardly a slum. Local merchants had in fact invested substantial funds in improvements: "In recent years," reported the *Los Angeles Times* in 1999, "concrete sheds with corrugated tin roofs have given way to Arabic-style minarets, plastic grape vines, and wall tapestries depicting the Turkish seaport Istanbul." Because many of the neighborhood's food stalls, shops, and restaurants occupied illegal additions that crowded Zengguang Street, a simple road-widening project would inflict a punishing blow to the community and its source of sustenance. This was precisely what authorities had in mind. On the morning of March 15, 1999, bulldozers began advancing on the street as police chased off reporters and merchants scrambled to salvage what they could from their doomed shops and stalls.[15]

When I visited Zengguang Street in October that year, it was a clean and spacious thoroughfare, with broad new sidewalks devoid of any markets or food stalls. On walls nearby, however, there was a plethora of protest graffiti, and the side alleys and lanes just off Zengguan Street now teemed with the very market activities purged from the front. The main drag had been ceded to the authorities, but the enclave survived—a resilient community indeed. Similar Orwellian acts of urban improvement took place elsewhere in the run-up to National Day—social engineering in the guise of city planning. Throughout the city, hundreds of acres of night markets, street stalls, restaurants, cobbler and bicycle repair shops, fruit stands, and other entrepreneurial accretia were leveled, all accused of being "the major cause," as the official Xinhua news agency put it, "of the untidy appearance and visual pollution in certain parts of the city."[16] Also purged in the interest of image were 300,000 migrant workers. These were not idle loafers but the very men and women who had polished and planted the capital for the fiftieth anniversary. Ten thousand such workers rushed to complete the gargantuan Oriental Plaza shopping center at Wangfujing so that it could be unveiled for National Day. The workers themselves were then spirited off to the

Zengguang streetscape cleared of merchants' stalls, 1999. PHOTOGRAPH BY AUTHOR

edge of town, for such poor ordinary people could not be allowed to sully the image of the People's Republic on its fiftieth birthday.[17]

Such actions were replayed more recently. Hundreds of families were removed from potential athletic facility sites before they were inspected by International Olympic Committee (IOC) officials during the candidacy process. In February 2001, Beijing officials even banned the use of coal-fired stoves for several days, forcing residents to endure freezing temperatures so that a visiting IOC delegation might be impressed by the relatively clean city air.[18] Once the 2008 Games were officially in hand, urban renewal began in earnest in the capital. By the spring of 2005, some 300,000 people had lost their homes to Olympic-related development projects, mostly in the vast, semirural district north of the city center chosen for the Olympic Green.[19] The destruction of the city's vernacular *hutong* fabric (with its narrow lanes and alleys), already well underway by 2001, was vastly accelerated in the rush to transform Beijing into a modern Olympic city. Hundreds of neighborhoods were identified as old, dilapidated, and in need of total upgrading—in other words, being scraped to the ground.[20]

The ensuing evictions caused tremendous ill will in the city, and even extraordinary acts of resistance. In late May 2005, two brothers threatened to blow up a work crew with a bearing-filled bomb in protest of redevelopment. Their home was one of many scheduled for demolition to make way for an unspecified Olympic facility in Shijingshan District. According to the *Beijing News*, the men doused themselves with gasoline and shouted "whoever dares to destroy our house will perish with us together"; the pair was arrested after a standoff with police and promptly disappeared.[21] A year earlier, another Beijing resident, Ye Guozhu, was sentenced to four years in prison after protesting forcible eviction, ostensibly for Olympics-related construction. His brother, Ye Guoqiang, imprisoned for an attempted protest suicide in Tiananmen Square, claimed that the family business was ruined by the eviction, and that the Olympics was only being used as a pretext to push forward lucrative real estate deals.[22]

Even as the Humanistic Olympics Cultural Relics Preservation Program was putting the finishing touches on a reconstituted Yongdingmen, Beijing's cultural heritage was elsewhere being destroyed in the name of the Games. Venerable neighborhoods east and west of Qianmen Street and nearby Meishi Street, one of Beijing's historic commercial centers, have been extensively redeveloped in the Olympic rush. These *hutong*-filled districts, just below the old south wall and front gate of the inner city, Zhengyangmen, were famous for their opera companies and acrobatic troupes, banks, guilds, former Qing Dynasty brothels, and boarding houses for young scholars in town to sit for the imperial examinations. One Qianmen institution, the Tong Ren Tang herbal medicine shop on Dazhalan Street, had been in continuous operation since 1669. Qianmen was also legendary for local Beijing culinary specialties, including *jiaozi* (dumplings) and Peking duck.[23]

But rather than assure its preservation, the coming of the Olympics only accelerated redevelopment of the historic area, despite its status as one of Beijing's twenty-five protected historic districts. "This neighborhood is the face of Beijing to the world," one local man put it. "They don't want foreigners to see this scarred old face."[24] What visitors will see instead are million-dollar neotraditional courtyard homes, a much wider Meishi Street, and gentrified, pedestrianized Qianmen and Nanxinhua streets, with cafés and restaurants much like the nearby arts shopping street, Liulichang, well known to every foreign tourist.[25]

The process of tarting up the old streets has been controversial in architectural circles, too. A junior professor at a prestigious local university was commissioned, for a staggering sum of money, to create a series of traditional building facades for the new Qianmen streetscape. The result was more set design than good urbanism, a jumble of traditional architectural motifs thrown together in a drunken romp through history. It has since been redesigned. The Qianmen demolitions, begun in early 2005, triggered a flood of protest from the increasingly vocal preservation community as well as local residents such as Zhang Jinli, a former steelworker and restaurateur in Qianmen's Dazhalan section, who was angry enough about losing his home and business to string up banners accusing the government and the courts of running roughshod over the people.[26]

These and other excesses are balanced, to some degree, by a range of Olympic-related public works and civic amenities. The most visible of these are located in the centerpiece of Beijing's Olympic transformation, the Olympic Green. Roughly three times the size of New York's Central Park, the 2,864-acre expanse incorporates the China National Garden and the Olympic Forest Park, the latter an ecological sanctuary for the city featuring a 300-acre Olympic Lake and an artificial mountain made of 140 million cubic feet of fill. Also in the Green are the Olympic Village; Media Village; a 2.8 million-square-foot hotel and convention center; extensive shopping, entertainment, and cultural facilities; and four new subway stations. Most importantly, the Green contains fourteen of Beijing's nineteen new Olympic competition venues, including the National Stadium and National Aquatics Centre.[27] The Green, laid out by Massachusetts-based Sasaki Associates, is located several miles above Tiananmen Square and caps a long northward extension of the city's old imperial meridian. The job of extending this great shaft of space, to physically and symbolically fuse the Olympic Green to the larger city, was given to none other than German architect and urban designer Albert Speer Jr.

Speer's father was, of course, Adolf Hitler's chief architect and minister of armaments. Though Speer Jr. hardly knew his father and obviously bears none of his guilt, being commissioned by an authoritarian regime to create a great urban axis awakened old ghosts.[28] For in the 1930s the elder Speer, then Inspector General of Building for the Reich Capital Berlin, used just such a device to give form to Welthauptstadt Germania, the megalomaniac city that was to be the seat of Hitler's thousand-year Reich. Speer's monumental Berlin

The Olympic stadium nears completion, 2007. PHOTOGRAPH BY PENG BO, VIART IMAGE STUDIO

axis was anchored at one end by the impossibly large Volkshalle (with a dome seventeen times the size of St. Peter's in the Vatican), extending through a great triumphal arch several times larger than the one in Paris. Speer never got to implement his grand axial vision; the closest he came was laying out a whimsical north-south axis to organize his tiny garden plot at Spandau Prison.[29]

The younger Speer's datum spans the gamut of Beijing, extending from a new railway station and the reconstructed Yongdingmen south of the Old City, and then running north of the Bell and Drum towers to the Olympic Green. There, the axis slips between the two main facilities for the Olympic Games, the National Aquatics Centre and National Stadium, calling forth another historical irony: one of the few structures actually erected in Berlin during the elder Speer's tenure as Nazi builder was Werner March's stadium for the 1936 Summer Olympic Games.[30]

The National Stadium and Aquatics Centre are the crown jewels of Olympic Beijing. The job of designing the 91,000-seat National Stadium was awarded, after an invitational competition, to the Swiss architects and Pritzker laureates Jacques Herzog and Pierre de Meuron, who worked on the project with iconoclastic Beijing artist and landscape architect Ai Weiwei. The Sino-Swiss

The Bird's Nest and the Water Cube straddle Albert Speer Jr.'s central axis.
COURTESY PTW·ARUP·CSCEC

collaboration yielded a remarkable building encased in a tracery of steel columns and resembling a loose-spun fiberglass cocoon, or, as it is now universally known, a bird's nest. Elliptical in shape, the stadium measures just over 1,000 feet on the long axis and is rotated at a slight angle, ten degrees off Speer's axis, to align it to the Asian Games site nearby. This move, only evident in plan view, was meant to symbolically link the Olympic site with the landmark complex built for Beijing's first high-profile international sporting event, in 1990.

The Bird's Nest is formed by a series of twenty-four interlocked steel column sets, each weighing more than a fleet of trucks. These constitute both the facade and the load-bearing structural system of the stadium; as Arthur Lubow described the stadium in the *New York Times*, "its skin is made of bones."[31] Where gaps between the twigs of a real bird's nest might be filled with leaves and grass, the cavities between the stadium's steel columns—those over the seating areas, at least—are filled with high-tech plastic panels. Ironically, the building's distinctive tracery—its most memorable feature—began as a means of concealing the structural supports for the retractable roof originally required in the competition précis but later dropped for budgetary reasons.

The Nest will host a number of key Olympic sporting events—most of the track-and-field competitions are scheduled to take place there. But the building's most memorable function will be as the site of the spectacle and fanfare bracketing the actual athletic events: the opening and closing ceremonies for the 2008 Summer Olympiad. The opening ceremony, especially, has become a singular event in the choreography of the modern Olympic games. For the host city—and nation—the ceremony is a chance to display cultural brilliance and technical mastery to a captive global audience. The opening of the 2008 Summer Games is scheduled to begin at the auspicious moment of eight o'clock on the evening of the eighth day of the eighth month of 2008. For the stadium's architects, the gala event presented a characteristically Chinese challenge—accommodating a huge, finely graded assembly of "very important persons," some 11,000 in all, including 700 VVIPS and 20 VVVIPS, presumably among them Hu Jintao, Wen Jianbao, and other senior leaders and heads of state.[32]

Just across Speer's axis from the Bird's Nest is the second major landmark of Olympic Beijing, the 754,000-square-foot National Aquatics Centre, better known as the Water Cube. The building utilizes the same pneumatic panels as the National Stadium, only here they are its defining feature; the Water Cube is entirely clad with them. These units, called ETFE panels, are essentially air-filled pillows, inflated by low-power electric pumps and sandwiched between two layers of a translucent Teflon-like membrane made of ethylene tetrafluoro-ethylene. The trapped-air panels provide insulation but also admit abundant natural light, and thus create a greenhouse effect to warm the interior of the natatorium. The Water Cube utilizes some 4,000 individual ETFE units, some nearly thirty feet across, set within a steel space frame arrayed in a seemingly chaotic pattern inspired by the geometry of biological cells and soap bubbles. The overall effect is that of a building made of suds.

The Aquatics Centre was designed by Australian architects PTW and engineered by the British engineering firm Ove Arup & Partners, one of the largest in the world.[33] Arup worked out the structural engineering for the National Stadium, too, and is also helping erect another major Beijing landmark scheduled for completion by 2008—the new headquarters for CCTV. Designed by Rem Koolhaas and Ole Scheeren for China's vast state media conglomerate, CCTV Tower resembles a skyscraper snapped in two places to make a self-contained loop; rather than pierce the sky, the building enframes it.

CCTV Tower, Beijing. COURTESY OF THE OFFICE FOR METROPOLITAN ARCHITECTURE (OMA)

Though only fifty-five stories (755 feet tall), it is a huge and programmatically complex building with a total floor area of some 4.31 million square feet—roughly equivalent to each of the twin towers of the late World Trade Center in New York. The CCTV tower is a self-contained media city, with offices, studios, and production and broadcasting facilities that will accommodate some 10,000 workers. Erecting the Koolhaas loop presented extraordinary challenges to Arup's engineers. One particularly poetic puzzle involved joining the two leaning towers. Because they are unequally exposed to the sun, differential expansion required that the union be consummated at dawn. Only then would the structures have cooled to roughly the same temperature, enabling them to line up perfectly. The CCTV Tower is an inventive piece of work; it literally upends many shibboleths regarding skyscraper design. If any of Beijing's new signature buildings has potential to become a city icon, this is it.

On the other hand, like nearly all recent monumental architecture in the capital, CCTV Tower is little more than a glorified piece of sculpture, a building almost wholly disengaged from the streetscape and an indifferent participant in the fabric of the larger city. It could have been built anywhere. This is not so much the fault of the architects as it is a function of Beijing's seeming ambition to turn itself into a Chinese version of Los Angeles or Houston, a city of automobiles, vast highways, and isolated architectural events. What makes this all the more ironic is that CCTV Tower has been positioned as one of the cornerstones of Beijing's official central business district (CBD), the capital's much-willed new "downtown."

Beijing, unlike most Western cities, has never had a dominant business district; it was, after all, a center of political, cultural, and administrative functions through most of its history.[34] Commercial functions were relatively limited and tertiary-sector services—banking, legal and financial services, insurance, and advertising—were virtually nonexistent until only the last thirty years or so. In most capitalist cities, market forces encourage firms to cluster together to facilitate exchange and maximize economies of scale. Clustering is centripetal and usually results in a vertiginous pileup of office and commercial space in the center of the city—the classic high-rise downtown. The center of Beijing, on the other hand, was dominated by an ancient palace complex and the ponderous governmental buildings set around Tiananmen Square. As the economy heated up in the reform era, demand for office space became acute. Developers responded by erecting commercial office buildings in whatever space was available in the Old City, and along the inner ring roads, where land was less expensive. The city's literally endless ring roads (they are closed loops, after all) were fast-sprouting edge city developments, none of which reached a point of sufficient critical mass to yield a CBD. Major retail activity—another typical function of CBDs—was itself split among several areas, including Xidan, Wangfujing, and Qianmen.

Beijing's planners concluded that the lack of an accessible, well-served central district was untenable for a world city, or at least unbecoming of one. They were also keenly aware that Beijing had no brand-image skyline, nothing that could compare to the magical towers of Hong Kong's Central District, or to the spectacular emergent skyline at Pudong. For most people, the first impression of a city comes from its signature against the sky. Stacked and rising skyscrapers, gathered on the horizon, signal our arrival in Chicago or Minneapolis or Boston; even sprawlish places like Atlanta, Houston, or Los Angeles can be pinned down from afar by their vertiginous centers. For many cities, that skyline is no less than a trademark. Beijing, having nothing of the sort, set out with characteristic audacity to create from scratch both a skyline and a CBD.

The place chosen for this—the Jiangguomen District east of the city center between the third and fourth ring roads—had in fact already evolved many such functions. But so had another emerging center—the Finance Street District on the city's west side. By the late 1990s Beijing was fast developing a split or "dual" CBD. Each served somewhat different needs: Jiangguomen, close to foreign embassies and a number of world-class hotels, was the favored location for foreign multinational corporations, while Finance Street, closer to central ministries and bureaus, was favored by domestic firms requiring more immediate access to the Chinese government.[35] Nonetheless, a 1.5-square-mile section of Jiangguomen was officially tagged as Beijing's future downtown.

The task of master-planning the area was awarded by competition to a small Los Angeles firm, Johnson Fain Partners, in April 2001. Their scheme called for more than 500 new buildings with a staggering 108 million square feet of floor space for office, residential, retail, and other uses. About half of this—some 54 million square feet—will be commercial office space, equal to roughly a quarter of all the office space in the Chicago metropolitan area. The center will eventually be anchored by a 140-story skyscraper, destined for a site one block south of the CCTV Tower. The Koolhaas gargantua may thus itself be one day dwarfed by one of the world's tallest buildings.[36]

Superdeveloper Pan Shiyi (center) on a billboard at SOHO Jianwai, Beijing, 2006.
PHOTOGRAPH BY AUTHOR

The CBD has also become Beijing's trendiest place to live, with a number of high-profile—and highly exclusive—residential estates opening in recent years. The most talked about of these is Renki Yamamoto's elegant SOHO Jianwai complex. With sharply rendered modernist towers set about an artfully spare landscape, SOHO Jianwai is an architectural step above most other mixed-use complexes in town, even if the buildings are rumored to be shoddily built. It is very popular with Beijing's ascendant professional class; units sell out within weeks as each new phase is completed. The complex flanks the south side of Chang'an Avenue, not far from the CCTV Tower, on a site that was once the largest machine-tool factory in Beijing.

A total of twenty high-rise towers—about half of them complete by press time—will eventually support a daily population of some 50,000 residents and workers at SOHO Jianwai. The development is one of several by Beijing supercouple Pan Shiyi and Zhang Xin, whose real estate company, SOHO China, was launched in 1995. It has since become one of the most successful in China (in terms of revenue, SOHO racked up more than half the real estate sales in the CBD in both 2002 and 2003).[37] Fabulously wealthy now, both Pan and Zhang began humbly enough; he grew up in rural Gansu Province, she was a Hong Kong émigré who worked in a factory as a teenager before studying at Cambridge University and pursuing a career as a Wall Street investment banker. The couple's rags-to-riches rise has made them folk heroes in China, the toast of the urban elite. The real key to their success was understanding and exploiting the market value of good design and brand-name architecture. Pan and Zhang have commissioned bold designs from some of the world's leading architects, including Steven Holl, Zaha Hadid, Peter Davidson, and Chang Yung Ho, now chair of MIT's Department of Architecture. Their Jianwai project follows a number of earlier successful developments, including SOHO New Town, also in the CBD, and a much-publicized upscale villa complex known as the Commune by the Great Wall.

★   ★   ★

Most major landmark buildings in Beijing, in the CBD and elsewhere, have been the work of foreign architects. This is often—and increasingly—the source of controversy. The CCTV Tower, for example, has been criticized as a big-ticket extravagance and even an engineering outrage (Rem Koolhaas himself admitted that the building "violates some of the sincerely held convictions about logic and beauty").[38] The Chinese public is a vocal and wickedly honest arbiter of architectural worthiness, capable of ruining the reputation of building—and maker—for resemblances alone ("boy, it sure looks like a..."). Of course, this works both ways. Xing Tong's Shanghai Art Museum, for example, was favorably likened to an ancient pottery vessel. John Portman's tri-towered Ritz Carlton hotel complex in Shanghai, completed in 1990 and one of the first major commissions by an American architect in the post-Mao era, happily resembles the Chinese character for "mountain" (*shan*). Shanghai residents have mostly positive things to say about the pagoda imagery in the Jin Mao Tower.

But not all imported architecture is so embraced, and the comparisons can be odious indeed. The British architects who designed Hong Kong's first high-rise office building, Jardine House (1973), made the singular but colossal error of using round windows on all four facades of the fifty-two-story tower. The local Cantonese population immediately labeled it "Sing Chin Ki Szee Fat Long"—the House of a Thousand Assholes. That it also

The Big Egg looms over an embattled *hutong*; Beijing, 2004. PHOTOGRAPH BY AUTHOR

headquartered a haughty English firm with a history of opium trafficking didn't help. An early version of Herzog & de Meuron's National Stadium in Beijing was said to resemble a child's toilet, and was then feverishly reworked to remove the ruinous similitude.[39] The CCTV Tower's "calligraphic swoop" has itself been likened to a donut, an intoxicated chicken, and a man brought to his knees.

More inglorious comparisons still have enveloped another big foreign-designed building just up the street, the French architect Paul Andreu's Grand National Theater. Proponents of the National Theater, an immense glass-and-titanium dome set in a pool of water, describe it as a phosphorescent pearl rising from a lake. Local Beijingers have been a bit less kind, claiming it resembles a colossal turtle egg or, worse, a floating silver turd from outer space. Viewed from what remains of *hutong* neighborhoods nearby, the National Theater does look every bit like a hovering starship, perhaps stopping by Beijing to pick up some steamed dumplings or a bootleg DVD.

One reason the National Theater has been such a target of criticism is its site. The Big Egg was laid in the very center of the Chinese capital, just behind the Great Hall of the People and a stone's throw from Tiananmen Square. The project came about as part of a rush of opera house projects that swept China in the late 1990s, sparked by Shanghai's decision to build one in People's Park. Not to be outdone by this mercantile upstart, Beijing decided to erect an even bigger and bolder opera house than the one Charpentier created for Shanghai.

Building an opera house at Tiananmen was not a new idea; Zhou Enlai, China's urbane and much-admired premier, first suggested it in the 1950s. Zhou, along with Deng Xiaoping, was one of dozens of idealistic young Chinese who studied in Paris in the 1920s, mulling over Marx and *L'Humanité* in Left Bank cafés. Even as (or perhaps because) the *tricolore* still flew over many a colony, radical politics flourished in France between the wars. But Zhou relished Parisian life, and he returned to China with an air of continental sophistication that contrasted sharply with his more earthy comrades. He also came home with a love of opera. At Zhou's insistence, a national opera house was designed for a site near Tiananmen, but it was never built due to a lack of funds. That French architects would design the two most famous new opera houses in China would have amused the premier. But if Charpentier's building at least nods to China's architectural past (its upswept form recalls the big roofs and deep eaves of traditional Chinese buildings), Andreu's makes no such show. It is truly an interloper from the Van Allen belt. For that matter, so too are the CCTV Tower and most of the Olympic set pieces. But none of these structures has been placed in the hallowed precincts of Tiananmen. Anything erected within sight of the Square, Zhongnanhai, or the Great Hall of the People will be subjected to much higher standards of contextual and cultural compatibility. On neither ground does Andreu's building measure up.

The theater, like so many recent projects in China, began with an international competition, one that eventually yielded sixty-nine schemes from architects around the world.[40] Two committees were then charged with selecting "a work of global significance and great originality" from the lot. The architectural jury consisted of eighteen designers (fourteen from mainland China, one from Hong Kong, and one each from Japan, Canada, and Spain), and the "proprietor's committee" was composed of officials from the municipal government, the Ministry of Construction, and the Ministry of Culture. In two rounds of deliberation, the committees shortlisted five entries and later added four more, for a total of nine finalists. Among them were submissions by Andreu, Terry Farrell, Arata Isozaki, HPP International, Wong & Ouyang, and teams from Tsinghua and Shenzhen universities. Three were to be chosen for presentation to the national leadership, but in narrowing down the options, the committees failed to reach a consensus. The proprietor's committee favored the Andreu scheme, which began as a rectilinear box but later evolved into a dome. The architectural jury argued that the Andreu proposed building was too expensive, impractical, and ill suited to the context of Tiananmen Square. But they were overruled, allegedly because the revised Andreu scheme was favored by Jiang Zemin, then premier. The architect's committee suddenly found itself sidelined; it would play no further role in the selection process.[41]

None of this would be particularly interesting were it not for a signal innovation in the design selection process: public input. In an unprecedented move, Beijing officials put all forty-four submissions on display and invited the people to inspect the drawings and comment on the various schemes. No more than a few dozen visitors were expected to show up on opening day, July 19, 1998; instead, the venue was mobbed by several hundred people.

Critics have charged that the event was a charade, orchestrated to make a big show of soliciting public input, when in reality officials had no intention of using it to choose a scheme. Others complained that the public itself was too caught up with the building's exterior appearance and too ignorant about functional and engineering matters to make a truly informed selection. The competitors themselves, many of whom were on hand to explain their work, grumbled that the exhibition layout gave preference to some schemes over others. The public straw poll favored the Isozaki entry, which was also highly regarded by the architectural jury. Political symbolism and the unhealed wounds of the past, however, virtually assured that no Japanese would ever be awarded such a prominent commission. In the end, the popular vote did not appear to influence the outcome of the competition. But for all its shortcomings, the exhibition established an important precedent for openness and public input that has since been followed with other major public works, most notably the Olympic Green and National Stadium.[42]

In the end, many people were unhappy with the choice of Andreu's design, among them a vocal and well-connected group of senior architects who took their protests to the press and the highest levels of government. They were inadvertently aided by a tragedy half a world away, when part of another Andreu building at Charles de Gaulle International Airport collapsed mysteriously in May 2004, killing several people—two Chinese nationals among them. The incident triggered a review of the National Opera and emboldened the anti-Andreu faction to even push for demolition of the half-built structure—an extreme act that would have added new meaning to the old Stalinist maxim, "You can't make an omelet without breaking eggs."[43]

Andreu's Egg may have been spared that fate, but much of ordinary Beijing has not been so lucky. In the city beyond Tiananmen, beyond the tourist buses and five-star hotels, the seemingly endless expanse of *hutong* neighborhoods and courtyard houses that blanketed the city for hundreds of years has fallen in one of the most rapid and convulsive periods of urban demolition in history. Even as Beijing erects singular architectural monuments to create a definitive identity for itself, it has largely rubbed out of existence the very fabric that gave the city such unique color, richness, and character.

CHAPTER FIVE

City of *Chai*

城市—拆了

On the northwest edge of metropolitan Beijing, far from the noise and dust of the Chinese capital, lies a theme park named "Old Beijing Miniature Landscape Park" (Lao Beijing). Here, spread across 124 acres in the city's suburban Changping District, is a detailed 1:15 scale reproduction of the Chinese capital at its urban architectural zenith during the late Ming and early Qing dynasties. Old Beijing is one of a number of "minilandscape" theme parks built in China in recent years (a subject explored more fully in Chapter 9, "Theme Parks and the Landscape of Consumption"). What distinguishes Old Beijing is its inclusiveness. Here the old city is presented as a whole—not only the great temples and palaces and towers, but the vast tapestry of courtyard houses and narrow lanes and alleys that long defined the capital's quotidian cityscape. I visited Old Beijing on a bright, cold winter morning in 1999. Smoke from a vendor's stove drifted over the miniature city, adding that acrid aroma of coal that is one of the olfactory trademarks of Chinese cities in winter. A handful of elderly men shuffled here and there along the paths, heads down and arms behind their backs as if engaged in the very kind of nostalgic retrospection urged by park advertisements: "Relive your long lost memories of Beijing." Yet even as I wandered through this garden of urban memory, wrecking crews in the city itself were tearing apart the very lanes and courtyard houses so finely reproduced here. One could consume a miniaturized rendition of old Beijing's cityscape even as the thing itself was being swept into the dustbins of history.

Extensive demolition of China's vernacular urban residential fabric has been a hallmark of the post-Mao era. Few cities have been spared, especially those in the booming coastal provinces. In Nanjing, only a handful of the city's

An elderly woman awaits removal from her demolished *hutong* neighborhood, Chongwen District, Beijing, 2004. PHOTOGRAPH BY AUTHOR

Old Beijing Miniature Landscape Park, 1999. PHOTOGRAPH BY AUTHOR

once numerous Ming, Qing, or Republican-era neighborhoods have survived the redevelopment onslaught. One of these stood until recently just below the office in which I wrote much of this book; the neighborhood, its one-story buildings canted to the odd angle of a long-gone street, progressively vanished in the summer and fall of 2006. A teeming urban neighborhood the year before, it was soon reduced to rubble, picked over for recyclables by migrant workers. In its place now stands a towering luxury condominium.

But Nanjing's losses pale in comparison to those of Shanghai or Beijing. Between 1988 to 1998, more than thirty million square feet of old housing stock in Shanghai was demolished.[1] The next four years saw an additional 162 million square feet of old neighborhoods cleared to make way for new development— 20 percent of the city's total residential area. By the mid-2000s, urban renewal in Shanghai had rubbed out an area of urban fabric equal in size to Venice.[2] The human impact of such extensive redevelopment is equally staggering: in just two years, from 1992 to 1994, some 200,000 families (approximately 640,000 people) were tossed out of Shanghai's inner-city districts—roughly equal to the population of Baltimore.[3] More recently, an additional 50,000 residents were relocated from Minhang District to make way for the main site of the 2010 World Exposition.[4] The destruction of vernacular urban fabric has been even more extensive in Beijing, where wholesale demolition of *hutong* neighborhoods has drawn the ire of architects and urbanists worldwide. The losses have also begun to strike a deep chord in China, at least among the educated. The vernacular urbanism of Beijing is significantly older than that of Shanghai, and more thoroughly Chinese, some of it dating back to the Ming Dynasty. The rapid elimination of this national heritage—by Chinese hands, no less—prompts unsettling comparisons to earlier episodes of self-inflicted cultural injury such as the Cultural Revolution.

According to an old Beijing saying, there were once more narrow lanes or alleys, *hutong*, in the Chinese capital than hairs on the back of a goat, and for centuries that was likely true. The origins of the *hutong* date back to the Mongol capital city of Khanbaliq (later renamed Dadu), founded in 1266 by Kublai Khan, the grandson of Genghis Khan. The word itself is rooted in the Mongolian term *hottog*, meaning "water well," which were typically situated in public lanes or alleys. The original *hutong* were located within the city walls of Dadu and inhabited by the gentry.[5] But in time, these quarters expanded beyond the city walls to suburban communities that formed in the vicinity of each of the twelve city gates. When it was conquered by Ming forces in 1368, Mongol Dadu was among the largest cities in the world, its numerous *hutong* home to as many as a million people.[6] After the demise of the Mongols and the end of the Yuan Dynasty, the third Ming emperor Zhu Di (the Emperor Yongle) moved the imperial throne from his native Nanjing to Dadu, now renamed Beijing.[7] In the subsequent centuries—from about 1420 to the end of the Qing Dynasty in 1911—Beijing's *hutong* fabric reached its greatest development, filling nearly all the space within the inner and outer city walls not occupied by the imperial palace and official buildings.

In plan view, the *hutong* collectively resemble the skeleton of a fish, with the east-west lanes (the *hutong* proper) radiating from either side of larger collector spines running north and south. Shops and stores typically line the latter streets, while the *hutong* themselves—generally thirty feet or less in width—are primarily residential.[8] The names of many *hutong* evoke a vanished era, referring to crafts or trades that once took place there—Carrying-Pole Hutong, Goldfish Hutong, Wet Nurse Hutong, and so forth. The basic architectural unit of this vernacular cityscape was the *siheyuan*, or courtyard house;

lined up side by side, the compounds formed the larger block structure of the city (oriented north-south), which was scored east-west by the interstitial *hutong*. Prior to 1949, *hutong* and *siheyuan* blanketed most of Beijing, covering as much as 3,212 acres.[9]

The courtyard house itself has deep roots in Chinese vernacular culture, appearing in a range of modified forms throughout China. Surely one of the coziest forms of habitation in the world, the courtyard house is the very picture of domestic sanctuary and an expression in architectural form of the traditional Chinese extended family structure. And while the scale and opulence of courtyard houses vary greatly, according to the wealth and position of their owners, they all shelter family members around one or more interior courtyards. In layout, the *siheyuan* follow many of the same principles of spatial organization and *feng shui* that guided the planning of the Imperial Palace and all royal Chinese cities. *Siheyuan* were typically structured about a north-south axis. The main pavilion, located at the top or north end of the compound, faced south and usually housed the master of the household and his immediate family. Buildings to either side of the courtyard were occupied by parents, families of the children, aunts, and uncles. Servants and persons of lower rank would often occupy rooms along the inside of the south or north exterior walls. Access to the complex was invariably through a gated portal on the south or east side, which opened onto a *hutong*.

The urbanism of *hutong* and *siheyuan* was one of splendid tension between the internalized shelter of the domestic realm and the busy public lanes and streets outside. Privacy was indulged in spite of high density. *Hutong* urbanism was also sustainable. The individual compounds, set alongside one another, formed a kind of megastructure that was protected from the wind and required less energy to heat than an equivalent number of isolated buildings. The open courtyards provided abundant natural light and ventilation and were often shaded by trees. Because most buildings were single-story, these courtyard trees (and those lining the larger streets) were often the tallest features in most neighborhoods, producing a luxuriantly leafy setting. The mixture of functions along the lanes and larger streets meant that most daily goods and services could be obtained within a short walk or bicycle ride. The high density of the *hutong* neighborhoods also fostered the formation of thick social networks, a human infrastructure that balanced the one of brick and mortar. In all, Beijing's *hutong* were a superlative example of humanistic urbanism, the very antithesis of the sprawling high-rise housing that has blanketed vast areas of urban China in recent years.

Of course, it is easy to be seduced by all this, especially as a foreigner who has never had to spend a cold winter night in an old *hutong* flat heated, if at all, by a tiny coal stove. It might make for good urbanism, but most housing in these old neighborhoods was terribly overcrowded, unsanitary, and unsafe. Decades of deferred maintenance took a heavy toll on the structures, and many units lacked running water, a kitchen, or private bathroom. Moreover, the defining feature of *siheyuan*—the spacious, tree-shaded courtyard—largely ceased to exist years ago due to clutter and infill. By the late 1970s, building floor space in the typical *siheyuan* complex had increased by 30 percent. Many of the new occupants were refugees from nearby Tangshan whose homes were leveled by the catastrophic earthquake of July 1976. To help solve the sudden housing crisis, government officials encouraged infilling the *siheyuan*.[10] The once-spacious courtyards were thus transformed into a maze of shacks and lean-tos; they were no longer called *siheyuan*, but *dazayuan*—"big cluttered courtyards." The overcrowding and chaos that ensued only helped cement the perception that old Beijing suffered from urban ills that nothing but demolition could cure.

Though some *hutong* neighborhoods were cleared for public works and new housing during the Mao era, most of this vernacular fabric was still relatively whole even into the early 1990s. Much of it would not, however, see the decade's end. The very real need to upgrade housing combined with the emergence of a real estate market and the ensuing development binge spelled its doom. Land in central-city Beijing soon became too valuable for the ordinary people living there. Even a well-intentioned initiative to upgrade the Old City's housing stock—later known as the Old and Dilapidated Housing Renewal program (ODHR)—was progressively undermined by rising property values. ODHR pilot projects were meant to rehouse original area residents in situ, while also providing a modest amount of market-rate housing to offset costs. Renewal sites were selected on the basis of need, targeting areas where existing housing was in particularly bad shape. The new housing was typically low in density and designed to maintain the scale and architectural character of the surrounding district. But as property values soared, the lure of profit overruled such niceties. The municipal government soon abrogated its responsibility to provide affordable new housing for residents in the Old City, and chose instead to fatten its coffers with lucrative land-lease fees and taxes on parcels released to developers. In the process, Beijing ridded itself of both "old and dilapidated housing" and the poor people inconveniently living in it.[11]

By the mid-1990s most Old City residents were no longer being rehoused on site, but were packed off to cheap new quarters far from the city center. The selection of redevelopment sites was also increasingly determined by market forces. Regardless of the condition of housing therein, priceless parcels close to Chang'an Avenue or the Forbidden City were suddenly deemed in need of housing renewal, and were soon cleared to make way for luxury residences, upscale office buildings, and shopping malls like Oriental Plaza. Any housing that was built on such land was almost always beyond the means of former residents; poor and working-class residents were thus replaced by affluent elites.

Even the pioneering early ODHR projects fell victim to the rush to profit. Among these, Ju'er Hutong was the flagship. Located near the Bell and Drum towers and east of the city's central axis, Ju'er Hutong was designed by Wu Liangyong and his colleagues at Tsinghua University. It ably translates the traditional *siheyuan* courtyard complex into a modern, multilevel housing prototype. Ju'er's preferential treatment of original residents, careful design, and emphasis on "metabolic change rather than total clearance" brought the project universal applause when its first phases were completed in 1992. It even won the prestigious World Habitat Award from the United Nations.[12] Yet by the mid-1990s even the project's exemplary social objectives had been "defeated by the market," as Dan Abramson has put it. Ju'er's original residents themselves contributed to this by finding cheap lodgings elsewhere and renting their new flats (at rates many times their monthly salaries) to affluent professionals. The international recognition Ju'er received made it a sought-after place to live, and by the late 1990s two thirds of Ju'er's residents were renters, half of whom were well-heeled expatriates from overseas. In a final indignity, the newcomers hardly used the spacious courtyards except to park cars.[13]

★   ★   ★

Central-city redevelopment in Beijing has thoroughly and permanently altered the character of the Chinese capital. A conservative estimate is that 40 percent of the Old City was pulverized between 1990 and 2002, eliminating in a decade an urban landscape that had endured 600 years of war, peace, and

Voice among the ruins—"Dear neighbors: Our elderly parents are deaf and mute; please take good care of them"; *hutong* demolition site, Chongwen District, Beijing, 2004. PHOTOGRAPH BY AUTHOR

revolution. In area, the demolition zones covered about 6,178 acres, roughly equivalent to all of Manhattan from Madison Square Garden to 125th Street in Harlem, including Central Park.[14] Some studies predict that as much as 90 percent of old Beijing will eventually be eliminated.[15] Save for war and earthquakes, the speed and totality of this urban holocaust has no equal in history. Beijing's decade-long wrecking ball brings vividly to mind Joseph Schumpeter's famous phrase "creative destruction." The Austrian economist used this seeming oxymoron to describe the dynamic upheaval inherent in free-market capitalism—"the never-ending cycle," as Max Page has put it, "of destroying and inventing new products and methods of production."[16] Or, to paraphrase Marx's famous observation about the evaporative effects of free-market capitalism, in Beijing nearly all that was solid melted into air, a fact made all the more extraordinary by Beijing's status as the capital of a nation still nominally committed to Lenin, Marx, and Mao.[17]

Preservation efforts have been virtually impotent against all this. In 1990 a Conservation Plan for 25 Historic Areas in Beijing's Old City outlined more than two dozen sites worthy of preservation in and around the Forbidden City and the Old City's historic north-south axis—all told, some 260 *hutong* and 2,000 *siheyuan* were included. The plan was hailed by preservationists; here was one of the first attempts in China of comprehensive heritage conservation, aimed at preserving the total urban environment—the fabric of the city—rather than isolated gems of singular architectural or historical interest. As Wu Liangyong put it, such "integrated conservation" was essential to heritage planning in historic capitals like Beijing, in order to protect "the organic order embedded in their physical environment."[18] But the conservation plan protected only about 2,565 acres of historic urban fabric—less than 17 percent of Beijing's Old City and a mere 5 percent of remaining *hutong* neighborhoods. The plan also had the unintended effect of concentrating—and speeding up redevelopment activity in those areas not tagged for conservation; it was, in effect, a death sentence for any district not officially listed. Moreover, several of the listed conservation areas were also part of the ODHR program, meaning that the buildings therein had to be both preserved and brought up to code. Incredibly, this task was interpreted in at least two instances as authorizing tabula rasa demolition of the historic building stock.

This happened partly because conservation status in China is often conferred for attributes other than architectural.[19] Exalted places in China tend to be valued more in terms of site than for the buildings erected thereupon, although numerous and important exceptions can be found. The site is earthbound and enduring; architecture is relatively fragile and ephemeral. Buildings at Buddhist pilgrimage sites, places of worship for a thousand years, have typically been reconstructed many times through the centuries; Western tourists are often startled to learn that the "ancient temple" they marvel at was proudly rebuilt in 1993 using reinforced concrete. This act of privileging site over building as the prime locus of value deviates from the prevailing Western concept of historic preservation, in which the burden of significance is more evenly distributed between the site and the original structure (and often leans toward the latter; many historic buildings moved to new sites retain much of their cultural value).[20]

Thus a conservation area in Beijing's Old City, so designated because it was traditionally a neighborhood of ethnic minorities, could be razed and rebuilt so long as the factor of significance—the minority community—remained in place. This is what happened to the historic Niujie (Ox Street) Hutong in Xuanwu District, southwest of the Forbidden City. The neighborhood, largely inhabited by Chinese Muslims of Hui ethnicity and anchored by a Song-era mosque, was leveled in 1998 to make way for high-rise residential towers.[21] The area was included in the twenty-five conservation areas plan specifically because of the mosque and Muslim community, both of which remained after the area's *hutong* and *siheyuan* were razed. The cultural significance of the neighborhood existed independently of its built environment, or so it was argued.

A similar fate awaited Nanchizi Street in Dongcheng District. Nanchizi was a crown jewel of both the twenty-five conservation areas plan and the ODHR program, largely because of its treasured central location just outside the moat of the Forbidden City and the walls of the Working People's Cultural Palace (the former Supreme Ancestral Temple). Originally part of the Imperial City itself, Nanchizi once housed porcelain, silk, meat, grain, and other supplies for the emperor's court, a history recalled in lane names such as Silk Storeroom (Duan Ku) Hutong, Porcelain Storeroom (Ci Qi) Hutong, and Lantern Storeroom (Deng Long Ku) Hutong.[22] The district was only opened to the public after the fall of the Qing in 1911 and the founding of the Republic. Nanchizi's unique setting, intimate scale, and unique history combined to make this an extraordinary place. As a Tsinghua University study conducted in the early 1990s described it, "Nanchizi Street itself is one of the very few with a perfectly preserved atmosphere of classic old Beijing: completely shaded by the branches of mature Chinese Scholar Trees and lined with mainly one-storey shops serving local residents. Among the side *hutongs* the environment is peaceful and quiet....The houses which crowd along the moat have a splendid view of the Imperial Palace, against whose formal, monumental grandeur their own chaotic, diverse and humble appearance contrasts sharply."[23]

Officially, at least, Nanchizi was not valued for its rich fabric of *hutong* and *siheyuan*, but because of its adjacency to the Forbidden City. In the 1993 Beijing Master Plan, the neighborhood on the west side of Nanchizi Street was designated a future park. It was to be cleared to open up views from Nanchizi Street to the moat, wall, and rooftops of the Forbidden City—to create, in effect, "an emerald necklace bedecking the Imperial Palace."[24]

It was a dubious strategy at best, reminiscent of an ill-considered effort by the U.S. National Park Service to give Independence Hall in Philadelphia "breathing room" and a more stately approach by bulldozing several blocks of nineteenth-century commercial architecture along Chestnut Street and north to the Benjamin Franklin Bridge. The resulting open space, dominated by Independence Mall, was meant to clarify and strengthen the visual presence of the diminutive Georgian landmark—to give it "a setting worthy of it preeminence," as a University of Pennsylvania administrator put it in 1935.[25] But in so favoring one epoch over another, the district's rich architectural legacy heritage was truncated and diminished, and a century's worth of urban history was lost.

The majority of Nanchizi lay on the east side of Nanchizi Street, however, and here the problem was not a planned park but the priceless real estate underneath. To exploit this, the local district government formed a company in the early 1990s to redevelop Nanchizi "as a low-density, luxury-standard neighborhood of one- and two-storey traditional-style courtyard houses."[26] For several years nothing happened, and by 1999 a growing outcry against the destruction of Beijing's *hutong*—from China's budding heritage preservation community, foreign observers, and impacted residents—prompted city officials to bolster conservation planning in the Old City. Actual plans guided by preservation principles were produced for each of the twenty-five conservation areas and seemed to promise just the kind of integrated conservation— of building and context as well as indigenous population—that Wu Liangyong and others had advocated for years.

But measured, context-sensitive preservation would not be easy. First, Nanchizi's *siheyuan* were typically overcrowded, making it impossible to rehouse all residents on the same site without dramatically increasing the height of the buildings. Moreover, upgrading Nanchizi's basic infrastructure would be exceedingly difficult and expensive; the costs would never be recouped if the site were redeveloped as single-story housing for working-class people. Displaced residents would also have to be rehoused somewhere else, at no small expense. It became Nanchizi's unenviable fate to serve as a test bed for working out a solution to all this. As one city planning official later put it, Nanchizi was to be "the paradigm for a new era of development for Beijing that would strike a balance between conservation and redevelopment."[27]

A thorough survey of the community was undertaken, and conservation guidelines were drafted by Tsinghua University and the Beijing Institute of Architectural Design and Research. Fully 82 percent of the existing buildings were deemed worthy of preservation; the balance could be redeveloped without diminishing Nanchizi's essence. Several schemes favoring gradual redevelopment were now proposed by Tsinghua University and other design institutes. But the local district government and Beijing's powerful vice-mayor for construction at the time, Wang Guan Tao, favored a scorched-earth approach, especially as it became clear that the alternatives would not break even financially. Wang and local officials argued that only a handful of buildings in Nanchizi were significant enough to merit saving; the planners, on the other hand, favored an inclusive, incremental approach intended to preserve Nanchizi as a place, rather than just a site.[28] But doing so would not be cheap, nor would it yield a polished, photogenic product of the sort politicians crave. A lovely park and new upscale housing would give more "face" to the vice-mayor and other officials than a handful of old houses, however well restored.

Caught up in all this were Nanchizi's more than 900 families, who, after enduring menacing visits by demolition and relocation service staff, were informed in May 2002 that they had one month to vacate their homes. Many of the residents—some 70 percent according to the 1993 Tsinghua study—had lived there for more than twenty years; naturally, many resisted abandoning their old homes. As one elderly man, a Nanchizi resident since 1947, complained, "This is all a real estate scam...they say our house is too old and falling apart, but they won't let us fix it up ourselves because they want the land."[29] By the end of June only a third of the families had left. The developer and its relocation contractor then took action to encourage the holdouts—known as "stubborn nail households" (*dingzi hu*)—to depart. When I visited Nanchizi with several of my MIT students in late June 2002, many of the houses were already partially wrecked by the demolition contractor; utility lines had been cut, windows smashed, and holes punched through walls and roofs—all to make life hell for the resisters and thus hasten their departure. We were ourselves soon ejected by security personnel when two students, working on a documentary about Beijing, were caught filming the damage.[30]

But the very qualities that made Nanchizi a treasured redevelopment site—a fifteen-minute walk from both Tiananmen Square and the Wangfujing Street shopping district—also assured that its destruction would be witnessed by many Beijing residents, not to mention nosy foreigners with cameras. Indeed, Nanchizi received an unprecedented amount of media attention, which stirred up more protest and eventually prompted municipal authorities and the Ministry of Construction to stop work. Nanchizi was, for many, the last straw in a decade-long drama of wreckage and renewal in the capital. Even UNESCO lodged a formal objection, arguing that Nanchizi was part of the buffer zone around the Forbidden City, a World Heritage Site. But by summer's end, nearly all the residents were gone, the media soon lost interest in the story, and contractors quietly resumed demolition, eventually razing some 900 old homes. Only nine of more than 240 *siheyuan* at Nanchizi were saved. Today a linear park, the "green necklace" envisioned in the master plan, occupies the west half of Nanchizi abutting the walls of the Working People's Cultural Palace. Across the street, dozens of new residences have been erected, designed to emulate the ancient buildings they replaced. Nanchizi, a stone's throw from Chairman Mao's placid gaze at Tiananmen, is now one of the most exclusive addresses in Beijing, with homes selling for more than $1 million.

The popularity of Nanchizi's neotraditional homes is itself part of a deeply ironic revival of interest in traditional residential architecture. Even as urban China's historic building stock is razed, living in a courtyard home has become the rage among affluent expatriate Chinese as well as foreign homebuyers in Beijing and other cities. At the peak of the *hutong* demolition frenzy in the 1990s, a number of prominent businessmen and socialites in Beijing, mostly foreigners or overseas Chinese, began purchasing and restoring historic *siheyuan*. Hong Kong legislator and businessman David Y. L. Chu spent $2 million restoring a courtyard house complete with sauna and karaoke room, and Chinese-American lawyer Handel Lee transformed a crumbling 7,535-square-foot complex into what has been described as "arguably the most luxurious courtyard house in Beijing" (he followed this by opening Shanghai's flagship Armani store in a bund building restored by American architect Michael Graves).[31]

Hong Kong's trendy China Club opened a Beijing facility in a sixteenth-century *siheyuan* on Xi Rong Xian Hutong, built by a descendant of the Qing ruler Kangxi and later home to Republic president and erstwhile emperor Yuan Shikai. Since 1959 the complex had been a Sichuan restaurant, famous as a favorite haunt of Deng Xiaoping's (it was there that Deng uttered his legendary "cat" allegory about political systems: "it doesn't matter if the cat is white or black, as long as it catches mice"). The club poured $8 million into restoring the complex, producing a facility described by *Asiaweek* as "possibly the swankiest watering hole in Beijing." Its September 1996 opening was attended by Kevin Costner, Michael Caine, and the Duchess of York.[32] Laurence J. Brahm, a New York–born businessman and author, has restored several Qing courtyard houses in Dongcheng District, both for his own home and for his campy

Newly built million-dollar *siheyuan* in Nanchizi, Beijing, 2006. PHOTOGRAPH BY AUTHOR

revolution-themed entertainment ventures—the Red Capital Club restaurant and a boutique hotel, Red Capital Residence.[33] Beijing's municipal government has even tapped this market as a means of realizing heritage conservation goals it failed to achieve on its own. In May 2004, it issued a "Circular Encouraging Groups and Individuals to Buy Siheyuan in Beijing's Old Districts and Cultural and Historical Conservation Areas," which offered tax breaks and other incentives to entice individuals or corporations to buy, sell, or lease such properties.[34] As of 2006 there were approximately 7,000 to 9,000 *siheyuan* on the market in Beijing, the best preserved and most valuable of which were in Xicheng and Dongcheng districts, where a single 21,528-square-foot complex near Shichahai, a chain of lakes in the Old City, sold in 2005 for nearly $5 million.[35]

More unlikely still are the entirely new subdivisions of traditional courtyard homes that have been built in the suburbs of Beijing and other cities in recent years. Cathay View (Guan Tang) in Chaoyang District, opened in 2004, is one of several such developments; homes there cost in the neighborhood of $800,000. Despite the high prices, a third of Cathay View's 350 properties sold in the first four months on the market. The neotraditional homes feature many of the architectural details and materials characteristic of Ming and Qing *siheyuan*—red-lacquered window tracery, walls of slate-grey brick, and heavy roofs with fluted tiles and upswept eaves—"all of which," notes a sales brochure, "add up to form an authentic cultural experience." Indeed, according to its developers, Cathay View's unique suburban homes are part of "a cultural renaissance of Chinese traditional architecture." The community, on the other hand, is rather a more hybrid artifact, with a full-size baseball diamond, tennis courts, a half-pipe for skateboarders, and an espresso café where residents can "get carried away by the rich aromas and the Viennese melodies playing in the background."[36] Like all upscale villa housing in the People's Republic, Cathay View is a gated community, making the courtyard houses within its walls doubly enclosed. While Cathay's homes are modeled on the indigenous architectural culture of Beijing, competing projects elsewhere in the city—Courtyard by the Canal (Yun He An Shang De Yuan Zi) in Tongzhou District or Yuefu Garden (Yuefu Yuan) and Fragrant Hills Estates (Xiang Shan Jia Di) in Beijing's western hills—have been modeled on the residential vernacular of Suzhou and southern China. Regardless of style, the courtyard homes have proven very popular with both expatriate and, increasingly, Chinese homeowners.[37]

★   ★   ★

The creative destruction of Beijing can be summed up with the singular Chinese character *chai* (拆)—to tear down, demolish, or tear apart. This ubiquitous sign of creative destruction is commonplace in every Chinese city today, but it has come to have particular symbolic power in Beijing. Dashed on the walls of condemned structures and often enclosed in a circle, *chai* is like a death's-head heralding the imminent demise of the *urbs corpus*. Encountered in an otherwise tranquil neighborhood, the sudden appearance of *chai* is deeply unsettling, reminiscent of the memento mori that chill idyllic scenes in classical poetry and paintings of Arcadia, a reminder of life's passage and the inevitability of death. Critics Zhao Xudong and Duran Bell have argued that the symbolic power of *chai* is also related to collective memories of past episodes of "legitimated destruction...of the old China for the sake of the new"—particularly during the Cultural Revolution, when Mao's campaign to rid China of the Four Olds led to the frenzied destruction of relics and landmarks nationwide.[38] Despite obvious differences of politics and motivation, there are clear and troubling parallels between the radical obliterations of the Cultural Revolution and the market-driven creative destruction of the post-Mao era. The analogy, provocative as it is, is especially apt when *chai* is seen painted on walls where faded slogans from the Cultural Revolution can still be read.

Artists have also exploited the iconography of *chai* to critique the dehumanizing impacts of urban demolition on Beijing and its people. In Huang Rui's *Chai-na / China* silk-screened collages, photographs of wrecked *siheyuan* are overlaid with the ubiquitous moving-company advertisements found plastered throughout condemned neighborhoods. These, in turn, are juxtaposed against the portrait of Chairman Mao at Tiananmen—a provocative indictment of the state and its complicit role in bringing about Beijing's destruction. In the center of Huang's paintings the word "China" is emblazoned, along with the characters *chai* (拆) and *na* (那), an allegorical device that situates urban demolition at the very center of Chinese identity by turning *chai* into a Chinese homophone of the nation's English name.

The sheer multiplicity of *chai* images in Wang Jinsong's 1999 photographic montage, *One Hundred Demolition Pictures (Bai Chai Tu)* transforms

Chai (demolish), Beijing, 2002. PHOTOGRAPH BY AUTHOR

the pragmatic, nominally apolitical character into a kind of graffito of resistance against the modernizing forces of redevelopment and binge-building. At the same time, the anguished urban context of the characters is muted by the beauty of line and color in the photos; here *chai* becomes calligraphic, an exquisite design drawn not on condemned city walls but richly textured backdrops. Wang's use of the word "one hundred" (*bai*) is both literal—the montage contains one hundred photographs—and figurative, evoking traditional use of *bai* to connote an immeasurable quantity. A traditional way of describing the masses is *lao bai xing*, literally "old hundred surnames." Spring festival prints of a "Hundred Children," known as *bai zi tu*, bring good luck and multiple offspring. Perhaps best known in the West is Mao's Hundred Flowers campaign of 1956 (Bai Hua Yun Dong), a brief interlude of liberalism when intellectuals were encouraged to speak out and critique the government (the campaign invoked an old poem: "Let a hundred flowers bloom; let a hundred schools of thought contend").

The character *chai* has also seen service as a true graffito, surreptitiously scrawled on new buildings and public structures to ridicule the architecture of New Beijing. While graffiti, or "tagging," as it is known in the United States, is rare in China, there is a long tradition of painting characters on walls for

Huang Rui, *Chai-na / China*, 2005, silk screen and oil on canvas. COURTESY OF THE ARTIST

both propaganda purposes and as an act of protest and resistance (the short-lived Democracy Wall of 1978 is perhaps the best-known example).[39] Graffiti received a powerful boost as a mode of expression in the mid-1990s when mysterious bald-head profiles began appearing on ruined buildings throughout Beijing. The anonymous creator of the works, artist Zhang Dali, did not reveal himself until 1998, after he had spray-painted some 2,000 heads around the city. The tags spurred considerable controversy and debate and were both condemned as vandalism and celebrated as bold acts of self-expression. Some people even concluded the faces were the mark of a sinister secret society that was infiltrating the capital.

In fact, Zhang's profiles were originally intended as an attempt to engage the city in a kind of conversation; as art historian Wu Hung has written, the work—collectively entitled *Dialogue*—represented "an intense negotiation between a public-minded artist and a rapidly changing city."[40] Zhang himself explained the images as "a condensation of my own likeness as an individual," a kind of artistic avatar that "stands in my place to communicate with this city."[41] By placing a human figure on the ruins of the city, often on the same walls where *chai* was painted, Zhang also succeeded in focusing people's attention on the convulsive, dehumanizing transfiguration of their city.

As Anne-Marie Broudehoux has observed, he literally "put a human face" on the anonymous urban ruins. That his profiles are featureless is also significant; "Zhang's blank faces invoke the ongoing fragmentation of Chinese society," writes Broudehoux, "and people's deepening alienation from their environment."[42]

Alienation and the dehumanizing effects of urban redevelopment are themes that have also been explored by a number of Beijing filmmakers and videographers, whose documentary explorations of the city's ruins constitute what anthropologist Robin Visser has termed an "aesthetics of disappearance."[43] Examples include Zhang Nian's *Demolition Beijing, 1990–2000* and Zhang Yuan's 1998 film *Dingzi Hu*, a reference to the "stubborn nail" families who refuse to leave their old neighborhoods (the English title of the film is *Demolition and Relocation*). Zhao Liang's video *Bored Youth* highlights the anomie of Beijing youth by placing the teenaged protagonist in an abandoned building on the verge of demolition; the boy wanders aimlessly through empty, darkened rooms while window panes are heard shattering in the background. Eventually the actor joins in the destruction, as if resigned to the inevitable tow of fate.[44]

Perhaps the most imaginative act of artistic protest against the destruction of vernacular Beijing was Sheng Qi's "living art" piece entitled *Old Haunts Revisited (Gu Di Chong You)*, truly a moving tribute to the city's vanishing heritage. Sheng's "material" included a late-model Jeep Cherokee and a scale model of a traditional wood-structure house (*mu jie gou*), built in part using drawings from Liang Sicheng's classic book, *A Pictorial History of Chinese Architecture*. In January 2002 the artist strapped his scale-model house to the roof of the SUV and over the next few weeks plied Beijing's expressways in an extraordinary attempt to awaken residents to the passing of their city's urban architectural legacy. *Old Haunts Revisited* literally took Sheng's art out of the gallery and thrust it into people's daily lives; the roof of the SUV became a kind of nomadic tableau, a platform upon which he could make very public artistic statements. The meaning of the work changed as the Jeep roved about the city, seen now against a backdrop of a luxury housing estate, now against the red walls of Tiananmen and the Forbidden City. Sheng hoped that as the little house "bobbed and dodged like an apparition in the city" it might perhaps jolt motorists and pedestrians into reflecting for a moment on the vanishing built environment and the corresponding loss of culture and collective memory.[45]

★   ★   ★

To many observers, the creative destruction of Beijing and other Chinese cities brings vividly to mind the American experience of urban renewal; there are clear and obvious parallels, to be sure. In the 1950s and 1960s, vast tracts of downtown urban land in American cities were cleared to make way for new development, a movement driven by a coalition of local government and private-sector interests whose chief aim was real estate development.[46] People caught in the way of this "growth coalition," mostly the poor and working classes, were swept around like so many autumn leaves. The fabric of historic downtown districts was torn and shredded, typically replaced—if replaced at all—by overscaled modernist buildings that impoverished the streetscape. Vacant land and parking lots from stillborn renewal schemes still scar many American downtowns.

Though some cities began renewal projects immediately after the Second World War, the urban renewal era began in earnest with the passage of the Housing Act of 1949, Title I of which made available huge sums of money to help cities "acquire and clear slum and blighted property in designated redevelopment areas and sell or lease it to private developers (or the public agencies) at below market value."[47] Cities formed redevelopment authorities with the power to take land and sell or lease it to private developers at fire-sale rates, with the federal government paying up to two-thirds of the land clearing costs. Title I was originally intended to upgrade and replace substandard residential housing in decaying center-city districts, a purpose not unlike that of Beijing's Old and Dilapidated Housing Renewal program. But the provisions were vague enough to sustain a variety of interpretations, some of which excluded affordable housing altogether.

Downtown real estate and business interests quickly exploited the vagueness of Title I to underwrite a wide range of luxury residential and commercial development. Municipalities, hungry for tax revenue, also backed such projects, as did many politicians, who—not unlike the officials who determined the fate of Nanchizi—were more interested in a photogenic legacy than housing poor people. The real hope underlying urban renewal was to make cities appealing again to affluent whites who followed the suburban dream out of town in the 1950s and 1960s. To do this, "slum housing" adjacent to downtown was condemned and cleared not for the benefit of the poor who lived there, but to maximize the value of the land beneath.

In many American cities, the homes of the poor were thus bulldozed to make way for fancy apartments, shops, and entertainment facilities close to downtown. In Kansas City, Missouri, for example, to achieve urban renewal's promise of middle-American "Dream City Without Slums" the city's Land Clearance for Redevelopment Authority dislodged hundreds of low income, mainly African American families.[48] As Robert Fogelson writes, the "overriding objective" in this and other renewal campaigns "was not to wipe out the slums in order to build decent housing and pleasant neighborhoods for low-income families. Rather it was to curb decentralization—to induce the well-to-do to move back to the center by turning slums and blighted areas into attractive residential communities—and, by so doing, to revitalize the central business district to ease the cities' fiscal plight."[49]

In the end, urban renewal failed in almost all its objectives. The historic cores of many American cities were left gutted and empty, tens of thousands of families were displaced, and few suburbanites returned to the city anyway. "With millions of new homes on the market during the 1950 and 1960s," writes Jon Teaford, "there was no compelling reason to opt for life amid the bulldozed wastelands of once-blighted areas."[50] Driving American urban renewal, therefore, was a perceived need to save "dying" central cities from economic oblivion. Renewal czars and mayors like New Haven's Richard Lee were hailed as the best hope for urban America ("He Is Saving a 'Dead City,'" gushed the *Saturday Evening Post* in 1958). Poor neighborhoods next to downtown—what Charles T. Stewart called "the dirty collar" around the central business districts—were condemned for redevelopment in an ill-fated attempt to jump-start the downtown economy and curb the flow of brains and capital to the suburbs.[51]

In China, the drivers of urban renewal could not be more different. Cities in China are in no danger of economic irrelevance or oblivion; instead, they have been the engines of China's explosive economic growth over the last two decades. Although inner-city land in China is similarly occupied by old buildings and poor people, urban land there is being redeveloped precisely because there is such huge demand for downtown living, not as the result of heavy subsidies provided by the government to stoke the private sector. Moreover, while there has been considerable sprawl and suburban growth on the peripheries of China's cities (a topic discussed in Chapter 7, "Suburbanization and the Mechanics of Sprawl"), it is nothing like the mass exodus of middle-class residents from American cities following the Second World War. By the 1960s, American cities, and their downtowns, especially, were indeed dying. In China today, the city reigns supreme. Developers stumble over themselves to have a chance at developing prime center-city properties; there is no need to entice them with below-market land prices.[52]

There are also significant differences between American urban renewal and the Chinese experience in terms of scale. American renewal projects had a devastating impact on inner-city communities, mostly populated by low-income blacks, white ethnics, or other minorities. Some of the losses were considerable in scale, especially in relation to the size of American cities at the time. Redevelopment of Pittsburgh's Golden Triangle and Lower Hill districts in the mid-1950s, among the earliest and largest urban renewal undertakings in the United States, displaced some 5,400 families, more than 28,000 people.[53] In the mid-1950s St. Louis planning chief Harland Bartholomew declared the city's Mill Creek Valley district a slum and slated it for urban renewal. Before long, this vibrant community—a hub of black culture in the Midwest and a cradle of ragtime and jazz—was reduced to a 465-acre wasteland nicknamed "Hiroshima Flats." Some 6,400 homes and forty churches were destroyed, and more than 20,000 people displaced, nearly all of whom were African American.

Equally catastrophic was the destruction in 1959 of Boston's West End neighborhood, the focus of several major studies on the human costs of renewal.[54] Though overcrowded and full of run-down buildings, the West End was a robust and diverse community with streets filled in summer with the sounds of Italian, Greek, and Yiddish. Like Mill Creek Valley, the destruction of the West End displaced more than 20,000 people, most of whom were scattered to working-class suburbs throughout the Boston area. Renewal in New Haven was more incremental, but still displaced 25,000 people between 1954 and 1969. By the time large-scale demolition ended in the early 1970s, urban renewal in the United States had forced one million Americans out of homes in 2,500 neighborhoods in 993 cities.[55]

The impacts of American urban renewal were significant, but they pale in comparison to those induced by center-city redevelopment in China, even when adjusted to the relative scale of cities. For example, given Pittsburgh's 1955 population of about 1.7 million, the displacement of 28,000 people would mean a proportional loss in Beijing of more than 180,000 people, just about the number of Beijing residents actually displaced by redevelopment projects in a single year, 2003, according to data from the Beijing Bureau of Statistics.[56] The very next year, 2004, an additional 20,000 households—about 68,000 people—were uprooted by redevelopment in the capital.[57] In other words, in a mere twelve months Beijing displaced a number of persons equal to the combined displaced population of some of the largest, most infamous American urban renewal projects of the postwar era: Mill Creek Valley in St. Louis, Pittsburgh's Golden Triangle and Lower Hill, and the West End of Boston. Estimates as to the total number of people displaced in the 1990s by urban renewal in Beijing vary widely, but it is likely close to one million people, or about the total displaced population of thirty years of urban renewal in the United States.[58]

Given the additional tens of thousands displaced by redevelopment in other cities, the total impact of urban renewal in China is staggering indeed. This is human upheaval on a scale seen previously only in time of war or extreme natural catastrophe. When a city sustains a devastating blow—whether from natural disaster, human agency, or a combination thereof—both the built environment and its human occupants are impacted. The degree of this impact varies considerably: some disasters will inflict near-total destruction on a city's built environment, leaving the population more or less unharmed (few people died in the Great Fire of London in 1666, for example, though some 80 percent of the city was ruined). Other catastrophic events, such as the Black Death of the European Middle Ages or the industrial disaster in Bhopal in 1984, do not really affect the built environment, but inflict grievous harm to the human population. Recovery from the latter is often much more difficult. Rebuilding a city's broken infrastructure is one thing; rebuilding broken lives and wrecked communities is quite another. Indeed, it may be that the real measure of urban resilience is not a city's capacity to reconstruct bridges and highways, but how well the people rebound and heal their communal networks and social fabric. Even now, several years after Hurricane Katrina slammed into New Orleans, the city's once-rich tapestry of neighborhoods and social fabric has yet to fully recover from the storm and flood.[59]

Clearly, the redevelopment of Beijing's Old City has had an immense adverse impact on the capital's physical landscape. But it has also eviscerated the city's human landscape, and the effects of this are more latent, more difficult to quantify, and less visible to most observers. How does one begin to calculate, for instance, the toll inflicted upon a man like the octogenarian professor introduced in the previous chapter, Zhao Jingxin, who was given only days by the Wangfujing Real Estate Development Company to abandon a 400-year-old courtyard house that was his home for nearly half a century? Redevelopment has inflicted trauma on tens of thousands of people like Zhao. The pain and suffering of such sudden uprooting from familiar social soil is compounded by the brutal manner in which residents are sometimes treated by relocation companies, and by the grimmer reality of a corrupt government full of greedy officials more interested in profit than providing affordable housing for the people.

Those who have dared resist the development juggernaut have been threatened with beatings and, afterward, deprived of due compensation as punishment for being uncooperative. Community input and public participation in the redevelopment process is virtually nonexistent. After informing a community of 15,000 residents near Tiananmen Square that it had six weeks to clear out to make way for a luxury residential development, the Kangtai Real Estate Development Company held a single thirty-minute "public meeting" in a local restaurant, during which its representatives refused to answer a single question.[60] In the following weeks many residents stubbornly stayed put, and in early January 2002 an Orwellian notice went up, stating flatly, "we have decided to require you to cooperate with us and move out as soon as possible." Shortly after, the remaining homes were flattened, often with the occupants' belongings still inside; one man was even forced out before he had a chance to put on his shoes. Others were physically removed by hired thugs or punched and kicked by men in unmarked uniforms. As one man put it, "I've never seen people who work for the government behave like thugs, except during the Cultural Revolution."[61]

Most Old City residents have not been rehoused on site or in quarters nearby—one of the original aims of the Old and Dilapidated Housing Renewal program. Dispossessed residents, such as those at Nanchizi, are usually offered three options: buy a unit in the new development at a discounted price (if it is indeed housing being built, and not an office or shopping mall); accept a lump-sum payment and be gone (the optimal solution from the developer's standpoint); or accept new housing provided by the developer elsewhere in the city.

Community telephone window in demolished *hutong* neighborhood, Chongwen District, Beijing, 2004. PHOTOGRAPH BY AUTHOR

Even with the price break, new housing on-site is typically well beyond the means of most old residents. Most choose new flats. Naturally, developers try to find the cheapest land possible for these resettlement units. Replacement housing is therefore invariably located on the city's suburban fringe, where development costs are much lower. Such housing varies greatly in size, quality, and locational amenities.

In their new homes far from the city center, residents typically have the space and modern conveniences their *hutong* homes lacked—a modern kitchen, private bath, heat and air conditioning, telephone, and sometimes even internet service. But such perks come at a steep price. Displaced residents are now often distant from their workplaces, in locales poorly served by public transportation, far from schools or hospitals, and lacking the wide range of shopping, dining, and cultural opportunities that were once at their fingertips.[62] In many instances relocated residents must commute as long as two hours to get to workplaces that were once a short walk or bicycle ride from home. Worse, people are removed from the long-standing family networks and social contacts that rooted them to their old homeplace. Though the practice of relocating whole neighborhoods to the same new housing estates eases this to some degree, the old neighborhood's deep social structure rarely survives transplanting.

In a paean straight from Jane Jacobs's *The Death and Life of Great American Cities*, one former Old City resident reminisced about her life in the thick of *hutong* Beijing; "We were like family," she said of her courtyard neighbors. "In the *hutong*, I had no qualms about leaving my daughter alone at home.... Our neighbors provided all the security she needed." Life in her high-rise on the suburban frontier was a different world; "Now I keep calling from work to make sure everything is okay."[63] Or as one Beijing factory worker, about to lose her *hutong* home, pondered to a reporter: "Neighbors...what will we do for neighbors?"[64]

Nobody yet knows what the long-term impact of all this will be on the many families displaced by redevelopment in Beijing—or in other Chinese cities, for that matter. Sociologists, health officials, and urban planners in China are just beginning to study relocated urban populations, work that promises to shed new light on urban trauma and human resilience. If past studies of renewal-related relocation in the United States are of any use, we can expect the psychological and emotional toll to be substantial. In his classic study of

Luxury housing on the site of a former *hutong* neighborhood, Chongwen District, Beijing, 2006.
This photo was taken from the same spot as the image on p. 144, two years later.

PHOTOGRAPH BY AUTHOR

Boston's West End, "Grieving for a Lost Home," Marc Fried argued that losing the community triggered a "grief response showing most of the characteristics of grief and mourning for a lost person." Fried, then a clinical psychologist at Massachusetts General Hospital (itself in the West End), worried that extensive urban relocation might well be "a crisis with potential danger to mental health." Among the West Enders he interviewed, Fried observed a wide range of negative emotional responses and concluded that "Grieving for a lost home is evidently a widespread and serious social phenomenon following in the wake of urban dislocation."[65]

Geographer J. Douglas Porteous uses the term "domicide" to describe the emotional, psychological, and social trauma caused by "the deliberate destruction of home by human agency in the pursuit of specified goals."[66] Porteous also determined that "bereavement-like symptoms of grief are common among those uprooted and relocated." He found that relocated residents "often improve their living standard dramatically, but pay for this in terms of considerable social and psychological disruption"—precisely what countless relocated Beijing residents have experienced in their expulsion from the Old City.[67] In *Domicide: The Global Destruction of Home*, Porteous makes a distinction between "extreme domicide"—the result of warfare, terrorism or violent state action— and "everyday domicide," associated with "development projects, large public facilities such as highways and airports, urban renewal" and other works usually undertaken for "the public good." Displacement in Beijing is obviously not "extreme domicide," at least by Porteous's definition. But "everyday domicide" also seems inadequate to describe the unprecedented scale of upheaval in the Chinese capital—and indeed most major cities throughout the rapidly urbanizing People's Republic.[68]

CHAPTER SIX

The Country and the City

城市與農村

An altogether different drama of loss and relocation unfolds every day in countless rural villages across China, one that brings new meaning to a sixth-century epic ballad "Southeast Fly the Peacocks" (*Kong Que Dong Nan Fei*). Described as "one of the most remarkable poems in the Chinese language," the narrative chronicles a domestic tragedy in Anhui Province. A beautiful and talented young wife, despised by her mother-in-law, is forced to leave her husband, a prefectural clerk who dutifully abides by his mother's wishes and sends his wife away. The young woman returns to her family home disgraced and heartbroken and her elder brother promptly begins making arrangements to find her a new spouse. The woman agrees to marry again, but reluctantly, for she is still deeply in love with her husband. She is consumed by sorrow in the end and drowns herself on the wedding day. Upon learning of this, her husband also takes his life, hanging himself from a courtyard tree. The pair are buried together beneath a grove of cypress and pine, united again by death. In the boughs above the grave a pair of mandarin ducks call out plaintively, as if to tell passersby the tragic tale.[1]

That an ancient poem about failed love and a mother-in-law from hell could have anything to with Chinese urban growth seems far-fetched. But the poem lends its name, and even some of its spirit, to the Chinese experience of migration, particularly of rural people to the city. The poem's first and most famous line—"A pair of peacocks fly to the southeast, but pause and look back every five *li*" (*Kong que dong nan fei, wu li yi pai huai*)—has come to symbolize the bittersweet moment of leaving one's beloved old home and striking out for new horizons. Forced out by circumstances to find a new place in the world, the

Grandfather and grandson in a migrant worker shack on demolition site, Nanjing, 2006.

youthful migrants look homeward with sorrow as their familiar world vanishes into the past.

One of the defining aspects of the post-Mao period has been an unprecedented migration of rural "peacocks" from the countryside into China's major metropolitan centers. By any measure, it is the largest mass movement of humanity in history, easily dwarfing the greatest migrations of the past. China is today the most rapidly urbanizing country in the world. But the path of Chinese urbanization has not been a smooth one, and the current city boom has been preceded by convulsive periods of growth and shrinkage during the Mao years. At the founding of the People's Republic in 1949, there were only fifty-eight cities in mainland China; these contained about 10.6 percent of the total population. The new Communist regime reclassified a number of counties as "urban," increasing the number of cities to 132. The urban population, meanwhile, increased by about thirty-five million people between 1949 and 1956, largely due to an influx of migrants from the countryside.[2]

Over the next decade this figure—and the number of cities itself—rose and fell with the vagaries of Maoist economic and social policy. There was some effort in the early 1950s to relieve the war-swollen population of China's cities by resettling people in the countryside and rural interior, but it was largely noncompulsory, and those who left could return at any time; cities continued to grow.[3] Following this was a brief period of fast urbanization at the outset of the Great Leap Forward: between 1958 and 1960, the number of cities in China rose by 42 percent, and the urban population increased by 30 million—from 14.6 percent of the total population in 1956 to nearly 20 percent in 1960.[4]

Behind this dramatic increase was an effort to develop an urban industrial base to transform China's cities from resource-hungry consumers to Marxian producers. Mao's vision of smokestack cities across China soon became reality as millions of peasants left the land to work in urban factories, foundries, and steel plants. Vast new industrial operations were built both on the urban fringe and in the city centers, where factories were shoehorned into old neighborhoods as part of self-contained live-work communes known as *danwei*. The point was to cultivate an urban proletariat, a revolutionary workforce like that in Soviet Union. Placing heavy industry in the heart of populous residential districts violates basic laws of real estate economics, not to mention good land-use planning. It was only possible now because the government controlled all urban land and could allocate its use irrespective of the marketplace and—especially—the center-to-periphery land rent gradient typical of capitalist cities. Land was, in effect, no longer a scarce resource, so traditional determinants of property value (location, location, location) no longer held: a site across from the Forbidden City was equal in value—theoretically at least—to a pigsty on the outskirts of town.[5]

Despite the labor needs of new state-run industries, the government was wary of unchecked urban growth and began developing a system by which a "blind flow" (*mang liu*) of rural people into cities could be limited. This led to an extraordinary social-control apparatus known as *hukou*. Inspired by the Soviet passbook system, *hukou* was first developed in the early 1950s and implemented as national policy by decade's end. The system required that every Chinese citizen be registered as part of a specific *hukou*, or household. *Hukou* registration, assigned at birth, was fixed to a particular locality and virtually impossible to change. Its chief purpose was to limit the size of cities by preventing "rural leakage into urban society."[6]

Hukou registration not only severely limited a person's freedom of movement, it also determined the kind of life he'd lead. City residents were given "non-agricultural" or urban *hukou* status (*feinongye renkou*), while those in the countryside had agricultural *hukou* status (*nongye renkou*). Because the state—again following Soviet precedent—took responsibility for the welfare of city residents only (farmers had plenty to eat, it was assumed), urban *hukou* status became a coveted thing: with it came all kinds of perks and entitlements unavailable to rural folk—not only rations of meat, rice, and oil (the famous "iron ricebowl") but access to housing, health care, schooling, pensions, and retirement benefits.[7] City people thus gained status and security at the expense of the farmer, whose already humble place in Chinese society dropped lower still—a particular irony given the supposed centrality of peasanthood in the identity of the Chinese Communist Party. Though it was several years before the *hukou* system was perfected and fully enforced, it eventually became a powerful means of controlling the mobility of the Chinese people, as well as the "central institutional mechanism defining the city-countryside relationship" in Maoist China.[8]

The Great Leap Forward ended in disaster, with profound and lasting implications for China's millions of rural peasants. Because so many peasants had been urged to labor in city factories or run makeshift foundries in the countryside, fields were untended and crops left to rot. The nature of the ensuing famine proved the dreadful effectiveness of the *hukou* system. Though strictly rationed, food was available in the cities throughout the crisis; urban residents received regular, if diminished, allotments of grain and other staples. But the peasantry had no such entitlements to fall back on. Millions of rural people began to starve. The scarcity of food in the countryside should have sent a wave of hungry people into China's cities, but fearful of social chaos and millions more mouths to feed, Mao took steps to prevent just such an influx. He was also desperate to jump-start the agricultural economy, which meant keeping as many farmers as possible on the land, famine or no famine. Thus, *hukou* enforcement was mercilessly ramped up, effectively immobilizing the rural populace and forcing millions to starve in place.[9] The result was history's greatest famine, in which as many as thirty million people died—a greater toll than the Black Death during the European Middle Ages.[10] The government further forced millions of peasants who had earlier been encouraged to work in urban factories to return to the countryside, in order to reduce its welfare burden.[11]

All this led to a dramatic reversal of the urban growth spurt of the late 1950s. In 1959 alone, 5 million city workers were sent back to the land; another 20 million were forced out between 1960 and 1962. China's urban population fell from a high of 130 million in 1960 to 89 million in 1965. Even the number of cities plummeted: in 1961 there were 208 cities by official count; three years later that figure had dropped to 169.[12] Strict enforcement of *hukou* regulations continued throughout the Mao era, blocking nearly all urban migration and artificially capping the population and physical expansion of Chinese metropoles. The *hukou* system has not been called "the world's most influential urban growth management instrument" for nothing.[13]

Efforts to limit the size and power of cities during the Mao era were also related to China's decision to "go it alone" after the great Sino-Soviet split of the early 1960s. The Soviet model of socialism, followed assiduously until then, emphasized heavy industry and the development of an urban proletariat. The Maoist "Chinese development model," on the other hand, favored agricultural production and focused more on the rural peasantry. Unlike the Bolshevik revolution, driven by an uprising of urban workers in St. Petersburg, communism in China began as a guerrilla movement and came of age in the countryside. True, its intellectual seeds were first sown in city soil—in exuberantly capitalist Shanghai, no less. But it was in rural Yan'an (Yenan) Province, among the peasantry, that Chinese communism evolved its fundamental characteristics—a closeness to the soil; values of simplicity, hard work, and self-sufficiency; a "spirit of rough egalitarianism." Rural China became a touchstone for the Party, even as it advocated a vast urban industrial development program. "After the communists took power in 1949," writes Michael Frolic, "they sought to apply to the whole of China what they had learned in Yenan, in effect taking a model of agrarian revolution in a small base area and integrating it with the classic Soviet model of large scale rapid industrialization." As the Sino-Soviet marriage fell apart, Mao rejected Lenin and returned to his roots, seeking a path to modernization that was "neither Manchester nor Moscow." As Frolic puts it, the Chinese path might prove "that mankind might modernize without passing through the fire and brimstone of massive urbanization, without a highly centralized command economy, and without ruthlessly subjecting the countryside to the rule of cities." The ideological focus of Chinese communism thus moved back to the countryside, mythified now as an "outpost of national culture and values amidst the destructive cosmopolitanism of industrial urban life."[14]

Another factor explaining Maoist under-urbanization was fear of war with the Soviet Union and possibly the United States. The 1960s were an anxious time for China, particularly in terms of international relations. A border dispute with India flared into armed conflict in 1962. Across the Taiwan Strait, Chiang Kai-shek seemed poised to attack, possibly with the help of American carriers in the Pacific at the time. U.S. troops were gathering not far from the Chinese border in Vietnam, where a fresh conflict would eventually require the commitment of some 350,000 Chinese troops. Most menacing of all was the breakdown of relations between China and the Soviet Union, which threatened to turn violent at any moment. If ever there was a time to make ready for war, this was it. The same fear of war that drove Mao to build bomb shelters beneath Beijing also led to an extraordinary campaign to decentralize Chinese cities and industry—a top-secret development program known as the Third Front. Launched in 1964, the Third Front was meant to put China on a war footing by moving strategic industrial assets and population out of harm's way—deep in the nation's mountainous interior and far from the vulnerable China coast.

At this time, 60 percent of civil industry and many defense assets were located along the coastal plain, as were the nation's largest and most important cities—a rich field of targets indeed for Soviet or American bombers. Diverting people and economic activity away from the coast was militarily prudent, but also intended to stimulate development in the impoverished western provinces. Third Front works were epic in scale: the great Panzhihua iron and steel production complex in Sichuan Province was among the largest undertakings of the Mao era; entire new rail systems were required to serve it. The campaign can also be seen as part of larger Maoist efforts at the time to reduce the size of China's cities. Hundreds of thousands of urban workers were moved from coastal cities to staff new and relocated factories in the remote interior.[15]

Ironically, the Third Front campaign is similar in many respects to American efforts to disperse cities and industry during the Cold War. The threat of a Soviet nuclear attack sparked an "urban dispersal movement" in the United States, which hoped to scatter urban residents to suburban new towns beyond the densely populated Boston-to-Washington "hot zone." Dispersal advocates such as Tracy B. Augur and Goodhue Livingston Jr. argued that in an age of Soviet ICBMs, extreme urban concentration was suicidal. The logic was sound enough: a nuclear device detonated over New York City would indeed kill millions and paralyze the American economy. As Livingston put it, dispersal was "the only real national insurance available against a surprise knock-out blow" (the *Bulletin of Atomic Scientists* similarly argued that dispersal was "the only measure which could make an atomic 'super Pearl Harbor' impossible").[16]

Closer still to Third Front objectives was the American Industrial Dispersion Policy. Approved by President Truman in 1951, the directive followed a National Security Resources Board report emphasizing that "dense agglomerations of industrial plants were inviting targets for the enemy and that plants separated in space would better survive an atomic attack."[17] The dispersalists failed in their bid to decentralize America's big cities, but there was really no need for all the effort in the first place—Americans spread out on their own in the 1950s and 1960s, moving to places like Levittown and Daly City in a great national rush to the suburbs.

The outlook for China's cities was even more bleak during the Cultural Revolution, a period of political extremism and social chaos that began around 1966 and only ended with Mao's death a decade later. In these years, *hukou* enforcement was stepped up and the "blind flow" of rural migrants to cities all but ceased. Urban development came to a standstill, and some cities even shrank in size. The central government kept the largest cities fiscally underfed to prevent them from dominating the national economy. Critical infrastructure fell into disrepair during the Cultural Revolution, as did urban housing stock, now mostly controlled by the state. Because it charged such low rents, the government had no funds to undertake basic maintenance.[18] The condition of the residential building supply, already overcrowded and in poor repair, quickly worsened, which helps explain why so much of China's historic urban fabric was beyond any hope of rehabilitation by the 1990s.

Eventually the State Housing Administration was shut down, and all urban planning activity brought to a halt.[19] Chinese cities entered a kind of urban architectural time warp during the Cultural Revolution. "By the late 1970s," writes Barry Naughton, "the central districts of Shanghai, Tianjin, and Guangzhou had an almost museumlike character, so little had they apparently changed from the 1930s." Most cities experienced almost no physical expansion in this period. The small amount of new housing built was limited to small inner-city parcels. Unlike the typical American city and its vast fringe of suburbs, the border between city and countryside in China became sharply drawn. Farmland lay within a stone's throw of dense urban districts, fostering a variety of economic symbioses (for example, night soil from urban latrines was used as fertilizer on nearby farms, increasing agricultural production while keeping cities clean). As we will see, this abundance of farmland so close to town also set the stage for wholesale urban sprawl in the 1990s.[20]

The draconian social policies of the Cultural Revolution also bled cities of population; although there was some flow of temporary rural workers to cities in this period, the outflow was even greater still.[21] From about 1967 to 1976 some thirty million urban residents were sent down to the countryside to be "rusticated" (*shang shan xia xiang*). This included an entire generation of urban youth as well as artists and intellectuals who were accused of counter-revolutionary tendencies. Forcing students and urban elites to endure the roughsimplicity of rural life was meant to flush away bourgeois habits and diminish the "three great disparities" (*san da cha bie*) that Mao wanted to purge from Chinese society: the disparity between manual and mental work; between the urban proletariat and the rural peasantry; and between the countryside and the city. If anything, forced rustication only produced a lot of bitter, overeducated pig farmers.

Though the Cultural Revolution ended in 1976, the period of urban stagnation lingered several more years until the start of the Deng Xiaoping era. Dramatic change was again in store: by the mid-1980s, the gray-blue Maoist

city was being flushed away by the free market, and China's cities came booming back. Both the number of cities and the urban population began an
extraordinary climb that hasn't stopped since. There were 193 cities in China
in 1978; by 1999 the figure had surged to 667—an increase of almost 246 percent. Many of these were at first little more than paper cities—towns or counties that were reclassified as urban but still provincial in spirit and function.
Elsewhere, existing cities incorporated nearby rural villages, rapidly extending
their land area and population and creating extraordinary city-country juxtapositions in the process—bullocks in Beijing, rice fields in Shanghai.[22]

But it was not a change in bureaucratic designation that made these new
places suddenly urban, it was all the people who began flocking to them to
work and live. Tens of millions of people have flooded China's metropoles in
recent decades. After a long winter, the Chinese urban population surged, dou-
bling between 1978 and the late 1990s. In 1950 about 17 percent of the total
national population lived in cities; by the 1990s this number was up to 27 percent, and today it exceeds 40 percent. Some studies show that by 2030, China's
urban population could be in excess of 60 percent.[23] If this proves right, the
People's Republic will eventually have an urban population two times the total
population of the United States. It will also have achieved in a single generation a level of urbanization that the United States needed almost a century to
attain: America's urban population was about 20 percent in 1860, and did not
reach 60 percent until the 1950s.[24]

★   ★   ★

In fact, China's urban revolution is likely even greater than most statistics
reveal. Nearly all official estimates, including the numbers cited above, do not
account for the largest and most crucial component of the urban population
boom—the rural migrant labor workforce that makes up as much as a quarter of the real population of China's cities today. The economic reforms of the
1980s unleashed a steady stream of rural migrants to China's cities, men and
women from impoverished agricultural villages, collectively known as the
"floating population" (*liudong renkou*).[25] The influx of these workers into the
booming coastal provinces began slowly at first but sped up in the 1990s, as
hukou restrictions were eased to meet industry's demand for workers. There
were 500,000 migrant workers in Shanghai in the summer of 1984; by 2000,

"My aspirations lie in the countryside," Cultural Revolution propaganda poster, 1973.
COURTESY OF MAOPOST.COM

that figure had increased to 3.87 million—equal to nearly a third of Shanghai's official population.[26] Beijing's floating population, a mere 200,000 in 1984, swelled to three million by 1998.[27]

Nationwide, the numbers are even more breathtaking. The annual influx of rural migrants to China's cities increased from 9 million in 1989 in to nearly 30 million a decade later. All told, there were some 25 million migrant workers in China's cities in the mid-1980s, and about 70 million ten years later. By 2003 the floating population was double this figure, and it remains in the neighborhood of 140 million people—fully 10 percent of China's total population. To put this in American perspective, an equivalent percentage of immigrants in the United States would number 30 million people, or nearly five times the number of undocumented Mexican nationals currently in the United States, according to the Pew Hispanic Center.[28]

In terms of scale, rural-urban migration in China today is unprecedented in history. All previous "great migrations," whether between or within nations, dwindle to insignificance in comparison. In 1998 alone, some twenty-seven million rural migrants made their way to China's cities, equal to the total number of emigrants from Europe to the United States over the 100 year period from 1820 to 1920, the peak decades of European emigration to America. The migrant worker population of Beijing is nearly equal to the total number of rural Americans who moved to cities between 1920 and 1930, or the number of African Americans who left the rural South in the decades following the Second World War—two of the most formative demographic shifts in American history.[29]

In addition to stimulating urban growth, the economic reforms of the 1980s also streamlined agricultural production. In 1979 a new program of family farming known as the Household Responsibility System replaced the rural collectives of the Mao era. Newly motivated by marketplace incentives, individual farmers competed now to get ahead; innovation led to higher crop yields and an overall increase in efficiency. Studies have credited the Household Responsibility System with nearly half of China's increase in agricultural output between 1978 and 1984.[30] But efficiency can be unkind. Fewer people were now needed to do the same work, and the result was a huge labor surplus in the countryside. As *hukou* restrictions were eased, millions of these idled farmworkers headed for the cities in search of work. Not only was work available in China's cities, but it also paid a lot better than anything in the countryside. A 2002 survey found that Shanghai's migrant workforce earned an average of ¥3,650 each year, nearly four times the ¥920 average annual income of rural people.[31]

Economic disparities between the countryside and city are, of course, nothing new; they have driven rural-urban migration for centuries. Leaving the land and coming to the city in search of opportunity is one of humanity's timeless dramas. Between 1840 and 1900, some three million people left rural towns during the second phase of the Industrial Revolution in England, and by 1851 there were more urban residents in England than rural—a "watershed demographic event" that marked the first time a modern nation had more city people than country folk.[32] Similarly, a decline in New England's agricultural economy in the middle years of the nineteenth century—caused in part by the opening of the Erie Canal—led many rural Yankees to find work in the mills of Lowell and Lawrence, Massachusetts. The influx helped raise New England's urban population from 7 to 36 percent between 1810 and 1860.[33] The millions of emigrants from Ireland and Italy who later flocked to America were themselves largely rural people. By 1920 the urban population of the United States already exceeded that of the rural countryside. After World War II, black sharecroppers put out of work by the mechanical cotton picker began moving in even larger numbers to the "Promised Land" of the urban North, an influx that continued well into the 1970s. In 1860, African Americans were a largely rural people; a century later, the tables had completely turned: most now lived in cities, as did the majority of Americans overall.[34]

Like Chicago at the end of the nineteenth century or New York in the Roaring Twenties, China's booming cities consume a steady supply of labor. Millions of hands are needed on construction sites and in factories, restaurants, and hotels, and to take on the thousand-odd thankless tasks that more permanent city residents are no longer skilled enough or have no desire to do—especially the so-called Three "D" (difficult, demeaning, and dirty) jobs such as janitorial services, street sweeping, building demolition, refuse collection, and recycling. Millions of rural and small-town migrant women, mostly young and single, gravitate to the restaurant and retail trades or find work on factory production floors and back-room sweatshops where they cut, sew, and assemble all the low-priced consumer products flooding world markets.

Male migrants are usually employed in more physically demanding or dangerous lines of work, most notably building construction. In Shanghai, nearly 27 percent of the migrant labor force in the late 1990s worked on construction sites.[35] Life as a migrant construction worker is hard and hazardous. Peasant life may have been regulated by the sun and moon, but construction sites are often active 24/7, illuminated at night by huge work lamps that brighten the city sky. Laborers usually reside on site, either in purpose-built temporary structures or condemned structures withheld from demolition until the last minute. On their one day off each week, workers may be seen milling about in the air-conditioned splendor of local shopping malls or supermarkets, marveling at cameras and televisions that cost six months' hard-earned wages. Construction is difficult, dangerous work even in the United States, where safety laws, powerful unions, and generous health benefits make it a parlor game compared to China. Though much improved in recent years, work-site conditions in China harken back to the American construction industry circa 1915. Site safety regulations are minimal, and independent labor unions are outlawed by a government well aware of the union roots of Poland's Solidarity Movement, which overthrew that nation's communist regime in the 1980s.

In China, it is commonplace to see men welding with no eye protection, wearing flimsy slipper-like shoes around ten-ton machines, or working just inches beneath swinging craneloads of steel with not a hardhat in sight. Injuries are common and catastrophic. A study of occupational accidents in Shunde, one of the booming cities of the Pearl River Delta, showed that building construction was the most dangerous work there in the early 1990s, with an average annual mortality of 54.8 per 100,000 workers—more than double the rate in the U.S. construction industry at the time.[36] The brutal life of Chinese construction workers is movingly rendered in Jia Zhangke's 2004 film *The World*. In one scene, a sweet young man, given to philosophic musings about life, is forced by circumstance to join his cousins working a construction site on the outskirts of Beijing. When he is mortally injured by a flying cable, his heartbroken parents come from their rural village to collect his body and last wages, which are paid out with icy efficiency by the crew boss. On the windswept expanse of the unfinished roof that evening, the family burns an offering to the boy's departed spirit.

In the eyes of many Chinese capitalists (and their foreign joint-venture partners), the migrant labor workforce is an ideal tool for wealth production— easily managed, easily replenished, and essentially disposable. Workers are usually single, young, and healthy and typically leave long before they get old and infirm. Migrants are disciplined and hardworking, tolerant of low wages and miserable work conditions; and—for the time being at least—they make few demands and expect little from their employers. They are politically unorganized and thus voiceless, although there is increasing evidence that this is beginning to change. Those workers who complain, get injured, or do not produce enough are summarily fired, and there is usually no shortage of eager replacements. Independent labor unions like those that have so much power in the United States are illegal in China; what unions do exist are more like government-run social clubs. Of course, migrants can vote with their feet, and often do—turnover is rapid and workers constantly move around in search of better work and living conditions. Sometimes they leave a job with nothing at all. In September 2004, the central government found that China's construction workers were owed some $43 billion in unpaid back wages. Some laborers had not been paid in years; in debt to their employers and living on the promise of payment, they had essentially become slaves.[37]

If the work is hard, the living is not much better. Some men and women, blessed with a knack for business, good *guanxi* (personal connections), and plenty of luck have indeed done well in cities; a small number have even made

Homeless laborer, Dalian, 2006. PHOTOGRAPH BY AUTHOR

fortunes. The Chinese popular press is full of stories, reminiscent of Horatio Alger's bootstrap tales, of once-poor *nongmin* (country bumpkins) who have conquered the city. The vast majority, however, struggle to make ends meet on a daily basis. Though most migrants bring in a good income compared to what they would earn back home, city life is expensive: rent, security deposits on tools or uniforms, taxes, work permit fees, and the occasional necessary bribe can keep workers in a constant state of debt. The lack of proper *hukou* status deprives migrants of a range of entitlements available to the local population, putting them at a further disadvantage. Migrants also face a gamut of cultural and institutional barriers that make it all but impossible to become fully vested members of the urban community.

Chinese society is extraordinarily homogeneous—more than 90 percent of the population is Han Chinese—and "otherness" is less a function of race or ethnicity than of class, income, birthplace geography, job, or *hukou* status. The migrant laborer is close to the bottom of China's urban social ladder. Migrants are derisively called *mingong*, a term roughly equivalent to the American "cracker" or "redneck." They are blamed for nearly every urban problem and stereotyped as ignorant rubes with a penchant for crime. They are routinely denied access to stores, shopping malls, or hotel lobbies, and often evicted wholesale in advance of high-profile events, especially in Beijing. Migrant families, though relatively few in number, have it especially hard. Without local *hukou* registration, their children have little or no chance to attend school, and teens are virtually barred from a university education. Little is gained by being born in a city, either. Like low-caste Indians, children of migrants inherit the mother's *hukou*, and are thus also excluded from the welfare benefits of the urban franchise.

The single men and women who make up the majority of the migrant worker population face additional challenges when it comes to mating and marriage. Marrying into the local population is uncommon in a Chinese society increasingly preoccupied with class and status. For men, the prospects of finding a mate in the city are especially dim. Mao-era progress in terms of gender equality has been countered somewhat by a return of traditional gender roles and a "re-feminization" of Chinese womanhood—especially among the middle and upper classes. The ruddy-cheeked factory girls on Maoist posters have largely traded in their gloves for makeup and motherhood. If print and television advertisements are any measure of cultural values, and they usually are, the prevailing image of domestic bliss in China today is very similar to that of the United States circa 1955—a handsome husband with a good income; a gifted and obedient child; a charming, effeminate wife who lunches with her girlfriends and hosts Tupperware parties (Tupperware is in fact very popular today with the emergent Chinese middle class, and Tupperware Brands operates some 1,900 franchised storefronts in 200 cities across the People's Republic).

Given this, the typical male migrant worker—with meager income, bad clothes, and the wrong *hukou* status—has little chance indeed of catching a city girl. His chances among the floaters are not much better, not only because of a gender imbalance among the migrant population—males predominate by a wide margin—but because migrant women are also looking to marry up the food chain. Workers' sexual needs are, inevitably, met by prostitution, which is rampant now in Chinese cities. The sex trade is typically carried on in small shops fronting as hair salons and often marked by pink or purple lighting (or, more obviously, by the fetchingly clad "hairdressers" therein). Invariably, such shops are staffed by country girls themselves trying to make it in the city.[38]

In spite of all these challenges, China's migrant workers are an extraordinarily resourceful and resilient lot and usually scrimp and save enough to send money back home to their families. Annual remittances from the migrant workforce are now a major part of China's rural economy, especially in poor rural provinces like Henan, Anhui, and Sichuan—the three provinces that provide the most migrant labor to China's cities. Studies have shown that the average migrant worker sends home up to ¥3,000 annually, more than three times the average annual income of rural workers. In 2003 China's migrant workforce sent home an estimated $45 billion.[39] This money has vastly improved the conditions of life in the Chinese countryside. The gleaming, tile-clad new homes rising amidst a dark backdrop of century-old structures—seen in villages throughout rural China today—are only the most visible effect of such grassroots economic infusions.

For most people, the immense scale of China's migrant worker population only becomes fully evident once a year, during the Lunar New Year holidays. New Year, which usually occurs in late January or early February, is the most important of the three "golden week" holidays of the Chinese calendar. In the days before the start of the festival, nearly all migrant workers head home to the villages and small towns of their birth to celebrate the holiday, sometimes traveling a thousand miles or more. Rail and bus stations become scenes of controlled pandemonium, and the nation's transport infrastructure is quickly pushed to the bursting point. Seats go almost instantly, and on many trains and buses passengers are forced to stand cheek-by-jowl for rides that often last all night. The busiest travel time of the American calendar—the days just before and after Thanksgiving, when airports are packed and highways thick with traffic—pales in comparison to China's annual New Year rush. In 2005 some 65 million Americans took to the road, rails, and air at Thanksgiving; Chinese officials estimated that some two billion people traveled in 2006 during the New Year holiday season, more than thirty times the Thanksgiving travel load in the United States.[40] History's greatest migration—of millions of rural people to China's cities—is thus is reenacted each spring in reverse, in what has itself become the greatest annual movement of humanity on the globe.

CHAPTER SEVEN

Suburbanization and the Mechanics of Sprawl

城郊化進程

The Venetian merchant-adventurer Marco Polo traveled to China with his father and uncle in the last quarter of the thirteenth century. He stayed for seventeen years, becoming a trusted advisor of Kublai Khan and a denizen of the imperial court. Many years later in Italy, having been captured by the Genoese, Polo is said to have dictated a dazzling account of his Cathay adventures to a fellow prisoner. The stories were eventually published as *Il Milione*, known in English as *The Travels of Marco Polo*. Though dismissed by some as an extravagant romance, the book was for centuries one of the only accounts in the West of the cities and landscapes of the Orient.

Polo's *Travels* is also our earliest account of Chinese suburbanization in Western literature. The adventurer's descriptions of the fabulous city of Khanbaliq (Cambuluc), the Mongol capital that eventually became Beijing, include a detailed account of development beyond the city walls. "There is a suburb outside each of the gates, which are twelve in number," wrote Polo; "and these suburbs are so great that they contain more people than the city itself [for the suburb of one gate spreads in width till it meets the suburb of the next, whilst they extend in length some three or four miles]." These were hardly dull bedroom communities, for therein—lodged in "numerous fine hostelries," wrote Polo—were "foreign merchants and travellers, of whom there are always great numbers who have come to bring presents to the Emperor, or to sell articles at Court, or because the city affords so good a mart to attract traders." All told, there were "as many good houses outside of the city as inside, without counting those that belong to the great lords and barons, which are very numerous."[1] We tend to think of suburban development as a

Security guards at entrance to Country Garden Villa estate, Guangdong Province, 1999.
PHOTOGRAPH BY AUTHOR

recent phenomenon; in fact, suburbs have been with us for centuries, as Polo's account well illustrates. In both China and the West, suburbanization—and what we today term "sprawl"—is as old as urban settlement itself; suburbs have been "a persistent feature in cities," writes Robert Bruegmann, "since the beginning of urban history." And in this, China is no exception.[2]

Of course, nothing Marco Polo witnessed at Khanbaliq comes close to the vast scale of suburban development in Beijing today. The "suburbs... so great" that he toured seven centuries ago have long been engulfed by the capital. But the legacy of those early suburbs lives on in the seemingly endless expanse of housing estates, gated villa subdivisions, shopping malls, and edge city office towers rising on the road-ringed periphery of Beijing—today one of the fastest-sprawling cities in the world. Between 1980 to 1990, some 77 percent of all new housing built in the capital was not in the center city but in its outlying suburban districts. In that same period, Beijing's central districts lost 82,000 people while its inner and outer suburbs gained nearly 1.7 million new residents. This pace increased dramatically over the next ten years: between 1990 and 2000 the city's core lost another 222,000 while the suburbs gained nearly three million people, many of whom were residents of *hutong* neighborhoods forced out by wholesale urban renewal.[3]

And Beijing is hardly alone in this. Every major coastal city, and many inland, has undergone rapid lateral expansion in recent years, making sprawl one of the hallmarks of contemporary Chinese urbanism—a phenomenon colloquially referred to as *tan da bing*—"making a big pancake." In Dalian, nearly 87 percent of all new housing built between 1991 and 1994 was in the city's suburbs.[4] Sprawl in Shanghai has been even more pronounced. Like most Chinese cities, Shanghai's built-up urban area covers only part of a municipal jurisdiction extending far out into the rural countryside. At the outset of the reform era, in 1982, that zone encompassed about ninety square miles; by 1995 the built-up area of Shanghai was sprawling across 794 square miles of the lower Yangtze Delta, a nearly ninefold increase in land area.[5] To obtain comparable growth, New York City would have to expand across all of Long Island and Westchester County, and into a sizeable chunk of northern New Jersey. Even during the Big Apple's most active period of suburban expansion—the quarter-century between 1960 and 1985—the New York metropolitan region grew in area by a mere 65 percent, with an overall population increase of only about 8 percent.

⋆ ⋆ ⋆

The factors driving sprawl in China and the lateral expansion of its cities are many and complex, related both to reform-era land economics and to the legacy of Maoist policies (discussed in the previous chapter) meant to cultivate urban industry and limit the population and physical size of cities. As we have seen, Chinese cities experienced near-zero growth during the Cultural Revolution, from 1966 to 1976. They remained compact and dense as a result, with an abundance of rural land close by. The transition between city and surrounding countryside was thus sharp and clean—without the broad intermediate zone of suburban development that was forming at this time around American cities.

Chinese cities in the Mao era also developed a unique spatial form based on the *danwei* communal work-unit model of social organization. Partly rooted in Soviet planning practice, the *danwei* was a kind of socialist production machine with a physical layout intended to facilitate shared living and cohesion among workers. The *danwei* model was employed not only in mills and factories, but in nearly every institution of modern life—universities, hospitals, schools, research institutes, government bureaus, and ministries. By the 1960s, some 90 percent of China's urban population belonged to a *danwei*. It became the basic unit of social and economic life in urban China—"the site," writes David Bray, "through which the state provided welfare, housing, education, healthcare and other social benefits."[6]

The architecture and urban design of the *danwei* underscored its comprehensive role in the lives of urban workers. The typical *danwei* included both workplace and residential accommodations, as well as day-care facilities, a school, infirmary, bathhouse, meeting hall, and a canteen for communal meals. These functions were typically set in a complex of buildings grouped about a series of orthogonal axes, with the entire compound enclosed by a perimeter wall. Spatially, then, the *danwei* compounds bore a striking resemblance to "ancestral" forms of Chinese urbanism—especially the courtyard house, which in turn miniaturized many of the spatial design principles seen in larger scale in Chinese walled cities. The recycling of such earlier urban architectural traditions is a function, Bray argues, of "a mimetic effect in which familiar forms are reinvoked to secure the boundaries of new modes of social life."[7]

In providing for the total life needs of workers, the *danwei* complex also evokes the tradition of neoutopian industrial town planning in the West. Among the earliest such efforts was Claude-Nicolas Ledoux's scheme, begun in the 1770s, for the French royal salt works at Chaux, Arc-et-Senans. Integral to Ledoux's facility were housing and amenities meant to yield a happier—and thus more productive—workforce. As with nearly all subsequent model towns, Chaux was also deeply paternalistic: the director's residence, for example, was placed at the center of a semicircular array of dwellings, enabling surveillance in a manner much like Jeremy Bentham's later Panopticon.[8] In the early nineteenth century, Scottish utopianist Robert Owen experimented with communal forms of social organization at his New Lanark spinning mills, while a French contemporary, Charles Fourier, placed all shared community functions in a live-work megastructure he called a "phalanstery." These experiments inspired such later English model towns as Port Sunlight, built for workers of the Lever Soap Company, and Bourneville, a project of the Cadbury Brothers chocolatiers.

In the United States, George Pullman developed a model industrial town for workers at his vast Chicago railcar works, but his attempts to control nearly every facet of community life were resented, and the experiment ended with a calamitous strike in 1894. In terms of spatial structure, perhaps the closest thing in the United States today to the Mao-era *danwei* complex are those older, in-town university campuses like those at Columbia or Harvard, where people live, work, and study in a communal environment defined—and separated from the city—by walls and gates. In China today, universities are in fact among the last institutions to retain the traditional *danwei* urban-architectural form, although an increasing number of faculty and staff now reside off campus.

Collectively, the *danwei* compounds—each a little world unto itself—formed a kind of patchwork quilt at the larger scale of the city. There was little interpenetration between the individual work units, nor much functional or administrative engagement between them and the larger city. "City-level government often had no control over the development of large-scale *danwei* within their urban jurisdiction," writes Bray, "and as a result, the socialist city became dominated by a cellular spatial structure where each cell...had very few horizontal links with any other part of the city. This gave rise to one of the most significant peculiarities of Chinese socialism: cities that were collections of independent workplace-based communities, rather than integrated urban environments."[9] Life in the Maoist city was thus introverted, with little of the vibrant street culture and teeming public markets that characterized Chinese urbanism in earlier eras. Walter Benjamin's *flâneur*, to whom the arcades and boulevards of Paris were a churning, kaleidoscopic spectacle, would have been quite bored in a Maoist Chinese city.

Moreover, city planning in the Mao era did not undertake broad-stroke exclusionary zoning of land uses, but was largely restricted to "grouping certain types of work-unit compounds in certain areas of the city."[10] While some larger institutional functions were indeed zoned—in Beijing, for example, universities were concentrated in the northwest quadrant of the city and foreign embassies were east of Tiananmen Square—Maoist urbanism was typified by a great mixture of uses at the micro- *danwei*-neighborhood level. Because the *danwei* was designed to accommodate in situ nearly all a resident's daily needs, each walled compound contained a range of urban functions and amenities that were once distributed over a wide area of the city. The Maoist city was thus really more a collection of tiny urban villages than a metropolis in the Western sense, with a heterogeneous, finely grained texture of land use.

This differed dramatically from American cities of the era, where functional zoning—first adopted in the 1920s—was increasingly used to spatially separate land uses considered incompatible, often for good reason. Zoning precluded, for instance, siting a fertilizer plant next to a primary school, or the construction of a supermarket in the middle of a residential street. In terms of the urban fabric, zoning created a coarser pattern of land use, with large, functionally homogeneous areas. Because the separation of manufacturing facilities from residential districts is one of the fundamentals of modern zoning, the typical Mao-era *danwei* complex would have been illegal in nearly every major American city (except, perhaps, Houston, Texas, which never adopted formal zoning).

This urban spatial structure had profound implications for traffic and transportation. As life became increasingly focused at the local level and the *danwei*, there was little reason for people to travel beyond their own self-contained work-unit world. Cities in the Mao era were in fact "planned on the assumption," writes Piper Gaubatz, "that most residents would rarely need to travel beyond their compounds. There were no private cars and few taxis. Wide monumental streets that ran between the high compound walls were traversed primarily by buses, trucks, and bicycles, but traffic was sparse."[11] All those vast Soviet-style avenues laid out in Beijing and other cities in the 1950s were only fully thronged during military parades and other state functions.

Those same once-empty thoroughfares are today jam-packed with cars and trucks, bicycles, buses, and motorbikes. People in China's cities are moving around more than ever, like atoms in a heated flask. Among the chief causes is the demise of the *danwei* as a live-work package, which has resulted in a growing spatial separation between workplace and residence. With urban redevelopment in the 1980s and 1990s, many state-owned enterprises were themselves forced to relocate to the urban fringe, usually without the extensive on-site housing and other residential facilities that characterized their earlier incarnations. Housing provided by the *danwei* was one of the pillars of the Chinese welfare state, but in the reform era the state scaled back its landlord role. Economists argued that housing should be provided by the free market, according to the laws of supply and demand.[12] Deng Xiaoping himself argued for market housing in a 1980 speech, urging measures to help "make people feel that buying a house is more worthwhile than renting."[13] The old system of in situ *danwei* housing was gradually abandoned in favor of subsidies and loans enabling workers to purchase market-rate housing anywhere in town. The change was largely welcomed, and by the late 1990s real estate, interior decorating, and home improvement had become chief passions of the Chinese middle class.[14] But often the new housing, especially the more affordable units, was far from the factory or office. Workers could no longer just roll out of bed and onto their desk or workbench; now they had to commute.

Property developers were quick to exploit the burgeoning demand for affordable housing. As new housing in center-city districts is often prohibitively expensive, developers began focusing on all that undeveloped land sitting on the urban fringe, the legacy of under-urbanization during the Mao era. As discussed in the last chapter, Chinese cities were fiscally undernourished in the 1960s and 1970s and underwent little or none of the sprawling outward growth so common by then in the United States. The result was a surfeit of rural land within easy reach of town—a tabula rasa upon which developers could now build a whole new suburban empire.

True to classic models of a center-to-edge land value gradient, land on the urban fringe was much cheaper than in the city proper because it was so much more plentiful. A study of suburban development in Shenyang, for example, found that the land-use prices in the urban periphery were one-tenth those of the center city.[15] Of course, there were usually farmers on this rural land who had to be relocated and compensated for their losses, but for developers this was nothing compared to the immense financial and logistical burdens related to resettling scores or hundreds of families on an urban site. On the suburban fringe developers could move quickly and profitably; they literally had a field day, carpeting mile after mile of once-productive agricultural land with vast housing estates. The structure of municipal governance itself helped lubricate this suburban development machine. The jurisdictional boundaries of Chinese cities are typically immense and include large areas of agricultural hinterland. The city limits of Beijing, for example, cover some 6,500 square miles, almost equal in size to the entire New York metropolitan area. Chongqing's city limits enclose a staggering 31,815 square miles, making it ninety-nine times the size of New York City and the largest city in the world in terms of land area. Within these vast jurisdictions there are scores of small towns and villages, themselves undergoing a process of urbanization, that will eventually become engulfed by the expanding sea of suburban development.

While all land in China is owned by the central government, responsibility for the management and administration of urban land was decentralized in the reform era to local municipalities—and this included authority to lease development rights to that land. At the same time, local governments were also made newly responsible for funding all sorts of infrastructure and public services in their jurisdictions—things the central government had long paid for. Municipalities thus began leasing land in their outlying urban districts, a lucrative source of revenue to help meet these new costs. "Since land is the most valuable 'commodity' under the control of a municipal government," writes Zhang Tingwei, "generating revenue from leasing land use rights and charging land use fees has become the most popular practice for local government." Leasing fees have yielded a rich bounty indeed for local governments nationwide—as much as ten billion yuan annually in the late 1990s. In Shanghai, land leasing in Pudong brought in $190 million between 1990 and 1995. Much of this windfall was ploughed back into the ground, to pay for infrastructure and site improvements that would make the district even more attractive to developers—or even to acquire and annex additional rural land from adjacent towns.[16]

Entry gate, Fortune Garden Estate, Beijing, 2002. PHOTOGRAPH BY AUTHOR

Predictably, the huge sums involved in land leasing have also led to corruption among municipal officials and rural village heads, who are themselves part of the urban political system and have little motivation to defend local peasants. As Frederic Deng and Youqin Huang have written, "Since these leaders are appointed and paid by the local government they are really not independent and behave more in the interest of local government than in the interest of peasants."[17] Not surprisingly, the losers in the land conversion game are families working the land. Peasants have virtually no voice in the eminent domain processes and are given paltry sums in compensation for the land they work— far less than what urban residents are typically awarded. This is because compensation is calculated by the average crop yield of the land and not its future value as real estate. Rural land conversion has in fact sparked some of the largest and most violent uprisings in China in recent years. Official estimates of "public order disturbances" rose from 10,000 in 1994 to 87,000 in 2005; most of these were peasant protests against development-related eviction.[18]

Development on the suburban fringe in the 1990s was not all driven by the new demand for commodity housing. Many municipalities also began converting outlying rural land to build suburban economic and technological development zones (*kaifa qu*) in the hopes of attracting domestic and foreign direct investment. The zones were modeled on the highly successful special economic zones created in the 1980s, and were also inspired by foreign precedents like the Stanford Industrial Park and North Carolina's Research Triangle Park. In the early 1990s hundreds of development zones appeared on the outskirts of China's cities. Their siting was often arbitrary and unplanned, conforming to no locational logic vis-à-vis regional transport networks and thus contributing to a particularly inefficient form of "leapfrog" sprawl.

In a single year—from 1991 to 1992—more than 2,500 new economic development or high-tech districts were created. Beijing alone had twenty-six such development zones by 2003, the largest of which was the Beijing Economic Development Zone. The majority of this development-zone acreage was land removed from agricultural production. Creating these zones required throwing many thousands of peasants off the land, prompting parallels between Chinese "zone fever" and the land enclosure movement that transformed rural England in the years leading to the Industrial Revolution. Worse, in many cases the promised high-tech industrial development never came, and the land remained vacant and idle. By the mid-1990s the Wild West pace of zone development led to a crackdown by the central government. Some 1,200 particularly ill-conceived development zones were abandoned and about 300,000 acres of land returned to agricultural use. But the fever soon returned, and by 2003 there were nearly 4,000 development zones on the suburban outskirts of China's cities, accounting for a total land area of nearly 14,000 square miles—more than New Jersey and Connecticut combined.[19]

★ ★ ★

Fueled by a roaring housing market, land conversion has contributed to a perfect storm of suburban expansion in China. Its collective impact on the Chinese landscape is so vast in scale that it can only be fully appreciated from space. In the 1960s it was often claimed (mistakenly) that the Great Wall of China was the only human-made object visible from space. Today it is the explosive suburban growth of China's metropolitan regions that dazzles orbiting eyes. Over the last two decades, Landsat and other remote-sensing satellites have been quietly documenting the surging tide of Chinese urban development. Satellite data gathered in the 1990s revealed that China's collective urban footprint—

the extent of actual building mass, not just administrative limits—grew by some 3,177 square miles in the course of the decade, an increase equivalent to ten times the land area of New York City.[20] Karen C. Seto's studies of the Pearl River Delta, also using Landsat imagery, revealed a 364 percent increase in urbanized land between 1988 and 1996, with a consequent loss of some 500 square miles of cropland.[21] An earlier study of Dongguan, one of Guangdong's fastest growing cities, showed that the land area of construction sites in and around the city increased by 974 percent between 1988 and 1993. Today, most of those construction sites have "hardened" into finished buildings.[22]

An equally compelling snapshot of Chinese sprawl and urban expansion was compiled using night imagery from the U.S. Defense Department Meteorological Satellite Program (DMSP). The program's satellites circumnavigate the globe close to the poles in a sun-synchronous, low-altitude orbit some 500 miles above the earth. They detect cloud luminescence but also pick up artificial light from the earth's surface (DMSP imagery was used to produce the popular "Nighttime Lights of the World" map). Using DMSP radiance data captured in 1996, University of Georgia geographer C. P. Lo created three-dimensional "illuminated urban area domes" of China's metropolitan areas. As expected, the brightest jewels were the cores of major cities. The data also revealed sprawling metropolitan growth in the areas of Beijing and Tianjin, Shanghai, Shenyang, and the Pearl River Delta.[23] Lo's study only verifies what any senior airline pilot with time in Asia will tell you: until the mid-1980s, mainland China at night was a sea of inky blackness; today its vast urban zones glow like supernovae strung together by shimmering highway-strands of light.

Urban sprawl and suburban development in the United States had a similarly dramatic impact on the landscape. But beyond this, suburbanization in China differs in important ways from the American model.[24] In the United States, suburbanization began in earnest after the Second World War, when a booming economy, plentiful jobs, mortgages subsidized by the federal government, and an expanding highway infrastructure put the American dream of home ownership within reach of millions. Developers like the Levitt Brothers, who applied principles of mass production to residential construction, churned thousands of acres of farmland and pasture into subdivisions of single-family homes. In the decade between 1948 and 1958, some twelve million people left America's cities for the suburbs, creating a vacuum that was subsequently filled by African Americans from the rural South and new immigrants from abroad.[25]

American suburbs in the postwar period were low in density and characterized by large-lot subdivisions, single-family homes, an extensive automobile infrastructure, and a high degree of segregation along class and racial lines.

American suburbs were also politically autonomous and fiscally independent of the city. They could tax themselves for a variety of public services and improvements that often made for a higher quality of life than the city could offer. Suburban school systems were stronger; police forces were better paid and better equipped; there was more reliable garbage collection; and the roads were well maintained and quickly cleared of snow. The very identity of American suburbia, too, formed independently of—and in opposition to—the city. By the late 1960s many Americans had come to believe that the city was no longer a good place to live.

This perception was partly colored by a hoary tradition of antiurbanism in American culture—a certain ambivalence toward cities and urban life that dates back at least as far as Thomas Jefferson. In its classic form, the American dream was not imagined in an inner-city setting, but in that mythified "middle landscape" of suburban bliss somewhere beyond city limits. But among new immigrants, too—even those with a long history of urban living in the "old country"—a preference for the suburbs has proven strong; Jews and Italians in New York, for example, were among the earliest and most enthusiastic suburbanites in the postwar period, when entire neighborhoods of Brooklyn and Queens seemed to be relocating to Levittown and New Jersey. In fact, there were hard and real reasons for suburban white flight in the 1960s. American cities then were faced with a range of seemingly intractable socioeconomic problems. A decade of disinvestment had left their infrastructure in ruins; there were increasing racial tensions that often erupted into riots and violent protest. By the 1970s, crime and vandalism were out of control.

In China, there has been no rampant street crime to run from, nor any deep-rooted philosophy of antiurbanism to coax urban flight. The city in China has never been stigmatized the way American cities were in the postwar era. This is not to suggest that Chinese cities are entirely blissful; indeed, there are many serious negative aspects to urban living in China today. Chinese cities have been in an almost perpetual state of demolition and construction in recent decades; the air is terribly polluted and filled with flying grit and dust. Jackhammers drown out the few remaining songbirds. Traffic is congested, drivers universally rude, and housing exorbitantly expensive; and in some cities—especially in Guangdong Province—burglaries and street crime are on the rise. But even if the air is cleaner and there are more trees and open space on the suburban fringe, the city is still the star about which all things orbit, the political and administrative hub of the metropolitan universe.

Unlike American suburbs, those in China are literally *sub*-urban: that is, subordinate to the city. They are, in effect, little more than outlying neighborhoods of cities whose vast administrative limits reach far into the countryside. Far flung from the center of things, the quality and range of public services in Chinese suburbs tends to be poor, even if the housing is rich.[26] Suburban housing estates and villa developments are little islands of order and privilege in a transitional landscape neither urban nor rural. Many have homeowner associations, and the property management company typically contracts out a wide range of services—security, maintenance, groundskeeping—that makes life within the compounds pleasant indeed. But the comforts and conveniences do not extend beyond the gates. The outlying districts of Chinese cities are typically short on cultural or educational amenities and underserved by public transportation.

Compared to their Chinese analogues, suburbs in the United States might more accurately be termed "exurbs," for they are only nominally subordinate to their adjacent city and enjoy great political and fiscal autonomy. In the postwar boom years, American suburban communities flourished as their tax bases swelled with the arrival of millions of former urbanites. Businesses soon followed the money out of town, setting up shop in suburban malls. Economically, the city's loss was the suburbs' gain; one bled to nourish the other. In China, suburban development has not come at the expense of the city; if anything, both have profited. As Yixing Zhou and Laurence J. C. Ma point out, "No such devastating impact on the central city's tax revenues has resulted from suburbanization in China because suburbanization has taken place entirely within areas that are under the administrative jurisdiction of the cities themselves." Indeed, Chinese suburbanization "has occurred while the city center is undergoing dramatic positive spatial and economic transformations.... Instead of urban environmental decline, social conflict, and the shift of fiscal resources to the suburbs that American cities have experienced, cities and suburbs in China have been flourishing at the same time."[27] Of course, America's older urban centers have undergone a great renaissance in recent years, and urban living is certainly back in vogue—especially among the so-called creative class. But the legacy of the postwar shift of economic fortunes is with us still; affluent suburban communities like Suffolk County, Long Island, not older urban centers, are the ones that routinely dominate quality-of-life polls and "best places" rankings.

Many jobs have also migrated to the suburban fringe in Chinese cities, which is another departure from the American experience. In the initial phases of suburbanization in the United States—from the 1920s through the 1960s—most people continued to work in the city, commuting downtown from an outlying bedroom community. Only later did businesses and corporations themselves begin to decentralize, eventually yielding a more complex pattern of intraregional commutation from suburban home to a workplace in an office park or edge city business district. In China, housing and employment opportunities have developed more or less synchronously on the suburban frontier, as industry and tertiary-sector jobs once located in the center city have relocated to less expensive suburban quarters.[28]

While many Chinese suburbanites continue to commute to center-city jobs—by bus, van pool, taxi, or bicycle—an increasing number work in the suburbs themselves and commute to their jobs by automobile. Even families who thought they might make do with public transportation or employer-provided van service often discover that life in the suburbs is a lot more convenient with a car. Sooner or later, the suburban condition makes motorists out of most who can afford it. A 2005 postoccupancy survey of one of the Vanke company's popular housing estates in suburban Shanghai—Holiday Town—revealed that nearly 70 percent of responding households owned a car, with 100 percent of adult residents under age 60 reporting in the affirmative. The majority of residents also reported a commute length of 49 to 60 minutes.[29] And as more and more knowledge workers move to the suburbs and buy cars, the firms they work for are also pulling up center-city stakes and relocating to office space on the urban fringe, where there is quick access to the metropolitan arterial system and plenty of on-site parking.

For all its presumed conveniences, a car is a demanding servant. Acquiring an automobile in China fundamentally alters a person's lifestyle and tends to change where people dine, shop, play, study, and perhaps even work. To an even greater degree than in the United States, car ownership in China also changes a person's relationship to the built environment. For one, Chinese motorists will often avoid the city center because of traffic congestion and the scarcity of parking. In Shanghai, for example, there is already an estimated shortfall of more than 60,000 parking spaces in the center city, expected to climb to 120,000 spaces by 2010.[30]

Of course, plenty of suburban Americans avoid downtown for much the same reasons, but American cities have evolved with the automobile for decades now, and are relatively accommodating of motorists. Chinese cities, on the other hand, have only recently been inundated with cars and are terribly ill-equipped to handle their surging numbers. You bump into evidence of this everywhere, literally, for Chinese motorists often simply park on the sidewalk. Such incursions are tolerated, however inconvenient and dangerous, because there is a strong element of class entitlement associated with automobile ownership in China. Unlike in the United States (where even illegal immigrants have cars), automobile owners are assumed to be rich and powerful, and are thus permitted to push around mere bipeds.

The form and structure of the evolving Chinese suburban landscape is also markedly different from the American model. The archetypal suburb in the United States is low in density, with generous lot sizes and detached single-family homes. In some regions of the country—southern California, the southwest, and parts of the southeast—many upmarket suburban developments are of the "gated" variety, where access is strictly controlled and limited to residents and their guests. Chinese "villa" complexes (*bie shu qü*), strikingly similar to gated American McMansion-type developments, began appearing on the outskirts of major cities in the early 1990s.[31] But far more numerous in China are gated housing estates of clustered mid- to high-rise apartment buildings (*zhu zhai xiao qü*), which have become the basic unit of suburban sprawl in China. This is, of course, sprawl with Chinese characteristics—much denser and much more "urban" than anything in suburban America, and more in line with the European model of dense public housing estates on the urban fringe. This creates a curious hybrid form of sub-urbanism that is not quite urban nor fully suburban, at least as far as those terms have been defined in the United States.

Chinese suburban housing estates, as well as the less dense, more upmarket villa estates, are planned residential complexes that are as isolated from the larger landscape—and from each other—as were the Maoist *danwei* compounds. Among their notable features are plentiful parking, lavishly landscaped common areas, a formidable perimeter fence or wall (often with

David Bray points out luxury villas in an aerial photo of suburban Beijing at the
Beijing Urban Planning Exposition Hall, 2006. PHOTOGRAPH BY AUTHOR

electronic security or surveillance apparatus), and an entry gate and guard
booth staffed around the clock. Most housing estates include a comprehensive
range of on-site amenities. As David Bray notes, housing in the typical suburban estate "is integrated with communal facilities like kindergartens, clinics,
restaurants, convenience shops, sports facilities and communications infrastructure all under the control of a professional property management company."³² In this respect, too, housing estates bear a certain kinship to the
danwei complex. Of course, the typical housing estate is not connected to a
place of work, and there is little or no chance of employment on site. It is, notes
Bray, "a privatized realm that residents have bought their way into. Unlike the
danwei, to which people were assigned, residence in a *xiao qü* is determined
largely by choice and the ability to pay." More money not only "buys a bigger
apartment in a better-serviced compound," writes Bray, but "peace of mind and
a greater sense of security."³³

   In a metropolitan landscape undergoing convulsive social and physical
transformation, China's suburban housing estates are advertised—and generally perceived—as clean oases of order and tranquility. As crime rises in step
with yawning disparities between rich and poor, the issue of security and safety

Luxury housing in Dalian, 2006. PHOTOGRAPH BY AUTHOR

looms in the minds of many homebuyers. Freedom from fear in an increasingly risky world is indeed one of the key selling points for villas and housing estates. Sales brochures nearly all emphasize this point, using stock images of well-starched guards standing stiffly at attention or peering into closed-circuit TV monitors. Amenities for children are also high on the list. Families with children are the biggest consumers of suburban housing, according to studies by Vanke.[34] With playgrounds and open space far from traffic, twenty-four-hour security, and an extra room for the in-laws or a nanny, housing estates are indeed self-contained sanctuaries for raising a family.

This is another way American suburbs and their Chinese cousins differ: in terms of the relative balance of lifestyle-related amenities and attractions that are found within versus outside the immediate community. Most American subdivisions are little more than a clustering of private homes on a public street. Upscale developments, gated communities especially, may have a community center of some kind, or a common pool or playground facility. But only the best New Urbanist projects offer a range of on-location communal facilities anything like those of the typical Chinese suburban housing estate. When looking for a good place to live, American homebuyers take the pulse of the larger community—studying quality-of-life benchmarks such as the reputation of local schools, proximity to parks, and frequency and severity of crime. In China, homebuyers focus more on the housing estate itself. Amenities in the local area certainly add appeal—quick access to the road network is important, for example. But what really sells these places is the quality and range of amenities provided by the property management company on site and within the gates—gym, spa, banquet hall, child-care center, computer room, karaoke parlor, billiard room, pool, tennis courts, landscaped grounds, and so forth.

All this means that marketing suburban residential property in China is about selling a lifestyle, not just a home. More so than their American peers, Chinese homebuyers are acquiring an identity—buying into a particular image of reality—when they choose one estate over another. Given the extreme competition in the property market, developers have become highly inventive in pitching lifestyle, or at least skilled in copying ideas and motifs from elsewhere. Indeed, this market-driven eclecticism scours the globe in search of the unique and memorable, the romantic or sophisticated—anything that might give an alluring spin to a piece of real estate.

Doing so often involves, at the very least, using an English name for the development, which may or may not be a direct translation of its Chinese appellation, and often has nothing at all to do with the architecture or actual appearance of the place. It may even make no sense in English. But neither is it meant to be taken literally, for the use of English is primarily intended to telegraph a certain degree of worldly taste and sophistication—comparable to the pretension of spicing up one's talk with the occasional French phrase. As one Beijing journalist explained it, upscale villa and townhouse projects are aimed at "the white collar office worker and successful people. Their English is not bad. They are naturally fond of [English] terms. Those who cannot understand foreign languages generally respect foreign words. Therefore, developers do not waste their efforts on translating the jargon into Chinese." Indeed, doing so can be risky; the phonetic Chinese translation of "townhouse" in the local Beijing dialect, for example, yields *tang hao zhi*, which sounds enough like "townhouse" but literally means "mouse in the soup."[35]

Officialdom itself occasionally grumbles about the provenance of real-estate nomenclature; in the fall of 2004, for example, Shanghai authorities passed a regulation giving property developers one year to get rid of all names— English and Chinese—deemed "feudal, aristocratic, foreign and immoral"

嫡传贵胄，观达府邸
Inherit nobility, mansion of aristocrat

Billboard advertisement at construction site of luxury housing development, Nanjing, 2007.
PHOTOGRAPH BY AUTHOR

in the interest of "national dignity." The law was roundly ignored.[36] Morality aside, many names simply invoke aspects of the Starbucks lifestyle favored by the panglobal urban elite and are not necessarily keyed to a specific place or geography. In Beijing, the more memorably named of these housing estates include Latte Town, Glory Vogue, Yuppie International Garden, Wonderful Digital Jungle, and—cutting to the chase—Top Aristocrat.

Others estate names are more specific in terms of place, time, and geography. References to New York City became especially popular in Beijing in the 2000s. There, Forest Hills, Park Avenue, Central Park, MOMA, SOHO, and Upper East City are all names of upscale housing estates in the city or its suburban belt. "In Chinese culture," one young man put it to a *Newsday* reporter, "we don't have all these iconic names that symbolize prosperity. So we borrow."[37] Geographer Fulong Wu refers to these derivative environments as "transplanted cityscapes." Such mimicry is a strategy used by property developers and marketing consultants who "imagine globalization as a 'new way of life'" and try to capture some of its magic to give their product a competitive edge. In name, graphic identity, and architectural design, these projects "actively exploit the symbolism of globalization" as they attempt to sell a distinctive lifestyle to upwardly mobile urban elites. "To boost authenticity," writes Wu, "developers adopt various innovative measures including employing global architects, mimicking Western design motifs, naming the roads and buildings with famous foreign names that are familiar to the Chinese, and even forging a relationship of sister communities with foreign towns."[38]

A good example of this manic eclecticism is a 2005 magazine advertisement for an exclusive housing estate on the west side of Nanjing. The ad features a Photoshopped skyline dominated by such global architectural icons as Notre Dame Cathedral, the United States Capitol, skyscrapers of lower Manhattan, and London's Big Ben and Houses of Parliament. Looming in the foreground of this eclectic cityscape is the grill and Spirit of Ecstasy hood ornament of a Rolls-Royce Silver Seraph. The Chinese name of the development—*Hai De Wei Chen*—is itself a study in eclecticism, referring to both London's Hyde Park and the Acropolis in Athens, and yielding something else altogether in the somewhat muddled English translation provided by the project's marketing team— "Acropdis Park." Buried beneath all these symbols of global affluence is a sole, small picture of the housing estate itself, which looks nothing like either of the cityscapes invoked in its name.

Transplanted geographies are only one of a number of strategies used to distinguish residential projects, sell a lifestyle, and create a market edge. Another is green architecture and sustainability. In 1998 the central government set new standards for environmental and energy conservation, partly in response to the 1997 Conference on Climate Change in Kyoto, Japan. Following Kyoto, global warming and related issues gained popularity as the press gave them more airplay. Soon enough, property developers were promising "green living" and new proximity to nature at housing estates. Green World Garden, Greenery Villas, and Beautiful Garden—all in Shenzhen—are just several of many examples.

The nexus between lifestyle marketing, architecture, and urban design is even more intensely exploited by developers of single-family luxury villas. Ironically, despite their clear American provenance and often striking resemblance to McMansions, these villas have a much longer history in China than the more ubiquitous mid-rise residential housing estates. In Guangzhou, Tianjin, Qingdao, Shanghai, Nanjing, and other treaty ports, spacious "international residences" were built in the early decades of the twentieth century for diplomats, businessmen, and government officials. Like today's projects, these early villa developments typically featured "detached dwellings on curving streets, garages for private vehicles, latest interior appointments and eclectic stylistic references on the houses' exteriors."[39] The 1899 town development plan for the port of Qingdao, ceded to Germany two years before by the Qing government, established a villa quarter on the slopes of Bismarck Mountain above Huiquan Bay, with homes designed in the German neo-Renaissance style.[40]

In Nanjing, American architect Henry Murphy helped draft plans for a new Chinese capital in 1929, and his proposals included at least one suburban district with Chinese-style villas, possibly modeled on an earlier residential project he laid out in Coral Gables, Florida.[41] While that particular scheme was never realized, a similar community of luxury homes, known as Yi He Lu, was built in Nanjing west of the Drum Tower on Beijing Road. Home to diplomats and ranking officials in both the National and Mao periods, Yi He Lu remains one of Nanjing's most gracious neighborhoods, thickly shaded by plane trees. Shanghai had several such villa and townhouse districts, the best of which were the work of Czech-Hungarian architect Laszlo Hudec. In 1930 Hudec, who later designed Shanghai's famed Park Hotel, laid out a subdivision for affluent Chinese businessmen known as Great Western Road Circle. This was followed two years later by a more ambitious project in the city's western suburbs, Columbia Circle. The brainchild of an American engineer-turned-developer named Frank J. Raven, Columbia was promoted as "an estate designed for garden homes" that combined "city conveniences with suburban comforts." Columbia Circle's suite of house styles was inspired by the vernacular architecture of France, Italy, and the English countryside, and, especially, the United States, which was represented by such finishing options as "San Clemente, California, Colonial, Florida, San Diego and Hollywood."[42]

Projects like Columbia Circle foreshadowed the stylistic eclecticism of Chinese villa design in the 1990s. The rush to gain an edge in a brutally competitive real-estate market has left virtually no architectural style, historical epoch, or geography unplundered—an enterprise vastly aided by such tools as digital photography, Photoshop, and the world wide web. A Shanghai development from the early 1990s, Wonderland Villas, used the famous live oak allée at Oak Alley Plantation in Vacherie, Louisiana, on the front cover of its sales brochure. In the Pearl River Delta, a highway billboard advertising Majesty Manor Villas, seen on the outskirts of Guangzhou in the late 1990s, was graced with a much-enlarged image of a New England village, complete with whitewashed church steeple and town green. Another development from this period, the Yuanming Yuan Garden Villas near Beijing's Summer Palace, offered stylistic confections ranging from Georgian Revival to Victorian, the pièce de résistance being a half-scale replica of the White House in Washington DC. The backdrops for the Yuanming Yuan homes in the sales brochure were even more random, and included a Maine forest scene in autumn, a palm-fringed golf course, and (yet another) plantation. Backdrops and buildings from opposite ends of the United States were thus digitally fused into a single seamless fantasy.

The developers of Rose Garden Villas, another Beijing project from the early 1990s, took this hectic eclecticism to the stars—literally. Developed by a businessman who made a fortune selling tonic for balding men, Rose Garden offered five home styles, each in a neighborhood "zone" of similar buildings set about a like-designed community center. The first four were straightforward enough—Northern European, Mediterranean, Japanese, and American (with a community center designed to resemble a Spanish colonial church). The fifth, however, was called "Outer Space," and featured spaceship-like homes reminiscent of the bright red *folie* at Parc de la Villette in Paris. As one project manager explained, the celestial homes were meant to appeal to youthful movers and shakers with a "space-age kind of outlook."[43] Far more common in the 1990s was the florid European "Continental style" (*ou lu feng*)—a variety of wedding-cake neo-Baroque architecture that is also well represented in Bangkok, Seoul, and Staten Island. The Continental style in China was especially popular between 1993 and 2001 and was meant to convey an air of wealth and taste. It has been applied to everything from five-star hotels to rural gas stations and remains still very much in use today for villas and housing estates.

The image-making and marketing savvy of villa developers has become much more sophisticated in recent years, and so has the architecture. Clean-lined modernist villas, some with truly innovative designs, have begun to make a mark, especially at higher price points. Perhaps best known is a project by SOHO known as "Commune by the Great Wall," where some of the leading young architects in Asia were commissioned to design a compelling array of homes nestled below the Great Wall north of Beijing. There are also now many more villa developments that feature traditional Chinese architectural themes. In the early 1990s, Hong Kong architect Nelsen Chen designed a villa community in Suzhou inspired by the region's unique vernacular

Billboard advertisement for a Continental-style villa estate in Nanjing, 2006.

PHOTOGRAPH BY AUTHOR

architecture, but the project was largely ignored at the time by homebuyers who felt the buildings looked "too old." A decade later, neotraditional Chinese developments have become popular with both local and overseas Chinese. The popular Cathay View Villas in Beijing is modeled on local *siheyuan*, while Tian Lun Sui Yuan in suburban Suzhou looks to the canal-laced local vernacular (in something of a reach, a second Tian Lun project used the same south China style for a development north of Beijing, a bit like erecting Spanish colonial homes in northern New Hampshire). One of Vanke's newest developments in Shenzhen, the Fifth Garden (Di Wu Yuan), also looks to regional Chinese building traditions for inspiration.

But the focus on foreign styles has also not abated; market research in 2003 found that 70 percent of property developments in Beijing at the time emphasized Western geographies and architectural motifs.[44] For every neotraditional Chinese villa there are a dozen projects like Roman Vision in Nanjing, Germany Villas in Suzhou, or Shanghai Czech Quarter, with its "Independent Garden Villas of Czech Style." Vancouver Forest in Beijing has craftsman bungalows mixed with Georgian, Tudor, and Prairie-style homes (in kindred north-woods spirit, another Beijing company offers custom-built log cabin villas).

New luxury homes at Cambridge Impression gated community, Wuxi, 2006.
PHOTOGRAPH BY AUTHOR

In Wuxi, a city in the Yangtse Delta at the north end of Taihu (Tai Lake), there is Cambridge Impression. One of several billboards advertising the project featured an array of black granite stones inscribed with names of Cantabrigian luminaries past and present: Wordsworth, Milton, Newton, Byron, Bacon, Wittgenstein, Darwin, Keynes, Hawking. Another displayed an aerial view of the finished product—a fragment of faux Britannia in the People's Republic. When I toured the project site in late 2006, construction was well underway; an English church steeple rose above a huddle of Tudor-style townhouses and mansions, still latticed with scaffolding. At the entrance of the "Sample District of British Lifestyle," a carefully positioned perspective rendering of the town flowed seamlessly to the completed buildings nearby—creating an optical illusion of an ersatz reality. Another billboard, with a flowery garden scene and English wrought iron furniture, carried the startling exhortation "TEA TIME, NOT KILL TIME."

References to high tea and English towns are exceptional. More common are villa projects that evoke sun-splashed geographies around the world. There is Sydney Coast in Beijing, where residents can enjoy a "seven-day Australian-style villa life."[45] Rancho Santa Fe is in Shanghai, in spite of its

Billboard advertisement for a Spanish colonial villa development, Nanjing, 2007.
PHOTOGRAPH BY AUTHOR

name. Mid-Mountain Acropolis in suburban Chengdu enables living "in the Mediterranean style," while nearby Vanilla Lake Town Houses urges "Let Us Return To Miami In A Dream." Property developers have been especially keen on the "Southern Californian" (Nan Jia Zhou) lifestyle spin. Affluent professionals can now "Live a Palm Springs Life" on Chongqing's north side, or tour California craftsman-style bungalows at nearby Burlington Town (the developer's website plays "Hotel California" in the background). Nansha Garden, an exclusive villa estate in the Pearl River Delta, makes it possible to "experience the seaside life of Southern California in America" while only a seventy-minute commute from Guangzhou. An earlier project in Huizhou, Regent-on-the-Park, offered "California" style homes for "free-spirited, independent people." Napa Valley and Yosemite are villa estates on the outskirts of Beijing, and not far away is Orange County (Ju Jun), a compelling simulacrum of both California culture and an American gated community. The idea for Orange County came to its developer, Zhang Bo, during a 1998 tour of California that included a drive around the original Orange County. Correctly surmising that the area's upscale Mediterranean-style homes would appeal to Beijing's nouveau riche, Zhang decided to import a subdivision's worth of the homes.[46]

Billboard advertisement for a Southern California–style villa community, Guangdong Province, 2006.

PHOTOGRAPH BY AUTHOR

The Chinese Orange County is an authentic knockoff indeed. It was laid out by the Newport Beach architectural firm Bassenian Lagoni, whose founder, Aram Bassenian, built a career designing production-model houses for tract builders around the United States. Bassenian, no mean emulator himself, spent years importing vernacular architectural motifs from Tuscany to Southern California. "In his 36 years as a production architect," writes June Fletcher, "Mr. Bassenian has borrowed plenty from that rural Italian style, inspired by frequent trips overseas, and has popularized stacked stone turrets, rough-hewn beams and waxed fieldstone floors in attached and detached homes."[47] Imported from Tuscany to the Golden State, Bassenian's Italianate aesthetic was then transposed to Beijing, making Orange County a true poster child for global culture. And while American homeowners buy China-made products at home-improvement stores, nearly all the materials used to decorate Orange County's homes were shipped from the United States—including American tile, wood siding, and wall sconces.

Zhang Bo's tour of America also involved a careful study of McMansions around the United States. This enabled him to provide a suite of upscale amenities unheard of in China until then, from basement poolrooms to outdoor barbeque consoles. The overall effect is convincing indeed. As the *Los Angeles Times* reported, "The interior of one model home looks like it was ripped from a Pottery Barn catalog. On the shelves are volumes of Encyclopedia Britannica and novels by Tom Clancy, James Michener and Judy Blume. A framed photo shows a couple laughing on their wedding day. Another is of Andy Griffith with Opie by his side. In the recreation room, the board game Sorry lies open on a table." On opening day, guests toured model homes while enjoying McDonald's cheeseburgers.[48]

Villa estates like Orange County afford residents a lifestyle not only light-years removed from that of nearby rural residents, but even from most city people. Theirs is a close approximation indeed of the lifestyle enjoyed by residents of the upscale gated McMansion communities that became popular in the United States in the 1980s. Residents of China's villa complexes nearly all have cars, and often several. They drive to work and drive their children to school in the morning. They shop at supermarkets with spacious parking lots and at suburban big-box stores like Wal-Mart, Carrefour, IKEA, Metro, and B&Q—the British home-improvement chain that has become China's answer to Home Depot. On weekends the family may load into the car and head to a local amusement park, theme park, or sports facility to watch their child's soccer match, and end the day with dinner at a suburban restaurant, or at McDonald's or KFC. Often such outings include three generations of family members, as in-laws frequently reside with their children and grandchildren.

A friend of mine in Beijing, an architect with whom I studied at Tsinghua University several years before, described to me with pride and satisfaction his life in the Chinese capital in the late 1990s. He and his wife had recently purchased a home beyond the city's third ring road. Soon they realized that one car was not enough to meet their commuting needs, so they purchased another one and now they were both driving to work. On weekends they used the cars to do the week's grocery shopping. Or she would take one car to meet with her girlfriends for lunch while he packed his radio-control model airplanes in the other vehicle and headed to his club's suburban flying field. What he described for me could well have been an account of suburban life in Phoenix or Atlanta or San Diego.

Of course, we love to parody and ridicule the auto-centric, suburban lifestyle here in the United States; and in China, too, its manifold ironies and contradictions have been critiqued with merriment. A series of cartoons

別墅误读之四——**大工业流水线式**（如果都是 copy 而来，别墅与公寓又有何区别呢）

"The Industrial Production Line," cartoon commentary on the Chinese suburban condition.
COURTESY OF *MARKET WEEKLY* MAGAZINE (AUGUST 2003)

published in a 2003 issue of *Market Weekly* (*Shi Chang*), a real estate magazine, is a case in point. One cartoon, entitled "Frog in a Well" (Jing Di Wa), commented on the social isolation of suburban life: two old classmates, now successful businessmen, run into each other on their commute home; caught up in reminiscing, they suddenly realize they are home and are in fact next-door neighbors in the same isolating complex of single-family villas. Another pokes fun at the opulence of villa architecture: a weary business traveler ambles into a resplendent McMansion thinking it is a hotel, only to be swiftly ejected by the outraged homeowners. In a third, entitled "The Industrial Production Line" (Da Gong Ye Liu Shui Xian), an elderly grandfather makes his way home in a villa subdivision; he has forgotten the address—No. 23— before, and so now mutters it to himself as he searches among the identical homes. Nonetheless, the gentleman ends up in No. 32, bursting in on a couple in flagrante delicto.[49] In a final cartoon, a suburban couple drives from their home to spend a relaxing afternoon in the city, only to encounter so much traffic that the pedestrians all around are moving faster than they. Exasperated, they finally get out of their expensive sedan and carry it into town.

CHAPTER EIGHT

Driving the Capitalist Road

行駛在資本主義大道上

The spatial order of China's emerging suburban landscapes is fundamentally and unapologetically oriented toward the motor vehicle, and this is helping drive a boom in automobility unlike anything in the world since America became a nation of motorists in the 1950s. As we have seen, the expanding metropolitan footprint encourages automobile use, which also fuels and is fueled by extensive highway construction. Abetting Chinese sprawl is much the same vicious cycle of road building that engulfed American cities decades ago: a highway is built to ease congestion, but the new facility only ends up encouraging that many more motorists to drive. Soon the new road is also congested, which of course leads to a new round of proposed highways. It's the urban transportation equivalent of a dog chasing its own tail.

Given that automobile ownership is also encouraged by the central government as a means of stoking GDP, it is hardly surprising that China has become the fastest-growing car market in the world. Despite the relatively high costs of ownership and maintenance, a car is the ultimate consumer dream today for millions of Chinese, and few things confer prestige as surely as a new luxury sedan. A twenty-city survey in the late 1990s by the Association of Chinese Customers found that one out of three urban families planned to purchase a car within the next three years (doing so became easier in October 1998, when the Construction Bank of China began offering the nation's first auto loans)[1]; another survey established that driving a car ranked along with English language proficiency and facility with a computer as the top three "basic and necessary skills in modern Chinese society."[2]

But convenience, status, and prestige do not fully explain the car's surging appeal in China. As any American teenager will tell you, an automobile

Elevated highway, Nanjing, 2006. PHOTOGRAPH BY AUTHOR

also represents freedom and independence. In a society where travel was once highly restricted and much of life circumscribed by the state, driving your own car—wherever and whenever you wish—offers a compelling sense of agency and self-determination. As one forty-something driver put it to a *China Daily* reporter, "Sitting behind the wheel, your body, your spirit feels like they're flying, and you have control of everything except the toll fee."[3] It may well be that the car is a kind of placebo for freedoms yet ungained in China. An automobile also provides a luxurious measure of privacy and personal space. In China, where even affluent families make do with dwelling space a fraction of the size of the average American home, an automobile is a piece of real estate as well as a means of getting about town. The modern sedan is also a well-appointed cocoon—climate-controlled, sealed off from the noise and pollution of the street, and often equipped with a sound system better than the one at home. All this suggests a point often overlooked in lamentations on commuting: many people in fact relish their drive to work, which may also be the only time all day they have to themselves.

Whatever the reason, this much is clear: China is going mobile with abandon. In 2005 the People's Republic surpassed Germany to become the third largest auto manufacturer in the world. That year some 5.92 million new vehicles were sold in China, more than double the number of sales in 2001 (2.73 million). Passenger vehicle sales in 2006 jumped by another 30 percent over the previous year (in contrast, passenger car sales in the United States, a saturated market, have been declining steadily since 1999). China's domestic motor vehicle market now ranks ahead of Japan's and is second in size only to that of the United States.[4] Industry analysts forecast that by 2020 China may be the largest producer and consumer of cars on earth, with total car ownership exceeding even than of America.[5]

Most of the new cars in China are where the money is: in and around the major coastal cities. Between 1990 and 2003, for example, the number of motor vehicles in Shanghai climbed from 212,000 to 1.2 million.[6] Beijing passed the million-car mark in the spring of 2002, when more than 1,000 new cars were being added to the city's roads each day; by October 2006, there were an estimated 2.7 million cars in the capital, reflecting an annual surge of some 15 percent.[7] The biennial Beijing Auto Show is one of the most popular events in the city. A record 550,000 people attended the ten-day exhibition in November 2006, with another 50,000 visiting a related auto-parts show

nearby. Beijing Goldenport Motor Park, located in the capital's northeast suburbs, is China's "first multi-functional, comprehensive auto theme park." In
2004 Goldenport hosted an "Automobile Culture and Fashion Week" to introduce would-be motorists to all aspects of car culture. The park boasts China's
largest drive-in cinema, an auto shopping mall, and, for those with pent-up
road rage, a pay-per-lap Formula Three track on which drivers can race against
each other in their own vehicles.

China's motoring boom is also evident in extensive suburban "auto-miles"
like those in American cities, as well as more uniquely Chinese "automobile
city" megamalls (*qi che cheng*). These temples of car culture are perhaps the
most telling harbingers of the Chinese motoring revolution underway, and
they are like nothing in North America. In the United States, car dealerships
typically only display a handful of top models in an interior showroom; most
are on the lot outside. This is rarely the case in China, due in part to the high
cost of vehicles but also because the heavily polluted air in most cities quickly
covers anything left outside with a layer of grit and grime (utility trucks, on the
other hand, are usually sold off open lots). One of the largest of these interior
motor malls is Hangzhou Automobile City, which opened on the outskirts of
the Zhejiang provincial capital in 2004. Its immense gull-winged roof covers
thirty-two acres of showroom floor, equal in area to two dozen American football fields. Automobile City sells half of the cars bought annually in the greater
Hangzhou area. The mall's manager told me in July 2005 that in the preceding
six months they had sold 30,000 automobiles, the majority to young professional women, who typically purchase a Chevy Spark, Chery QQ, Volkswagen
Beetle, or other *nu che*—"woman's car."[8]

But a trip to the motor megamall is hardly needed to understand China's
infatuation with all things auto. The car has pervaded nearly every corner of
cultural production—from TV shows and billboard advertisements to dozens of glossy motoring magazines and tea-table folios like *Appreciation of World
Famous Autos* and *Family Sedans Tempt China*.[9] In the 1990s road-trekking
auto clubs became the rage and driver education academies began opening all over China; one was even the setting of a popular 1996 movie—*Signal
Left, Turn Right* (*Da Zuo Deng, Xiang You Zhuan*), Huang Jianxin's brilliant sat-
ire about contemporary Chinese society. The Beijing Longquan Driver Training
Center trains some 22,000 students a year on a sprawling fifty-two–acre campus. The even larger Haidian School, in the suburbs northwest of the city,

Brochure illustration for Hangzhou Automobile City, 2004.

had 500 instructors on staff in the late 1990s (one boasted to a reporter, "I've trained many killers!"). Between January and April 2002, more than 90,000 would-be Beijing motorists, many of them graduates of driving academies, sat for their driver's-license exam.[10] A popular radio program launched in Beijing in the 1990s advised motorists on the ins and outs of owning and operating a car in the capital. Originally hosted by Wang Liang, the program was a kind of sinofied version of NPR's *Car Talk*—"all cars, all day on AM 92.7."[11]

Not surprisingly, China's automobile boom has come at the expense of other, greener forms of transportation. Bicycles may still be the vehicle of choice for millions of city folk, but they are increasingly shunted aside to make way for all the cars. There were an estimated 540 million bicycles in China in the 1990s—that's two for every person living in the United States. Beijing, with eleven million bikes in 2001, had more than any city on earth. At the outset of the reform era Deng Xiaoping even famously promised "a Flying Pigeon in every household"—a reference to the venerable Chinese bicycle brand Feige.[12] But today bicycles—and the popular battery-powered "e-bikes"—are banned on major thoroughfares in Shanghai, Beijing, and other cities, and new roads are often laid out without the generous bike lanes that have long

"No Bicycle," Dalian, Xinghai District, 2006 (Dalian World Expo and Convention Center in background).
PHOTOGRAPH BY AUTHOR

distinguished Chinese streetscapes. Guangzhou authorities even attempted an outright ban on bicycles in the center city in the 1990s, but outraged residents turned the measure back. Shanghai officials also toyed with a center-city all-bike ban that was to take effect by 2010, though wisdom prevailed there, too; transportation experts were able to convince authorities that such a ban would only increase traffic congestion as more people took cars and taxis.[13] More recently, Guangzhou enacted a ban on motorcycles, ostensibly to reduce traffic congestion and improve air quality; in reality it was more about keeping up appearances—the machines are popular with poor migrant workers and associated with thieves and criminal gangs.[14]

But bike bans are hardly necessary; the number of bicyclists in Chinese cities has plummeted in recent years—dropping by 26 percent between 2001 and 2006. This is partly because more people are driving, but also because the growing number of cars makes cycling more difficult and dangerous. Most amateur motorists in Chinese cities (and many professionals) are relatively new to the road and often lack basic driving skills. Moreover, a culture of courtesy and etiquette—especially toward nonmotorists—has yet to form in China, to put it kindly. Chinese drivers rarely give way to pedestrians in a crosswalk, for example. Drivers will often push their way through a crowded intersection, with most pedestrians hustling passively out of the way. In New York or Boston such rudeness would result in a fight or a broken windshield. Each year, thousands of Chinese cyclists are killed or maimed by automobiles; injuries are often terrible, as bicyclists almost never wear helmets. Fully one-third of the estimated 83,000 traffic fatalities in China in 2000 involved bicyclists.[15]

Image is also contributing to the bicycle's demise. For many Chinese, the bicycle is an antiquated relic and a symbol of poverty and underdevelopment— the antithesis of its image in the West as an icon of sustainability and physical fitness. As one Beijing cabbie put it to a reporter from the *Washington Post*: "What kind of country would we be if we were all still riding bicycles? This is progress. This is development....Who wants to ride a bicycle when you can drive a car."[16] Precisely the opposite set of questions is asked these days in Chapel Hill, Cambridge, and other progressive communities.

A car is only as useful as the roads available to it, and toward that end China has launched the greatest road-building campaign since the American Interstate Highway System. Even into the late 1980s, China's highway system consisted of less than 200 miles of modern high-speed, limited-access motorway; by 2006 the National Trunk Highway System spanned 25,480 miles, making it second in length only to that of the American interstates. The pace of construction is also nearly that of the American interstate construction program at its peak, when some 41,000 miles were built between 1957 and 1969; China's highway mileage more than doubled between 2001 and 2005, extending the system by 15,350 miles in four years.[17] Transportation planners have promised to plug every major Chinese city into this system by 2010, and it is estimated that by 2020 China's National Trunk Highway System will include 53,000 miles of modern highway, besting by a long shot the American Interstate Highway System (currently about 46,800 miles) and thus stealing its title as "the greatest and the longest engineered structure ever built."[18] A good portion of this network will consist of urban expressways, which have been laced about and around every major city, none more visibly so than Beijing, whose multiplying ring roads have turned it into a kind of Los Angeles in concentric form.

In the United States we have come to regard large-scale urban arterials as destroyers of communities—and for good reason. In China, many more people's lives have been disrupted or destroyed by such road projects, yet highways, elevated expressways, even flyovers and cloverleaf interchanges, are widely hailed as icons of progress and modernity. Popular full-color folios are often published to celebrate a new piece of infrastructure. One such book, *Bridges of the Century*, was published in 1994 to commemorate completion of the first two spans across the Huangpu River between Shanghai and Pudong—to "eulogize the selfless devotion of the bridge builders" much the way the builders of the Brooklyn Bridge were cheered in 1888. Another, *Highway Interchanges of Beijing*, is filled with two-page photo spreads featuring cloverleaf intersections on the capital's outer ring roads. These arterial appliances are indeed strikingly beautiful, and often artfully landscaped. A hefty tome published in advance of the fiftieth anniversary of the People's Republic of China in October 1999— *Tremendous Changes in the Ancient Capital*—offers a visual record of Beijing's half-century metamorphosis into a "comprehensive metropolis" and features flattering aerial photos of the city's eight-lane ring roads and interchanges. Yet another tea-table tome, *Marvelous Ways in the West*, commemorates highway building in Tibet and China's remote western provinces. These books are not specialized trade publications, but the equivalent of American gift books celebrating, say, Cape Hatteras, puppies, or a New England autumn.

Of course, Americans went through a similar phase of infrastructure worship in the past; the United States was, after all, the first society to be smitten with motoring. A quick perusal of eBay will reveal numerous vintage souvenir books, pamphlets, postcards, pennants, ashtrays, dinner plates, shot glasses, beer steins, and tumblers commemorating the Pennsylvania Turnpike, New Jersey Turnpike, Verrazano-Narrows Bridge, and other landmarks of American motoring. Even if the United States was not alone in developing the automobile, it was the first nation to build them fast and cheap, and to transform its very culture and identity to accommodate the new machine. And in China, too, Americans helped set the stage for the current motoring revolution. Detroit swooned over the possibilities of the China market more than a century ago— a "virgin field," one writer put it, that "should absorb in years to come all the automobiles that America and other countries produce over and above their own actual needs."[19] As early as 1913, the *New York Times* reported that "on any pleasant day" in Shanghai, "you meet mandarins and merchants with their families, behind well-groomed chauffeurs, enjoying themselves exactly like prosperous Americans."[20] Americans stole the show at China's first automobile exhibition, held in a series of bamboo sheds in Shanghai in 1921 where half the vehicles on display were from the United States.[21] As industry analyst William Irvine observed in 1923, the Chinese "no longer regard the automotive vehicle as a foreign freak fit only for the use of the white man" and promised that the "propagation of the automotive idea has borne and will continue to bear fruit" for Americans.[22]

It would bear fruit for China, too. Sun Yat-sen considered development of a domestic automobile industry essential to China's growth. In a 1924 letter to Henry Ford, Sun commended the Michigan industrialist on his "remarkable work" putting Americans on the road and encouraged him to do the same in the Orient: "I think you can do similar work in China," wrote Sun, "on a much vaster and more significant scale."[23] Though he never responded to Sun's missive, Ford was keen on China, too, and that year hosted a visit by China's trade commissioner, Chang Chien Jr., who gave a speech—in Chinese—to a large group of Ford's Chinese service trainees then in residence at the Highland Park plant. Chien predicted an extraordinary future for motoring in China: "More than 100,000,000 automobiles, or five times the present world total," he noted, "would be required to provide China's 400,000,000 people with the same ratio of cars as Iowa."[24]

American automobiles quickly dominated the China market and by 1922 accounted for 95 percent of all motor vehicles imported to north China and 75 percent of sales in Shanghai. By the 1930s, American vehicles were outselling British models by a factor of ten, in spite of clear British advantages. The English custom of driving on the left side of the road, for example, had been introduced in China through the treaty ports, and gave British automakers an edge over the Americans, who were forced to retrofit their vehicles for the China market.[25] Even the British Chamber of Commerce in Shanghai had to concede that "one only has to walk the streets of this city to see the undeniable predominance of the American car."[26] Detroit simply offered a better product—lighter and less expensive than British vehicles, and also sturdier and more powerful.

The pole position of Yankee automakers was also the result of creative marketing. American salesmen drove their cars up the ramps of Beijing's city walls and dispatched convoys to remote corners of China. "As this always calls for journeys over almost impassable roads or where roads do not exist," wrote Irvine, "it affords a fine advertisement of the ability of the cars."[27] Hewlett Johnson reported that even in Xi'an, still a remote city in the 1930s,

American auto dealers were "straining every nerve to gain a footing." He was also surprised to encounter a team of U.S. car salesmen in Tibet, an "expedition of adventurous young men" drumming up publicity for the Dodge Motor Company.[28]

Though Americans were also at the forefront of the Good Roads movement in China and helped build some of China's first modern motorways, China in fact had developed an advanced road system many centuries before. An office of road construction was established during the Zhou Dynasty, as early as 1129 BC, which developed a five-part hierarchy of arterials—from horse trails and cart paths to chariot roads. Evidence from the *Guo Yu* (Discourse of the States), written during the Warring States period (475–221 BC), indicates that many of these early roads were planted with shade trees. After unifying China in 221 BC, the emperor Qin Shi Huang (also known as Shi Huangdi), later buried with the famed terracotta army, built roads from his capital at Xianyang, just north of present-day Xi'an, to Beijing, Guangzhou, Chengdu, and other cities; many of these Qin-era routes were shaded by pine trees planted at thirty-foot intervals. These early roads were later widened and improved for military use, and during the Yuan Dynasty, China's Mongol rulers repaired and upgraded some 2,000 miles of royal arterials. But by the late Ming period, many of these "splendid old imperial highways" had fallen into ruin, as Viola Smith and Anselm Chuh put it in 1931, "until to-day a bit of causeway and a half-hidden stone pavement are all that remain."[29]

By the early years of the twentieth century, there were few automobile-accessible roads in China outside of the treaty ports. American industry analysts understood that if China's automobile market was to be maximized, good roads would have to be built quickly. But there were also altruistic reasons why the United States helped China build a modern highway infrastructure. To facilitate shipment of food and medical supplies to famine-struck regions of Shandong, Henan, Hebei, and Shanxi provinces in 1920, the American Red Cross oversaw the construction of nearly 1,000 miles of simple tamped-earth motor roads. Tens of thousands of laborers were employed on these works, which were credited with significantly reducing mortality due to the famine.[30]

The man who directed much of the Red Cross relief work was another Michigan native, Oliver J. Todd, a civil engineer who had earlier helped build the Hetch Hetchy Dam in the Sierra Nevada mountains and the Twin Peaks Tunnel in San Francisco. Todd spent a total of eighteen years in China and supervised the construction of some 3,000 miles of motor roads in four-teen provinces. Not all these roads were in rural areas. In Guiyang, capital of Guizhou Province, Todd engineered an eight-mile loop road around the city in 1926, which was then built by soldiers and "all able-bodied students over the age of fourteen" in town (the boys worked one week, the girls the next). The motorway became the city's pride and joy. Ahead of opening day, a brand-new American sedan was hauled in pieces across the mountains from Guangzhou; reassembled in town, the car was paraded about by the provincial governor while 10,000 local troops and a military band serenaded Todd, the guest of honor, with a rendition of "Swanee River" and the "The Red, White and Blue."[31]

Todd's roads were primitive by today's standards, but they were a vast improvement upon existing conditions. "By tamping and rolling the damp earth as it was thrown up in 6-in. layers," Todd recounted, "new roads were made hard enough for immediate use so that autos could traverse them at 30 miles an hour."[32] Todd saw the motorways as modernizing agents, essential to China's economic development and the spread of stable government. As Jonathan Spence has written, Todd hoped "that one day trucks would roar down them, carrying grain and rice to stricken areas, while the private cars of officials and merchants would speed by with the promises of fairer administration and wider trade."[33] Of course, it is likely that Todd had American commercial interests in mind as well. After all, he was a Michigan boy, and he could only have been pleased to see his state's native industry flourishing in China: "American autos are being brought in to be used on these roads," he observed with approval; "American mining machinery will follow as will a hundred other things American."[34] Todd himself proposed a "Michigan in China" program to train young Chinese road builders—a "school in the field," as he described it, "mobile and highly practical."[35] He later handed supervision of a 350-mile road from Guiyang to Changsha to a Chinese assistant engineer who had studied at the Ford plant, and who in turn trained eighty cadet engineers—China's next generation of road builders.[36]

Todd's roads brought the ancient Chinese imperial road system into the twentieth century and became "a nucleus on which more roads have been built," as Todd put it in 1926.[37] The expanding network of motorways was cheered by the Good Roads Association of China, launched in Shanghai in 1920. The association advocated widening city streets and replacing old

stone cobbles with smooth concrete, and also urged that "all the city walls...
be demolished to construct loop highways." Led by Shanghai physician C. T.
Wang, the association formulated a development program that included "a triangle of roads" linking Shanghai to Suzhou and Hangzhou and eventually
Nanjing, where even more innovative road building efforts were underway.[38]

There, American city planner E. P. Goodrich introduced to China an influential early American road—the Bronx River Parkway. Goodrich, a founder of
the American Institute of Planners, was retained by the Nationalist government in the late 1920s to help make Nanjing "the most beautiful and the most
scientifically planned capital in the world."[39] Among other things, Goodrich
proposed building a scenic motor route around the city modeled on the
recently completed parkway in Westchester County, New York. That seminal
route, the first modern highway in the world, was designed by landscape architects Hermann W. Merkel and Gilmore D. Clarke and completed in 1925. In
China, Goodrich proposed using a variety of "Oriental landscape adaptations"
to adapt the road to its new culture, which included placing "pagodas and
gate houses at intervals along the way, with the beautiful bamboo trees which
the Chinese highly esteem." As with the Bronx River Parkway, the Nanjing
road was meant to be the start of a metropolitan system of parks and parkways. Nanjing officials requested copies of the Westchester Park Commission's
annual reports, and later sent the city's chief engineer to personally tour the
Westchester roads.[40]

The fact that today China drives on the right side of the road is also the legacy of an American—a U.S. Army general named Albert C. Wedemeyer, whom
President Franklin D. Roosevelt chose to replace Joseph Stilwell as commander
of the China theater in 1944. Wedemeyer's main task was to advise Chiang
Kai-shek in driving the Japanese out of China. Toward this end he drafted an
offensive, code-named "Carbonado," to culminate in the liberation of Hong
Kong and the south China coast. Carbonado was a massive operation and
required marshalling two full divisions of American-trained Chinese troops
airlifted from Burma. Thousands of men and vehicles had to be moved south
from Sichuan Province toward the Pearl River Delta, a 700-mile trek. To support their China operations, the Americans had brought in American-made
jeeps and other vehicles, but because traffic in China at the time moved to the
left, thanks to the British, the American vehicles were in effect being driven
on the wrong side of the road. So many traffic accidents occurred in bringing

supplies to the front that the Army launched a driver-education program for the troops, to little effect.[41]

Wedemeyer then determined that more drastic measures were necessary. If the vehicles themselves could not be easily retrofitted, why not just change the traffic pattern? Wedemeyer proposed to Chiang Kai-shek that, simply, "all traffic in China be transferred to the right side of the road." The generalissimo approved, and Wedemeyer ordered a publicity campaign in the spring of 1945. "Posters were placed on telephone poles and shop windows," Wedemeyer recalled in his memoirs, "showing diagrammatically how traffic would move and giving instructions to pedestrians in order to minimize accidents. Articles were published in newspapers throughout the country." But there was resistance. Shortly after the plans were announced, Wedemeyer learned that "articles were appearing in the vernacular press strongly criticizing the idea of breaking an old Chinese tradition and urging the Generalissimo to reconsider and uphold the old and the tried method of moving traffic."[42]

At first these appeared to be innocuous, but Wedemeyer was suspicious. He ordered an intelligence officer to investigate the source of the articles, which was traced to none other than the British Embassy. The British were certain Wedemeyer was surreptitiously paving the way for another kind of invasion—an invasion of American automobiles. Nonetheless, the new traffic law went ahead as planned, even after the Japanese surrendered and Carbonado was called off. On New Year's Eve 1945, Wedemeyer "had the thrilling experience of standing on the balcony of my tower apartment in the Cathay Hotel in Shanghai," as he later wrote, "to watch the traffic at midnight change over to move along the right side of the road." When Mao and the Communists took control of China several years later, they retained the new traffic pattern, which had the added convenience of also being the pattern used by the Soviet Union.[43]

★   ★   ★

The Guangzhou-Shenzhen, or Guangshen, Expressway (GSE), one of the first and most influential modern highways in the People's Republic, is itself a product of American prototypes.[44] The road was the brainchild of Hong Kong developer Gordon Y. S. Wu. As he was born into a family that operated the largest taxi fleet in Hong Kong, it was perhaps inevitable that Wu would one day help put China on the road. But Wu discovered his vocation half a world away, as an engineering student at Princeton University in the 1950s. Wu was particularly fascinated with a new highway that passed about ten miles east of campus, the New Jersey Turnpike. The road, running 118 miles from the Delaware River to the George Washington Bridge, was not yet the butt of Jersey jokes, or a symbol of America's overreliance on the automobile. Rather, it was hailed as a land-mark of the motor age and a masterpiece of engineering. Even the road's steel overpasses—all 400 of them—used state-of-the-art structural techniques. New Jersey's governor, Alfred E. Driscoll, called the turnpike "the finest high-way in the world."[45] Indeed, the road set standards that would be applied to interstate highways for decades—from the width and curve radii of carriage-ways to the ubiquitous green-and-white highway signs. The turnpike also stimulated residential development all along its route, transforming the wood-lands and dairy farms into a vast suburban kingdom that was itself cheered as a brave new world. For Gordon Wu, the New Jersey Turnpike was a vision of things to come.

The turnpike was also one of the first strands of a vast system of national highways that was about to be laced across the American landscape. The United States in the 1950s was in the midst of a sunny period of optimism born of unprecedented economic growth. Veterans were marrying and hav-ing babies, setting up suburban nests in places like Levittown, and buying new cars to get them to work and their families on the road for holiday vacations. In Congress a bill was making the rounds that would eventually become the Federal-Aid Highway Act of 1956, authorizing $25 billion to build a "National System of Interstate and Defense Highways." In New York City, Robert Moses was at the apogee of his power, realizing his longtime ambition to stitch up "the loose strands and frayed edges of New York's metropolitan arterial tapes-try."[46] Moses had already built a dozen bridges and tunnels and more than 600 miles of highway throughout the metropolitan region and was about to begin constructing the Cross Bronx Expressway. In the spring of 1955, Gordon Wu had a chance to meet this American Haussmann—an event of no mean sig-nificance for a young man besotted with highways. Wu was part of a group of engineering students invited by a society of construction industry profession-als known as the Moles to a dinner and lecture by Moses. Afterward, the guest of honor met with the student engineers and talked about highways and public works. More influential still was the summer Wu toured the nation by road with

Gordon Wu on the February 23, 1994, cover of *Princeton Alumni Weekly*.

COURTESY OF THE MAGAZINE

three Princeton classmates, ferrying a new Buick to California.[47] Following U.S. Route 30 across the Great Plains and over the Rocky Mountains, the junket carried the boys through a world that would soon be changed forever by the interstate highways. In 1958 Wu headed back across the Pacific, a Princeton diploma in hand and a head full of ideas. In his studies of history he learned how the Erie Canal had changed the course of American empire in the nineteenth century by enabling the port of New York to tap a vast and bountiful hinterland. Canals, railroads, roads—infrastructure meant access, and access meant trade, commerce, and prosperity. It was a lesson he would call upon many years later.

Back in Hong Kong, Wu helped his father launch a real estate venture known as Central Enterprises Company. Not long after, he founded his own engineering office—Gordon Wu and Associates—and in 1963 launched a construction company to build what he designed. He called it Hopewell Construction, after a New Jersey town close to Princeton. Wu's timing was perfect, for Hong Kong was about to enter the greatest construction boom in its history. By the late 1970s Wu was one of the biggest builders in the British colony. Wu and his engineers imported a technique of high-rise building construction, the concrete slip-form method, that made it possible to erect a floor every three days. In 1980 Wu crowned the city's skyline with the sixty-six-story Hopewell Centre—then the tallest building in the territory. The soaring white cylinder was the opening act in what would eventually become the most spectacular urban skyline in the world.

After Hopewell Centre, Wu began casting about for opportunities across the border, in the long-closed People's Republic of China. He was one of the first to understand that the extraordinary economic growth of Shenzhen and the greater Pearl River Delta could never be sustained without a modern transportation infrastructure. In the early 1980s there was not a single mile of high-speed, limited-access motorway in Guangdong Province. The region was indeed blessed with an abundance of rivers and canals—a natural infrastructure that had long facilitated trade with the outside world. But now the roaring economy demanded an extensive road network that could reach factories and farms in even the most remote corners of the region.

Already, people and goods were moving around as never before. The number of bus passenger trips in the delta nearly tripled every year between 1978 and 1986.[48] Factories and industrial plants were being built farther and farther away from historic water routes, severely overloading the region's cobbled-together maze of rural roads, many of which were unpaved and all of which were also used by pedestrians, oxcarts, and farm equipment. Worse still, the most important corridor in the Pearl River Delta—between Hong Kong and Shenzhen and the provincial capital of Guangzhou to the north—lacked direct arterial connection. It took a typical container truck seven hours to get from Shenzhen to Guangzhou, a distance no more than that between Manhattan and Trenton, New Jersey.

The solution, as Gordon Wu saw it, was to build something very similar to that vanguard motorway that passed just east of his old Princeton dormitory—the New Jersey Turnpike. If Deng Xiaoping opened China's door to the world, Gordon Wu would roll a six-lane carpet to its front door, all the way from Guangzhou to the Hong Kong border. But to his dismay, Chinese officials in Beijing were unimpressed with his planned road. The railroad ministry opposed it categorically, pointing out that China had few trucks and fewer cars, and that trains would do well enough to carry China into the future.

But Wu did not give up. He argued that while rail was perfectly suited to a centrally planned economy, the emerging entrepreneurial scene—fluid and dynamic—would demand a much more extensive network of regional penetration. With good roads, container trucks could take material straight from factory to buyer. Villages and rural collectives far from a rail line could tap into the economy and contribute to regional and national growth. He explained to senior ministers how the American interstate highway system worked, and how roads like the New Jersey Turnpike had reconfigured the economic geography of North America. In June 1983 he even led a delegation of Chinese officials—including the deputy minister of highways—on a road trip across the United States—a replay of his collegiate junket many years before. They started in San Francisco, where Wu purchased a used Dodge van, and then headed across the United States on a two-week tour of the American highway system. The group stayed in cheap motels, ate bad roadside food, and arrived in New Jersey in time for Wu's twenty-fifth college reunion.[49] The trip was a great success. By the time the Chinese officials returned home, they were smitten with cars and had all become evangelists for an American-style highway system. The following year, Gordon Wu gained the endorsement of both the central government and Guangdong's provincial authorities for his highway. The light had turned green.

Now the real work began. There are easier places on earth to build a major highway than the soggy, low-slung Pearl River Delta. The tropical monsoon climate of the region draws some eighty inches of rainfall annually. More than a thousand miles of rivers, creeks, and canals drain a hydrologic system extending across an area roughly the size of California.[50] The geographer George D. Hubbard called the Pearl River Delta "drowned topography"—a vast coastal plain submerged over the course of millennia and tilting toward the South China Sea.[51] The roadbed would have to crawl across duck ponds and rice paddies and busy shipping channels. There was also the matter of getting around or through densely populated villages and townships. As Wu's engineers worked out details for the road itself, he negotiated right-of-way agreements with local officials and landholders all along the route—a painstaking process that took most of a decade and all his *guanxi* (personal connections) to get right. In places where the road crossed property leased to private companies or rural collectives, Wu was forced to negotiate with landholders on an individual basis.

Local authorities could easily have condemned the needed property but refused to do so for a simple reason: to make the "rich foreigners" pay extortion-level compensation in exchange for the land use rights—literally, highway robbery. At one place Wu was even pressured to direct the highway corridor not away from a densely settled area, but straight toward one, which would force him to acquire scores of buildings and pay out immense sums in compensation. In an even more extreme case, developers got wind of the coming highway and proceeded to erect villas right in the planned path of the road. Having thus improved their land, the leaseholders proceeded to demand a bloated payout in compensation for their "losses." In spite of such roadblocks, Wu was able to patch together a workable—if costly—corridor for his highway. Construction, once it finally began, proceeded rapidly. More than one-third of the highway had to be elevated on pylons and bridges because of surface water. Nearly fifty-three million cubic feet of cement was used to construct the road. The project also required more than 43,000 beams, each weighing as much as ninety tons. To lift these into place, Wu's engineers designed a special launching gantry that would move along the construction route like a giant mechanical spider. Building the level stretches of the highway required moving more than one billion cubic feet of earth, enough to bury 3,000 football fields six feet deep. Though beset by these and other challenges, the road was completed in only twenty-two months. At the peak of operations, more than 30,000 men and women labored on the project around the clock. The Guangzhou-Shenzhen Expressway officially opened in July 1994. Its builder was hailed as a hero and knighted three years later by Queen Elizabeth for services to Asian infrastructure. [52]

★ ★ ★

Much as the New Jersey Turnpike did half a century ago, Gordon Wu's highway triggered extensive urban sprawl and created all along its flanks a landscape of motoring and motorists. Similar transformations can be seen throughout the coastal region. On the road-laced suburban fringes of China's booming cities, the alchemy of asphalt and automobiles has yielded a range of artifacts and environments catering to the car. These, too, often bear a striking similarity to American-style sprawl and the commercial "strip" culture that dominates the outskirts of every American city—shopping malls and supermarkets, big-box retail stores adrift in a sea of parking, drive-through fast-food restaurants, and budget chain motels. Even icons of America's early motor age have been resuscitated in China. The drive-in cinema, a rarity now in the United States, has been welcomed by Chinese motorists much the way it was in America in the 1950s.[53] China's first drive-in was the Maple Park Motor Cinema in Beijing, which opened in 1998 with a single screen and a parking lot covered with recycled meter-square concrete pavers removed from Tiananmen Square during its fiftieth-anniversary facelift.

I took a taxi to the cinema late one afternoon in 1999, and the youthful parking attendants—dressed in Desert Storm battle fatigues—told me I could rent a car across the street in which to enjoy the evening show. Indeed, Maple Park founder Wang Qi Shun soon figured out that he could extend his market by enabling carless couples arriving by bicycle to also enjoy the delights of a drive-in date. During the SARS outbreak in 2003, when restaurants and theaters throughout the capital were locked down, Maple Park was literally the only show in town. In the next few years a number of other drive-ins opened in Guangzhou, Zhengzhou, Shanghai, and Nanjing.

A more ubiquitous feature of China's evolving suburban motoring scene is the big-box and warehouse-style store, which debuted with Hong Kong–based GrandMart in Shenzhen in 1993.[54] German-based Metro, Thai-invested Lotus,

Maple Park Motor Cinema, Beijing, 1999. Note the recycled concrete pavers from Tiananmen Square.

PHOTOGRAPH BY AUTHOR

and the French company Carrefour were among the first such stores in many Chinese cities, quickly followed by competitors such as Wal-Mart, PriceSmart, and the Taiwan-based Jin Run Fa and Hao You Duo. Wal-Mart, which has sourced products in China for years, opened its first Chinese stores in 1996, initially in Shenzhen and Fuzhou. By the end of 2006 there were sixty-six Wal-Mart Supercenters and three Sam's Clubs in thirty-four Chinese cities, against some seventy-eight Carrefour stores then operating in the People's Republic. Industry analysts predict that by 2020 Wal-Mart's retail business in China could exceed in scale the company's North American operations.[55]

As with McDonald's, KFC, and other suburban standards, Wal-Mart enjoys considerably more prestige in China than in North America. None of these brands has a particularly highbrow image in the United States. But in China, all three are fairly expensive and thus patronized by relatively affluent families, and are roughly analogous to Target or Starbucks in the United States. Many big retailers opened first in center-city locations in China, adding outlying stores only when automobile ownership and the suburban population reached a critical mass—a tipping point that came in the mid-2000s in many cities. For example, the popular Su Guo supermarket chain began in the center of Nanjing and still operates dozens of twenty-four-hour convenience shops and community stores throughout town; but it has recently begun opening larger stores in car-convenient locales to tap the lucrative suburban market. Other big-box retailers in China—IKEA, the popular warehouse-club superstore Metro, and British-based home-improvement giant B&Q, for example—made their initial market entries in suburban locales, a deployment strategy more similar to the exclusively suburban focus of Wal-Mart, Target, Costco, and other megaretailers in the United States.[56]

China's motoring middle class also now enjoys some of the largest shopping malls in the world, commercial behemoths that have upstaged North American heavyweights like West Edmonton Mall or Mall of America. It is predicted that by 2010 seven of the ten largest shopping malls on earth will be in China. Golden Resources Shopping Mall (Jin Yuan) in Beijing snatched the title from West Edmonton when it opened on the outskirts of the capital in October 2004, between the third and fourth ring roads. With interiors designed by an Atlanta-based architectural firm, Golden Resources contains 230 escalators and more than 1,000 shops and restaurants, and its 6 million square feet of leaseable floor area make it significantly larger than Mall of America (at 2.5 million square feet). But alas, its reign was brief, and a year later Golden Resources was dethroned by the even larger South China Mall in Dongguan, with a total of some 7 million square feet of leaseable space (discussed in Chapter 9, "Theme Parks and the Landscape of Consumption"). As of 2005, two projected 10-million-square-foot monster malls were under development in China (Mall of China and Triple Five Wenzhou Mall), by none other than the Ghermezian Brothers of Canada, builders of both the Mall of America and West Edmonton Mall.[57]

The popularity of shopping malls in China, while certainly due to rising discretionary income, is also a function of Chinese residential urbanism: shopping malls, restaurants, and city spaces in general are flooded with people partly because most apartments are small, and many life activities are externalized to the public realm. People are "propelled," writes John Hannigan, "towards activities outside the home such as shopping, dining and moviegoing."[58] In China the city street and, increasingly, the semipublic space of the suburban shopping mall supply amenities and entertainments that in the United States are usually found right at home—in the media room or home gym, or the privacy of the typical teenager's bedroom, thumping with music.

Golden Resources Shopping Mall, Beijing, 2005. PHOTOGRAPH BY WU WEI

B&Q home-improvement store, Nanjing, 2006.

PHOTOGRAPH BY AUTHOR

In China's evolving suburbs, people generally enjoy more living space, but the popularity of the public promenade remains.

Another uniquely Chinese aspect of suburban commercial development is the vast single-purpose retail centers that have appeared on the peripheries of most larger Chinese cities: miniature shopping "cities" formed by economies of scale and agglomeration and unlike anything in the United States. Every major Chinese city now has a sprawling "furniture city" (*jia ju cheng*) or "home -improvement city" (*zhuang shi cheng*) on the outskirts of town—the Jinsheng market area west of Nanjing is just one example. These "cities" are similar in spirit to the clusters of goods and service providers traditionally found in Chinese cities, only now the clientele is largely auto-mobile. They often comprise several hundred shops and stores ranging in size from family-run stalls to huge lumber yards and big-box retailers like B&Q and its domestic competitors Home Way and Home World.

Big-box retailers and supermalls have been joined on the urban fringe by a variety of other commercial institutions aimed at suburban motorists. A number of budget motel chains operate in China now, including Motel 168, Seven Days Inn, Home Inns, and U.S.-based Super 8 Motels, which had facilities in

Nanjing's first drive-through fast-food restaurant, 2006.
PHOTOGRAPH BY AUTHOR

twenty-six Chinese cities by 2007. Although McDonald's has been in China for more than a decade, it only opened its first drive-through restaurants in 2006, beginning in Dongguan and Shanghai—cities that, not coincidentally, also boast the highest rates of automobile ownership in China. The company's first drive-in restaurant in Beijing opened on January 19, 2007, accompanied by traditional lion dancers and Ronald McDonald (speaking Chinese, of course). McDonald's had some 780 locations in China by 2007 and plans to use the drive-through format for most of its new restaurants. It is hardly surprising that, toward this end, McDonald's has recently entered a partnership with Chinese oil giant Sinopec, which currently operates some 30,000 service stations throughout China (and is building more than eleven new ones each week). "The deal," reported Reuters, "will take advantage of the fuel company's nationwide network of 30,000 service stations to serve China's rapidly growing population of motorists."[59] Nanjing's first drive-through, one of some 2,000 KFC stores nationwide, opened in 2006, just across the street from a sprawling home-improvement center and big-box supermarket. Were it not for the Chinese characters on the signs, the scene could well be suburban Atlanta.

CHAPTER NINE

Theme Parks and the

Landscape of Consumption

印象體驗與過度消費

China's motoring middle-class consumers also enjoy an extraordinary diversity of themed landscapes on the expanding suburban frontier. The advent of such postmodern spaces of consumption is, of course, first a function of the consumer revolution that has transformed China in the post-Mao reform era. Gone is the blue-gray world of Mao suits and state-run department stores, infamous for their surly clerks and lack of variety. By the late 1980s China's cities erupted with pent-up entrepreneurial zeal and commercial activity. From roast-yam vendors to Rolls-Royce dealerships, Chinese urban life today is defined by the rush and churn of the marketplace. China's surging economy has expanded at an average annual rate of 9.4 percent since 1978 and is now second only to that of the United States in terms of purchasing power parity (a measure of a currency's marketplace mileage, perhaps best known from the *Economist*'s "Big Mac Index").

This growth has created an immense middle class, or "middle stratum," to use the term preferred by Chinese officialdom. Estimates in 2002 by BNP Paribas Peregrine put the number of middle-class households at about 50 million nationwide, while projections by the China National Bureau of Statistics suggest that 25 percent of China's population, about 170 million people, could reach such status by 2010.[1] The Chinese Academy of Social Sciences (CASS) has predicted that by 2020, as much as 40 percent of China's total population (projected to exceed 1.5 billion by then) could meet the criteria for middle-class status; this, by official definition, means families with assets between 150,000 to 300,000 yuan ($18,072 to $36,144). If these estimates are correct, a generation from now there will be 600 million middle-class people in China, far more

Golfer at Grand Epoch City with 1/6-scale reproduction of a Beijing city gate
(Andingmen) in background, Xianghe, Hebei Province, 2006. PHOTOGRAPH BY AUTHOR

than the entire current populations of the United States, Canada, and Mexico combined.[2]

Newly affluent societies tend to pass through a period of spirited compensatory consumption, as new wealth mingles with the memory of scarcity. Now the hardships are past and it's time to enjoy the good life. This often comes along with an increase in leisure time. In China, the six-day workweek, standard for decades, was shortened to five and a half days in 1994 and to five days in March 1995. Rising incomes and added playtime ignited a boom in domestic tourism and holidaymaking. Thirty years ago, a week-long family vacation to a distant part of China (let alone a foreign country) was unheard of; most leisure and recreation activity took place locally and was organized by one's work unit. Today China boasts the largest domestic tourism market in the world and sends out more tourists to destinations in Asia than any other country. In 1995 there were approximately 615 million domestic tourists in China. By 2003 the figure reached 870 million, and two years later it was up to 1.2 billion.[3] As a result, the Chinese are in the midst of a grand rediscovery of their own national landscape and cultural heritage, with tourism to "scenic spots" of regional or national significance exploding in recent years. When I visited the famed Yangtze River Delta "water towns" of Zhouzhuang and Tongli in the early 1990s, local people were still plying the old ways of life. Visitors at the time were few in number except during major holidays. I returned in 2005 and found both villages utterly transformed by the booming tourist trade. Streets were packed with swarms of visitors, including the inevitable tour groups led by guides with flags and bullhorns. Every shop on every street in the center of town was now catering to tourists. The vast majority of these visitors were mainland Chinese tourists.

China is also quickly rising in rank as an international travel destination. Until the early 1970s only well-connected foreigners from the West, mostly academics or diplomats, could secure permission to visit China. By 1999 the number of visiting overseas nationals topped 8 million, and in 2005 more than 20 million people visited the People's Republic from abroad. If tourists from Taiwan, Macau, and Hong Kong are added, the figure jumps to 120 million. The World Tourism Organization estimates that by 2020 China will be the largest tourist market in the world, well ahead of the United States, France, Spain, and other current leaders.[4]

Growing affluence and leisure time, and the rapid global dispersion of life-style trends from the West and elsewhere, has reproduced in China nearly all the forms of sport, recreation, and leisure enjoyed by advanced industrial societies. Many of these require spaces and facilities of a kind never before seen in the People's Republic. Since the early 1990s affluent Chinese have taken up golf, tennis, backpacking, mountain biking, camping, paragliding, off-road trekking, rock climbing, whitewater rafting, snowboarding, snow skiing and water skiing, sailing, surfing, canoeing, horseback riding, hot-air ballooning, and bungee jumping. Teenagers have taken up skateboarding with a vengeance, and Shanghai now has the world's largest skate park. Go-kart fever swept the city a few years earlier, after China's first indoor kart track opened there in the late 1990s. Bowling became a national phenomenon around the same time, and between 1977 and 1997 the number of public bowling lanes in Chinese cities jumped from zero to 10,000.[5] True to form, China now boasts the largest single-floor bowling alley in the world—at the Gongti 100 Bowling and Tennis Center in Beijing.

Survival Island, also in the suburbs of the capital, is a 124-acre back-to-nature park where visitors can build character through such activities as archery, weaving, pottery throwing, papermaking, and tie-dyeing fabrics (they can also pursue a variety of "military sports" and learn about farming within sight of peasants who farm to survive). Recreational hunting has also made a debut. The Nanfang Hunt Club, opened in 1996 on a small island off the coast of Zhejiang Province, is a kind of hunter-gatherer theme park where patrons can choose from thirteen different hunting grounds stocked with "wild" animals. In its first year of operation some 4,000 would-be killers visited the park, bagging 150,000 ducks, 20,000 rabbits, and 6,000 pigs, all specifically raised for the hunt. In Shanxi Province the Oriental International Hunting Ground was one of five such parks under development there in the late 1990s.[6] Closer to the coast, in Hebei Province, is an equestrian-themed vacation village known as Cowboy City. Situated about halfway between Beijing and Tianjin, it is China's first subdivision of time-share holiday homes, developed by a businessman who learned of the time-share concept while studying in the United States. Cowboy City is something of a cross between Levittown and a dude ranch, where small homes with lawns and white picket fences cozy up to a sprawling corral and riding complex. The developer's website sports pictures of lanky American cowboys, horses on the open range, and a pearl-handled Colt 45.[7]

Skiing, snowboarding, and other winter sports also arrived in China in the 1990s, and with them a range of purpose-built leisure landscapes. Although references to skiing appear in Chinese literature as early the Han Dynasty, there were only a handful of skiers in the country in the early 1990s. Today there are several million, with more than 1,000 committed snowboarders in Beijing alone. China's first ski resort, or "snow park," opened in 1995 in Heilongjiang Province. Ten years later there were more than 200 such facilities operating in thirteen provinces.[8] China's largest ski resort is Xiling Snow Mountain Resort, at Mt. Daxuetang in the Xiling Mountains of Sichuan Province, about a two-hour drive from the provincial capital of Chengdu.[9]

But Sichuan is a long haul from most coastal Chinese cities. In an effort to make skiing more accessible to well-heeled urban families, entrepreneurs have opened indoor ski centers in a number of Chinese cities, first in Shanghai. The largest and most advanced is Beijing's Qiaobo Ice and Snow World, which began operating in the summer of 2005. The facility, set in the capital's north-eastern suburbs, allows skiers and snowboarders to pursue their avocation even in the middle of Beijing's hot, dry summers. The immense structure contains two slopes, one of which is 853 feet long and as tall at one end as a ten-story building. The facility is the fruit of an unlikely partnership between a Canadian refrigeration firm and none other than the architecture department at Tsinghua University, China's most esteemed institution of higher learning.[10]

At 17,598 feet Mt. Daxuetang receives plenty of natural snow all winter. Urban ski parks, on the other hand, must resort to making snow, a particularly dubious enterprise given a looming nationwide water crisis. China's annual water shortfall is in the area of 1.4 trillion cubic feet, and hundreds of cities face water shortages, especially in the north. In the area around Beijing, where a dozen or more ski parks were operating by 2005, snow- and ice-making equipment consumed an estimated 134 million cubic feet of water, roughly what 42,000 of the city's residents consume each year.[11]

Like a ski slope (the outdoor kind at least), a golf course may look natural but is in reality a highly engineered landscape. And no nation has built more or larger golf courses in the last twenty years than the People's Republic. Golf is as much a status symbol as it is a game, and nowhere more so than in China. There is no such thing as low-brow golf in the People's Republic, no open-to-all municipal courses like those in many American cities. As Charles McGrath put it in the *New York Times*, golf in China did not work its way upscale; it "arrived full-blown, in its high-end and even slightly decadent form." It is a game for the super elite, and unapologetically so. "Golf and the imagery of golf, which you see all over, on TV commercials and highway billboards, are a kind of code for the new China, the one where...hordes of newly minted millionaires are not the least embarrassed about flaunting their wealth. Much more than in America, golf in China stands for money, power and social exclusivity."[12]

Upwardly mobile entrepreneurs and business professionals look to golf not as a pastime but a passport to success. This has even led some universities to introduce the game to their students. China's first collegiate golf association was founded in 2005 at Peking University, whose administrators then announced plans to build a practice green right on campus—to help prepare MBA students "for a commercial world where deals are often made on the links." In October 2006, Xiamen University even made golf a required course for students majoring in economics and computer science, in order to "improve their job prospects."[13]

Though the royal and ancient game appeared in China more than a century ago, introduced to treaty-port Shanghai by the British, it was later purged by Mao as a decadent bourgeois pastime. Perhaps to drive the point home, the Communists turned Shanghai's most famous course into a zoo.[14] Golf resurfaced in the post-Mao reform era, this time on Chinese terms. In 1979 a government ban on the game was lifted, and five years later China's first modern course opened—the Chung Shan Hot Spring Golf Club in the Pearl River Delta. Built by Hong Kong billionaire Henry Fok to designs by Arnold Palmer, the course was graded by more than a thousand laborers using hand implements.[15] By the early 1990s some forty golf courses were either open or under construction in the Pearl River Delta alone, and by 2006 more than 300 courses were operating nationwide.

Appropriately enough, China's flagship course, Mission Hills Golf Club, opened in Shenzhen only months after Deng Xiaoping's historic 1992 inspection tour of the special economic zone. A huge billboard advertisement for Mission Hills was erected at the Lo Wu border crossing from Hong Kong, giving countless China-bound travelers an unlikely first impression of the mighty People's Republic: Jack Nicklaus swinging a nine-iron above the Shenzhen River. Mission Hills has since become one of the top golf resorts in

Asia. It was the site of the 41st World Cup of Golf in 1995, said to be the first uncensored television event broadcast from the People's Republic; and it hosted the Tiger Woods China Challenge in November, 2001.[16]

The Mission Hills facility is to golf what Las Vegas is to entertainment. It features a 300,000-square-foot clubhouse, five-star hotel, pools, spa, fifty-one tennis courts, a 3,000-seat tennis stadium, three driving ranges, and four pro shops. There is also a country club and palatial residential villas where the "grace of Tuscan forms combines with Hawaiian architectural themes." But the real draw is the greens. Mission Hills' ten championship courses beat out Pinehurst, North Carolina's eight-course complex, in 2004 to become the largest golf resort in the world. An army of 30,000 workers moved 30 million cubic yards of earth and rock in a record eighteen month's time to construct five new courses in 2002.[17] Golf at Mission Hills is made more pleasant by more than 2,000 caddies, nearly all young women, equipped with red shirts and long-billed hardhats to protect against wayward drives. The courses at Mission Hills were designed by some of the world's most celebrated golfers—among them Jack Nicklaus, Vijay Singh, Nick Faldo, Annika Sorenstam, José Maria Olazábal, and Greg Norman ("the Norman is by far the toughest," one golf critic observed: "extremely penal").[18] With its "Ten Signature Courses of the World," Mission Hills is a kind of golf theme park, in which a variety of experiences are presented for consumption.

Of course, there is an element of ersatz pastoralism in every golf course; all are distant heirs of the game's protolandscape in the fog-bound Scottish isles. But the virtuality of golf is heightened in China by the often extreme contrasts between idyllic fairways and nearby working farms or grimly polluted industrial scenes. Chinese courses "seem as if they were rolled out like a magic carpet on alien ground," writes McGrath; even Mission Hills "feels like a virtual landscape, or a golf fantasy—calendar art come to life—and when you board the shuttle bus and head down the hill, out the gate and past the factories and bleak concrete apartment buildings, dodging bicycles and flocks of pedestrians trudging along the road, it's like waking from a reverie."[19] In this sense, the Chinese golf course is a tranquil green lull in a landscape undergoing cataclysmic change, a kind of garden in the machine. This otherworldly aspect is often amplified by references to imagined geographies of status and prestige even farther afield. Mission Hills takes its name from a well-known course in Palm Springs, California, one of the first residential golf communities.[20] Long

Island Golf and Country Club is not in affluent Nassau County but in suburban Dongguan; and on the outskirts of Nanjing there is Harvard International Golf Club, where the $30,000 membership fee coincidentally costs about the same as a year's tuition at Harvard College. Shanghai International Golf and Country Club, with a course designed by Robert Trent Jones II, features an English-manor clubhouse by the same architectural office that produced some of Shanghai's most famous buildings of the 1930s. Sheshan Golf Club, also in Shanghai, offers players "a little slice of Tuscany," while nearby Tomson features a Japanese-designed course with hazards evoking the Great Wall and Mt. Fuji.[21]

China's golfing boom is not without controversy. For all their greenery and natural appearance, golf courses are highly managed landscapes, and their construction and maintenance can have substantial negative impacts on the local environment. In at least one respect, however, Chinese courses are more ecologically friendly than those in the United States: herbicide use is relatively low because it is cheaper to hire workers to pick weeds than apply costly chemicals. Water consumption is a more serious matter, especially in China's arid north. The thirty-plus courses in Beijing, a city with looming water supply problems, require a vast quantity of water to keep the ponds full and the fairways green. In south China, water is more plentiful, but golf courses there have consumed a significant amount of prime agricultural land—especially around Shanghai and in the Pearl River Delta.

Course development in Guangdong Province in the early 1990s ate up more than 1,300 acres of crop fields and rice paddies and forced the removal of hundreds of peasant families. In 1993 irate farmers blocked the Guangzhou-Shantou Highway in protest of land lost to golf development, delaying the opening ceremonies at a just-completed resort for seven hours.[22] In Hebei Province, elderly women in the village of Longan defied bulldozers in protest of a new golf development and the illegal clearing of land they had signed thirty-year leases to farm.[23] Ironically, local peasants whose livelihoods are ruined by golf-course development often secure new work weeding or clearing stones off the fairways that cover the land they once farmed.

The government has not been deaf to the golf menace. In November, 2006, China's state-run Xinhua news agency issued a commentary warning that "too many golf courses had been built in China, taking up badly needed farmland, sucking up scarce water and even running counter to the creation of a harmonious society."[24] Authorities have attempted to restrict golf-course development, usually to little effect. Beijing issued a nationwide golf-course moratorium in the spring of 2004, but eight of the ten courses under construction right in the capital had no governmental approval. For developers, the return on investment is so high it usually makes proceeding without permits worth the risk, and very often the approval of local officials can be bought (perhaps with a complimentary golf membership).[25]

★   ★   ★

China's new suburban landscape is also home to places where reality and fantasy are brought together as a setting for euphoric consumption. Just as China has become the world's top producer of highways and tall buildings, it is also churning out more theme parks than any nation on earth. Between 1990 and 2005 some 2,500 theme parks opened in China, though many have been short lived.[26] And just as property developers use imagined lifestyles and borrowed landscapes to sell upscale housing, theme park developers have plundered the globe in search of cultures and geographies to market as outright attractions, or to lubricate secondary consumption of some kind (as in a themed shopping mall or restaurant). Nothing is off limits or beyond the commodifying reach.

The setting of the great Chinese literary classic, *Dream of the Red Chamber*, has been reified at Grand Prospect Garden near Shanghai. Jinmeng Gold Theme Park in Beijing, opened in 2001, features a defunct mine where visitors learn about gold extraction, smelting, and production and can even try their hand at mining. Numerous wild animal and "safari" theme parks opened in the 1990s, including several dedicated to a single type of animal—snakes, crocodiles, even dinosaurs. The city of Zigong in Sichuan Province, well known to paleontologists for the many fossils excavated there since 1972, boasts a Jurassic-themed park known as Dinosaur Kingdom Garden, designed by the same American park planners who created Busch Gardens in the 1970s.[27]

At Shenzhen's Dapeng Bay a fossil of another sort—a 42,000-ton defanged Soviet aircraft carrier—forms the centerpiece of Cold War–themed Minsk World. Parked near the ship are MIG-23 fighters and helicopters with battle scars from the Soviet misadventure in Afghanistan. A "traditional Russia" shopping street and a troupe of Russian folk dancers round out the attractions. In 2002 *China Daily* reported that another decommissioned Soviet aircraft

American Dream Park, suburban Shanghai, 1999. PHOTOGRAPH BY AUTHOR

carrier, the *Kiev*—best known to American readers for its role in Tom Clancy's *The Hunt for Red October*—would be the focal point of "the world biggest military-theme park" in Tianjin, the Binhai Aircraft Carrier Theme Park.[28]

Even catastrophe has been mined for themes. The Tangshan International Earthquake Garden provides visitors an opportunity to learn about the earthquake that flattened the sprawling industrial city on July 28, 1976, killing at least 250,000 people. Visitors can experience tremors on an earthquake simulator, while the names of lost loved ones can be engraved—for a fee—on one of nine massive granite memorial walls. Though many have paid to have lost family included, others accused the developers of profiting from tragedy and were particularly enraged when the company offered a "group rate" to families who had lost six or more relatives in the disaster.[29]

The popular revival of Buddhism in recent years has also been commodified in the form of commercial theme parks. An immense Sakyamuni Buddha—at a lucky 88 meters (289 feet), nearly twice the height of the Statue of Liberty—lords over a Buddhism theme park at Lingshan in suburban Wuxi. The Lingshan colossus was made of 700 tons of copper and tin and erected near the site of a Tang Dynasty temple. It is the largest standing Buddha in the world, and a truly awesome spectacle when spied between hilltops from afar. At the foot of the mountain, far below Sakyamuni's feet, a spectacular, dynamic sculpture, *Nine Dragons Bathing the Baby Buddha*, erupts several times a day with water jets and symphonic music as the infant deity emerges from a giant mechanical lotus blossom.

An even loftier statue of the female bodhisattva Guan Yin rises 354 feet from the South China sea at another Buddhism theme park at Sanya, Hainan Island. The three-faced statue of the Goddess of Mercy is not without politics, however poetically rendered. Though it has a single body, Guan Yin's three faces are oriented, in turn, toward the world at large, mainland China, and Taiwan. During a ritual enshrining ceremony in April 2005, a gathering of 108 monks from mainland China, Hong Kong, Macau, and Taiwan prayed "for prosperity and peace across the Straits and the world."[30] Though nominally religious, these Buddha sites are hardly nonprofit: a ticket to the Wuxi Lingshan Buddha theme park in 2006 cost a hefty ¥88, about $11—nearly two full days' wages for local construction workers. A towering statue of a rather more secular luminary, Chinese American martial arts hero Bruce Lee, is the projected centerpiece of a $25 million theme park in the town of Shunde in Guangdong Province, ancestral home of Lee's family. The amusement park, which broke ground in November 2006, will feature a martial arts academy, Bruce Lee robots, and a roller coaster that emits the actor's signature screams.[31]

Much has been written about the cultural significance of theme parks, shopping malls, and related manifestations of modern consumer urbanism.[32] Their origins can be traced, at least in part, to the arcades of nineteenth-century Europe—pedestrian streets sheltered from the elements by a glass-and-iron roof and typically lined with cafés, shops, restaurants, and other places of amusement. Many European cities had arcades by mid-century, but no place more fully embraced the building type than Paris, where some 300 arcades stood in the years before Baron Georges-Eugène Haussmann gutted the city with his mighty plexus of boulevards. The great interpreter of the arcade was Walter Benjamin, whose essays about Paris between the wars are essential reading for anyone seeking the roots of contemporary urban culture. By the time Benjamin wrote about the Passage des Panoramas and other arcades in the late 1920s, they had long ago become obsolete, their trade siphoned off by fashionable new shopping streets like the Avenue des Champs-Élysées. The arcades were now places of dusty repose, a kind of attic of Parisian

The mighty Lingshan Buddha, Wuxi, 2006. PHOTOGRAPH BY AUTHOR

Detail revealing the immense scale of the Lingshan Buddha, Wuxi, 2006. PHOTOGRAPH BY AUTHOR

memory filled with half-empty pawn shops and wax museums. To Benjamin, the arcades were a glimpse into the collective psyche of the city, full of fabulous juxtapositions and "secret affinities"—a hair dryer next to the Venus de Milo, "the revolver above the goldfish bowl."[33] Benjamin also understood that the arcade, however passé, had once been a herald of the future. In the arcade were the seeds of a whole new social order, of a profound societal transition "from a culture of production to one of consumption." To Benjamin, the arcade in its prime was a kind of dream-inducer, stoking a yearning for material things that went beyond need and into the realm of fetish. The arcade manufactured desire. "Like the factories that produced the wares sold there," writes Herbert Muschamp, "the arcade was an industrial machine [that] relied on display, advertising, newspapers and the other new technologies of consumer manipulation."[34]

The shopping mall and the theme park are direct descendents of the arcade. There, too, eye-catching displays and clever advertising make us hunger for the imagined succor of stuff. The visual feast seduces us, encouraging us to consume things we don't need but "can't live without"—what Marx identified as commodity fetishism. As Michael Dutton put it in *Streetlife China*, post-Mao shopping spaces are "brightly adorned glass, mirror and chrome monuments to the capitalism of the gaze," architecture configured "to enchant and enhance." The pedestrian enters this consumer space "as though entering a dream. Everything is made desirable and everything is for sale."[35]

Souvenirs notwithstanding, theme parks traffic in even more ethereal stuff—that of experience. To paraphrase Dean MacCannell, at the theme park "pure experience, which leaves no material trace, is manufactured and sold like a commodity." Extending Marx's concept of commodity fetishism, MacCannell argues that one of the distinguishing aspects of postmodern, information-rich society is that such things as "programs, trips, courses, reports, articles, shows, conferences, parades, opinions, events, sights, spectacles, scenes and situations of modernity" are not valued for the labor necessary to produce them—the traditional Marxist reading—but in terms of "the quality and quantity of *experience* they promise." Moreover, many physical things too—automobiles, skis, iPods, cellphones, even real estate—are now valued primarily for their capacity to induce or enable an experience. "The commodity has become a means to an end," writes MacCannell, that end being "an immense accumulation of reflexive experiences which synthesize fiction and reality into a vast symbolism."[36] In this reading, the theme park is not just a particular place and time, but a kind of spatial delivery mechanism for manufactured euphoric experiences.

China's rising middle class has been a particularly eager consumer of this ethereal new commodity, for a variety of reasons. On a pragmatic level, many people now simply have the time and money to take the family on holiday, often in the family car, and suburban theme parks are a convenient venue for such outings—especially when the parents and in-laws come along. The experiential cornucopia available in the theme park is also particularly intoxicating when considered against the backdrop of recent scarcity and deprivation. All but a handful of Chinese today were poor thirty years ago, and many, especially the generation that came of age in the 1950s and 1960s, recall all too well just how challenging daily life had become by the end of the Mao era. The remembered paucities of the past—cultural and intellectual as well as material— have helped drive experience-consumption in the post-Mao era. The start of the reform era found people in China hungry to experience the world, to steal a glimpse of life beyond the *danwei* and beyond even China. Rising affluence, seeded by a steady flow of globalized information, has further massaged this longing. However derivative or cheesy, theme parks speak to this new yearning to experience the great world and life's rich bounty.

The theme park is also especially appealing in the face of convulsive change; its landscape is, quite literally, a sanctuary from reality, an escapist space where the problems of life can be checked at the gate. "Every theme park is a controlled utopia, a miniature world," writes Ian Buruma, "where everything can be made to look perfect."[37] It is no accident that the boom years of Disneyland and other early American theme parks were during the Cold War and the "urban crisis" of the 1960s. This escapist dimension was something Walt Disney well understood; the company's original mission statement talked about capturing "the essence of America as we know it," cultivating nostalgia, and offering "exciting glimpses of the future." But Disneyland was also meant to be a refuge from the "complexities of the present," a line that was later deleted from the company's corporate policy.[38]

As we have seen throughout this book, China is in the midst of an extraordinary period of social and cultural transformation. The unsettling metamorphoses its cities have undergone in recent years have disrupted millions of lives, and there is little prospect of peace and tranquility in the near future. The affluent can buy respite in a gated villa or housing estate, or on the fairways of a golf course. Those of more modest means must settle for the make-believe utopia of the theme park. In an urban China rattled by creative destruction, the world of the theme park is comforting indeed.

That said, it is only appropriate that the first theme parks of the post-Mao era—Splendid China, Folk Culture Villages, and Window of the World—were built in that bellwether of Chinese urban revolution, Shenzhen. Splendid China (Jinxiu Zhonghua) opened in 1989 and was China's first modern theme park. Described in tourist material as the "World's Largest Miniature Scenic Spot," Splendid China was the first of many places to miniaturize distant geographies and reconstitute them in theme-park form. At Splendid China, a selection of architectural landmarks and natural landscapes from the Middle Kingdom are presented in miniature form on a seventy-four-acre site. As a tourist brochure puts it, Splendid China compresses "5,000 years and 10,000 miles" of Chinese civilization into a package easily consumed in an afternoon.

It is a masterpiece of the miniaturist's art. The exquisite models, mostly at a scale of 1:15, are constructed with tiny bricks, rare woods, carved stone, and gold leaf; grounds are landscaped with bonsai and hand-clipped tiny hedges. Some 50,000 figurines, attired in costumes researched by the Central Academy of Fine Arts in Beijing, populate the various displays.

The miniaturized natural landscapes are set about the gardens "roughly according to their position in China," with "mountains, high plateaux, deserts and basins" on the west side of the park and "fertile plains, green hills...lakes and rivers" in the east.[39] Famous buildings include the Temple of Heaven, Tibet's Potala Palace, and the Forbidden City, which was constructed in Beijing and shipped to Shenzhen in fifteen truckloads. A rambling model of the Great Wall, six feet high and made of six million little bricks, snakes its way around the edge of the park. Today an even greater wall lies just beyond. When I first visited Splendid China in 1992, the area outside the park was largely undeveloped; now the little world is hemmed in to the east and north by lofty residential towers, adding another dimension to the park's surreality.

Splendid China is a true product of the open-door era; it is a choreographed introduction to China for foreign tourists, especially overseas Chinese returning to or visiting the "motherland" for the first time. For this reason it was built in a district on the west side of the special economic zone known as the Overseas Chinese Town. As one of the park's original designers, Ma Chi Man, explained it, Splendid China was meant to be "a miniature scenic spot in which China's renowned scenic attractions and historical sites could be concentratedly [sic] displayed so that people could admire and know more about China's beautiful wonders, splendid history and culture, as well as various national customs and habits in shorter time." The minipark format itself was inspired by Ma's 1985 visit to Madurodam "Lilliputian Land" in the Netherlands.[40]

In fact, Splendid China presents a much-edited version of Chinese space and time, an unblemished and politically neutral vision of national heritage. As Ann Anagnost has observed, Splendid China demarcates a space "within which the nation can be represented as a total concept, a timeless essence."[41] Splendid China is the China of the deep past—the Celestial Empire or Middle Kingdom. There are no tiny statues of Chairman Mao, no state-owned factories or Great Hall of the People. The only representative of China's convulsive twentieth century is a model of the Sun Yat-sen Mausoleum in Nanjing. The park's historical depth is underscored by the setting: "the miniature landscape compresses five thousand years of history into a tiny space," wrote Anagnost in 1993, "but it does so enclosed within the larger space of Shenzhen, a place whose history as an event spans only a decade."[42] Equally ironic is the fact that some natural landscapes reproduced at Splendid China no longer exist in reality. The model of the Three Gorges of the Yangtze River, for example, depicts the place as it was before a massive hydroelectric dam—five times the size of Hoover Dam—was completed at Xiling Gorge in 2006. The Gorges described in the park's promotional material—"breathtaking beauty, magnificent precipitous peaks...deep, fascinating valleys and whirling rapids"—are mostly now under water.[43]

The edited content of the replica park did not travel well to the United States, where a second park—Florida Splendid China—opened in Orlando in 1993, not far from Disney World. The park was quickly attacked from both sides of the political spectrum. Conservatives blasted it as a Communist propaganda park—"an attempt by Peking to infiltrate American society," wrote Kenneth Timmerman in the *American Spectator*, "designed to convince kids, and their unwitting parents, that the Communist dictatorship is simply heir to 5,000 years of imperial splendor."[44] The Left took equal umbrage at the park's inclusion of the Potala Palace in Tibet and landmarks from Inner Mongolia and East Turkestan. Activists picketed the park, and a boycott was mounted. In fact, the impact of Florida Splendid China was minimal because hardly anyone visited the place. Compared to nearby attractions like Disney World and the EPCOT center, Sea World, and Universal Studios Florida, the minipark was dull fare indeed. Florida Splendid China finally closed quietly in 2003.

Not far from Splendid China is another early theme park of the post-Mao era, Shenzhen Window of the World (Shi Jie Zhi Chuang), opened in 1994. Like the earlier project, Window of the World was developed as a joint venture between China Travel Service and Shenzhen World Miniature Company. If Splendid China compresses the Middle Kingdom primarily for tourists from abroad, Window of the World compresses global time and space for a domestic audience; it is Splendid China turned inside out and upside down.

Window of the World's 120-acre site contains replicas of some of the world's most famous architectural monuments and natural landscapes—from the White House to the Taj Mahal, the Tower of London to Ayer's Rock, the Grand Canyon, and the pyramids of Egypt. Most are significantly larger than the structures in Splendid China and built at scales ranging from 1:15 to 1:1. The one-third-scale model of the Eiffel Tower, built by China's Major Bridge Engineering Bureau of the Ministry of Railways, still ranks among Shenzhen's tallest structures.

In the years following its completion, Window of the World was copied throughout China—replicas of a replicant landscape. Beijing World Park in the

Window of the World, Shenzhen, 1994. PHOTOGRAPH BY AUTHOR

capital's Fengtai District is the best known of these, as it was the setting for Jia Zhangke's celebrated 2004 film *The World* (*Shi Jie*). Jia uses the bleak setting of the theme park in winter to tell the story of one of its employees, a young woman straining against her role as a cog in the machinery of China's expanding consumer society. A smaller-scale replica park is Little World at Yangcun, about halfway between Beijing and Tianjin, where five "continents" and four "oceans" set the stage for 137 views from eighty different nations.

If Splendid China put selected Chinese treasures on display for a newly invited world to enjoy, "world parks" such as those at Shenzhen and Beijing present a sampling of treasures from abroad for the consumption of Chinese nationals. Like all theme parks they can be interpreted at several levels, first and simply as places of amusement. But Chinese world parks can also be read through the lens of China's unique geopolitical status today. These parks seem to be telling the rising generation of young Chinese (especially those born with the open-door reforms, who are already savvy consumers of world culture) that the great world beyond the South China Sea, so long closed off, is increasingly their oyster. They provide a glimpse of the community of nations, indeed a "window" on a world that must now make room for China and accept that the Chinese are destined to play an increasingly significant role in shaping a global future.

If China's economic growth, collective ambition, and immense population mean anything, the People's Republic may well one day inherit the earth. In this "oyster thesis" sense, the Shenzhen and Beijing parks represent a figurative claiming of the world. The representation of iconic landmarks and spaces from around the globe (in literally diminished form) is an act of symbolic appropriation that recalls in spirit the imperial "theme parks" of the past, where celebrated landscapes from throughout the Middle Kingdom were reified in gardenesque form—as an aesthetic exercise, but also to demonstrate that they were subjects of the realm.

★   ★   ★

Indeed, the miniaturized representation of borrowed landscapes is a practice deeply rooted in Chinese culture. Classical Chinese garden design often re-created celebrated scenes and famous landscapes from afar, frequently in highly stylized form; this in turn played a formative role in the development of

Mini-U.S. Capitol at Beijing World Park, 2002. PHOTOGRAPH BY AUTHOR landscape gardening in the West. As Ian Buruma notes, the classical Chinese garden inspired "equally fantastic English garden parks, filled with fake Gothic and classical ruins, as well as chinoiserie bridges and pagodas."[45] Chinese imperial gardens took mimesis to even greater lengths. Yuanming Yuan, the "Garden of Perfect Brightness" that served as the old Summer Palace and was located in the northwest corner of Beijing, was a kind of imperial theme park built in the early eighteenth century by the Emperor Kangxi. Expanded and enhanced by Kangxi's grandson, the Emperor Qianlong, this extraordinary "Garden of Gardens" dazzled visitors from the West. "To depict all the splendours," wrote Maurice Irisson in 1860, "I should need to dissolve specimens of all known precious stones in liquid gold for ink, and to dip into it a diamond pen tipped with the fantasies of the oriental poet."[46] Qianlong simulated at Yuanming Yuan scenery from Hangzhou's West Lake, the famed gardens of Suzhou and Wuxi, and other places he visited during tours of his realm.

Such representations of distant Chinese geographies were not merely playful, but had a clear political dimension. Yuanming Yuan featured a series of islands known as Jiuzhou Qingyan—"Nine Lands United and Prosperous." As Anne-Marie Broudehoux writes, this symbolic gardenscape referred "to an ancient verse which described the mythological integration of the nine lands, alluding to the legendary unification of China," and was meant to carry "the subtle political message that a united China would bring prosperity."[47] Qianlong was also fascinated by exotic lands and foreign cultures and employed a number of Jesuit missionaries—among them painter Giuseppe Castiglione and mathematician Michel Benoist—to endow the palace grounds with pavilions, fountains, mazes, aviaries, belvederes, and other *folies* inspired by Versailles and the villas of Baroque Italy.[48]

More extraordinary still was a miniature Peking built by the Emperor Kangxi at the beginning of the eighteenth century in the middle of Yuanming Yuan that faithfully reproduced the urbanism and street culture of the old city. Father Jean-Denis Attiret, a French Jesuit missionary who became a painter at Qianlong's court, described this "little Town in the Midst of the whole Inclosure," laid out in the form of a square with "each Side...near a Mile long." "It has Four Gates, answering the Four principal Points of the Compass; with Towers, Walls, Parapets, and Battlements. It has its Streets, Squares, Temples, Exchanges, Markets, Shops, Tribunals, Palaces, and a Port for Vessels. In one Word, every thing that is at *Pekin* in Large, is there represented in Miniature."[49]

Reconstituted ruins at New Yuan Ming Palace, Zhuhai, 1999.
PHOTOGRAPH BY AUTHOR

Anticipating questions from his readers, Attiret explained that the "principal End" of this mimetic Peking—as well as simulated portions of Suzhou's main market street nearby—"was to procure the Emperor the Pleasure of seeing all the Bustle and Hurry of a great City in little, whenever he might have a mind for that sort of Diversion." As the Son of Heaven, he could never mingle with mere mortals; the emperor was, as Attiret put it, "too much a Slave to his Grandeur ever to shew himself to his People."[50]

The chimerical delights of Yuanming Yuan all came to end on the night of October 6, 1860, when the palace was sacked and looted by an expeditionary force of French and British troops led by James Bruce, Eighth Earl of Elgin (and son of Lord Elgin, who absconded with the Parthenon marbles in 1806). The punitive action was initially meant to hasten compliance with the treaty of Tianjin, forced on the Qing court several years earlier after China's defeat in the Second Opium War. After several foreign prisoners were subsequently killed by the Chinese, Elgin unleashed the full fury of his troops on Yuanming Yuan, burning it to the ground and leaving behind only the crumbled ruins of the garden's masonry European-style pavilions.[51]

In spirit at least, Yuanming Yuan is the great progenitor of the Chinese theme park. It is wholly fitting, then, that Yuanming Yuan itself has been reproduced in the form of a vast theme park in Zhuhai, just north of Macau on the west side of the Pearl River Delta. Just as the original Yuanming Yuan brought together the scenic delights of distant lands, the New Yuan Ming Palace (Yuan Ming Xin Yuan) reproduces the reproduction, often at a scale of one-to-one. The 148-acre park opened in 1997 and is described in tourist literature as a "patriotism education site"—meant to both celebrate a lost jewel of Chinese civilization and remind a new generation of China's past humiliations at the hands of foreigners. Driving home the point is an elaborate performance staged nightly at the park entitled *Burning Down the Palace*, which reenacts Elgin's rampage in a calculated appeal to feelings of nationalism and national pride.

The miniature Peking at the original Yuanming has itself been reproduced not far away, at Grand Epoch City (introduced in Chapter 3, "The Politics of the Past"), though admittedly without the simulated bustle and grit that distinguished Kangxi's mimesis. In addition to its golf course and vast conference and hotel facilities, the one-sixth scale replica of Ming Beijing features yet another reproduction of Qianlong's playground: "eight scenic views of Yuanmingyuan imperial garden."

More recently, themed borrowing of distant geographies has been used in the design of shopping malls. The most extraordinary example is South China Mall, located in Dongguan's Wanjiang New District. Erected on what were banana groves and sugarcane fields as recently as 2001, South China Mall is the largest shopping mall on earth, with a total floor area that, at seven million square feet, makes it bigger than the Pentagon. Put another way, South China Mall encloses as much space as about 3,000 average-sized American houses. Described as the "First Super-mega Theme Shopping Park of China," the mall applies the world-park strategy of cultural appropriation to encourage consumption on an unprecedented scale. The mall, which also includes China's largest indoor amusement park and the nation's first "Teletubbies Edutainment Centre," is the brainchild of Hu Gui Rong, a Guangdong magnate who made a fortune in the food business before jumping into real estate in 1988.[52]

Located just minutes from Gordon Wu's Guangzhou-Shenzhen Expressway, South China Mall is meant to one day be the centerpiece of the city's vast, fast-forming suburban belt. From the highway, arrival at the megamall is signaled

Aerial perspective rendering of the South China Mall complex, Dongguan.

COURTESY CHEN WEN JUN, SOUTH CHINA MALL

not by signage but by a singular architectural apparition that hovers above the suburban skyline—a full-scale replica of the campanile at Piazza San Marco in Venice. The tower is accompanied, appropriately, by a version of the Palazzo Ducale (Doge's Palace) alongside a miniature lagoon plied by Venetian gondolas. But the mall's developers didn't limit themselves to Italy; South China's customers are seduced by a true panoply of "worldwide sights and feelings," from a reconstituted Egypt to an ersatz San Francisco Bay, all strung together by a 1.3-mile canal that wends its way through the entire mall complex—a watery datum through time and space (traveled throughout by the persistent Venetians).

At the center of South China's European district is an Arc de Triomphe, nearly as tall as the Parisian original, which terminates an abbreviated Champs-Élysées where shoppers indulge in "Helvetic crystal, Korean fashionable hairdressing and Cuban cigars."[53] The Arc anchors a central square named, in spite of its geometry, "European Fashion Circle." From here two high-end shopping streets—the Via Condotti and Florence Street—lead west to the Venice Lagoon and an adjacent Caribbean District featuring a

South China Mall's replica of the campanile at Piazza San Marco, Venice, 2006. PHOTOGRAPH BY AUTHOR

cavernous salsa club. Amsterdam Street, just north, features a serpentine canal lined with colorful Dutch-style buildings, while south of Fashion Circle is an Egyptian plaza guarded by sphinxes. This in turn—and inexplicably—leads to a replica of the famous fountain at the Court of the Lions in the Alhambra, the fourteenth-century Moorish palace in Granada. But instead of an exquisite enclosure of filigreed screens and slender columns, the stone lions are framed on one side by the Nile Villa Hotel and on the other by the lumberyard of a big-box home-improvement store.

I first toured South China Mall a few days before Christmas in 2006 and watched hotel workers painstakingly cover all the landscaping around the lion fountain with cotton wool. Thus unfolded a scene that could only occur in contemporary China: rural migrant laborers at an Egyptoid hotel applying a layer of synthetic snow to a replica of a Moorish relic from Spain, all against the orange-and-white backdrop of a Home Depot knockoff. And in the background "Frosty the Snowman" played over and over again.

The mall was still partially under construction at the time. A battalion of security guards practiced martial-arts moves in the Fashion Circle, their Plexiglas antiriot shields laid down in an orderly grid nearby. Another group of young men, also clad in combat fatigues, were learning to roll fire hoses on the Via Condotti. Our guide from the Sanyuan Yinghui Company, South China Mall's developer, was the project's general manager—a thoughtful forty-something graduate of Peking University with a love of history and tea culture who also wrote a book about education. South China Mall had jumped into the headlines several months earlier, in April 2006, when *Newsweek* magazine named it one of the "seven new wonders of the world," part of a sundry sampling of "man-made gems" that also included Houston's gargantuan Lakewood Church and the International Space Station.

★   ★   ★

Beyond the allure of a world long off-limits, the popularity of theme parks in China can also be explained in terms of a yearning to recover the Chinese past, to reclaim ground lost during the Cultural Revolution. As we have seen, a resurgent interest in history animates many Chinese theme parks, as well as a range of other efforts to reclaim historic urban settings and even entire villages for the purposes of tourism and themed consumption. Mao's attempts to get rid of all things old, to wipe away all traces of China's feudal past, have only stoked a longing to retrieve and repossess the Chinese past, even if in ersatz, commodified form. Of course, the People's Republic was intended to bring about a radically new kind of society, a socialist utopia where all things old were regarded as obsolete. This ideology led Mao to undertake monumental acts of urban vandalism himself—the destruction of Beijing's ancient walls, for example. But even more damage was done in his name (and with his blessing) by the Red Guards.

In their frenzied efforts to purge China of its own history, the youthful Red Guards tore apart the very fabric of Chinese society. They defaced landmark buildings and destroyed precious artwork, smashed and burned antiques, and pillaged the homes of former elites, confiscating jewelry and searching for incriminating evidence of counterrevolutionary sentiments. As in the case of Liang Sicheng, intellectuals, especially historians and scholars of China's past, were similarly persecuted, and even lynched. At Zhongshan University in Guangdong Province, "the faculty and students who had not been sent to the countryside awoke one morning," writes Anne Thurston in *Enemies of the People*, "to find the entire senior faculty of the history department murdered, hanging from the trees that line the university entrance."[54]

Mao's vilification of history and the predations of his Red Guards effectively erased much of China's collective memory; it created a kind of blank spot in the historical consciousness of the Chinese people, as though precious photographs had been torn from a treasured scrapbook. People yearn to fill in these voids, to heal the rift with history and reconnect to past ages and traditions. Some do this by consuming the Chinese past at history-themed parks, restaurants, and urban heritage districts, regardless of how synthetic or superficial such places may be. Doing so helps still the anxieties brought about by rapid societal transformation; theme parks offer a moment of seeming order in a field of flux and change. Those that trade in history are doubly reassuring, for they offer both spatial sanctuary from the creative destruction all about as well as the comforts of the *longue durée*. The version of the past they offer, however contrived or artificial, serves as an unyielding anchor that stabilizes the turbulence of the present; theme parks literally put things in perspective, at least for the length of a visit. As Marshall Berman has observed, the consumption of history speaks to our "longing to create and to hold on to something real even as everything melts."[55] Satisfying such a yearning explains, at least

Tang Paradise, Xi'an, 2007. PHOTOGRAPH BY AUTHOR

in part, why historically oriented theme parks such as New Yuan Ming Palace, Grand Epoch City, Splendid China, and Folk Culture Village have been so popular among Chinese tourists.

In recent years, the sophistication and accuracy of these historical theme parks has greatly improved. One of the best is Tang Paradise (Da Tang Fu Rong Yuan) on the south side of Xi'an, surely one of the most beautiful theme parks in China. Built within sight of the fifth-century Big Wild Goose Pagoda (Da Yan Ta), this "Garden of History" opened in April 2005 on a 165-acre site where twelve "scenic regions" yield "a perfect exhibition of the grandness, prosperity and brilliance of the culture of the Tang Dynasty."[56] Indeed, the Tang Dynasty (AD 618–907) was an epoch of profound creativity in literature, the arts, and architecture and is widely regarded as a golden age of Chinese civilization. Its capital was Chang'an, terminus of the Silk Road and one of the world's great cities at the time (it was the predecessor of modern Xi'an). The architectural landmarks at Tang Paradise are exquisite, made doubly so at night by spectacular lighting. The buildings are largely the work of Zhang Jinqiu, one of the most respected senior architects in China and a master of historical styles. One of Liang Sicheng's last students, she often incorporates Tang-era historical references in her work, exemplified by her designs for the Shaanxi Museum of History and the Bell and Drum Tower Plaza in Xi'an.[57]

More recent chapters of Chinese history, including the National era and the early years of the People's Republic, have also been themed for commercial consumption. Most enigmatic are those celebrating aspects of Maoism or the Cultural Revolution—the very causes, after all, of China's historical amnesia. In these, even suffering and hardship have been commodified by the alchemy of affluence and nostalgia. In the mid-1990s a number of Cultural Revolution–themed restaurants opened in Chinese cities, including Worker, Farmer, Soldier in Zhongshan and Black Earth in Beijing. Founded by a group of former Red Guards, the latter featured plain but wholesome "hardship cuisine," the restaurant's walls were decorated with Mao badges, and its rooms were designed to resemble the rough wooden huts students lived in during their "rustication" experience in the Chinese countryside in the 1960s.[58]

Mao's Hunan Province hometown, Shaoshan, was a popular place of pilgrimage during the Cultural Revolution. Since then, local entrepreneurs and even the Communist Party have capitalized on the town's Maoist legacy. "Mao family restaurants" are commonplace, serving dishes once favored by the Great Helmsman, and in 1994 a Chairman Mao memorial theme park opened. As Michael Dutton has written, the park "shows the Communist Party tactically employing consumption to promote its politics in an enterprise that almost leads to vaudeville." A circuitous trail through the park replicates in garden-esque form the 6,000-mile Long March of 1935. This enables visitors, according to a 1990s park brochure, "to experience the revolutionary process in China for themselves by walking down the revolutionary road."[59]

Another Long March theme park (Hong Jun Chang Zhen Bo Lan Cheng) opened in Zhejiang Province in October 2005, where some forty key sites and 170 buildings along the storied route have been replicated. A similar development has been built in suburban Beijing—Red Army Theme Park (Dong Hong Jun Gong Yuan), acronymized in promotional material and souvenir T-shirts as "R.A.T.P." Developed by Beijing Long March Investments Limited, the park features another rendition of the revolutionary trek, wound about a 148-acre site in the capital's Chaoyang District.[60] All these parks are now part of a tourist trail of sites nationwide associated with the rise of the Chinese Communist Party—"part of a drive," as one writer put it, "to restore Marxist-Leninist faith in a population increasingly awash in consumerism." The entire system—a kind of distributed theme park at the scale of the nation—encompasses some 150 tourist sites that collectively brought in some twenty million visitors in 2004. Party officials also hope the attractions will bring in some 100 billion yuan ($12.5 billion) by 2010.[61]

Stoked by rising affluence, the new yearning to consume the past has also led to the transformation of entire urban streetscapes into stage sets for history-themed consumption. Though a staggering amount of China's built heritage has been lost in the last two decades, developers have recently begun to recognize the rich market potential of place and past—the value, to quote Jeffrey W. Cody, of "making history pay."[62] Heritage urbanism, decades old in the United States, is a new trend in China; as elsewhere, it involves the restoration (or "tarting up," to put it less kindly) of historic buildings and streetscapes for the purposes of commercial development, typically to host upscale retail and entertainment uses.

The earliest of these consumer-oriented heritage redevelopments in China actually date back to the beginning of the reform era. Among the most famous is Liulichang Culture Street in Beijing's Qianmen District, well known to anyone who has gone on a packaged tour of the city. Liulichang, which means "Glazed Tile Works," was originally the location of firing kilns used to produce colorful glazed tiles and other decorative components for palace buildings in the Yuan and Ming dynasties. After the kilns were moved in the late eighteenth century, Liulichang developed into a book market, and eventually became famous throughout Asia as an emporium for literary works, calligraphy, art, and antiques. Liulichang was also the center of China's publishing industry until Shanghai eclipsed it in the 1890s. The rehabilitation of the legendary market street was approved by the State Council in 1979, at the very start of the reform era. Over the next ten years, what original shops remained at Liulichang were rebuilt from the ground up to recall their glory years during the Qing Dynasty. The street was itself effectively removed from the gritty surrounds of Qianmen and transformed into a themed shopping space complete with spacious pedestrian mall and tour-bus drop-off zone. Liulichang quickly became a major tourist attraction in Beijing and, unlike the city's more colorful Dirt Market (Pan Jia Yuan), is still a place where authentic art and antiques can be found.

Other urban heritage projects of the early reform period were carried out in Shanghai and Nanjing. The district surrounding the sixteenth-century Yu

Yuan garden, at the center of Shanghai's old walled "Chinese city," was redeveloped in the 1980s into a popular tourist attraction and later extended with a new Ming-themed shopping avenue known as Shanghai Old Street (Laojie). An even more ambitious effort was undertaken at Fuzi Miao (Temple of Confucius) in Nanjing. Fuzi Miao straddles the narrow Qinhuai River as it flows through the city toward the Yangtze River nearby. The district is a part of Nanjing that served briefly as the capital of the Southern Tang dynasty (AD 937–975), close to the southernmost corner of the city's Ming-era defensive wall and its southern gate (Zhonghuamen). Fuzi Miao's centerpiece and namesake is a Song Dynasty Confucian temple built around AD 1034 and burned, razed, and reconstructed many times since (the name is derived from the philosopher's Chinese name, Kong Fuzi, latinized in the West as Confucius).

The temple was erected on the north bank of the Qinhuai to complement the Jiangnan Examination School next door, where entrance examinations for the imperial civil service were administered. Over the centuries the school expanded into a vast complex with thousands of tiny individual examination cells. It produced some of the most important intellectuals of the Ming and Qing dynasties and helped establish Nanjing as a center of learning in China. Because it was easily accessible by boat, the district also evolved a thriving marketplace; this, together with the famed temple and school, made Fuzi Miao a legend throughout China. Fuzi Miao figured prominently in descriptions of Nanjing in classical literature, especially from the city's glory years as one of two capitals of the Ming Dynasty (by 1375 it was the largest city in the world, with an estimated population of one million).[63]

Though the imperial examination system was abandoned in the final years of the Qing Dynasty, Fuzi Miao retained most of its historic market functions well into the twentieth century. The temple was burned during the Japanese occupation of the 1930s and extensively vandalized during the Cultural Revolution; after all, to the Red Guards, Confucius was the ultimate symbol of the ossified, stultifying past. By the late 1960s the district was largely derelict, though it still sustained some market functions. Then, in the mid-1980s, Fuzi Miao became the focus of a vast effort by the Nanjing municipal government to bring back the district's vibrant market culture. Though certainly meant to contribute to the city's economy, the project was envisioned first as an act of recovery and only secondarily as a profit-making venture. The Confucius

Fuzi Miao, Nanjing, 2007. PHOTOGRAPH BY AUTHOR

temple was restored and several adjacent market streets were laid out. New buildings were designed in the spirit of the regional vernacular architectural style, marked by a predominance of whitewashed walls, red-lacquered woodwork, and dark, tiled roofs with upswept eaves. Much of the work was done by architecture faculty at nearby Southeast University, in consultation with city engineers and design staff.

The new Fuzi Miao was an overnight success and quickly began drawing immense crowds. By the mid-1990s much of the surrounding area had been filled in to extend the network of pedestrianized shopping streets. The additional development led to extreme traffic congestion in this already densely packed section of town, and also raised issues about the very meaning of the place: should, for example, KFC or McDonald's be allowed to lease prominent quarters in the heart of the temple precinct? Fuzi Miao is the most successful urban cultural heritage redevelopment in China and remains one of the most popular tourist sites in the country. Its streets and alleys are packed with shoppers and tourists every weekend, and it is an especially popular destination during the mid-Autumn and Lunar New Year holidays.[64]

By the late 1990s developers began to turn their attention to the routinely overlooked—and fast vanishing—quotidian built environment of more recent eras. Older residential neighborhoods as well as industrial buildings and spaces from the treaty-port and Nationalist eras have been transformed into profitable stage sets for themed consumption in a number of Chinese cities. The market-driven resuscitation of neglected cityscapes started in the United States in the 1970s. Savvy developers figured that affluent Americans were tiring of the dullness and conformity of suburbia. They understood that, given the right attractions, people might even venture back downtown—to the same impoverished, rust-belt urban centers that white middle-class Americans had been fleeing for a generation. If a piece of historic downtown real estate could be cleaned up and made safe and stocked with upscale shops and restaurants, the suburbanites might well come back to the city.

This is indeed what happened. Developer James W. Rouse led the trend. In collaboration with architect Benjamin C. Thompson, Rouse began developing upscale retail complexes not in the suburbs (something he had already made a fortune doing) but in old city centers dismissed by many at the time as economically hopeless. Rouse correctly surmised that not only would people come to such "festival marketplaces," they would happily pay more for an item or a meal there because it was delivered in a setting imbued with history and a sense of place. The first Rouse-Thompson project involved a run-down warehouse and market complex in Boston close to the waterfront, which was transformed into the Faneuil Hall Marketplace. The Faneuil Hall–Quincy Market complex opened in 1976 and eventually became the Rouse Company's most profitable venture. Rouse and Thompson perfected their festival-marketplace formula, undertaking equally successful projects such as Baltimore Harborplace, New York's South Street Seaport, and Jacksonville Landing in Florida. Common to all these Rouse-Thompson collaborations was an emphasis on built heritage and history as a theme for upmarket consumption; they used reclaimed historic buildings or created new structures sympathetic to their historic waterfront settings.

The festival-marketplace approach to urban revitalization was emulated by cities coast to coast and succeeded where many urban renewal czars and their modernist architects had failed. Rouse himself was hailed as a visionary and was featured on the front cover of *Time* magazine in 1981, with the words

"Cities are Fun!"[65] The heritage theme remains popular today, so much so that American developers have even attempted to transport the grit and color of inner-city industrial scenes to the suburbs, creating de novo shopping malls such as the Streets at Southpoint in North Carolina. Developed by the Rouse Company on a suburban site in the Research Triangle, the vast retail complex is anchored by an ersatz smokestack and a "Main Street" formed by fake renditions of the red-brick tobacco warehouses in nearby downtown Durham, complete with faded period advertisements for cornflakes and Bull Durham tobacco.

Both the festival-marketplace approach to downtown revitalization and the creation of pedestrianized shopping streets—also popular in the United States in the 1970s—have become popular strategies for creating upscale consumption spaces in Chinese cities in recent years. In Zhongshan, city officials transformed a major thoroughfare in the old town center, Sun Wen Xi Road, into a heritage-themed pedestrian mall that opened in 1996. The avenue had been punched through the old walled city in the 1920s, part of a nationwide wave of urban modernizations carried out in the early years of the Republic. The new street was lined with arcaded shop houses three or four stories in height—a building type popular throughout the region in this era.[66]

As the greater Guangdong economy took off in the 1990s, Zhongshan officials turned to the street as a mechanism for revitalizing their long-neglected town center. They commissioned historical research on the street and its shops and sent city planners abroad to see at first-hand heritage-themed pedestrian streets in Europe, Australia, and the United States. These studies helped formulate an intervention reminiscent of Fuzi Miao a decade earlier, only now the main attraction was an ordinary commercial streetscape and not an esteemed temple. The thoroughfare was sealed off from traffic, paved with brick, and signed "Sun Wen Xi Road Tourism Zone." Shops were refurbished and painted lively colors, their facades flushed with floodlights at night; historical photographs of the street were mounted along the arcade; and street furniture and public art, mostly of the whimsical human-figure sort, were placed along the way. Once-gritty Sun Wen Xi Road thus morphed into a "cosmetic heritage" consumer zone; it was an overnight success, and so popular that the pedestrian street was later extended another third of a mile to Yue Lai Road. Interviews conducted in 2000 found that visitors uniformly regarded the street as a pleasant and attractive place to shop and even a symbol of Zhongshan.[67] The Sun

Zhongshan Street, Zhongshan, 1999. PHOTOGRAPH BY AUTHOR

Wen Xi Road project was followed by similar heritage street redevelopments in Guangzhou, Foshan, and elsewhere.

But the apotheosis of consumer-oriented heritage urbanism in China came several years later with the first-phase completion, in 2001, of Shanghai's Xintiandi shopping district (literally, "New Heaven and Earth"). The importance of this project, built around a core of restored buildings from the treaty-port era, cannot be fully appreciated outside of its Chinese context. In the West, consumer-oriented urban heritage redevelopment projects are nothing new; Xintiandi's builder, Vincent H. S. Lo, would hardly be hailed as a visionary in New York or Los Angeles. But the furious pace of development in recent years has all but rubbed out China's vernacular urban heritage, so even the smallest reversal of this tabula rasa trend must be cheered. Xintiandi, however contrived, however ersatz, seems to promise a new day in which China's urban architectural past is spared the usual fate of wholesale destruction, even if this means being dolled up and turned into a platform for consumerism.

Vincent Lo cut his teeth developing projects that had little or nothing to do with urban heritage. His Shui On Group, launched in Hong Kong with a loan from his father in 1971, made its name building modernist complexes such as Richland Gardens in Kowloon Bay and the company's own steel-and-glass headquarters, Shui On Centre. In the late 1990s, Lo secured development rights to a 128-acre parcel in Shanghai's Taipingqiao District, just south of Huaihai Road. The area was well stocked with a hybrid Western-Chinese form of housing built throughout the city around the turn of the nineteenth century known as *shikumen* (literally, "stone gate"). As with Beijing's *siheyuan*, much of this fabric—which once housed as much as 80 percent of Shanghai's population—had already been razed by the late 1990s. Lo was prepared to do much the same with his parcel.

That he chose otherwise must be credited to the American architect Lo hired to lead the project, Benjamin Wood. Wood convinced Lo that the *shikumen*, rather than dirty old relics, were a kind of urban Chinese equivalent of the Tuscan hilltowns Lo loved and admired. With Wood's guidance, the developer began to see in the sooty buildings and packed streets not an impediment to future development but its very key. Rather than clear the entire site and cover it with new buildings, Wood applied a strategy of reversed infill, selectively removing structures and restoring others to create a more spacious streetscape and yield a clarified, gentrified version of the old neighborhood—purged now,

Site of the First National Congress of the Chinese Communist Party (July 23, 1921),
Xintiandi, Shanghai, 2007. PHOTOGRAPH BY AUTHOR

of course, of its original residents and ready for new service as a stage for
upscale consumption. Indeed, Xintiandi's shops are secondary in importance
to the spectacle of the place. People go to Xintiandi to see and be seen as much
as to eat and drink, "to present themselves," as Tom Doctoroff has observed of
Starbucks in China, "as modern Chinese in a public setting."[68] Xintiandi effectively sold old Shanghai "back to its own residents," as Jen Lin-Liu has written—or at least to those who could afford it.[69]

The Wood-Lo collaboration is more than a little reminiscent of that
between Thompson and Rouse, and for good reason. Wood began his career
working for the cocreator of the American festival marketplace. After graduat-
ing from MIT in the 1980s, Wood took a job in Ben Thompson's Cambridge,
Massachusetts, office; he helped plan South Street Seaport and was the firm's
director of design by the time Thompson was awarded the Gold Medal by
the American Institute of Architects in 1992.[70] As Wood himself described
his relationship with Lo, "Everything I did previously in my career prepared me to work with this guy.... I'd done things that involved making destinations out of urban streetscapes, as opposed to making destinations out of
shopping malls."[71]

"1912," a Xintiandi-style entertainment district in Nanjing, 2006. PHOTOGRAPH BY AUTHOR

Though Xintiandi has received numerous awards and accolades in recent years, many critics see it as little more than a tarted-up simulacrum of the urban past. Orthodox preservationists are correct when they point out that Xintiandi's buildings have a disembodied, stage-set quality to them, that they seem disconnected from the surrounding urban fabric. Wood, who emphasizes that he is not a preservationist, has himself pointed out that many of the "original" buildings were in fact torn down and reconstructed. But despite its shortcomings, Xintiandi's appeal is considerable and multivalenced. As Wood himself has observed, Xintiandi is a place where China goes to see the West and the West goes to see China, where the old go to see the future and the young to see the past. If nothing else, Xintiandi helped make history cool—and prove that reclaiming the past can be big business.

Certainly it has been a major hit in Shanghai, and is easily the trendiest spot in a city with no shortage of hip and cool. Xintiandi's boutiques, cafés, and pubs do a brisk business serving crowds of both expatriates and affluent Chinese professionals. Xintiandi is packed on almost any evening of the week. It is hard to believe that when Jiang Zemin toured the place in 1999 scores of Chinese actors had to be hired to fill the shops and restaurants and thin out

Xinghai Castle, Dalian, 2006. PHOTOGRAPH BY AUTHOR

the preponderance of foreign faces—a scene that would have upstaged the good prince Grigori Potemkin himself.[72] Just as ironic is the presence—right in the middle of this trendiest of themed consumer spaces—of the diminutive meeting hall where, in the summer of 1921, the Chinese Communist Party held its First National Congress.

Much as the success of Faneuil Hall Marketplace led Rouse and Thompson to New York, Baltimore, and elsewhere, Lo and Wood have been asked to "Xintiandi" sites in more than two dozen Chinese cities. To date, they have only undertaken one other similar development, Xihutiandi on the waterfront of West Lake in Hangzhou. But much like a bootleg DVD, the Xintiandi idea has been copied around China; even the name has come to be used as a general descriptor, much like "festival marketplace."[73] Nearly every major Chinese city now has a knockoff Xintiandi-style heritage district either opened, planned, or under way. In Nanjing, a handful of Nationalist-era buildings alongside the old presidential compound inspired an elaborate historicist development known as "1912" (a reference to the year Sun Yat-sen founded the Republic of China). New construction in the complex is virtually indistinguishable from the few authentic period pieces—a single block of modest row houses on the site's west side. Tenants at 1912 are similar to those at Xintiandi: an upscale array of cafés, shops, and restaurants with exposed brick, low-voltage lighting, and over-priced drinks.

Developers in Dalian have taken the Xintiandi trend a step further, building from scratch a new "historic district" on the waterfront at Xinghai. This Xintiandi—the name is identical to the Shanghai project—features French Renaissance–style edifices artfully arranged about a plaza with fountains and a spectacular view of the sea. On a hillside above sits an even more incongruous example of themed extravagance in China—a colossal Bavarian castle, bristling with turrets and towers and crenellated battlements. Even in a nation full of ersatz architectural wonders, the sheer audacity of this supercastle defies belief—never more so than when one learns it was erected by city officials to improve the district's *feng shui* and contains nothing more than a little seashell museum.

China Reinvents the City

重生的城市

To summarize a revolution-in-progress is a fool's errand. Rather than attempt such a task, I have instead sketched out here six defining aspects or characteristics of contemporary Chinese urbanism and the evolving Chinese cityscape. These include speed, scale, spectacle, sprawl, segregation, and—on a final, hopeful note—sustainability. While, individually, many of these attributes are not wholly new in the annals of urban development, taken together they yield a pattern and process of city making that is largely without precedent. They are the hallmarks of an urban transformation unlike anything the world has seen before; a wholesale reinvention of the city as we know it.

Speed

China is the most rapidly urbanizing nation in the world, and perhaps in history. Never have so many urban settlements grown so fast, nor has more urban fabric been razed and reconstructed with such haste. In a single extraordinary generation, China has undergone a process of urban growth and transformation that took a century to unfold in the United States—itself a nation whose speed once awed the world. Chicago, after all, was the Shenzhen of the nineteenth century. Chicago's spectacular growth, especially after the Great Fire of 1871, made it the fastest-growing city in America, just as Shenzhen became the hasty pacesetter of post-Mao China. All through the 1980s and 1990s, Chinese cities strained to meet or beat "Shenzhen tempo"—a pace set by workers on the International Foreign Trade Center and defined as a finished building floor every three days. Appropriately enough, that mark was shattered a decade later by workers on another Shenzhen tower, who knocked a full half-day off the previous record.

Dongguan Public Library, Dongguan administrative district, 2006. PHOTOGRAPH BY AUTHOR

Today, most of China moves at warp speed. In the hours it took to read this book, probably another thousand apartments units were readied for occupancy across the People's Republic; a dozen new shopping centers were likely opened; a score more office towers and housing estates topped off. Sinopec, the Chinese oil conglomerate, will likely open another 500 gas stations this year on China's roads and highways, as it has done for several years now. In 2007 alone, McDonald's opened 100 new restaurants in Chinese cities, many equipped for drive-through service.[1]

In China, whole new towns are conceived, planned, and constructed in the time it takes to get a small subdivision through the permitting process in the United States. China built its first Maglev rail system in Shanghai in just two years. It took a decade to build a similar line in Germany, and in the United States we still only dream of such space-age stuff. In England, once ruler of the seven seas, it took thirteen years for Heathrow Airport's new Terminal Five to see the light of day. The new terminal at Beijing Capital International Airport, the largest in the world, was built in thirty-six months.

Of course, speed is stunning, but it can also be stupid. Haste makes waste and tends to come at the cost of quality, longevity, and even safety. The frenetic pace with which Chinese cities are being built and rebuilt has struck many observers, foreign and Chinese, as reckless and chaotic. At least one critic, a geographer at the Chinese Academy of Science, compared the present cyclone of creative destruction to the excesses of the Great Leap Forward, a period of political turmoil and misguided policy that led to, among other things, the worst famine in human history.[2] It is for good reason, usually, that it takes a month of Sundays to build anything in the United States. We have a vast system of checks and balances meant to slow things down, to rule out binge-building and architectural excess. Colossal urban renewal and expressway projects in the 1960s pushed one too many citizens around and led to a backlash against "master plans" and the "physical planners" who concocted them. The planning profession in turn rejected urban design and snuggled closer to the social sciences. New theories of advocacy planning, community development, and public participation helped make developers and municipalities accountable for their actions.

This is just now beginning to make its way to China, where urban planning is mostly still about spiffy drawings and spectacular visions. There are few, if any, mechanisms to assure public participation in the development

Rapid obsolescence: early 1990s building razed for new high-rise, Nanjing, Gulou District, 2007.

PHOTOGRAPH BY AUTHOR

process. The Maoist dictum that the individual should be subordinate to the collective will has been handily exploited to excuse all sorts of abuses in the name of national progress. In mid-1990s Shanghai, residents who protested their eviction for the Inner Ring Road were excoriated for selfishly impeding China's development and modernization. But with the exception of occasional (and increasingly common) "stubborn nails" like Wu Ping, the refusenik of Chongqing, the development juggernaut faces little opposition. In the United States, democratic institutions at the state and local levels act like a giant sea-anchor on development. The resulting torpor can be frustrating, and the community input process is all too often hijacked by ignorance, fear, and not-in-my-backyard self-interest. But, just as often, going slow yields a better project. Unchecked, speed is costly and can even kill. Countless Chinese buildings, thrown up in haste, have already outlived their usefulness. The life span of architecture in China is measured in dog's years. In 2006 I counted half a dozen office towers in center-city Nanjing that were scheduled for demolition or in the process of being razed; all had been built in the late 1980s and early 1990s. In most places, a building of such recent vintage would still be considered new.

While there have been significant improvements in recent years, construction quality is still often abysmal, even on tony commercial projects. Binge-building yields a high quotient of urban junk. A Beijing realtor to whom I was praising the spare, elegant architecture of a trendy housing estate in the central business district shook her head and advised me not to look too closely at how it was all put together. Upmarket housing on the outskirts of Nanjing, built in late 2000, looks today as if it had been built in the 1960s: crumbling staircases, facades streaked and stained. Even Paul Andreu's signature Pudong International Airport, opened in 1999, was visibly aging when I was there in 2006. Shoddy construction, a lack of code enforcement, and poor building maintenance is not only wasteful, but has killed many people—such as the dozen shoppers who lost their lives when a Dongguan shopping mall collapsed in December 2000.

Scale

Bigness is another defining aspect of China's contemporary urban landscape—and of Chinese ambition generally. Like speed, scale too was once an American specialty. A century ago, visitors from England and the Continent were enraptured—or dismayed—by the sky-piercing loft of American commercial architecture, or by the vast power embodied in American industrial landscapes. Europeans were awed by the steel works of Pittsburgh, Gary, or, earlier, the sprawling textile mills of Lowell or Lawrence. The Chicago stockyards, a stygian merger of pastoralism and industry, held the greatest concentration of livestock on earth and was also as much a stop on the tourist circuit as Niagara Falls. From the Columbian Exposition to the Hoover Dam, the Empire State Building to the Interstate Highway System, the United States has long been the sultan of size. Its overreaching ambition was never more aptly summarized than by Daniel Burnham's famous dictum: "Make no little plans."

The pinnacle of American achievement in this regard—the Apollo Program and the first few moon landings—came, poetically enough, just before the fall. By the early 1970s, the cultural tide had turned against bigness and ambition—a turn greatly expedited by the American misadventure in Vietnam. Suddenly, small was beautiful, and so were small plans; Burnham, purged by followers of Jane Jacobs, went down with Robert Moses and Edward J. Logue and the rest of the Great White Planners. We still do things in a big way in the United States; we invented the internet, after all, and have hardly checked our global scale of military adventuring. But when it comes to large-scale urban projects, China has largely displaced the United States, and the West in general.

There is hardly any category of building type, infrastructure, or amenity that China has not built in its largest incarnation. China is home to three of the five largest shopping malls on earth, two of the three longest bridges, five of the world's ten tallest buildings, and the world's new largest urban plaza (even Tiananmen Square has been displaced). It has built the largest dam and the biggest gated community and is well on its way to having the world's most extensive national highway network, greater in extent than even the American interstate system. China has the world's highest rail line and the world's longest, largest bus (half as wide as a football field, with room for 300 passengers). It has the biggest airport terminal and the largest bowling alley, the biggest tennis complex and the most expansive golf course, the largest skateboard park, and even the world's largest lamp. China has built the biggest Buddhas on earth and, in Henan Province, even the world's largest dragon: a thirteen-mile tourist colossus meant also to protect the city of Zhengzhou from wind-blown sand. For a time, China even boasted the world's largest McDonald's restaurant. But, appropriately enough, the behemoth—which opened in

1990 just off Chang'an Avenue in Beijing—was itself rubbed out to make way for something bigger still: Oriental Plaza Shopping Center, also one of Asia's largest.

China has also built more housing in the last twenty-five years than any nation in history, indeed, more than most nations' total housing stock—more than 70 billion square feet nationwide between 1981 and 2001 (equivalent to some 30 million average-sized American houses).[3] Shanghai alone created 208 million square feet of new housing between 1990 and 2004. The human dimension of China's urban transformation is also immense in scale. Since 1992, some forty-six Chinese cities have joined the million-plus population club; there are but nine American members. Wholesale redevelopment of center-city neighborhoods in China has displaced more urban residents than anything else in the peacetime history of the world. The number of people who have migrated to China's cities in the last twenty-five years is greater than the entire population of the United States, and China's middle class alone could well be as big as the entire current population of Europe by 2020.

As Burnham understood, bigness has a life force and spirit all its own. Jovian architectural and urban interventions are deterministic by virtue of scale alone; they create their own weather, if you will. The enormous political and financial muscle necessary to get a big project rolling also gives it almost unstoppable forward momentum, while the simple act of clearing so vast a site fundamentally changes the context of a big project; "big schemes overrun the territory they require," writes Dana Cuff, "leaving no trace of the former land use."[4]

Such tabula rasa city making has particular appeal to an authoritarian regime, and to developers keen on turning a quick profit. Bigness is also seductive from a theoretical perspective. In an influential 1994 interview in *Artforum*, Rem Koolhaas claimed that urban-architectural bigness was an antidote to the chaos and disorder of the fin de siècle metropolis, and that only very large architectural works could sustain in a single urban container the "promiscuous proliferation of events" that make a city what it is. "In a landscape of disarray, disassembly, dissociation, disclamation," he argued, "the attraction of Bigness is its potential to reconstruct the Whole, resurrect the Real, reinvent the collective, reclaim maximum possibility." The big project might be destructive at the outset—the thousands of families dislodged for colossal projects in Beijing or Shanghai would wholeheartedly agree—but it also seems to promise greater things still; "it can reassemble," noted Koolhaas, "what it breaks."[5] Though it's unlikely that very many developers or government officials in the People's Republic have read Koolhaas, they might well be comforted to know their big plans could be so eloquently justified. And so, too, those from the West who come East to satisfy their inner Daniel Burnhams. For China is the last refuge of architectural audacity, the last place on earth (tiny Dubai aside) where ego, scale, and ambition can still be indulged in brick and mortar. In China the sky can still be pricked and poked far from the zoning officials and community activists and the picky planning boards that govern what gets built in America.

Spectacle

The issue of scale is closely linked to that of spectacle. The contemporary Chinese city is spectacular in the literal sense of the word; it is meant to dazzle and awe, and to do so both internally and to a larger world audience. Spectacle in citymaking is nothing new, and the use of architecture and urban design to create a sense of wonder or fear can be traced back to the earliest urban settlements. Doing so was often related to faith or politics or, in the case of colonial regimes, to make an indelible statement of power and control to a subject people. In modern capitalist societies, architectural spectacle is typically a function of the marketplace. The flashy corporate office tower is, of course, the most obvious example; the staggered skylines of Chicago or New York or Los Angeles are, in this sense, bar graphs of competing corporate ego. In China, urbanistic spectacle results from a more complex set of ego inputs, one that certainly involves private real estate developers, but is also driven by party cadres and local officials eager to make their mark on the skyline. Cities flush with money from land leasing, taxes, and development fees have embarked on a range of civic improvement projects, many of extraordinary scale, luxury, and extent. Many visitors to Chinese cities have been deeply impressed by all this—by airports and opera houses; museums and convention centers and exposition halls; public recreation facilities, extensive new parks, waterfront promenades, and vast urban plazas studded with fountains and public art.

At Xinghai, a booming part of Dalian just southwest of the city center, municipal officials have created the largest public plaza in the world, a spectacular oval-shaped space slashed by axes with a star at the center and embroidered all about with arabesque parterres that can only be fully appreciated from

Xinghai Square, Dalian, 2006. PHOTOGRAPH BY AUTHOR

the air. The open space is at least two times larger than Tiananmen Square, and three Pentagons could easily fit within it with room to spare. Xinghai Square is enframed by luxury housing towers and anchored on one side by the sprawling Dalian World Expo and Convention Center, begun in 2003 and designed by French architect Emmanuel Delarue.

In Xi'an, city officials built a spectacular new plaza to showcase the Tang Dynasty Big Goose Pagoda. But what really makes the scene is a vast fountain complex whose hundreds of shooting water jets, synchronized to music and illuminated at night by lasers and floodlights, is a sight not soon forgotten (nor is the incongruity, sharply noted by local residents, of such aqueous indulgence in an arid region and in a city challenged with perennial water shortages).

One of the most dazzling examples of grand public works in China is Dongguan's new administrative center, built about a 230-acre, mile-long terraced plaza anchored at one end by a monumental City Hall and at the other by a trapezoidal Youth and Children's Center—a relationship that says perhaps more about China's keen commitment to education than it does about its obsession with political order. Also on axis, on the north side of the Children's Center, is a lake—nothing extraordinary, perhaps, until it is revealed to also be the roof of a vast parking garage. Deployed on either side of the axis is a remarkable ensemble of signature buildings—the kind of architectural trophy collection that every city mayor dreams about. Among the larger buildings is the Yulan Theater, Dongguan Science and Technology Museum, a conference center grand enough to serve as a national capitol, and the well-appointed Dongguan Public Library—the latter as much a bibliotechnic statement of arrival as was McKim, Mead & White's Boston Public Library more than a century ago. Dongguan is certainly not alone in building a glorious administrative headquarters for itself; equally spectacular districts have been built or are being developed by municipalities throughout the Pearl River Delta and coastal China.

There are also public works of relatively more modest scale in China's cities that are dazzling nonetheless as public improvements. Hangzhou officials, for example, transformed that city's once derelict, swampy lakefront into a splendid example of urban design, with miles of boardwalk promenades, teahouses, and gardens strung along the shore. Nanjing recently completed an extensive complex of new parks and pedestrian trails on Purple Mountain in the vicinity of Pipa Lake and the Sun Yat-sen Mausoleum.

Conference center, Dongguan administrative district, 2006. PHOTOGRAPH BY AUTHOR

All these public works spectacles appear to be the fruits of municipal largesse (not to say affluence) unlike anything seen in the United States since the New Deal. But caution is needed in assessing these projects, or at least the intentions of the responsible officials. Despite real and measurable benefits to the people, grand public works in China are often conceived with more self-serving interests in mind. They are typically undertaken by city and provincial officials to impress Party superiors and, especially, the leadership in Beijing. In China, officials have no democratic constituencies to please; they are rewarded and promoted based largely on what they do, and nothing brings rewards faster than having a spectacular new opera house or convention center to show a visiting VIP from the central government. For this reason, costly public works of the kind described above are commonly referred to in China as "face" or "image" projects (*xing xiang gong chen*).

This yearning for "face" plays out on a larger, global stage as well. China is a nation on the rise, keen on making its mark on the world and erasing the legacy of its past humiliation at the hands of the West and Japan. Like the self-made parvenu, China is striving to outbuild and outshine those who long kept her on her knees. This is, of course, the prime motive force behind China's fervent preparations for the 2008 Olympic Games. It is also clearly at work in the preparations for World Expo 2010 in Shanghai. The money and effort being poured into this event are more than a little reminiscent of the World's Columbian Exposition of 1893. The Columbian Expo, which nominally marked the 400th anniversary of Columbus's voyage to the New World, was really a coming-out party for the United States, thrown to celebrate the triumph of American industrialization, the closing of the frontier West, and the phoenix-like rebirth of Chicago after the Great Fire. In effect, it marked the start of the "American Century."

Shanghai's World Expo 2010 is just as ambitious, and it is expected to draw the largest number of visitors of any world's fair in history. Just as Pullman's coaches served the Chicago fair on their very own rail spur, Shanghai is building its second high-speed Maglev rail line to shuttle regional visitors to the Expo site. Even the theme of the Shanghai fair, "Better City—Better Life," is reminiscent of the Chicago event, whose "White City" set new standards for architecture and urban design that shaped American space for decades to come. That Shanghai should host this event is also poetically appropriate; Shanghai today is just as adrenaline-pumped as Chicago was a century ago—a harbinger of things to come that visitors will gaze upon with an unsettling mix of fear and wonder.

Sprawl

Cities in China are spreading out rapidly upon the landscape, undergoing a process of rapid centrifugal expansion. As explored in Chapter 7, "Suburbanization and the Mechanics of Sprawl," China-style sprawl differs in keys ways from its American cousin. For one, Chinese suburbs are far more dense than anything in the suburban United States; even single-family "villa" developments are, on average, much more thickly laid upon the land than most American McMansion subdivisions. Chinese suburbs also lack the political and administrative autonomy that characterizes American suburban communities; they are, by and large, no more than outlying districts of a city whose administrative boundaries typically reach far into the hinterland (Chongqing, for example, encompasses 31,815 square miles—the largest city in the world in terms of land area).

While many affluent people are moving to the suburbs in China, they are accompanied on the urban fringe by those of lesser means—including workers whose places of employment have relocated to the edge of town and low-income urban residents displaced by wholesale redevelopment of the center city. Between 1990 and 2000 in Beijing, the city center lost 222,000 people while suburban districts gained some three million people, including many residents of *hutong* neighborhoods forced out by urban renewal.[6] Chinese suburbanization is also largely devoid of the underlying cultural ambivalence toward cities that helped drive urban flight in America, especially in the 1960s and 1970s. In China, cities are hot. But they are also increasingly expensive places to live, and this factor alone has driven millions of former city dwellers to seek less costly accommodations on the urban periphery. The homes they choose are also very different from those in the suburban United States. The single-family residence on a spacious lot is still only for the superrich in China. Much more common is the gated mid- to high-rise housing estate—the standard unit of Chinese suburban sprawl.

But there are also key commonalities between Chinese and American sprawl. As in the United States, sprawl in China has consumed an immense amount of productive agricultural land. Chinese sprawl is also a function of rising car ownership, for the People's Republic is going mobile with abandon. China is the fastest-growing automobile market in the world, and by 2020 may well be both the largest producer and consumer of cars in the world, with total ownership exceeding even that of the United States. This means a surfeit of highway asphalt, and it is also yielding a whole new exurban landscape oriented to motorists, one in which many of the forms and spaces of American-style suburban sprawl—from big-box retail stores and drive-through restaurants to motels and megamalls—have been reproduced, now with Chinese characteristics.

Segregation

Chinese urban space is fast segregating along new lines of income, class, and social status. Maoism, for all its numerous shortcomings, did succeed in creating a society in which all people were equal, at least in theory. Today the tycoon has replaced the worker or soldier—or Chairman Mao—as the new cult hero in China. Chinese bookstores overflow with "How I Earned My Fortune" titles by self-made millionaires like Pan Shiyi of SOHO China or Wang Shi, the former People's Liberation Army soldier who founded Vanke. China may still be nominally a socialist nation, a republic of the people still led by a communist regime, but in reality China has become one of the most stridently ambitious capitalistic societies on earth, a nation on the make, hungry to get rich. I often joke with my students that progressive cities like Chapel Hill or Cambridge are far more socialistic today than the People's Republic of China.

In the last thirty years economic reform and rising affluence in China have lifted hundreds of millions of people out of poverty, more perhaps than in any nation in history. Yet at the same time the ideals of social justice and equality that China has long purported to uphold have all but vaporized. Disparities between rich and poor, between the haves and have-nots, are increasing rapidly and seem to promise that kind of bifurcated society that has long typified Latin America or India. China today is a brutally competitive, almost Darwinistic place; the weak, feeble, unintelligent, or unskilled are quickly crushed and cast aside. Migrant workers especially are ruthlessly exploited by the machinery of wealth production—the very men and women whose labors make the factories hum and the skyscrapers rise. China's migrant workers, idled by an agricultural economy made more efficient by market reforms, come to the cities in search of a better life and to escape the crushing poverty of the rural countryside. This "floating population" has streamed into China's urban regions by the tens of millions in recent years, and may number as much as 140 million people nationwide. Migrant workers typically have no health care or insurance, let alone any sort of social-service net to fall back upon or unions to take up their case.

Expanding class and economic disparities are increasingly mirrored in the built environment. The city of the rising elite is one of bright lights and big ambition, of gated, guarded housing estates and glitzy shopping malls. But in the midst of such privilege is often another urban world, one inhabited by the poor and disenfranchised; the densely packed "urban villages" trapped in the middle of Shenzhen, Guangzhou, and other cities are only the most visible example.

Sustainability
In December 2006 it was widely reported in the global media that the Chinese river dolphin, the *baiji*, was extinct. The species, once abundant in the lower Yangtze River, had come under severe stress in recent years as a result of increasingly heavy ship traffic, dam construction, runoff, and pollution. Only

a handful of the animals had been sighted in the previous decade, none since 2004. The dolphin, once known as "the goddess of the Yangtze," was the first large aquatic mammal to go extinct since the 1950s. The passing of this odd-looking creature, news of which barely caused a ripple in the People's Republic, is symbolic nonetheless of China's looming environmental crisis—a problem of truly global proportions. China's environmental problems are legion. Nearly all of the most terribly polluted cities in the world are in China, and vital air and water resources are fast becoming toxic. Nanjing, renowned for its street trees, parks, and universities, is practically smothered most evenings by an acrid-smelling smog blown in by nocturnal winds from chemical plants on the outskirts of town. In Xi'an, a combination of Gobi Desert dust and smoke from farmers burning wheat fields in the surrounding countryside makes for near zero visibility at certain times of the year. Beijing on the best of days struggles with some of the highest levels of motor-vehicle-borne carbon emissions in Asia.

China is also consuming natural resources at a ferocious clip and scouring the planet in search of raw materials. It is now the second largest consumer of oil in the world and burns through more fossil fuel than Russia and India combined. As Thomas L. Friedman has pointed out, this hunger for oil has led China into making deals with some of the least savory regimes on earth, in Sudan, Zimbabwe, Angola, and elsewhere.[7] Although Chinese money pouring into sub-Saharan Africa has awakened the region's long-dormant economies and stimulated growth unseen in decades, China's Africa play is wholly absent humanitarian impulse and is driven exclusively by rising demand for oil, coal, copper, iron, timber, and other natural resources.

From South America to Central Asia, China is literally consuming the world. All this comes at the very moment when the United States, Japan, and Western Europe—long the chief polluters of Spaceship Earth—have finally begun to end their decades of bad environmental behavior. Yet scientists have argued that even if all greenhouse gas emissions were to stop tomorrow, it would take centuries to reverse the damage already done. This daunting prospect is made more so by the likelihood, according to statistics from the Chinese government itself, that by 2008 China will eclipse the United States as the world's leading producer of greenhouse gases—an Olympian achievement indeed. "Today's global warming problem has been caused mainly by us in the

West," observes David Fridley of the Lawrence Berkeley National Laboratory's China Energy Group, "but China is contributing to the global warming problem of tomorrow."[8]

When it comes to the environment, China and the West are moving in opposite directions, and at blinding speed. As recently as 2001, for example, China's total greenhouse gas emissions were only 42 percent of what the United States was producing at the time; just five years later that number was up to 97 percent.[9] China's usual response to such criticism is to claim exemption as a developing country, and to point out the hypocrisy of Western—and especially American—pots calling the Chinese kettle black. China's per capita energy consumption, after all, is a mere fraction of America's. Why should China hobble its growth, people ask, when the West got rich plundering the planet?

The answer, of course, is that China has no choice. Even if Beijing cares not a whit about the well-being of other peoples and nations, it cares greatly about keeping its own economy on an upward trend, and it has increasingly come to see that doing so will require taking positive steps to protect the environment and reduce its galloping pace of resource consumption. For China, "going green" is not the lifestyle option it is often construed to be in the United States. Spoiled by its enormous wealth, land, and resources, America has long been a wasteful and inefficient nation; only recently has it begun to take seriously the nexus between environmental health and future economic viability. For China, reducing resource consumption is an even more urgent matter. China is trying to run a marathon at a sprinter's pace. The nation's current course of fast growth and expanding resource use is utterly unsustainable. Moreover, its increasing dependence on foreign commodities exposes China to the uncertainties of global geopolitics and the whims of other countries. With the possible exception of social instability from the growing gap between rich and poor, nothing more fully threatens the future of the People's Republic than the prospect of catastrophic environmental collapse or the economic meltdown that would result from a sudden lack of oil. As George Perkins Marsh demonstrated in his book *Man and Nature* (1864), mighty civilizations have ground to a halt for less.

There are indeed encouraging signs that China has begun to take environmental matters seriously. And it need only look back to its own past for inspiration. China is a civilization with a long and rich history of harmonious and often sublime coexistence with the natural environment, perhaps best exemplified by the ancient gardens of Hangzhou or Suzhou. Vernacular architecture in nearly every region of China embodies centuries of environmental wisdom and includes some of the best examples of sustainable design and "green building" anywhere in the world.[10] One is the *yao dong* courtyard house of the loess plateau regions of Shaanxi, Henan, Shanxi, and Gansu provinces, among the oldest form of human habitation on earth. The cave-like hillside dwellings, landscape architecture in the truest sense, are set about excavated courtyards and provide a suprisingly comfortable living environment in all seasons; the houses are cool in summer and warm in winter. China's grassroots-level sustainability can also be seen on nearly every city street, in the old woman collecting empty water bottles or the rural migrants pedaling unbelievably overloaded tricycles full of recycled cardboard or Styrofoam. Every building demolition site in China is also a massive recycling operation. Anything that can be reused is set in neat piles to be carted off for new life—bricks, wiring, pipes, doors, window frames, scraps of structural timber, even mangled jumbles of reinforcement bar. Most such materials would end up in a landfill in the United States.

Of course, these and other examples of street-level sustainability in China are more a function of poverty than a strong ethic of environmental stewardship. As such, unfortunately, they are both stigmatized and bound to decline as China becomes increasingly affluent. Bicycle use has been falling in most cities for these very reasons; bikes are seen as a poor-person's transport option and are quickly thrown aside as families make their way up the socioeconomic ladder. In Henan and Shaanxi provinces, rural families who have lived in *yao dong* dwellings for generations yearn to move to fancy new high-rise flats with air conditioning and a modern kitchen. Architects in the region, such as Xia Yun and Liu Jia Ping of Xi'an University of Architecture and Technology, have been working to prevent this by developing a workable prototype of an updated, modern *yao dong* house.

In similar spirit, China's central government itself has launched a string of promising reforms in recent years aimed at reducing China's collective environmental impact. In a rare example of self-criticism in January 2007, the central government even admitted that China failed to meet its own goals for environmental protection, its "ecological modernization" lagging far behind economic and other achievements.[11] One of the most promising pieces of legislation is the Renewable Energy Promotion Law, passed in 2005 and implemented a year

Building material recycling at a *hutong* demolition site, Chongwen District, Beijing, 2004.
PHOTOGRAPH BY AUTHOR

later. As conveyed by Article I, the law was intended "to promote the development and utilization of renewable energy...diversify energy supplies, safeguard energy security, protect the environment, and realize the sustainable development of the economy and society." Especially emphasized were renewable energy sources—wind, solar, tidal and hydroelectric, geothermal and biomass. The central government has further set itself a target of 12 percent of total power capacity from renewable energy sources by 2020.[12]

Indeed, despite the fact that a new coal-fired power plant opens every ten days in China, the nation may yet show the world how to go green. For all the automobiles crowding onto its city streets, China is also building more miles of subway and light-rail public transportation than any nation on earth. China already has the world's largest biofuels plant and the world's largest solar plant, a 100-megawatt facility in Dunhuang, Gansu Province, that dwarfs its closest rivals—a 12-megawatt plant in Germany and an 11-megawatt facility under construction in Portugal. In February 2007 China announced plans to earmark some 200 million acres of woodland for biomass production and to plant trees on more than 600,000 acres of land in Yunnan and Sichuan

New *yao dong* housing, Da Ping village, Henan Province, 2007.
PHOTOGRAPH BY AUTHOR

provinces for similar purposes. China's installed wind-power capacity has been growing exponentially, and the Global Wind Energy Council has predicted that by 2020 China could be drawing 150 million kilowatts of energy from the wind, surpassing Germany, Spain, and the United States to become the world's leading producer of wind power.[13]

China already boasts some 60 percent of the world's installed solar water heater capacity, and an estimated thirty million households nationwide use solar power in one form or another. Ready-to-install A-frame solar units come complete with a water tank and are sold at any major home-improvement store, displayed out front the way garden sheds are at American stores. Needless to say, no such ready-built solar equipment is available in the United States, where low-voltage garden lights are about the only solar-powered thing readily available at home-improvement stores. In September 2005, Shanghai officials approved a measure to install more than one million square feet of solar panels on rooftops across the city, in addition to several solar power plants.[14] In the early morning, from my twelfth-floor office window in Nanjing, I could see the

Rooftop solar water heaters, Xi'an, 2007. PHOTOGRAPH BY AUTHOR

sunlight glinting off hundreds of solar water-heating units on the rooftops of the city below—a comforting sight indeed.

The same economies of scale that have rockbottomed the cost of everything from air conditioners to Christmas ornaments may well also produce photovoltaic arrays affordable enough to make solar electricity a viable option for homeowners around the world. As architect William McDonough has put it, "When China comes on line with solar collectors that are cheaper than coal, it will be one of the greatest gifts to the United States"—and to the world. Making solar power more cost-effective than burning coal is, McDonough argues, "the assignment of our species at this moment in history. And China is the only place where this can happen."[15] It is a promising sign indeed that one of China's richest men, Shi Zhengrong of Suntech Power, a graduate of the School of Photovoltaic and Renewable Energy Engineering at the University of New South Wales, made a fortune manufacturing photovoltaic cells for solar panels.

China may well also show the world how to build a truly sustainable city. One of the most ambitious—and promising—urban development projects in the world today is planned for Chongming Island, a fifty-mile-long spit of land in the middle of the Yangtze River near Shanghai. Chongming is a largely rural landscape, but in coming decades it is to be transformed into a self-sufficient green city known as Dongtang. Powered by energy from wind turbines and biofuels derived from farm waste, Dongtang is meant to source 30 percent of its energy from renewables by 2020 and eventually achieve an overall carbon-emission level of zero. No fossil-fueled cars or trucks will be permitted on the island, where transportation will be handled instead by solar-powered water taxis and buses running on hydrogen fuel cell technology. The urbanized portion of Dongtang will be compacted into three "villages" built with energy-efficient green building technology. Large portions of the island will be forested or used for organic farming. The local economy will be sustained by eco-tourism and low-polluting, high-tech industry. In its first phase, Dongtang will accommodate 25,000 people, but it is expected to eventually be home to as many as 500,000 by 2040.[16] The project is, of course, not without its critics and potential problems. It could well end up just a green theme park for eco-curious tourists from Shanghai. But the very fact that China has chosen to invest in such an ambitious experiment is much to its credit, and even if it fails to achieve every goal, Dongtang could well serve as a laboratory for green urbanism elsewhere.

Though environmental stewardship has a long and rich history in China, it is, as yet, surely not characteristic of contemporary Chinese urbanism. At present, sustainability in Chinese cities is no more than a faint spark against a vast, dark field. But again, the sheer scale of Chinese ambition potentially makes even this a beacon for the world; "a glimmer in China," as McDonough put it to me recently, "is a bright light in the world indeed."[17] So I end this exploration of the new Chinese landscape on a somewhat hopeful note: that, whatever its motivations, China will reinvent the city as a more sustainable entity, and thus perhaps show the rest of this fast-urbanizing planet a new and greener approach to urban settlement and urban life. The continued growth of the Chinese economy—indeed the very viability of the People's Republic—surely depends upon it. And so do we all.

NOTES

The Urbanism of Ambition

1. See Howard W. French, "Homeowner Stares Down Wreckers, at Least for a While," *New York Times*, March 27, 2007; Joseph Kahn, "China Backs Property Law, Buoying Middle Class," *New York Times*, March 16, 2007. Eventually the building was pulled down, but not before its owner won generous compensation from the developers.

2. Photographer Edward Burtynsky captures the awesome scale of the Three Gorges project and the landscapes it doomed. See http://www.edwardburtynsky.com.

3. Piper Gaubatz, "China's Urban Transformation," *Urban Studies* 36, no. 9 (1999): 1515.

4. Ian Johnson, "Moving a Mountain to Clear the Bad Air in Lanzhou, China," *Wall Street Journal*, August 7, 1997.

5. The total housing stock in the United States in 2005 was 218,654,766,000 square feet; from U.S. Census Bureau, Current Housing Reports, Series H150/05, American Housing Survey for the United States, http://www.census.gov/hhes/www/housing/ahs/nationaldata.html. Also see Shruti Gupta, "China: Building a Strong Foundation," *Frost & Sullivan Market Insight*, September 16, 2004.

6. In 2004, GDP of sub-Saharan Africa at market prices was approximately $529 billion; see "Sub-Saharan Africa Data Profile," *World Development Indicators Database* (World Bank Group, April 2006), http://devdata.worldbank.org.

7. David Barboza, "China Builds its Dreams, and Some Fear a Bubble," *New York Times*, October 18, 2005.

8. In 2004 China's construction industry employed about 24 million people; *China Statistical Yearbook* (Beijing: China Statistics Press, 2004).

9. See Daniel B. Wood, "Cement Shortage Hits US Housing Boom," *Christian Science Monitor*, August 17, 2004; Sandra Fleishman, "China's Expansion Squeezes Cement Supply," *Washington Post*, September 18, 2004.

10. For an introduction to the subject of Chinese highways, see the three-volume compilation *Highways in China* (Beijing: Ministry of Communication, 1990, 1995, 2000). For an American perspective, see Rob Gifford, *China Road* (New York: Random House, 2007).

11. "China Plans Everest Highway for Olympics Event," *CNN News*, June 19, 2007.

12. Accurate data on urban-renewal displacement in China is difficult to find. I based this estimate on measurements of the actual road channel using aerial photographs, combined with population density data from the Wendell Cox Consultancy (www.demographia.com).

13. Chinese Academy of Engineering, National Research Council, et al., *Personal Cars and China* (Washington, DC: National Academies Press, 2003), 228.

14. "China Stands as World's 2nd Largest Auto Market," *People's Daily*, January 13, 2006; Eric Baculinao, "China's Auto Industry Takes Off," *NBC News*, January 12, 2007.

15. Chia-Liang Tai, "Transforming Shanghai: The Redevelopment Context of the Pudong New Area" (unpublished masters thesis, Columbia University, Faculty of Architecture and Planning, May 2005), 54; "Beijing's Private Autos Top One Million," *Xinhua News*, May 22, 2002.

16. Between 1978 and 1995, approximately 11 million acres (17,375 square miles) of cultivated land in China were lost to development; another 17 million acres (26,562 square miles) vanished between then and 2004. See Jonathan Watts, "China's Farmers Cannot Feed Hungry Cities," *Guardian Unlimited*, August 26, 2004. Also see Chengri Ding and Gerrit

The Urbanism of Ambition
continued
Knaap, "Urban Land Policy Reform in China," *Land Lines* (Lincoln Institute of Land Policy) 15, no. 2 (April 2003).

17. Watts, "China's Farmers Cannot Feed Hungry Cities," August 26, 2004.

18. Li Conghua, *China: The Consumer Revolution* (New York: Wiley, 1998), 5.

19. GDP measured at purchasing-power parity; Pam Woodall, "The Dragon and the Eagle," *Economist*, September 30, 2004. See also "The Real Great Leap Forward," *Economist*, September 30, 2004.

20. Approximately 29 million people emigrated from Europe to the United States between 1820 and 1920, while about five million African Americans moved out of the rural South between 1940 and 1970. Approximately 6.5 million Americans moved from farms and rural areas to cities between 1920 and 1930.

21. As the *Los Angeles Times* pointed out, Yao's NBA salary alone makes him "one of China's most profitable exports to the United States." Ching-Ching Ni, "Working-Class Hero? NBA Star Nets China's Proletarian Award," *Los Angeles Times*, April 28, 2005.

22. Joseph Kahn, "China's Elite Learn to Flaunt It While the New Landless Weep," *New York Times*, December 25, 2004.

23. Hannah Beech, "Wretched Excess," *TIME Asia Magazine* 160, no. 11 (September 23, 2002).

24. The bronze likeness shows Li gesturing toward the horizon with his palm facing down, as if hailing a far-off friend. As Li explained in a 2002 interview, to have cast himself with palm raised up and outward would have been politically provocative; it is still a gesture reserved for likenesses of Mao Zedong. Craig S. Smith, "For China's Wealthy, All but Fruited Plain," *New York Times*, May 15, 2002. See also Rupert Hoogewerf, "Li Qinfu, Size XL," *Forbes.com*, November 11, 2002.

25. Daniel Abramson, "'Marketization' and Institutions in Chinese Inner-city Redevelopment," *Cities* 14, no. 2 (1997): 71n; Nancy Lin cites similar statistics (1:30,400 in China; 1:3,120 in the United States) in "Architecture Shenzhen," in Chuihua Judy Chung, Jeffrey Inaba, Rem Koolhaas, Sze Tsung, et al., eds., *Great Leap Forward* (Köln: Taschen, 2001), 158–61.

26. James, who wrote *The American Scene* upon his return from a twenty-year hiatus in Europe, understood the ephemerality and impermanence of the skyscraper city: "They never begin to speak to you, in the manner of the builded majesties of the world as we have heretofore known such—towers or temples or fortresses or palaces—with the authority of things of permanence or even of things of long duration. One story is good only till another is told, and sky-scrapers are the last word of economic ingenuity only till another word be written." Henry James, *The American Scene* (London: Chapman & Hall, 1907), 76–77.

Thunder from the South

1. This translation is from Peter Hessler, *Oracle Bones: A Journey Between China's Past and Present* (New York: Harper Collins, 2006), 83.

2. Ezra F. Vogel and Steven I. Levine, eds., *Deng Xiaoping Shakes the World: An Eyewitness Account of China's Party Work Conference and the Third Plenum* (Norwalk, CT: EastBridge, 2004), 145.

3. Ibid., 147.

4. Ibid., 143.

5. Ibid., xvii.

6. On the nexus between resistance to the opium trade and the Taiping rebellion, see Frederic Wakeman Jr., *Strangers at the Gate: Social Disorder in South China, 1839–1861* (Berkeley: University of California Press, 1966).

7. John K. Fairbank, *China: A New History* (Cambridge, MA: Harvard University Press, 1998), 192.

8. Ezra F. Vogel, *Canton Under Communism* (Cambridge, MA: Harvard University Press, 1969), 18.

9. Ibid., 21.

10. Mihai Craciun, "Ideology Shenzhen," in Chuihua Judy Chung, Jeffrey Inaba, Rem Koolhaas, Sze Tsung Leong, et al., eds., *Great Leap Forward* (Köln: Taschen, 2001), 85.

11. Ezra F. Vogel, *One Step Ahead in China: Guangdong Under Reform* (Cambridge, MA: Harvard University Press, 1989), 2, 85–86.

12. Anthony Gar-On Yeh, "Urbanization Trend in China: Coastal, River, and Interior Cities in China's Development," in *Chinese Cities and China's Development*, ed. Yeh and Chai-Kwong Mak, 149–82 (Hong Kong: University of Hong Kong, Centre of Urban Planning and Environmental Management, 1995).

13. "Per-capita Income of Shenzhen Farmers Near 10,000 Yuan," *People's Daily*, January 18, 2001; income figures are from the China National Bureau of

Statistics; see http://www.allcountries.org/china_statistics/10_20_per_capita_annual_net_income.html.

14. See Yue-man Yeung and Xu-wei Hu, eds., *China's Coastal Cities: Catalysts for Modernization* (Honolulu: University of Hawaii Press, 1992); also see David K. Y. Chu, "The Politico-economic Background to the Development of the Special Economic Zones," in *Modernization in China: The Case of the Shenzhen Special Economic Zone*, ed. Kwan-Yiu Wong and David K. Y. Chu, 37–39 (Hong Kong: Oxford University Press, 1985).

15. Shahid Yusuf and Weiping Wu, *The Dynamics of Urban Growth in Three Chinese Cities* (New York: Oxford University Press, 1997), 28.

16. Vogel, *One Step Ahead*, 151, 126–27.

17. Lai Pingyao, "Foreign Direct Investment in China: Recent Trends and Patterns," *China & World Economy* no. 2 (2002): 26, 29; Yan Cui, "Development of Foreign Banks in China," *China & World Economy* no. 4 (2001): 5.

18. Kwan-Yiu Wong et al., "Shenzhen: Special Experience in Development and Innovation," in *China's Coastal Cities: Catalysts for Modernization*, ed. Yue-man Yeung and Xu-wei Hu, 265 (Honolulu: University of Hawaii Press, 1992). Also see Hessler, *Oracle Bones*, 83.

19. Zhou Ding, "Review of the Urban Planning and Development of Shenzhen," *China City Planning Review* 3, nos. 1–2 (1987): 11.

20. These figures include all five districts of the Shenzhen Metropolitan Region (formerly Bao'an County), three of which constitute the SEZ proper. See Jianfa Shen, "Urbanization in Southern China: The Rise of Shenzhen City" (paper presented at the International Geographical Union, Commission on Urban Development and Urban Life, Mexico City, August 11–15, 1997), 2, 7. The early figures are from David K. Y. Chu, "Population Growth and Related Issues," in *Modernization in China*, ed. Kwan-Yiu Wong and David K. Y. Chu, 131 (Hong Kong: Oxford University Press, 1985).

21. "Shenzhen Has 8.27 Million Population," *Shanghai Daily*, April 26, 2006; Shenzhen Government Online, "Citizen Life: Proportions of Population," http://sz.gov.cn.

22. Nancy Lin, "Architecture Shenzhen," in *Great Leap Forward*, 161.

23. Vogel, *One Step Ahead*, 137–38.

24. Tom Vanderbilt, "Talking About a Revolution," *Metropolis*, August/September 1998.

25. Emperor Kangxi undertook tours in 1684, 1689, 1699, 1703, 1705, and 1707; Qianlong's were launched in 1751, 1757, 1762, 1765, 1780, and 1784. See Michael G. Chang, "Fathoming Qianlong: Imperial Activism, the Southern Tours, and the Politics of Water Control, 1736–1765," *Late Imperial China* 24, no. 2 (December 2003): 51n.

26. For a wonderful interpretation of the imperial scroll paintings, see David Hockney's 1988 film, *A Day on the Grand Canal with the Emperor of China*. Also see Maxwell K. Hearn, "Document and Portrait: The Southern Tour Paintings of Kangxi and Qianlong," in *Chinese Painting under the Qianlong Emperor*, ed. Ju-his Chou and Claudia Brown (Tempe: College of Fine Arts, Arizona State University, 1991).

27. Sheryl WuDunn and Nicholas D. Kristof, *China Wakes: The Struggle for the Soul of a Rising Power* (New York: Times Books, 1994), 122–23.

28. For an in-depth examination of Deng's *nanxun* and its political ramifications see John Wong and Zheng Yongnian, eds., *The Nanxun Legacy and China's Development in the Post-Deng Era* (Singapore: East Asian Institute, National University of Singapore, 2001).

29. Hessler, *Oracle Bones*, 86.

30. See Yan Song, "Housing Rural Migrants in China's Urbanizing Villages," *Land Lines* (Lincoln Institute of Land Policy) 19, no. 3 (July 2007): 2–7. See also L. Zhang, S. X. B. Zhao, and J. P. Tian, "Self-help in Housing and Chengzhongcun in China's Urbanization," *International Journal of Urban and Regional Research*, 2003, 27.

31. "Kowloon Walled City," *Newsline: Columbia University Graduate School of Architecture, Planning and Preservation* 3, no. 2 (2003). Also see Ian Lambot and Greg Girard, *City of Darkness: Life in Kowloon Walled City* (Surrey, UK: Watermark Publications, 1999).

32. Jianfa Shen, "Urbanization in Southern China," 1–2.

33. Zhou Ding, "Review of the Urban Planning and Development of Shenzhen," *China City Planning Review* 3, nos. 1–2 (1987): 11; Vogel, *One Step Ahead*, 137.

34. Anthony G. O. Yeh, "Physical Planning," in *Modernization in China*, ed. Kwan-Yiu Wong and David K. Y. Chu, 108–9, 117–23, 124 (Hong Kong: Oxford University Press, 1985).

35. Zhou Ding, "Review of the Urban Planning and Development of Shenzhen," 10–13.

36. Mihai Craciun, "Ideology Shenzhen," in *Great Leap Forward*, 117. Also see "Planning Havoc Hits Cities," *South China Morning Post*, February 16, 1994.

37. Anthony Walker, *Land, Property and*

Thunder from the South
continued
Construction in the People's Republic of China
(Hong Kong: Hong Kong University Press, 1991), 35–
39, 40, 44.

38. Chengri Ding and Gerrit Knapp, "Urban Land
Policy Reform in China's Transitional Economy," in
Emerging Land and Housing Markets in China, ed.
Chengri Ding and Yan Song, 13–14 (Cambridge, MA:
Lincoln Institute of Land Policy, 2005).

39. Ibid., 21.

40. Anthony G. O. Yeh, "Pudong: Remaking
Shanghai as a World City," in *Shanghai:
Transformation and Modernization Under China's
Open Policy*, ed. Yue-man Yeung and Sung Yun-wing,
275–76 (Hong Kong: Chinese University of Hong
Kong Press, 1996).

41. Anthony G. O. Yeh, "The Dual Land Market
and Urban Development in China," in *Emerging Land
and Housing Markets in China*, 39–45. Technically
speaking, there is yet another layer here—a tertiary
market—in which end users purchase flats or office
space from real estate developers. Only in these
latter two do actual free-market mechanisms operate.

42. The phrase "metropolitical corridor" is from
John R. Stilgoe, *Metropolitan Corridor: Railroads and
the American Scene* (New Haven: Yale University
Press, 1983).

43. Gregory E. Guldin, "Desakotas and Beyond:
Urbanization in Southern China," in *Farewell to
Peasant China: Rural Urbanization and Social Change
in the Late Twentieth Century*, ed. G. E. Guldin, 62
(Armonk, NY: M. E. Sharpe, 1997).

44. Yu Wong, "China's Road Program Carries
New Perils," *Wall Street Journal*, December 28, 1998.

45. See Pan Haixiao, "Impact Study of Freeway
on the Adjacent Areas in Suburban Shanghai" (paper
presented at the World Planning Schools Congress,
Shanghai, 2001). The colloquial expression "gone
downhill" is derived from the experience of New
England hill towns bypassed by railroads in the mid-
nineteenth century. As the rail lines were built through
the level valleys, communities in the hills above were
newly disadvantaged and eventually abandoned as
people moved "downhill" to the new centers of
economic activity.

46. Gary Cheung, "Bridge to Lift Delta Economy
by HK\$110 Billion," *South China Morning Post*, April
23, 2002.

47. Michael J. Enright, Ka-mun Chang, Edith E.
Scott, and Wen-hui Zhu, *Hong Kong and the Pearl
River Delta: The Economic Interaction* (Hong Kong:

2022 Foundation, 2003), 223–24; also see Enright et
al., *Regional Powerhouse: The Greater Pearl River
Delta and the Rise of China* (New York: Wiley, 2005).

48. Lim Siong Hoon, "Bridge Building Faces a
Cash Crunch," *South China Morning Post*, July 19,
2003. Also see "China Builds World's Longest Trans-
oceanic Bridge," *People's Daily*, August 22, 2003.

49. See Tunney F. Lee et al., *Linking the Delta:
Bridging the Pearl River Delta* (Hong Kong: 2022
Foundation, 2003).

50. Manuel Castells, *The Rise of the Network
Society* (Oxford: Blackwell Publishers, 1996), 403.

51. Ibid., 407.

52. Ibid., 408.

53. Ibid., 409.

54. Import data is from the U.S. Customs Office.
The number of light sets imported from China in 1999
was 128,013,881. Assuming an average length of 12
feet per set, this yields about 290,940 miles; average
distance between the earth and moon is about
239,000 miles.

55. Interview with Edith E. Scott by Christopher
W. Runckel (2005), see http://www.business-in-asia.
com/greater_pearl.html.

56. Wu Wei and Thomas J. Campanella, "China's
Global Beacon," *Metropolis*, December 2006, 40.

57. Howard W. French, "New Boomtowns
Change Path of China's Growth," *New York Times*,
July 28, 2004.

Reclaiming Shanghai

1. John K. Fairbank, *The United States and China*,
4th ed. (Cambridge: Harvard University Press, 1983),
162.

2. John K. Fairbank, *Trade and Diplomacy on the
China Coast: The Opening of the Treaty Ports, 1842–
1854* (Cambridge: Harvard University Press, 1953),
49–52, 63–73.

3. Ibid., 155. Additional ports were forced open
after the Second Opium War in 1860.

4. Ibid., 156n.

5. Kerrie L. MacPherson, "Shanghai's History:
Back to the Future," *Harvard Asia Pacific Review*,
Spring 2002, 38.

6. Ibid.

7. See Kerrie L. MacPherson, *A Wilderness of
Marshes: The Origins of Public Health in Shanghai,
1843–1893* (Hong Kong: Oxford University Press,
1987).

8. Nicholas R. Clifford, *Shanghai, 1925: Urban
Nationalism and the Defense of Foreign Privilege*

(Ann Arbor: Center for Chinese Studies, University of Michigan, 1979), 4; Kerrie L. MacPherson, "Designing China's Urban Future: The Greater Shanghai Plan, 1927–1937," *Planning Perspectives* 5 (1990): 43.

9. George Woodcock, *The British in the Far East* (London: Weidenfeld and Nicolson, 1969), 160, quoted in Clifford, *Shanghai*, 5–6.

10. Clifford, *Shanghai*, 2.

11. MacPherson, "Shanghai's History," 41–42.

12. In 1952, St. John's merged with several other Shanghai institutions, and is now the campus of East China University of Politics and Law.

13. MacPherson, "Shanghai's History," 41–42.

14. Seng Kuan, "Image of the Metropolis: Three Historical Views of Shanghai," in *Shanghai: Architecture and Urbanism for Modern China*, ed. Seng Kuan and Peter G. Rowe, 94n (New York: Prestel Verlag, 2004).

15. Kuan, "Image of the Metropolis," 87; Yang Yongsheng, ed., *Noted Architects in China* (Beijing: Contemporary World Press, 1999), 49.

16. Kerrie L. MacPherson, "Designing China's Urban Future," 44.

17. Quoted in Michael Tsin, "Canton Remapped," in *Remaking the Chinese City: Modernity and National Identity, 1900–1950*, ed. Joseph W. Esherick, 29 (Honolulu: University of Hawaii Press, 2000).

18. On the Boxer fellowships, see Michael H. Hunt, "The American Remission of the Boxer Indemnity: A Reappraisal," *Journal of Asian Studies* 31, no. 3 (May 1972).

19. Joseph W. Esherick, "Modernity and Nation in the Chinese City," in *Remaking the Chinese City: Modernity and National Identity, 1900–1950*, ed. J. W. Esherick (Honolulu: University of Hawaii Press, 2000), 1–18. See also Ruth Rogalski, "Hygienic Modernity in Tianjin," 30–46 in the same volume.

20. On the demolition of city walls for roads and highways, see Jeffrey W. Cody, "American Planning in Republican China, 1911–1937," *Planning Perspectives* 11 (1996); also see Thomas J. Campanella, "'The Civilizing Road': American Influences on the Development of Highways and Motoring in China, 1900–1949," *Journal of Transport History* 3, no. 26 (March 2005).

21. MacPherson, "Designing China's Urban Future," 47; also see Li Kai-guang, "The Identity and Conflict of the Members in the Shanghai Local Self-Government Movement," *Shi Lin* (*Historical Review*) 5, no. 74 (2003).

22. A small section of the wall survived demolition, at 269 Dajing Road, near the old Small North Gate (Xiaobeimen); it is now part of a museum.

23. Cited in Clifford, *Shanghai*, 4.

24. Ibid., 7–8

25. MacPherson, "Designing China's Urban Future," 45–46.

26. V. K. Ting, quoted in A. M. Kotenev, *Shanghai: Its Municipality and the Chinese* (Shanghai: North-China Daily News and Herald, 1927), 70.

27. A. M. Kotenev, *Shanghai: Its Municipality and the Chinese* (Shanghai: North-China Daily News and Herald, 1927), 70.

28. Ting quoted in Kotenev, *Shanghai*, 71.

29. Sun Yat-sen (Sun Zhong Shan), *Sun Zhong Shan Xuan Ji*, vol. 1 (Beijing: Remin Chu Ban She, 1981 [1919]), 209–11. Also see Kerrie L. MacPherson, "Head of the Dragon: the Pudong New Area and Shanghai's Urban Development," *Planning Perspectives* 9 (1994): 61–85.

30. MacPherson, "Head of the Dragon," 66–68.

31. MacPherson, "Designing China's Urban Future," 50.

32. Ibid., 50–54.

33. Quoted in Cody, "American Planning in Republican China," 366.

34. Wang Chun-hsiung, "The Greater Shanghai Plan: A Nationalist Utopia," *Dialogue*, February 1999, 64.

35. Ibid., 64–65.

36. See Jeffrey W. Cody, *Building in China: Henry K. Murphy's "Adaptive Architecture," 1914–1935* (Hong Kong: Chinese University of Hong Kong Press, 2001). Also see relevant sections of Yang Yongsheng, ed., *Noted Architects in China* (Beijing: Contemporary World Press, 1999).

37. Kuan, "Image of the Metropolis," in *Shanghai*, ed. Kuan and Rowe, 89.

38. MacPherson, "Designing China's Urban Future," 47–49

39. Zheng Zu'an, "The Fall of New Civic Center of Greater Shanghai in 1937" (paper presented at the ECAI [Electronic Cultural Atlas Initiative] Shanghai Conference, May 2005, Center for Historical Geographic Studies, Fudan University).

40. The aerial imagery readily available now via Google Maps or Google Earth is an extraordinary tool for studying Chinese cities. Aerial photographs have long been highly restricted in China; possession could once get you a very long prison sentence. Now anyone with internet access can pull up such views, a remarkable fact considering that the government

Reclaiming Shanghai

continued

routinely blocks blogs and other websites considered threatening to security or the social order.

41. "Shanghai Xin Jiangwan Cheng Gui Hua Xin Xian Chun Lun," *International Architecture*, September 9, 2004.

42. Zhou Zuyi, "Skateboard Showdown," *Shanghai Daily News*, September 8, 2005; "Venue for Extreme Sports Unveiled in Shanghai," *People's Daily*, June 25, 2004; David Goldenberg, "A Skate Park Rises in the East," *Wired* 14, no. 1 (January 2006).

43. Quoted in MacPherson, "Head of the Dragon," 76.

44. Yeh, "Pudong," 276–79.

45. Ibid., 289.

46. MacPherson, "Designing China's Urban Future," 43.

47. Chia-Liang Tai, "Transforming Shanghai: The Redevelopment Context of the Pudong New Area" (unpublished masters thesis, Columbia University, Faculty of Architecture and Planning, May 2005), 14.

48. Kris Olds, "Globalizing Shanghai: The 'Global Intelligence Corps' and the Building of Pudong," *Cities* 14, no. 2 (1997): 115–16.

49. French Back-Up Group for the Development of Shanghai-Pudong, "Shanghai International Consultation on the Lu Jia Zui Business Centre in Pu Dong: Outline of the Dossier," May 1992, 1.

50. The group consisted of IAURIF; Ministère Français de l'Equipement, Direction des Affaires Economiques et Internationales; and Etablissement Public d'Aménagement de la Région Défense. See "Outline of the Dossier," 24.

51. Olds, "Globalizing Shanghai," 115–17.

52. Yang Yongsheng, ed., *Noted Architects in China* (Beijing: Contemporary World Press, 1999), 228–29.

53. Other Chinese architectural landmarks that have been recalled in rooftop superstructure include I. M. Pei's Bank of China Tower in Hong Kong; the Central Plaza building in Hong Kong's Wanchai District, with its pyramidal roof; and, more recently, Charpentier's Shanghai Grand Opera House, best known for its immense upswept roof, which is itself evocative of Terry Farrell's earlier Peak Tower in Hong Kong.

54. Quoted in Thomas J. Campanella, "The Visible City: Shanghai," *Metropolis*, March 1995, 33–38.

55. Chinese Academy of Engineering, National Research Council, et al., *Personal Cars and China* (Washington: National Academies Press, 2003), 225–28.

56. See, for example, Howard W. French, "In Chinese Boomtown, Middle Class Pushes Back," *New York Times*, December 18, 2006.

57. Asian Development Bank, "Project Performance Audit Report on the Shanghai-Nanpu Bridge Project (Loan 1082-PRC) in the People's Republic of China," November 1999, 11n.

58. "Work Begins on Bridge," *Shanghai Daily*, August 31, 2005.

59. Chia-Liang Tai, "Transforming Shanghai: The Redevelopment Context of the Pudong New Area" (unpublished masters thesis, Columbia University, Faculty of Architecture and Planning, May 2005), 54.

60. Chinese Academy of Engineering, *Personal Cars and China*, 224.

61. "Six New Bridges, Tunnels on Shanghai's Drawing Board," *People's Daily*, September 21, 2003.

62. For a critique of the four schemes, see Kuan, "Lujiazui International Consultation," in Kuan and Rowe, *Shanghai*, 96–103.

63. Olds, "Globalizing Shanghai," 117–18.

64. Ibid.

65. "Century Boulevard" (Shi Ji Da Dao) (Shanghai: Shanghai Pudong Real Estate Development Company and Shanghai Lujiazui), 4–6, 24.

66. "Century Park" (Shanghai: Shanghai Century Park Administration Co.); "Briefing on Pudong Century Park Plan," (http://www.shld.com/brief/company/spld/005g.htm).

67. Tao Ho, "The Development of Pudong with Special Focus on Lu Jia Zui" (paper presented at IAIA 1993, Shanghai).

68. See Max Page, *The Creative Destruction of Manhattan, 1900–1940* (Chicago: University of Chicago Press, 1999).

69. Thomas J. Campanella, "Jin Mao Tower, Shanghai," *Architectural Record*, January 2000, 82–89.

70. Ibid.

71. Ibid.

72. This closes at least one circle: in 2000, former Chinese premier Li Peng cancelled a visit to the real Althingi in Iceland because a crowd had gathered at the building to protest China's human rights record. Ulrika K. Engström, "Luodian—a Slice of Sweden in China," *Sweden.se*, February 10, 2006, http://www.sweden.se/templates/cs/Article___13712.aspx.

73. Shiuan-Wen Chu and Ruurd Gieterna, "Dutchness at Your Service," *Archis #5: Archis is... DUTCH* (Amsterdam: Stichting Artimo, 2002).

74. Jonathan Watts, "Shanghai Surprise: A New Town in Ye Olde English Style," *Guardian*, June 2, 2004.

75. Quoted in Hannah Beech, "Ye Olde Shanghai," *Time Asia*, February 14, 2005; Clifford Coonan, "Shanghai Surprise," *Irish Times*, September 30, 2006.

76. Richard Spencer, "The Chinese Have Shanghaied My Pub," *Telegraph*, September 15, 2006.

77. Beijing, too, has a spectacular urban planning exhibition hall, just off Tiananmen Square. It features a miniature-scale model nearly as large as Shanghai's and an illuminated glass floor with aerial photographs of the entire city, allowing the visitor to stride about the capital like a giant.

The Politics of the Past

1. See Anthony S. Pitch, "Patriotism and the Reconstruction of Washington, DC, After the British Invasion of 1814," in *The Resilient City*, ed. Vale and Campanella, 97–98 (New York: Oxford University Press, 2005). Actually, the Americans did much the same thing the year before in York; British admiral George Cockburn's plan was meant as retaliation.

2. Wu Liangyong, "Conservation and Development in the Historic City of Beijing," *Ekistics* 64 (1997): 240.

3. Jeffrey F. Meyer, "Traditional Peking: The Architecture of Conditional Power," in *Journal of Developing Societies* 2 (1986): 264.

4. Meyer, "Traditional Peking," 266. Also see Meyer, *Dragons of Tiananmen: Beijing as a Sacred City* (Columbia: University of South Carolina Press, 1991).

5. Meyer, "Traditional Peking," 277. See also Paul Wheatley's seminal treatise on traditional Chinese city planning, *The Pivot of the Four Quarters* (Chicago: Aldine Publishing Company, 1971).

6. Ibid., 266.

7. Ibid., 268, 275–76. Meyer quotes a Confucian saying that summarizes the astral symbolism of the emperor: "He who rules by moral force (*te*) is like the polestar which remains in place while all the lesser stars do homage to it."

8. Nancy S. Steinhardt, "Why Were Chang'An and Beijing So Different?," *Journal of the Society of Architectural Historians* 45, no. 4 (December 1986):

342; also see Steinhardt, *Chinese Imperial City Planning* (Honolulu: University of Hawaii Press, 1990), 33.

9. Meyer, "Traditional Peking," 264; Steinhardt, *Chinese Imperial City Planning*, 4–10. A clean geometric layout was easier to achieve on the level plains of north-central China than in the hilly south, hence the pure form of northern capitals like Xi'an and Beijing (or smaller cities like Pingyao in Shanxi Province or Shangqiu in Henan Province). Nanjing, on the other hand, is highly organic in form, its walls following the undulations of the terrain. Hangzhou, capital of the Southern Song Dynasty, also had an irregular layout. See Sen-Dou Chang, "Some Observations on the Morphology of Chinese Walled Cities," *Annals of the Association of American Geographers* 60, no. 1 (March 1970): 69–70.

10. Meyer, "Traditional Peking," 271–72.

11. Jianying Zha addressed this facet of Beijing urbanism in her 1996 book *China Pop*: "Everywhere within the city were the walls of courtyard houses, from the biggest—the royal palaces at the very center of the city—down to the humblest cottages. The social status of an inhabitant dictated the size of his house and the length of his walls. In some ways, old Beijing was a magnificently walled-in courtyard with an infinite succession of smaller walled-in courtyards." See Jianying Zha, *China Pop: How Soap Operas, Tabloids and Bestsellers Are Transforming a Culture* (New York: New Press, 1996), 59–60.

12. Edward N. Bacon, *Design of Cities* (1967; New York, Penguin, 1976); Bacon worked for Murphy as a draftsman in his Shanghai office from April 1933 to April 1934; see Jeffrey W. Cody, *Building in China: Henry K. Murphy's "Adaptive Architecture," 1914–1935* (Hong Kong: Chinese University of Hong Kong Press, 2001), 2, 220n.

13. Wu Hung, *Remaking Beijing: Tiananmen Square and the Remaking of a Political Space* (Chicago: University of Chicago Press, 2005), 59, 63–64.

14. Ibid., 173, 172–75. The painting is also famous for the many times its cast of characters changed in accordance with political winds and whims; as officials fell in and out of favor, they were removed or added to the group of leaders on the balcony.

15. Albert C. Wedemeyer, *Wedemeyer Reports!* (New York: Henry Holt, 1958), 287.

16. In fact, the relationship between China and the Soviet Union was never one of equals, and by 1960 the two countries had an epic falling out that nearly led to war.

The Politics of the Past
continued

17. Victor F. S. Sit, "Soviet Influence on Urban Planning in Beijing, 1949–1991," *Town Planning Review* 67, no. 4 (1996): 465–71. Also see Greg Castillo, "Cities of the Stalinist Empire," in *Forms of Dominance: On the Architecture and Urbanism of the Colonial Experience*, ed. Nezar AlSayyad, (Aldershot, UK: Avebury, 1992), 261–87.

18. Quoted in Sit, "Soviet Influence," 469.

19. Sit, "Soviet Influence," 463–64; also see James H. Bater, *The Soviet City: Ideal and Reality* (London: Edward Arnold, 1980).

20. Sit, "Soviet Influence," 466.

21. Wu Liangyong, *Rehabilitating the Old City of Beijing* (Vancouver: University of British Columbia Press, 1999), 17.

22. Li Shiqiao, "Writing a Modern Chinese Architectural History: Liang Sicheng and Liang Qichao," *Journal of Architectural Education* 56, no. 1 (2002).

23. Wilma Fairbank, *Liang and Lin: Partners in Exploring China's Architectural Past* (Philadelphia: University of Pennsylvania Press, 1994), 23–29, 49–50.

24. The *Ying Zao Fa Shi* was not a style manual per se, but rather described "systems and methods of quantity survey and material calculation...used by the Imperial Government to control construction materials and avoid waste." "It is highly unlikely," writes Ma Qingyun "that they were used as [a] resource for the production of architecture. They were equivalent to today's cost estimate manuals and code books." Ma Qingyun, sidebar in Chung et al., *Great Leap Forward*, 191.

25. Li, "Writing a Modern Chinese Architectural History," 35–36; Nancy S. Steinhardt, "The Tang Architectural Icon and the Politics of Chinese Architectural History," *Art Bulletin* 86 (2004).

26. Fairbank, *Liang and Lin*, 169.

27. Ibid., 137.

28. Liang Sicheng and Chen Zhanxiang, "Proposal for the Location of the Administrative Central Area of the PRC Central People's Government," in *The Complete Works of Dr. Liang Sicheng*, ed. Yang Yongsheng, vol. 5, 65 (Beijing: China Construction Industry Press, 2001). I used an English translation by Colin Zhang; page numbers refer to the published Chinese edition.

29. Ibid., 64.

30. Ibid.

31. Ibid., 67.

32. Ibid., 66–68.

33. Ibid., 64.

34. Ibid., 65.

35. Ibid., 61.

36. Ibid., 62.

37. Ibid., 62.

38. Nikolai Voronin, "Reconstruction of the Reoccupied Soviet Union Areas Formerly Occupied by the German Invaders," quoted in Liang and Chen, "Proposal for the Location of the Administrative Central Area," 62.

39. Voronin quoted in Liang and Chen, "Proposal," 80.

40. Ibid., 81. Liang's choice of Soviet references was strategic: Voronin and Schusev were no lightweights. Voronin's studies of Russian architecture earned him the Lenin and State prizes, two of the Soviet Union's highest state honors, and Schusev was the dean of Soviet architects by the time he died in 1949. He helped plan Moscow after the 1918 revolution and designed the Lenin Mausoleum in Red Square; his name today graces the Schusev State Museum of Architecture.

41. Wu Liangyong, *Rehabilitating the Old City of Beijing*, 23.

42. Sen-Dou Chang, "Beijing: Perspectives on Preservation, Environment, and Development," *Cities* 15, no. 1 (1998): 14.

43. Liang and Chen, "Proposal," 60.

44. Wu Liangyong, *Rehabilitating the Old City of Beijing*, 18. Wu also argues that Chiang Kai-shek's General Command for the Suppression of Communists also operated in the area west of the Old City, further tainting the district.

45. Wu Hung, *Remaking Beijing*, 8.

46. Chen Zhanxiang, "Yi Liang Sicheng Jiaoshou" [Remembering Professor Liang Sicheng], in *Liang Sicheng xianshen danchen bashiwu zhounian jinian wenji* [Papers presented to Mr. Liang Sicheng on his eighty-fifth birthday] (Beijing, 1996), quoted in Wu Hung, *Remaking Beijing*, 8; Wang Jun, *Cheng Ji* [Story of a City], 177, cited in Wu, *Remaking Beijing*, 246n.

47. Wu Liangyong, *Rehabilitating the Old City of Beijing*, 18–19.

48. Wu Hung, *Remaking Beijing*, 8–9.

49. Ibid., 64–65.

50. Ibid., 18–24.

51. Ibid., 22–24.

52. Ibid.

53. Ibid., 111–12.

54. Ibid., 109.

55. Sit, "Soviet Influence," 467–69.

56. Sen-Dou Chang, "Some Observations on the Morphology of Chinese Walled Cities," 64n.

57. On the subject of walled cities, see Ronald G. Knapp, *China's Walled Cities* (New York: Oxford University Press, 2000).

58. Ibid., 64, 64n; Alfred Schinz, *The Magic Square: Cities in Ancient China* (Stuttgart: Axel Menges, 1996), 325.

59. Chang, "Some Observations," 69.

60. Schinz, *Magic Square*, 315, 325.

61. Chang, "Some Observations," 64.

62. Han-Veng Woo, "Design of Streets and the Use of City Walls in the Development of Highway Systems in the Municipalities of China" (unpublished masters thesis, Iowa State College, 1930).

63. It's possible that Woo, whose thesis focused on Nanjing, derived this idea from Henry Murphy. As Jeffrey Cody has shown, Murphy was commissioned by Chiang Kai-shek's Nationalist government to help plan the nation's new capital. In the spring of 1929 he repeatedly urged the National Capital Reconstruction Planning Committee to preserve the city's majestic walls. To make the idea more palatable, Murphy showed how the top of the structure could easily be converted into a motorway, thus turning an antiquated liability into a modern asset. He illustrated this with a perspective drawing not unlike the one Woo drew for his thesis. Jeffrey W. Cody, "American Planning in Republican China, 1911–1937," *Planning Perspectives* 11 (1996): 355–58.

64. J. Morgan Clements, *China: Automotive Conditions and the Good Roads Movement*, Trade Information Bulletin No. 2 (Washington: Department of Commerce, 1922), 13–15.

65. Ibid., 3, 18–19; Jeffrey W. Cody, "American Planning in Republican China," 342–43.

66. A. Viola Smith and Anselm Chuh, *Motor Roads in China*, Trade Information Series No. 120 (Washington: Department of Commerce, 1931), 7.

67. Woo, "Design of Streets," 23.

68. William I. Irvine, *Automotive Markets in China, British Malaya, and Chosen*, Special Agents Series—No. 221, Department of Commerce, Bureau of Foreign and Domestic Commerce (Washington: Government Printing Office, 1923), 32.

69. The hoax was not fully disclosed until after the death of last of the four reporters. See "Will China's Wall Come Down," *New York Times*, June 27, 1899; Harry Lee Wilber, "A Fake That Rocked the World," in *Great Hoaxes of All Time*, ed. Robert Medill McBride

and Neil Pritchie, 17–24 (New York: Robert C. McBride, 1956).

70. Henry W. Lawrence, "Origins of the Tree-Lined Boulevard," *Geographical Review* 78, no. 4 (October 1988): 355.

71. See Carl E. Schorske, *Fin-de-siècle Vienna: Politics and Culture* (New York: A. A. Knopf, 1980).

72. Wu Hung, *Remaking Beijing*, 250n.

73. Quoted in Fairbank, *Liang and Lin*, 43.

74. Liang Sicheng, "Discussion on the Problem of Preservation or Demolition of the City Wall of Beijing," in *The Complete Works of Dr. Liang Sicheng*, ed. Yang Yongsheng, vol. 5, 85 (Beijing: China Construction Industry Press, 2001). English translation by Colin Zhang; page numbers refer to the published Chinese edition.

75. Ibid., 86.

76. Here, too, Liang's case may have been haunted by Japanese actions during the occupation. To connect the Old City to their new center to the west and an industrial suburb in the east, the Japanese in 1939 opened two new gates in the city walls—Fuxingmen (originally Chang'anmen) in the west, and Jiangguomen (originally Qimingmen) in the east. These allowed Chang'an Avenue to pass through and eventually become Beijing's principal east-west thoroughfare. See Wu Hung, *Remaking Beijing*, 251n.

77. Liang, "Discussion," 86–87.

78. Ibid., 88. The walls of Smolensk were constructed around 1600.

79. Ibid.

80. Jianying Zha, *China Pop*, 62.

81. Orville Schell, "Glimpses of Old China in Modern Beijing," *New York Times*, October 4, 1987.

82. Emily Honig, "Socialist Sex: The Cultural Revolution Revisited," *Modern China* 29, no. 2 (April 2003): 148.

83. Lin Zhu, cited in Fairbank, *Liang and Lin*, 180–81.

84. Ibid., 178–86.

85. Henry James, *The American Scene* (London: Chapman & Hall, 1907), 408, 77.

86. Zhang Wen, interview by author and Wu Wei, Zheng'An Palace Hotel, Xianghe, Beijing, November 4, 2006; also see *Di Yi Cheng* (sales brochure) (Xianghe: CITIC Guoan Grand Epoch City Conference & Exhibition International Company, 2006).

87. Erik Eckholm, "Restoring an Ancient City's Glory Brick by Brick," *New York Times*, September 30, 2002.

The Politics of the Past
continued

88. "Beijing's Imperial Past to be Restored," *China Daily*, September 25, 2004.

Capital Improvements

1. Ryan Ong, "New Beijing, Great Olympics: Beijing and its Unfolding Olympic Legacy," *Stanford Journal of East Asian Affairs* 4, no. 2 (Summer 2004): 39–41.

2. Deyan Sudjic, "The City That Ate the World," *Guardian*, October 16, 2005.

3. On the nexus between the Olympic Games, urban design, and city form, see Julian Beinart, "From Olympia to Barcelona: Themes of Permanence and Transience," *Spazio e Società* 50 (April–June 1990): 34–54.

4. Stephen Essex and Brian Chalkley, "Olympic Games: Catalyst of Urban Change," *Leisure Studies* 17 (1998): 195–96.

5. Brian Chalkley and Stephen Essex, "Urban Development through Hosting International Events: A History of the Olympic Games," *Planning Perspectives* 14 (1999): 369–70.

6. "Trees Spring Up at Night as Beijing Goes Green," *South China Morning Post*, July 5, 1999; Tang Min, "Millions of Trees Planted in Capital," *China Daily*, May 18, 1999; Jasper Becker, "Rule of Noise as Beijing Spruces Up," *South China Morning Post*, July 3, 1999.

7. "Tiananmen Square Reopens Minus Kites," *South China Morning Post*, June 29, 1999.

8. Mark O'Neill, "Home of Reformers Becomes a Thing of the Past as Demolition Squad Arrives," *South China Morning Post*, September 27, 1998.

9. Feng Ke and Zhang Yan, "To Redevelop Beijing or to Destroy Beijing," 1999, revised version of "Beijing at the Crossroads," *Architect* 84 (1998), by the same authors.

10. Mark O'Neill, "Deng's Scholarly Neighbour Ousted from Historic Home," *South China Morning Post*, October 28, 2000; "Battle for Beijing's Ancient Courtyards," *South China Morning Post*, August 27, 1998; Teresa Poole, "City Life: Peking," *Independent* (London), September 14, 1998. The story of Professor Zhao, and the larger struggle to save old Beijing, is well told by Ian Johnson in *Wild Grass: Three Portraits of Change in Modern China* (New York: Vintage Books, 2004).

11. "The Widening of Ping An Avenue: Making Decisions about Historic Preservation" (Kennedy School of Government Case Program [C15-99-1525.0], 1998), 2–6.

12. For an overview of Beijing's peasant enclaves, see Chaolin Gu and Haiyong Liu, "Social Polarization and Segregation in Beijing," in *The New Chinese City: Globalization and Market Reform*, ed. John R. Logan, 198–211 (Oxford: Blackwell Publishers, 2002). Also see Laurence J. C. Ma and Biao Xiang, "Native Place, Migration and the Emergence of Peasant Enclaves in Beijing," *China Quarterly* 155 (September 1998): 546–81. A particularly thorough study of Zhejiang Village is Li Zhang's *Strangers in the City: Reconfigurations of Space, Power, and Social Networks Within China's Floating Population* (Stanford: Stanford University Press, 2001). The relationship between occupation and regional origin among migrant workers is also explored in Chaolin Gu and Jianafa Shen, "Transformation of Urban Socio-Spatial Structure in Socialist Market Economies: The Case of Beijing," *Habitat International* 27 (2003): 107–22. For a more general work on the formation of peasant enclaves in cities of the developing world, see Bryan R. Roberts, *Cities of Peasants: The Political Economy of Urbanization in the Third World* (London: Sage, 1978) and *The Making of Citizens: Cities of Peasants Revisited* (Ultimo, Australia: Halstead Press, 1995).

13. Li Zhang, *Strangers in the City*, 4.

14. "1,000 Evicted in Games Bid," *South China Morning Post*, June 22, 1993.

15. Anthony Kuhn, "Beijing Starts Razing Muslim Area," *Los Angeles Times*, March 16, 1999.

16. Cited in "Demolition Clean-up for Capital," *South China Morning Post*, March 11, 1999.

17. There was some justice, however; within in a few months most of the evictees—and many more—had returned. "Beijing: A New Cultural Revolution," *China Economic Review*, October 23, 1998; Erik Eckholm, "As Beijing Pretties Up, Migrants Face Expulsion," *New York Times*, April 18, 1999.

18. Paul Wiseman, "Beijing Residents Pay Price for Olympics Push," *Chicago Sun-Times*, July 12, 2001.

19. Jane Macartney, "Thousands of Homes Destroyed to Make Way for Olympic Tourists," *Times Online*, May 26, 2005.

20. See Ou Ning, "The Story of Zhang Jinli," *Kulturstiftung des Bundes* 7 (2006), translated from the Chinese by Yu Hsiao-hwei.

21. "Two Arrested Over Bomb Threat at Beijing Olympic Site" *Agence France Presse*, June 12, 2005.

22. Ibid.

23. "Demolition Begins in Old Beijing Pleasure District," *Asian Economic News*, January 31, 2005; "Beijing's Historic Qianmen District Goes Under the Wrecking Ball," *Agence France Presse*, April 28, 2005.

24. Jim Yardley, "Olympics Imperil Historic Beijing Neighborhood," *New York Times*, July 12, 2006.

25. Ibid.

26. Ou Ning, "The Story of Zhang Jinli"; also see Ou Ning, "Street Life at Da Zha Lan," *Urban China* (2006), http://www.dazhalan-project.org/news-en/2006-07-11.html.

27. "Beijing Awaits New 'Back Garden,'" *China Daily*, July 7, 2006.

28. Oliver August, "Beijing Signs Up Son of Hitler's Architect," *Times Online*, February 14, 2003.

29. The prison garden is mentioned in Albert Speer, *Spandau: The Secret Diaries* (New York: Macmillan, 1976).

30. On Speer's plans, see Stephen D. Helmer, *Hitler's Berlin: The Speer Plans for Reshaping the Central City* (Ann Arbor, MI: UMI Research Press, 1985).

31. Arthur Lubow, "The China Syndrome," *New York Times*, May 21, 2006.

32. Ibid.

33. Tristram Carfrae, "Engineering the Water Cube," *Architecture Australia*, July/August 2006.

34. On the structural differences between Asian cities and those in the West, see also Barrie Shelton, *Learning from the Japanese City: West Meets East in Urban Design* (Oxford, UK: Taylor & Francis, 1999).

35. Yu Zhou, "Beijing and the Development of Dual Central Business Districts," *Geographical Review* 88, no. 3 (July 1998): 429–36.

36. Danny King, "Plans for Huge China Tower Undeterred," *Los Angeles Business Journal*, November 5, 2001.

37. Colleen Ryan, "They Bought Beijing," *Australian Financial Review*, October 27, 2005. The couple was the subject of a flattering *New Yorker* profile; see Jianying Zha, "The Turtles," *New Yorker*, July 11, 2005.

38. Though he has also asserted that "a refusal of the Promethean in the name of correctness and good sense could foreclose China's architectural potential." Rem Koolhaas, "Beijing Manifesto," *Wired*, August 2004, 125, 129.

39. Lubow, "The China Syndrome."

40. See *A Collection of Design Schemes for the International Architectural Competition of the National Grand Theater* (Beijing: China Architecture and Building Press, 1999).

41. Mark O'Neill, "Architects Stage Revolt," *South China Morning Post*, April 17, 2000.

42. Zhang Hong Jiang, "Public Commentary About National Theatre," *Life Times*, July 21, 1998; Zhang Jie, "Journalists Cause Trouble During National Opera Exhibition," *Life Times*, July 22, 1998.

43. George Watson, in *The Lost Literature of Socialism* (Cambridge, UK: Lutterworth Press, 1998), attributes the "omelet" maxim to Beatrice Potter Webb, the vanguard English socialist, eugenics advocate, and Soviet apologist. New York masterbuilder Robert Moses often used the phrase to defend his huge public works.

City of *Chai*

1. Yun Cheng, "Land Leasing and its Impact on Urban Renewal in Shanghai" (paper presented at The Future of Chinese Cities conference, Shanghai, July 1999).

2. Hannah Beech, "Appetite for Destruction," *Time Asia*, February 26, 2001; see also Beech, "Shanghai Swings!" *Time Asia*, September 20, 2004.

3. "Angry Shanghai Residents Make Way for Development," *South China Morning Post*, December 14, 1994.

4. Neha Sami, "Local Labor for Global Exposition," in *Conference Proceedings* (China Planning Network [CPN] Third Annual Conference, Urban Development and Planning in China, June 2006), 217.

5. Choong Tet Sieu and Anne Naham, "Home Truths: As Beijing's Old Houses are Swept Away, a New Lifestyle Is Emerging," *Asiaweek*, October 30, 1998, 59.

6. Alfred Schinz, *The Magic Square: Cities in Ancient China* (Stuttgart: Axel Menges, 1996), 288–92.

7. Ibid., 315–18.

8. Wu Liangyong, *Rehabilitating the Old City of Beijing* (Vancouver: University of British Columbia Press, 1999), 12–13, 76.

9. Zhang Jie, "Informal Construction in Beijing's Old Neighborhoods," *Cities* 14, no. 2 (1997): 88.

10. Zhu Jiaguang and Fu Zhijing, "Planning and Design Concept for the Renewal of Number 265, Deshengmen Nei Dajie," *Beijing Guihua Jianshe* [Beijing Planning and Construction], 3, cited in Wu Liangyong, *Rehabilitating the Old City of Beijing*, 59; Zhang Yan, "Urban Design in the Inner City of Beijing:

City of *Chai*
continued

Poetics and Politics of Housing Reform" (unpublished seminar paper, Massachusetts Institute of Technology, Department of Urban Studies and Planning, 2000), 13. The great Tangshan earthquake of July 1976 leveled about 80 percent of that city and killed upward of 250,000 people. See Lawrence Vale and Thomas J. Campanella, *The Resilient City: How Modern Cities Recover from Disaster* (New York: Oxford University Press, 2005), 9–10.

11. Daniel Benjamin Abramson, "'Marketization' and Institutions in Chinese Inner-City Redevelopment: A Commentary of Lü Junhua's *Beijing's Old and Dilapidated Housing Renewal*," *Cities* 14, no. 2 (1997): 72n.

12. See Wu, *Rehabilitating the Old City of Beijing.*

13. Abramson, "'Marketization,'" 74; Zhang, "Urban Design in the Inner City of Beijing," 13.

14. "Beijing: The Fate of the Old," *China Heritage Newsletter* (China Heritage Project, Australian National University) 1 (March 2005).

15. Eric Eckholm, "A Burst of Renewal Sweeps old Beijing Into the Dumpsters," *New York Times*, March 1, 1998.

16. Max Page, *The Creative Destruction of Manhattan* (Chicago: University of Chicago Press, 1999), 2.

17. The original phrase was "all that is solid melts into air."

18. Wu Liangyong, "Conservation and Development in the Historic City of Beijing," *Ekistics* 64 (1997): 244.

19. Jasper Goldman, "From Hutong to High-Rise: Explaining the Transformation of Old Beijing, 1990–2002" (unpublished masters thesis, Massachusetts Institute of Technology, Department of Urban Studies and Planning, September 2003), 86.

20. The Chinese model is similar in many respects to premodern Western concepts of the exalted place, especially sites of religious pilgrimage. Clearly the Temple Mount in Jerusalem as an esteemed site has outlasted many of the architectural monuments built to celebrate its significance.

21. Zhang Yan, "Urban Design in the Inner City of Beijing," 19.

22. Nan Xiang Hong, "Nanchizi Zhi Jie," *Nan Fang Zhou Mo*, July 4, 2002.

23. Lü Junhua, "Beijing's Old and Dilapidated Housing Renewal," *Cities* 14, no. 2 (1997): 66–67.

24. Ibid., 67.

25. George E. Nitzche quoted in Constance M. Greiff, *Independence: The Creation of a National Park* (Philadelphia: University of Pennsylvania Press, 1987), 29–62.

26. Lü, "Beijing's Old and Dilapidated Housing Renewal," 67.

27. Quoted in Goldman, "From Hutong to High-Rise," 88.

28. Ibid., 83–94; Lü, "Beijing's Old and Dilapidated Housing Renewal," 67.

29. Quoted in Robert J. Saiget, "Beijing Defends Destruction of Inner City Amid Widespread Dissatisfaction," *Agence France Presse*, August 15, 2003.

30. A videotape was confiscated, but the film was made anyway—*Beijing: From Hutong to High-Rise* (2002), directed by Jasper Goldman and Beatrice Chen.

31. Choong and Naham, "Home Truths," 59.

32. "China Club Beijing Opens," *Asiaweek*, September 27, 1996.

33. Aryn Baker, "Cashing in on Mao-stalgia," *Time Asia* 161, no. 5 (February 10, 2003).

34. "Individuals Encouraged to Buy Courtyard Houses," *Beijing This Month*, May 15, 2004.

35. Chen Nan, "Siheyuan: Old Beijing Style Appeals to Many," *Beijing This Month*, April 14, 2006.

36. "Cathay View: The Heart of Beijing's Central Villa District" (sales brochure); also see "Cathay View Courtyard Residences," Villas China website, http://www.villaschina.net/beijing/CathayView.htm.

37. Jia Hepeng, "Chinese-Style Villas Emerge in Market," *China Daily*, September 24, 2004.

38. Zhao Xudong and Duran Bell, "Destroying the Remembered and Recovering the Forgotten in *Chai*," *China Information* 19, no. 3 (2005): 489–503.

39. Anne-Marie Broudehoux, *The Making and Selling of Post-Mao Beijing* (New York: Routledge, 2004), 236n–37n. Residents protesting the imminent destruction of their homes have occasionally emblazoned their walls with grievances.

40. Wu Hung, "Zhang Dali's Dialogue: Conversation with a City," *Public Culture* 12, no. 3 (Fall 2000).

41. Quoted in Wu Hung, "Zhang Dali's Dialogue," 749.

42. Broudehoux, *The Making and Selling of Post-Mao Beijing*, 221–25.

43. Robin Visser, "Spaces of Disappearance: Aesthetic Responses to Contemporary Beijing City Planning," *Journal of Contemporary China* 13, no. 39 (May 2004): 277–310.

44. See Meike Behm, "China: Dynamics of the Public Space," *NY Arts Magazine*, March/April 2005.

45. Sheng Qi, "Guan nian he yi shu: *Gu di chong you*" [A statement of artistic concept by Sheng Qi regarding *Old Haunts Revisited*], Beijing, March 8, 2002, www.c12000.com/guard/rebirth/concept/shengqi/wen4.shtml; also see "You mu zai cheng shi de yi shu" [Nomadic city art], *Zhong Guo Jiao Tong Bao*, December 19, 2002.

46. Harvey Molotch, "The City as a Growth Machine: Toward a Political Economy of Place," *American Journal of Sociology* 82 (1976): 309–30.

47. Robert M. Fogelson, *Downtown: Its Rise and Fall, 1880–1950* (New Haven, CT: Yale University Press, 2001), 376.

48. Kevin Fox Gotham, "A City Without Slums: Urban Renewal, Public Housing and Downtown Revitalization in Kansas City, Missouri," *American Journal of Economics and Sociology*, January 2001, 302.

49. Fogelson, *Downtown*, 378.

50. Jon C. Teaford, "Urban Renewal and its Aftermath," *Housing Policy Debate* 11, no. 2 (2000): 450.

51. Quoted in Fogelson, *Downtown*, 319.

52. However, developing center-city parcels in Beijing has, in the last few years, become less profitable and more cumbersome, partly due to growing historic preservation advocacy and the mounting cost and complexity of dealing with and re-housing current site residents.

53. Redevelopment of the Lower Hill "displaced over 8,000 residents; 1,239 black families, 312 white." I used these figures to determine typical family size in the project area (about 5.2 persons), and thus estimate the total displaced population at about 28,080. See *Pittsburgh Neighborhood Atlas: The Hill* (Pittsburgh: Pittsburgh Neighborhood Alliance, 1977), 2. The 5,400 figure for Golden Triangle is from Peter Hall, *Cities of Tomorrow: An Intellectual History of Urban Planning and Design in the Twentieth Century* (New York: Blackwell Publishing, 1988), 231.

54. The definitive works are Herbert J. Gans, *The Urban Villagers* (New York: Free Press, 1962); Marc Fried, "Grieving for a Lost Home," in *The Urban Condition: People and Policy in the Metropolis*, ed. L. J. Duhl (New York: Simon and Schuster, 1963), expanded in *The World of the Urban Working Class* (Cambridge, MA: Harvard University Press, 1973); and Chester Hartman, "The Housing of Relocated Families," *Journal of the American Institute of Planners* 30 (November 1964): 266–86.

55. Martin Anderson, *The Federal Bulldozer: A Critical Analysis of Urban Renewal, 1949–1962* (Cambridge, MA: MIT Press, 1964); also see Mindy T. Fullilove, *Root Shock: How Tearing Up City Neighborhoods Hurts America, and What We Can Do About It* (New York: One World/Ballantine Books, 2004).

56. In 2003 some 53,000 families were displaced by redevelopment projects, about 182,300 people calculated using the average family size of 3.4 persons.

57. "Beijing: The Fate of the Old," *China Heritage Newsletter* (China Heritage Project, Australian National University) 1 (March 2005).

58. See Mark O'Neill, "Human Cost of Development," *South China Morning Post*, April 7, 2000.

59. Lawrence Vale and I explored this subject in *The Resilient City: How Modern Cities Recover From Disaster* (New York: Oxford University Press, 2005).

60. Michael A. Lev, "Beijing's Poor Pay Price for Urban Renewal," *Chicago Tribune*, January 13, 2002.

61. Quoted in Lev, "Beijing's Poor."

62. As suggested earlier, this is not the way it was supposed to be. In its original formulation the Old and Dilapidated Housing Renewal program was meant to rehouse a significant percentage of residents on site, not in distant suburbs. New housing units were offered to returning residents at a price that covered the cost of construction, already low due to tax breaks and reduced infrastructure fees. See Lü Junhua, "Beijing's Old and Dilapidated Housing Renewal," 59–61.

63. Quoted in Choong and Naham, "Home Truths," 59.

64. Ibid.

65. Fried, "Grieving for a Lost Home," 151–52, 167.

66. J. Douglas Porteous and Sandra E. Smith, *Domicide: The Global Destruction of Home* (Montreal: McGill-Queen's University Press, 2001), 12.

67. J. Douglas Porteous, "Domicide: The Destruction of Home," in *The Home: Words, Interpretations, Meanings and Environments*, ed. David N. Benjamin, 159 (Brookfield, VT: Ashgate Publishing Company, 1995); also see Lorna Fox, "The Meaning of Home: A Chimerical Concept or a Legal Challenge?" *Journal of Law and Society* 29, no. 4 (December 2002): 580–610.

68. Kenneth Hewitt's review of *Domicide: The Global Destruction of Home* in *Canadian Geographer* 48, no. 2 (2004): 245.

The Country and the City

1. Hans H. Frankel, "The Chinese Ballad 'Southeast Fly the Peacocks,'" *Harvard Journal of Asiatic Studies* 34 (1974): 248.

2. Tiejun Cheng and Mark Selden, "The Origins and Social Consequences of China's Hukou System," *China Quarterly* 139 (September 1994): 653.

3. Ibid., 648.

4. Lü Junhua, Peter G. Rowe, and Zhang Jie, eds., *Modern Urban Housing in China, 1840–2000* (New York: Prestel, 2001), 146.

5. Yixing Zhou and John R. Logan, "Growth on the Edge: The New Chinese Metropolis," in *Urban China in Transition*, ed. John R. Logan. (London: Blackwell Publishers, 2007). Page numbers refer to an earlier draft of this chapter, entitled "Suburbanization of Urban China: A Conceptual Framework," 1–2.

6. Xi Zhang, "Migration, Household Registration System and Urbanization" (conference paper presented at Asian Studies on the Pacific Coast, Eugene, Oregon, 2004), http://mcel.pacificu.edu/aspac/home/papers/uz.php3.

7. Cheng and Selden, "The Origins and Social Consequences of China's Hukou System," 650.

8. Ibid., 644.

9. Xi Zhang, "Migration, Household Registration System and Urbanization."

10. See Jasper Becker, *Hungry Ghosts: Mao's Secret Famine* (New York: Free Press, 1996).

11. Yixing Zhou and Laurence J. C. Ma, "Economic Restructuring and Suburbanization in China," *Urban Geography* 21, no. 3 (2000): 209.

12. Cheng and Selden, "The Origins and Social Consequences of China's Hukou System," 666; Lü et al., eds., *Modern Urban Housing in China*, 147.

13. Chengri Ding and Gerrit Knaap, "Urban Land Policy Reform in China," *Land Lines* (Lincoln Institute of Land Policy) 15, no. 2 (April 2003).

14. B. Michael Frolic, "Reflections on the Chinese Model of Development," *Social Forces* 57, no. 2 (December 1978): 384–88. Whether Mao and the Chinese communists were outright antiurbanists is a matter of debate among sinologists. Kam Wing Chan has argued, for example, that Maoist antiurbanism has been largely a figment of the Western imagination. Mao did voice ambivalence toward big cities, though he also said "the peasants are the future industrial workers of China and tens of millions of them will go to the cities. For if China wants to build a great number of large modern cities, then she will have to undergo a long process of transformation in which the rural population become residents of the cities." It may be more accurate to describe the Mao regime as "semiurbanist" than outright "antiurbanist." The Mao quote is cited in R. J. R. Kirkby, *Urbanization in China: Town and Country in a Developing Economy* (New York: Columbia University Press, 1985), 21. Also see Kam Wing Chan, *Cities With Invisible Walls* (Hong Kong: Oxford University Press).

15. Barry Naughton, "The Third Front: Defence Industrialization in the Chinese Interior," *China Quarterly* 115 (September 1988): 351–54, 357; Naughton, "Cities in the Chinese Economic System: Changing Roles and Conditions for Cutonomy," in *Urban Spaces in Contemporary China*, ed. Deborah S. Davis et al., 67 (New York: Cambridge University Press, 1995). Naughton claims the term "Third Front" was first used by Lin Biao at a party meeting in 1962. The First Front was China's coast, while the Third Front was the deep interior; between the two was the Second Front.

16. Goodhue Livingston Jr., "The Blight of Our Cities," 261; Ralph E. Lapp, "Industrial Dispersion in the United States," 256; "The Only Real Defense," 242. These were all published in a special issue of *Bulletin of Atomic Scientists*, September 1951. Also see Robert Kargon, "The City as Communications Net: Norbert Wiener, the Atomic Bomb, and Urban Dispersal," *Technology and Culture* 45, no. 4 (October 2004): 764–77.

17. Harry S Truman, "Memorandum and Statement of Policy on the Need for Industrial Dispersion," August 10, 1951. From John Woolley and Gerhard Peters, *The American Presidency Project* (Santa Barbara: University of California, http://www.presidency.ucsb.edu/ws/?pid=13875).

18. Zhou and Logan, "Suburbanization of Urban China," 1–2.

19. Lü et al., eds., *Modern Urban Housing in China*, 171–73.

20. Barry Naughton, "Cities in the Chinese Economic System," 70, 73.

21. Thomas Scharping, "Urbanization in China Since 1949," *China Quarterly* 109 (March 1987): 108.

22. See Kam Wing Chan and Ying Hu, "Urbanization in China in the 1990s: New Definition, Different Series, and Revised Trends," *China Review* 3, no. 2 (Fall 2003): 49–71.

23. Gordon Anderson and Ying Ge, "Do Economic Reforms Accelerate Urban Growth? The Case of China," *Urban Studies* 41, no. 11 (October 2004): 2201–02.

24. See U.S. Census Bureau, *1990 Census of Population and Housing*, "1990 Population and Housing Unit Counts: United States," Table 4 ("United States Urban and Rural Population, 1790–1990").

25. The floating population technically includes anyone living away from their official *hukou* residence for more than a year. Conversely, migration is officially "permanent" only with a formal transfer of *hukou* registration to the new location. In fact, an urban *hukou* can be purchased, but the enormous cost—as much as $200,000 for Shanghai—makes this an impossibility for nearly all migrants. Although the term is mostly used in reference to the rural migrants, the floating population technically also includes the millions of relatively affluent, educated people in China who are working in places apart from the birth-defined *hukou* registration. See Daniel Goodkind and Loraine A. West, "China's Floating Population; Definitions, Data and Recent Findings," *Urban Studies* 39, no. 12 (2002): 2237–50; also see Feng Wang and Xuejin Zuo, "Inside China's Cities: Institutional Barriers and Opportunities for Urban Migrants," *American Economic Review* 89, no. 2 (May 1999): 279.

26. Zheng Guizhen et al., "A Preliminary Inquiry into the Problem of Floating Population in Shanghai City Proper," *Renkou Yanjiu* 3, nos. 2–7 (May 29, 1985); Tai-Chee Wong et al., "Building a Global City: Negotiating the Massive Influx of Floating Population in Shanghai," *Journal of Housing and the Built Environment* 20 (2005): 30.

27. Chaolin Gu and Jianfa Shen, "Transformation of Urban Socio-spatial Structure in Socialist Market Economies: The Case of Beijing," *Habitat International* 27, no. 1 (March 2003): 112.

28. In all likelihood the size of the Chinese floating population is considerable higher; the marginal legal status of migrant workers—who, by definition, are supposed to be somewhere else—makes them an elusive quarry for researchers and census takers. "China's Floating Population Tops 140 Million," *China Daily Online*, July 27, 2005, http://english.people.com.cn/200507/27/eng20050727_198605.html. Also see Goodkind and West, "China's Floating Population: Definitions, Data and Recent Findings," 2243.

29. About 29 million people emigrated from Europe to the United States between 1820 and 1920, while about five million African Americans moved out of the rural South between 1940 and 1970.

30. Justin Yifu Lin, "Rural Reforms and Agricultural Growth in China," *American Economic Review* 82, no. 1 (March 1992): 34–39.

31. Tai-Chee Wong et al., "Building a Global City," 32.

32. Jason Long, "Rural-Urban Migration and Socioeconomic Mobility in Victorian Britain," *Journal of Economic History*, March 2005. I refer here to a version of this essay presented at the October 2002 meeting of the Economic History Association.

33. Eric Foner and John A. Garraty, eds., "Internal Migration," "Urbanization," *The Reader's Companion to American History* (New York: Houghton Mifflin, 1991).

34. See Nicholas Lemann, *The Promised Land: The Great Black Migration and How It Changed America* (New York: Vintage, 1992).

35. Kenneth D. Roberts, "The Determinants of Job Choice by Rural Labour Migrants in Shanghai," *China Economic Review* 12, no. 1 (2001): 28.

36. The Shunde study found that 274 construction workers were killed over the five-year period from 1989 to 1993; see Tak-sun Ignatius Yu et al., "Occupational Injuries in Shunde City," *Accident Analysis & Prevention* 31, no. 4 (July 1999): 313–17. The fatality rate for the U.S. construction industry between 1980 and 1989 was 25.6 per 100,000 workers; see "Occupational Injury Deaths—United States, 1980–1989," *Morbidity and Mortality Weekly Report* 43, no. 14 (April 15, 1994): 262–64.

37. Jim Yardley, "In a Tidal Wave, China's Masses Pour From Farm to City," *New York Times*, September 12, 2004; see also Roberts, "Determinants of Job Choice," 15–39; and Roberts, "Female Labour Migrants to Shanghai: Temporary 'Floaters' or Potential Settlers?" *International Migration Review* 36, no. 2 (2002).

38. Tai-Chee Wong et al., "Building a Global City," 41; Feng Wang and Xuejin Zuo, "Inside China's Cities: Institutional Barriers and Opportunities for Urban Migrants," *American Economic Review* 89, no. 2 (May 1999): 277. Also see Jianfa Shen and Yefang Huang, "The Working and Living Space of the 'Floating Population' in China," *Asia Pacific Viewpoint* 44, no. 1 (April 2003): 51–62. Some have argued that living conditions among the migrant workforce are not as bad as commonly believed, and certainly China has avoided the extensive slums or squatter settlements often associated with rapid urbanization in the developing world; see Leiwen Jiang, "Living Conditions of the Floating Population in Urban China," *Housing Studies* 21, no. 5 (September 2006).

The Country and the City
continued

39. Yardley, "Tidal Wave."

40. Xin Li, "Millions Travel Home to Ring in Lunar New Year," *Washington Times*, January 30, 2006; John Helton, "Holiday Travel: 'Take the Car,'" *CNN.com*, November 2, 2006, http://www.cnn.com/2006/TRAVEL/11/01/holiday.travel.overview/index.html.

Suburbanization and the Mechanics of Sprawl

1. *The Book of Ser Marco Polo: The Venetian Concerning Kingdoms and Marvels of the East*, "Chapter XXII: Concerning the City of Cambaluc and its Great Traffic and Population," translated and edited by Colonel Sir Henry Yule (London: John Murray, 1903).

2. Robert Bruegmann, *Sprawl: A Compact History* (Chicago: University of Chicago, 2005), 18.

3. Yixing Zhou and Laurence J. C. Ma, "Economic Restructuring and Suburbanization in China," *Urban Geography* 21, no. 3 (2000): 223.

4. Ibid.

5. Tingwei Zhang, "Land Market Forces and Government's Role in Sprawl: The Case of China," *Cities* 17, no. 2 (2000): 125–28. The 1995 figure includes the previously rural counties Pudong, Baoshan, Jiading, and Shanghai.

6. David Bray, "Urban Design and Community Governance in China: A Study of Space and Power," in *Comment vivre ensemble*, ed. Paola Pellegrini and Paola Viganó, 83 (Venice: Università Iuav di Venezia, 2006); Bray, *Social Space and Governance in Urban China: The Danwei System from Origins to Reform* (Stanford: Stanford University Press, 2005), 94.

7. Bray, *Social Space and Governance*, 199–200.

8. Bentham's prison, circular in form with a central watchtower, allowed a single guard to keep an eye on scores of prisoners simultaneously.

9. Bray, "Urban Design," 84. Also see Laurence J. C. Ma, "Economic Reforms, Urban Spatial Restructuring, and Planning in China," *Progress in Planning* 61 (2004): 239.

10. Piper Rae Gaubatz, "Urban Transformation in Post-Mao China: Impacts of the Reform Era on China's Urban Form," in *Urban Spaces in Contemporary China*, ed. Deborah S. Davis et al., 30–31, 34–37 (New York: Cambridge University Press, 1995).

11. Piper R. Gaubatz, "Changing Beijing," *Geographical Review* 85, no. 1 (January 1995): 2.

12. Ya Ping Wang and Alan Murie, "The Process of Commercialisation of Urban Housing in China," *Urban Studies* 33, no. 6 (1996): 972. Also see Yan Song et al., "Housing Policy in the People's Republic of China: An Historical Overview," in *Emerging Land and Housing Markets in China*, ed. Chengri Ding and Yan Song, 163–72 (Cambridge, MA: Lincoln Institute of Land Policy, 2005).

13. Ya Ping Wang and Alan Murie, *Housing Policy and Practice in China* (New York: St. Martin's Press, 1999), 143, cited in Song et al., "Housing Policy," 169–70.

14. Zhou and Logan, "Suburbanization of Urban China," 5 (draft).

15. Zhou and Ma, "Economic Restructuring and Suburbanization," 219.

16. Tingwei Zhang, "Land Market Forces," 130.

17. F. Frederic Deng and Youqin Huang, "Uneven Land Reform and Urban Sprawl: The Case of Beijing," *Progress in Planning* 61 (2004): 225. Also see Peter Ho, "Who Owns China's Land? Policies, Property Rights and Deliberate Institutional Ambiguity," *China Quarterly* 166 (2001): 394–421.

18. Hannah Beech, "Seeds of Fury," *Time Asia*, March 6, 2006; see also Edward Cody, "In Chinese Uprisings, Peasants Find New Allies," *Washington Post*, November 26, 2005.

19. Deng and Huang, "Uneven Land Reform and Urban Sprawl," 214–19, 227.

20. Jiyuan Liu et al., "China's Changing Landscape During the 1990s: Large-Scale Land Transformations Estimated with Satellite Data," *Geophysical Research Letters* 32 (January 2005): 1–5.

21. See Karen C. Seto et al., "Monitoring Land-Use Change in the Pearl River Delta Using Landsat TM," *International Journal of Remote Sensing* 23, no. 10 (2002): 2001–02.

22. Anthony G. O. Yeh and Xia Li, "Economic Development and Agricultural Land Loss in the Pearl River Delta," *Habitat International* 23, no. 3 (1999): 374–76.

23. C. P. Lo, "Urban Indicators of China from Radiance-Calibrated Digital DMSP-OLS Nighttime Images," *Annals of the Association of American Geographers* 92, no. 2 (2002): 225–40.

24. I use the terms "sprawl" and "suburbanization" interchangeably, though some urbanists might object to this. I take both words to mean the process of metropolitan expansion into formerly rural or agricultural land on the urban fringe, resulting in a new spatial order that is relatively low in density and

structured by highways and oriented to an automobile population. Zhou and Ma make a useful
related distinction between "suburbanization" and
"suburban development." The latter "refers to the
transformation of suburban land to more intensive
industrial, commercial, and housing developments
regardless of where the impetus for such changes
comes from," and can occur whether the city center
is booming or in decline. The motive force behind
suburban development may be centrifugal, coming
either from the city center itself, or centripetal,
"coming from more distant places owing to the
attractiveness of the central city and its suburban
areas." On the other hand, "suburbanization" "refers
to the growth of suburbs resulting from the
decentralization of population and economic activities
from the urban core after the core has experienced an
extended period of economic growth and reached a
high level of population concentration and intensive
land use." See Zhou and Ma, "Economic
Restructuring and Suburbanization," 206–07.

25. Albert I. Gordon, *Jews in Suburbia* (Boston:
Beacon Press, 1959), 1.

26. Zhou and Logan, "Suburbanization of Urban
China," 9 (draft).

27. Zhou and Ma, "Economic Restructuring and
Suburbanization," 226.

28. Ibid., 220–22.

29. Tunney F. Lee et al., eds., *Vanke Vision:
Sustainable Residential Development in Shanghai
Urban Planning and Design Handbook*, Vol. 1—
Research Seminar and Field Survey (Cambridge,
MA: MIT Department of Urban Studies and Planning,
February 2006), 127.

30. Ibid., 24.

31. Anthony D. King explores the Chinese villa
phenomenon in "Villafication: The Transformation
of Chinese Cities," in *Spaces of Global Cultures:
Architecture, Urbanism, Identity* (New York:
Routledge, 2004), 111–26.

32. Bray, "Urban Design," 88.

33. Ibid., 89. It was actually the central
government's Ministry of Construction that first
developed the basic *xiao qū* (literally "small area")
site plan in the late 1980s. Drawing partly on Clarence
Perry's "neighborhood unit" theory, ministry planners
sought to provide not only housing but a variety of
communal facilities meant to "promote attributes like
social cohesion (*ningjuli*), neighborliness (*linli
guanxi*) and feelings of security and belonging."
Government-built *xiao qū* housing later served as a

model for the private-sector development community.
See Zou Denong, *A History of Modern Architecture in
China* (Tianjin: Tianjin Science and Technology
Press, 2001), 459–65 (in Chinese), cited in Bray,
"Urban Design," 88.

34. Lin Shao Zhou, "Development and Design of
the Low-Density Residence Community," (in
Chinese) *Bai Nian Jian Zhu Ping Lun* [Architecture
Century Commentary] 1 (2002): 34–39.

35. Fulong Wu, "Transplanted Cityscapes: The
Use of Imagined Globalization in Housing
Commodification in Beijing," *Area* 36, no. 3 (2004):
229; Tang L., "Talking about Beijing's Townhouse,"
Beijing Evening, cited in Wu, 230.

36. Cited in Hannah Beech, "Shanghai Swings!,"
Time Asia, September 20, 2004.

37. Quoted in Ted Anthony, "New York, China: The
City So Nice, They're Building it Twice," *Newsday*,
April 17, 2004.

38. Fulong Wu, "Transplanted Cityscapes," 229,
232.

39. Jeffrey W. Cody, "Columbia Circle: An
Obscured Shanghai Suburb, 1928–1932," *Dialogue* 23
(February 1999): 134.

40. Torsten Warner, *German Architecture in
China: Architectural Transfer* (Berlin: Ernst & Sohn,
1994), 199.

41. Jeffrey W. Cody, *Building in China: Henry K.
Murphy's "Adaptive Architecture," 1914–1935* (Hong
Kong: Chinese University of Hong Kong Press, 2001),
188–89.

42. Cody, "Columbia Circle," 132–33.

43. Billy Adams, "Space-age Living on the
Mainland," *South China Morning Post*, July 21, 1993.

44. Elisabeth Rosenthal, "North of Beijing,
California Dreams Come True," *New York Times*,
February 3, 2003.

45. Daniel Elsea, "China's Chichi Suburbs:
American-style Sprawl All the Rage in Beijing," *San
Francisco Chronicle*, April 24, 2005.

46. For more on this theme, see Eric Heikkila and
Rafael Pizarro, eds., *Southern California and the
World* (Westport, CT: Praeger, 2002).

47. June Fletcher, "Designing America," *Wall
Street Journal*, October 6, 2006.

48. Mike Anton and Henry Chu, "Welcome to
Orange County, China," *Los Angeles Times*, March 9,
2002.

49. "Di San Zhi Yan Kan Bie Shu," [An Objective
View on Villas] *Market Weekly*, August 2003, 55–57.
In Chinese.

Driving the Capitalist Road

1. "China Allows Car Loans For First Time," *Jinrong Shibao* [China Financial Times], October 13, 1998.

2. Cited in Philip P. Pan, "Bicycle No Longer King of the Road in China," *Washington Post*, March 12, 2001.

3. Cited in Song Mo and Wen Chihua, "Driving Ambition," *China Daily*, September 2, 2006.

4 "China Stands as World's 2nd Largest Auto Market," *People's Daily*, January 13, 2006.

5. Eric Baculinao, "China's Auto Industry Takes Off," *NBC News*, January 12, 2007.

6. Chia-Liang Tai, "Transforming Shanghai: The Redevelopment Context of the Pudong New Area" (unpublished masters thesis, Columbia University, Faculty of Architecture and Planning, May 2005), 54.

7 "Beijing Registers More New Cars Than Other Cities," *Xinhua News*, October 5, 2006; "Beijing's Private Autos Top One Million," *Xinhua News*, May 22, 2002.

8. Luo Rong Hua, interview by author and Wu Wei, Hangzhou Automobile City, Hangzhou, July 21, 2005. Luo was senior manager of Automobile City at the time.

9. See "Drive-in Theaters, Auto Shows, Magazines Reveal China's Auto Infatuation," *China Online—Industry News*, April 27, 1999.

10. "Beijing's Private Autos Top One Million," *Xinhua News*, May 22, 2002.

11. Lance Dickie, "Driving Madame Gou: China Bets on the Auto," *Seattle Times*, March 10, 1998. Also see MacLeod and Gesterland, "Autofocus," *China Online News*, June 8, 2000.

12. The heavy old Flying Pigeons (Feige) are still occasionally seen on streets and campuses. The bike has a revolutionary pedigree. Manufactured in a former Japanese artillery plant in Tianjin, the Flying Pigeon was the brainchild of a model worker named Huo Baoji who, filled with revolutionary ardor, built a prototype of a "people's bicycle" and presented it to party officials on July 5, 1950. Four years later, the Flying Pigeon was awarded first place in the nation's first quality appraisal for bicycles. The heavy steel bicycle, available in any shade of black, went on to become as much an icon of the People's Republic as the once-ubiquitous Mao jacket.

13. Pan Haixiao, interview by author, Shanghai, June 12, 2007. Pan is a professor of urban planning at Tongji University.

14. Jim Yardley, "Uneasily, Booming China City Reaches Milestone," *International Herald Tribune*, January 14, 2007.

15. In Beijing in the 1990s, studies revealed that nearly 70 percent of all traffic accidents involved bicycles, and bicyclists accounted for more than 30 percent of traffic fatalities in the city. Elders were found to be especially at risk; those over age sixty were five times more likely to become an accident victim. See X. Liu, L. D. Shen, and J. Huang, "Analysis of Bicycle Accidents and Recommended Counter Measures in Beijing, China," in *Transportation Research Record 1487* (Washington, DC: TRB, National Research Council, 1995), 75–83.

16. Cited in Pan, "Bicycle No Longer King." Also see Geoffrey York, "Cars Conquering the Bicycle Kingdom," *Globe and Mail*, January 20, 2007; Henry Chu, "Beijing Street's Bike Ban Deflates Cyclists," *Los Angeles Times*, October 27, 1998; "Media Blackout on Bicycle Suit," *South China Morning Post*, January 10, 2007. There has been some push-back from bicyclists and environmentalists in recent years. In October 2006 in Beijing, a middle-aged expatriate cyclist became an overnight celebrity when she refused to move for a motorist entering a designated bicycle lane; she stood her ground even after the driver got out and flung her bike aside. Eventually he apologized. See "Foreign Auntie Challenges Rule-Breaking Vehicle," *Nanfang Daily*, October 20, 2006.

17. Calum MacLeod, "China's Highways Go the Distance," *USA Today*, January 29, 2006; also see Wang Ting, "In China, a Rush to Get Behind the Wheel," *Washington Post*, June 6, 2002.

18. The phrase is from Tom Lewis, *Divided Highways* (1997; New York: Penguin, 1999), ix.

19 "Auto Exports Show Marked Increase," *New York Times*, May 8, 1910.

20 "Mandarins Like Motor Cars Now," *New York Times*, January 26, 1913.

21. William I. Irvine, *Automotive Markets in China, British Malaya, and Chosen*, Department of Commerce, Bureau of Foreign and Domestic Commerce Special Agents Series—No. 221 (Washington, DC: Government Printing Office, 1923), 32.

22. Ibid., 1.

23. Mira Wilkins and Frank Ernest Hill, *American Business Abroad: Ford on Six Continents* (Detroit: Wayne State University Press, 1964), 149–50. Ford automobiles were not actually manufactured in China, which is what Sun was pressing for. They were

assembled in Japan and "knocked down" for shipment to China—an arrangement that would become increasingly problematic as the relationship between the two countries deteriorated in the 1930s.

24 "Chinese Ready for Autos Says Commission Head," *Ford News* 3, no. 16 (March 22, 1924).

25 "Build Roads for Autos in China," *Ford News* 2, no. 5 (January 1, 1922). In 1934 Britain imported 301 cars to China, the United States, 3,014; see "China's Import of Motor Trucks, Buses, and Motor Cars for the Years 1933–June 1936 Inclusive," in Bureau of Roads, *Highways in China: Tables, Charts and Maps* (Nanking: National Economic Council, April 1935).

26. Irvine, *Automotive Markets*, 32.

27. Ibid.

28. Hewlett Johnson, "The Civilizing Road," *Times of London*, July 26, 1932, reprinted in Oliver J. Todd, *Two Decades in China* (Peking: Association of Chinese and American Engineers, 1938), 263; also see Johnson, "What I Saw in China," *Listener*, September 1934, reprinted in Todd, *Two Decades*, 348.

29. A. Viola Smith and Anselm Chuh, *Motor Roads in China*, Trade Information Series No. 120 (Washington, DC: Department of Commerce, 1931), 4–6.

30. Oliver J. Todd, "Modern Highways in China," *Journal of the Association of Chinese and American Engineers*, September 1926, in *Two Decades*, 219; Basil Ashton et al., "Famine in China: 1958–61," *Population and Development Review* 10, no. 4 (December 1984).

31. Oliver J. Todd, "Motor Roads for South China," *Oriental Engineer*, May 1927, 223–28; Todd, "The Good Roads Movement in Kweichow," *China Weekly Review*, December 24, 1927, 229–31; Todd, "Highways in a Land of Barriers," *Asia*, January 1929. Page numbers refer to the articles as reprinted in Todd, *Two Decades*. Also see "Kweichow's First Auto," *New York Herald Tribune*, February 12, 1928; and Jonathan Spence, *To Change China: Western Advisors in China, 1620–1960* (Boston: Little, Brown and Company, 1969), 211–12.

32. Todd, "Famine Relief and Road Building in Shantung," *Journal of the Association of Chinese and American Engineers*, November 1921, in *Two Decades*, 204–05, 211.

33. Spence, *To Change China,* 210–12.

34. Cited in Spence, *To Change China*, 215–16.

35. Oliver J. Todd, "A Practical Education Movement," *China Weekly Review*, January 26, 1929, in *Two Decades*, 316–19.

36. Todd, "The Good Roads Movement," 229–31.

37. Todd, "Modern Highways in China," 218–19.

38. J. Morgan Clements, *China: Automotive Conditions and the Good Roads Movement*, Trade Information Bulletin No. 2 (Automotive Division) (Washington, DC: Department of Commerce, 1922), 3–19.

39. Han-Veng Woo, "Design of Streets and the Use of City Walls in the Development of Highway Systems in the Municipalities of China" (unpublished masters thesis, Iowa State College, 1930), 23–25.

40 "China Plans Park System," *Daily Argus* (White Plains, New York), August 6, 1929; "Nanking Layout of Parkways Similar to County System," *Daily Argus*, September 10, 1929.

41. Albert C. Wedemeyer, *Wedemeyer Reports!* (New York: Henry Holt, 1958), 221, 328–32. Wedemeyer was originally to be assisted in the Carbonado operation by General George S. Patton, with whom he had worked in North Africa; Patton was preparing to join Wedemeyer in Chongqing when he was killed in a traffic accident in Germany on December 21, 1945.

42. Ibid., 354–55.

43. Ibid., 355–56.

44. China's first modern superhighway was the Shenyang-Dalian Expressway, opened in 1990. See Li Conghua, *China: The Consumer Revolution* (New York: Wiley, 1998), 111.

45. Quoted in Steve Anderson, "The Roads of Metro New York: New Jersey Turnpike," http://www.nycroads.com/roads/nj-turnpike/.

46. Quoted in Sam Roberts, "Reappraising a Landmark Bridge, and the Visionary Behind It," *New York Times*, July 11, 2006.

47. Sir Gordon Y. S. Wu, interview by author, Hopewell Centre, Hong Kong, April 16, 1999, passim.

48. Ezra Vogel, *One Step Ahead in China: Guangdong Under Reform* (Cambridge, MA: Harvard University Press, 1989), 221–22.

49. Rosemary Sayer, *Gordon Wu: The Man Who Turned the Lights On* (Hong Kong: Chameleon Press, 2006), 64–66.

50. R. J. Neller and K. C. Lam, "The Environment," in *Guangdong: Survey of a Province Undergoing Rapid Change*, ed. Y. M. Yeung and David K. Y. Chu, 438 (Hong Kong: Chinese University Press, 1994).

51. George D. Hubbard, "The Pearl River Delta," *Lingnan Science Journal* 7 (1929): 24.

52. Leo K. K. Leung, interview by author, Hopewell Centre, Hong Kong, August 10, 1999.

Driving the Capitalist Road
continued
Leung, executive director of Hopewell Holdings,
managed much of the day-to-day road-building work.

53. The drive-in was patented in 1933 by Richard
Hollingshead Jr. of Riverton, New Jersey, who
envisioned "a new and useful outdoor theater" in
which cars "constitute an element of the seating
facilities of the theater." See Kerry Segrave, *Drive-In
Theaters: A History From Their Inception in 1933*
(London: McFarland & Company, 1992).

54. Jon Woodier, "GrandMart to Open in
Shenzhen," *South China Morning Post*, August
29, 1993.

55. "Wal-Mart Poised for Major China Expansion,"
CNN Money, March 19, 2006.

56. Prof. Ji Guo Hua, interview by author,
Nanjing University, Graduate School of Architecture,
December 15, 2006.

57. David Barboza, "The Great Malls of China,"
New York Times, May 25, 2005; also see Robert
Marquand, "China's Supersized Mall," *Christian
Science Monitor*, November 24, 2004. Floor area
data is from "World's Largest Shopping Malls," http://
www.easternct.edu/depts/amerst/MallsWorld.htm.

58. John Hannigan, *Fantasy City: Pleasure and
Profit in the Postmodern Metropolis* (New York:
Routledge, 1998), 177.

59. "McDonald's, Sinopec in China Drive-thru
Store Deal," *Reuters*, June 20, 2006.

**Theme Parks and the Landscape of
Consumption**
1. Xin Zhigang, "Dissecting China's 'Middle
Class,'" *China Daily*, October 27, 2004.

2. "CASS: Chinese Middle Class Swelling,"
Xinhua News, March 30, 2004.

3. *China Domestic Tourist Market* (Singapore:
China Knowledge Press, 2005).

4. *China Tourism Industry Report*, 2006, http://
www.okokok.com.cn/Abroad/Class126/
Class111/200611/111909.html; also see *The Tenth Five-
Year Plan of the Travel Agency Industry and its
Development*, http://www.chinadaily.com.cn/
bizchina/2006-04/18/content_570798.htm.

5. Ron Gluckman, "Thrill to a New Industry,"
Asiaweek 26, no. 45 (November 17, 2000).

6. "Beijing Develops Survival Island Tourism
Base," *China Travel News and Events*, May 6, 1999;
"'Hunting Island' Off East China," *Far Eastern

Economic Review 41 (October 9, 1997): 42; "Shanxi
Plans to Construct Large Hunting Grounds," *China
Travel News and Events*, December 3, 1999.

7. See Cowboy City website, http://www.
m66s.com.

8. Kelvin Chan, "No Business Like Snow
Business," *Weekend Standard*, July 9, 2005.

9. "Large Ski Resort in Southern China," *China
Travel News and Events*, March 17, 2000.

10. Chan, "No Business Like Snow Business."

11. "Boom in Beijing Ski Resorts Sparks Water
Supply Worries," *China Ski Press*, August 5, 2005.

12. Charles McGrath, "How Do You Say Shank in
Mandarin?," *Play Magazine—New York Times*,
February 2006, 104.

13. "Golf Criticized in China," *Globe and Mail*,
November 26, 2006.

14. McGrath, "How Do You Say Shank in
Mandarin?," 104.

15. John Crean, "Build It and They Will Come,"
Asian Golf Monthly, November 2004.

16. Larry Olmsted, "Mission Accomplished," *Cigar
Aficionado*, July/August 2006.

17. Ibid.; McGrath, "How Do You Say Shank in
Mandarin?," 107.

18. Larry Olmsted, "Bigger Is Better," *USA
Today—The Golfer's World*, October 26, 2006.

19. McGrath, "How Do You Say Shank in
Mandarin?," 106, 114.

20. The golf community concept was pioneered
by the late Desmond Muirhead, one of the leading
golf course architects in the United States and "father
of private golf communities." See Kate Orff,
"Landscape," in Chuihua Judy Chung, Jeffrey Inaba,
Rem Koolhaas, Sze Tsung Leong, et al., eds., *Great
Leap Forward* (Köln: Taschen, 2001), 398; Curtis
Lum, "Golf-course Designer Desmond Muirhead
Dead at 79," *Honolulu Advertiser*, July 30, 2002.

21. McGrath, "How Do You Say Shank in
Mandarin?," 106.

22. Daniel Kwan, "Farmers Angry Over Land
Loss," *South China Morning Post*, June 8, 1993.

23. "Farmland in Capital Illegally Cleared for Golf
Course," *South China Morning Post*, July 9, 2000.

24. "Golf Criticized in China," *Globe and Mail*,
November 26, 2006.

25. "China Axes Golf Course Projects to Curb
Fast Loss of Arable Land," *People's Daily*,
March 20, 2004.

26. Tang Yuankai, "The Theme of Things to
Come," *Beijing Review* 48, no. 42 (October 20,
2005).

27. Michael Ma, "Dinosaurs Make Return in Sichuan Theme Park," *South China Morning Post*, June 3, 2000.

28. "Tianjin to Build World's Biggest Military-Theme Park," *People's Daily*, June 6, 2002.

29. The developers were notified by Tangshan city officials in late 2005 that as the whole park had been built without the requisite permits, the site would have to be vacated. See Guo Xun, "Tangshan Urban Planning Department Claims Earthquake Memorial Wall Illegal" (in Chinese), *Hua Xia Shi Bao*, August 1, 2006.

30. Xiao Feng, "Giant Buddhist Statue Enshrined in Hainan," *China Daily*, April 16, 2005.

31. "Bruce Lee Theme Park Set to Open in Guangdong," *China Daily*, November 30, 2006; John Harlow, "Screaming Rollercoaster Will Kick off Bruce Lee Theme Park," *Los Angeles Times*, September 3, 2006.

32. See, for example, Michael Sorkin, ed., *Variations on a Theme Park: The New American City and the End of Public Space* (New York: Hill and Wang, 1992).

33. Walter Benjamin, "The Arcades of Paris," in *The Arcades Project*, 874. Benjamin never completed this monumental work, which he referred to as "the theater of all my struggles and all my ideas." As Herbert Muschamp has written, "Over time, the project mutated into the literary equivalent of its subject: a discontinuous maze, composed of brief insights and digressions, along with quotations that glitter from the pages like wares in a shop window." See Muschamp, "Walter Benjamin: The Passages of Paris and of Benjamin's Mind," *New York Times*, January 16, 2000.

34. Muschamp, "Walter Benjamin."

35. Michael Dutton, ed., *Streetlife China* (New York: Cambridge University Press, 1998), 230.

36. Dean MacCannell, *The Tourist: A New Theory of the Leisure Class* (London: Macmillan Press, 1976), 21–23.

37. Ian Buruma, "Asia World," *New York Review of Books*, June 12, 2003, 55.

38. Keith Marchand, "Walt's Schmaltz: Not a Mickey Mouse Exhibit," *Montreal Mirror*, July 3, 1997. Walt Disney eventually parlayed this vision into an experimental city-building program known as EPCOT-Experimental Prototype Community of Tomorrow. Desmond C. K. Hui, "Building a Dream," *Xpressions* 25 (March 1999): 2–4.

39. Tang Jun, "Introducing Splendid China," in *China Tourism* (Hong Kong: China Tourism Press, 1993).

40. Ma Chi Man, "Let the World Know More About China," in *Shenzhen Splendid China: Miniature Scenic Spot*, ed. Shen Ping and Cheung Yuet Sim, 3 (Hong Kong: China Travel Service Hong Kong Limited, 1994).

41. Ann Anagnost, "The Nationscape: Movement in a Field of Vision," *Positions* 1, no. 3 (1993): 586.

42. Ibid., 588.

43. "Three Gorges of the Changjiang River," in *Shenzhen Splendid China: Miniature Scenic Spot*, ed. Shen Ping and Cheung Yuet Sim, 86 (Hong Kong: China Travel Service Hong Kong Limited, 1994). In a further irony, China Travel Service, the state-owned company that developed Splendid China, also operated a luxury cruise liner on the Yangtze River that brought tourists to the Three Gorges. The 300-foot ship, with a superstructure designed to resemble an imperial palace compound, was itself named *Splendid China*. See "'Splendid China' Cruises Three Gorges," *China Daily*, September 25, 1994.

44. Kenneth R. Timmerman, "Florida Splendid China," *American Spectator* 32, no. 3 (March 1999): 26–33.

45. Buruma, "Asia World," 54.

46. Maurice Irisson, Comte d'Hérisson, *Journal d'un interprète en Chine* (Paris: Ollendorf, 1886), translated and cited in Anne-Marie Broudehoux, *The Making and Selling of Post-Mao Beijing* (New York: Routledge, 2004), 54.

47. Anne-Marie Broudehoux, *The Making and Selling of Post-Mao Beijing* (New York: Routledge, 2004), 53–54.

48. Ibid., 50, 54–55.

49. Jean-Denis Attiret S. J., "Lettre à M. d'Assaut, 1er novembre 1743," in *Lettres édifiantes et curieuses écrites des missions étrangères par quelques missionnaires de la compagnie de Jésus* (Paris: Guérin, 1749), 27:1–61. English translation of 1752 by Joseph Spence [Sir Harry Beaumont], *A Particular Account of the Emperor of China's Gardens near Pekin*; reprinted in *The English Landscape Garden*, ed. John Dixon Hunt (New York and London: Garland Publishing, 1982).

50. Ibid. One of the highlights of this quotidian theme park was the enactment, several times a year, of all the "Commerce, Marketings, Arts, Trade, Bustle, and Hurry...even all the Rogueries" of a great city. The actors were palace eunuchs, who would put

Theme Parks and the Landscape of
Consumption *continued*
on "the Dress of the Profession or Part which is
assigned to him." A vast simulacrum would then
unfold, complete with choreographed chaos and "all
the Confusion of a Fair." Writes Attiret: "The Vessels
arrive at the Port; the Shops are open'd; and the
Goods are exposed for Sale. There is one Quarter for
those who sell Silks, and another for those who sell
Cloth; one Street for Porcelain, and another for
Varnish-works. You may be supply'd with whatever
you want. This Man sells Furniture of all sorts; that,
Cloaths and Ornaments for the Ladies: and a third
has all kinds of Books, for the Learned and Curious.
There are Coffee-houses too, and Taverns, of all
sorts, good and bad...'Tis all a Place of Liberty and
Licence; and you can scarce distinguish the Emperor
himself, from the meanest of his Subjects."

51. See Young-tsu Wong, *A Paradise Lost: The
Imperial Garden Yuanming Yuan* (Honolulu: University
of Hawaii Press, 2001).

52. Chen Wen Jun, interview by author and Wu
Wei, South China Mall, Wanjiang, Dongguan,
December 20, 2006. Mr. Chen was general manager
of South China Mall at the time.

53. South China Mall promotional brochure.

54. Anne F. Thurston, *Enemies of the People: The
Ordeal of the Intellectuals in China's Great Cultural
Revolution* (Cambridge, MA: Harvard University
Press, 1988), 133.

55. Marshall Berman, *All That Is Solid Melts into
Air: The Experience of Modernity* (New York: Viking
Penguin, 1988), 13–14.

56. "Tang Paradise," *Travel Guide China*, http://
www.travelchinaguide.com/attraction/shaanxi/xian/
tang-paradise.htm.

57. Peter G. Rowe and Seng Kuan, *Architectural
Encounters with Essence and Form in Modern China*
(Cambridge, MA: MIT Press, 2002), 176–82.

58. Geoffrey Crothall, "Eat Black Earth with Red
Guards, Drink Coke with Your Comrades," *South
China Morning Post*, October 18, 1993.

59. Dutton, *Streetlife China*, 232–34.

60. "Introduction to the Red Army Theme Park
Project," *Beijing Chaoyang Travel News*, March 3,
2006: http://www.bjtravel.gov.cn/biz/bizitem/
bizitem23485.htm. Also see project website at http://
www.redarmypark.com.cn. For Zhejiang project see
http://news.xinhuanet.com/photo/2005-10/20/
content_3653510.htm.

61. Hamish McDonald, "Chinese Tourists Urged to
See Red History in the Making," *Sydney Morning
Herald*, March 12, 2005.

62. Jeffrey W. Cody, "Making History (Pay) in
Shanghai," in *Shanghai: Architecture and Urbanism
for Modern China*, ed. Seng Kuan and Peter G. Rowe,
139 (New York: Prestel, 2004).

63. Nancy S. Steinhardt, *Chinese Imperial City
Planning* (Honolulu: University of Hawaii Press,
1990), 166.

64. Prof. Zhao Chen, interview by author, Nanjing
University, Graduate School of Architecture,
December 17, 2006.

65. For an overview of Rouse's career and
contributions, see Howard Gillette, "Assessing James
Rouse's Role in American City Planning," *Journal of
the American Planning Association* 65, no. 2 (Spring
1999); also see Nicholas Dagen Bloom, *Merchant of
Illusion: James Rouse, America's Salesman of the
Businessman's Utopia* (Columbus: Ohio State
University Press, 2004).

66. Jeffrey W. Cody and Wallace P. H. Chang,
"Cosmetic Heritage: The Fabrication of Pedestrian
Shopping Streets in South China, 1993–2000," in
Sites and Agents of Globalization, IASTE Working
Papers Series, vol. 126, 1–24.

67. The interviews were part of a study led by
Cody and Chang in June 2000. The term "cosmetic
heritage" is theirs, as well.

68. Quoted in Geoffrey A. Fowler, "Converting
the Masses: Starbucks in China," *Far Eastern
Economic Review*, July 17, 2003.

69. Jen Lin-Liu, "Xintiandi: Wood + Zapata
Reinvents Shanghai's Future by Including Its Past,"
Architectural Record 192, no. 3 (March 2004): 96,
cited in Cody, "Making History (Pay) in Shanghai."

70. Ben Wood, interview by author, Xintiandi,
Shanghai, June 16, 2007.

71. Cited in "Lo and Behold," *Post Magazine*,
January 11, 2004.

72. Ben Wood, interview by Bert de Muynck,
Commercial Real Estate in China, http://cre-china.
com/info.php?id=39&cid=2.

73. This may be taken literally. A 2006 *New York
Times* article about Wood noted that "back-alley copy
shops...sell duplicates of the computer discs that
architects drop off for reproduction. It may be only a
matter of hours before a Power Point presentation of
a new design is available for sale in a pirated edition."
See Julie V. Iovine, "Ben Wood, Our Man in
Shanghai," *New York Times*, August 13, 2006.

China Reinvents the City

1. "McDonald's Opens Drive-thru in Beijing" *International Business Times*, January 19, 2007.

2. This was reported in *Nan Feng*, July 13, 2006.

3. Yang Jianxiang, "Building Dreams in Bricks and Mortar," *China Daily*, September 14, 2004; The housing stock in the United States in 2005 was about 219 billion square feet; see U.S. Census Bureau, Current Housing Reports, Series H150/05, American Housing Survey for the United States, http://www.census.gov/hhes/www/housing/ahs/nationaldata.html.

4. Dana Cuff, *The Provisional City: Los Angeles Stories of Architecture and Urbanism* (Cambridge, MA: MIT Press, 2002), 4–5.

5. John Rajchman, "Thinking Big—Dutch Architect Rem Koolhaas—Interview," *Artforum*, December 1994.

6. Yixing Zhou and Laurence J. C. Ma, "Economic Restructuring and Suburbanization in China," *Urban Geography* 21, no. 3 (2000): 223.

7. Thomas L. Friedman, *The World Is Flat: A Brief History of the Twenty-First Century* (New York: Farrar, Straus & Giroux, 2005), 409.

8. Robert Collier, "A Warming World: China About to Pass U.S. as World's Top Generator of Greenhouse Gases," *San Francisco Chronicle*, March 5, 2007.

9. Ibid.

10. Ronald G. Knapp has written extensively on the subject of Chinese vernacular housing. See, for example, *China's Vernacular Architecture: House Form and Culture* (Honolulu: University of Hawaii Press, 1989) and Knapp and Kai-Yin Lo, eds., *House Home Family: Living and Being Chinese* (Honolulu: University of Hawaii Press, 2005).

11/ "China Admits Failure to Make Environmental Progress," *Reuters*, January 29, 2007.

12. People's Republic of China, "Renewable Energy Law" (unofficial version) from the Renewable Energy and Energy Efficiency Partnership.

13. Alex Pasternack, "China Could Be World's Biggest Wind Power by 2020," *Treehugger: Science and Technology,* January 26, 2007, http://www.treehugger.com/files/2007/01/china_could_be.php.

14. "Shanghai to Install Solar Panels on Building Roofs," *Shanghai Daily News*, September 15, 2005.

15. "Q&A with William A. McDonough," *Urban Land*, January 2007, 119.

16. "Visions of Ecopolis," *Economist*, September 21, 2006.

17. William A. McDonough, phone interview by author, April 11, 2007.

INDEX

Page numbers in bold indicate images

A

Abramson, Daniel, 150

agricultural land, 17, 194–97, 247, 293; land conversion, 194–97

Ai Weiwei, 132

airports, 14, 46, 70, 123–24, 125, 142, 171, 187, 282, 284, 285, 287. *See also individual airports*

Alexey Schusev, 103–104

Anagnost, Ann, 255–56

Andreu, Paul, 140, 141–43, 284

Anhui Province, 127, 173, 187

architects: American, 81–85, 131, 137, 139, 156, 208, 213, 272, 275–76, 300; British, 73, 123, 139; Chinese, 22–24, 61, 63, 66–67, 73, 80, 89, 102, 106, 132, 141, 209, 268, 271, 297; foreign, 23–24, 61, 72–73, 79, 88, 131–32, 134, 136, 139, 140, 141–42, 207, 208, 209; French, 72–73, 79–80, 115, 140–41, 142–43, 290; Japanese, 73, 141–42; Soviet, 103–04. *See also specific names*

Asian Games, 125, 133

automobiles, 16–18, 54, 63, 78, 80, 88, 103, 136, 150, 194, 214–15, 217–228, 232, 234–36, 239, 253, 293, 298; dealerships, 219, **220**; driving academies, 219–20; emissions, 125, 295, 301; history in China, 109–10, 193, 223–28; manufacturing, 88, 218; ownership, 17, 201–02, 214, 217–18, 235, 239, 293; in popular culture, 214–15, 219–20

B

B&Q home improvement store, 18, 214, 236, 238, **238**

Beijing, 17, 20, 75, 78, 88, 93–119, **97, 113, 118,** 121–43, **122, 132, 135, 140, 144,** 145–163, **151, 157, 168,** 170, 177, 184, 186, 189–90, 197, 218–19, 219–220, 223, 234, **235,** 236, **237,** 239, 243, 244, 247, 258, **259,** 260, 262, 269–70, 275, 284, 285–86, 295, **298;** central business district, 136–39, 284; city walls, 95, **97,** 102, 106–108, **111,** 111–114, **113,** 117–119, **118,** 147, 189, 224, 266; cosmology, 94–96; history, 93–106, 147–48; population, 20, 103, 181, 182, 190, 293; redevelopment, 126–31, 143, 149–56, 166–71, 190, 293; sprawl, 190, 195, 198; suburbs, 190, **196, 203,** 206, 209–13, 269, 293; urban planning, 93–96, 98–106, 112–13, 115, 136–39, 147–48, 193–94, 222, 268. *See also* Olympic Games, Summer 2008

Beijing Capital International Airport, 123–24, 282

Belmont, Joseph, 72–73, 80, 84, 88

bicycles, 16, 201, 220–22, 297; bicycle lanes, 220

big box retail stores, 17, 18, 214, 234–36, 238, 239, 265, 293

border, Shenzhen–Hong Kong, 32, 34–35, 45, 231, 232, 245

bowling alleys, 14, 116, 243, 285

Boxer Rebellion, 110; Indemnity Fellowships, 63, 101, 108

Bray, David, 191, 192–93, 203

bridges, 14, 45–48, 54, 71, 77–79, **78,** 80, 223, 233, 285

Broudehoux, Anne-Marie, 162, 260

bund (Shanghai), 61–62, **62,** 65, 73, 76, 77, 81, 87, 91, 156, **335**

Burj Dubai, 86

Buruma, Ian, 254, 260

C

Cantonese, 29, 30–31, 139. *See also* Guangdong Province

Cantopop, 35

Carrefour, 214, 235

cars. *See* automobiles

Castells, Manuel, 50

CCTV Tower, 134–36, **135,** 137, 138, 139, 140, 141

Century Avenue (Shanghai), 79–80

Century Park (Shanghai), 80

chai (demolish), 159–62, **160;** in art, 159–62, **161**

Chang Jiang. *See* Yangtze River

Chang, Wallace, 18

Chang'an, 29, 267–68. *See also* Xi'an

Chang'an Avenue (Beijing), 14, 105, 106, 125, 126, 138, 150, 286

Changsha, 49, 226

Changzhou, 44, 108

Chapel Hill, North Carolina, 35, 51, 222, 294

Charpentier, Jean-Marie, 57, 80, 141

Chen Zhanxiang, 101, 102–03

Chiang Kai-shek, 98, 115, 177, 227, 228

Chicago, 24, 35, 57, 81–84, 110, 137, 183, 192, 281, 285, 287, 292

Chinese Communist Party, 18, 21–22, 27–28, 38, 52, 88, 102, 121, 126, 175, 176–77, 268–69, 276, 279, 293. *See also* communism

Chinese diaspora, 19, 31, 156, 210, 242, 255

Chongqing, **13**, 195, 212, 284, 292

city models. *See* urban planning: exposition centers

civic improvements, 54–55, 57, 66–68, 123–24, 125–26, 131–34, 140–42, 287–92

Cody, Jeffrey W., 269

communism, 27, 31, 177; government, 38, 96, 174, 177, 228, 256, 293–95; movement, 69, 98, 176. *See also* Chinese Communist Party

Confucius (Kong Fuzi), 95, 270

construction industry, 15–16, 22, 183–84, 229, 231, 250, 284

consumerism, 17–18, 217, 218, 241–42, 250–53, 258, 269, 273, 275, 279, 293

Cornell University, 101

corridor urbanization, 18, 44, 234

Costco, 18, 51, 236

Country Garden housing estate, **21, 188**

courtyard houses, 96, 130, 143, 145, 147–49, 150, 191, 297. *See also* Siheyuan

Craciun, Mihai, 31, 42

creative destruction, 15, 151, 159, 163, 254, 266, 282

Cross Bronx Expressway, 16, 24, 229

Cultural Revolution, 18, 31, 35, 54, 100, 114–15, 147, 159, 167, 178–179, 191, 265, 268, 270; propaganda, **181**

D

Dadu. *See* Beijing

Dalian, 20, 33, **185**, 190, **204**; Xinghai district, **221, 278**, 279, 287–90, **288–289**

Danwei, 99, 174, 191–94, 202–03, 253; comparison to suburban development, 202–03

Dazhai (Maoist commune), 18, 54

Dazhalan Street (Beijing). *See* Qianmen District

De Meuron, Pierre, 24, 132–33, 140

demolition, 41, **74**, 77, 100, 105, 127–31, 142–43, **144**, 145–47, 149, 150–56, **151**, 159–71, **168, 172**, 183, 199, **283**, 284, 297, **298**; of city walls, 63, 108–14, 115–16, 118–19, 227. *See also chai* and urban renewal

Deng Xiaoping, 18–19, 21, **26**, 27–28, 30, 32, 33, 35, 37–40, 50, 66, 71, 85, 86, 141, 156, 179, 194, 220, 245

Doctoroff, Tom, 276

Dong Dayou, 66–67, 68

Dongguan, 31, 46, 51, 52, 54–55, 198, 236, 239, 247, 262, **263, 280**, 284, 290, **291**

Dongtang, 301

Dong Xiwen, 96–98

drive-in cinemas, 18, 126, 219, 234, **235,** 239

drive-through restaurants. *See* fast-food restaurants

Dubai, 15, 86, 287

Dutton, Michael, 252–53, 268

dynasties. *See individual names*

E

East Asian Tigers, 19

economy, Chinese, 22, 50, 44–45, 51, 123, 174, 176–78, 187, 191, 197, 200, 226, 231, 232, 296, 298; disparities, 20–21, 182, 184–85, 203, 247, 250, 254, 294; growth, 14, 19–20, 27, 28, 31–32, 35, 40, 44, 54–55, 127, 136, 164, 217, 229, 232, 258, 294, 301; reform, 18, 19, 27, 28–35, 38–40, 42–43, 66, 136, 180, 182, 196–97, 294. *See also* migrant workers, Special Economic Zones

entrepreneurs, 15, 19, 21–22, 32, 116, 138–39, 241, 244, 245, 262, 268, 293–94

environment, 20, 48, 247–48, 294–96; reforms, 207, 297–98; renewable energy, 297–301; sustainability, 24–25, 207, 222, 281, 294–301

F

Fairbank, John King, 58, 59

Fairbank, Wilma, 102

farmers, 20, 28, 32, 175–76, 179, 182, 195, 247, 295

Farrell, Terry (architect), 141

fast-food restaurants, 18, 214, 234, **235,** 239, **239,** 271, 282, 293. *See also* McDonald's

Feng Baohua, 118, **119**

feng shui, 85, 94–96, 148, 279

festival marketplace, 272–73, 276, 279

floating population. *See* migrant workers

Forbidden City, 94, 95–96, 102, 105, 119, 150, 151, 153, 156, 162, 175, 255

foreign investment, 19, 31, 33–34, 35, 43, 50, 71, 72, 110, 184, 196–97

formula racetracks, 88, 219

Foshan, 31, 52, 54, 275

Foster, Norman, 24, 73, 123
Four Olds, 115, 159, 266
Frolic, Michael, 177
Fujian Province, 32, 127
Fuksas, Massimiliano, 73
Futurama, 24, 57
Fuzhou, 20, 32, 33, 59, 235
Fuzi Miao (Nanjing), 270–72, **271**, 273

G

gardens, imperial, 260–62
Gaubatz, Piper, 193–94
Goldenport Motor Park (Beijing), 219
golf, 14, 18, 116, 117, 209, **240**, 243, 244–48, 254, 262, 285
Good Earth, The, 17
Goodrich, E. P., 227
Grand Epoch City, 116–17, **117**, **240**, 262, 267
Grand National Theater ("The Egg"), **140**, 140–43
Greater Shanghai Plan, 66–70, **68**
Great Leap Forward, 106, 114, 174–76, 282
Great Wall, 17, 40, 96, 107, 139, 197, 209, 247, 255; hoax, 110
Gross Domestic Product (GDP): of China, 19, 35, 217; of Guzhen, 52
Guangdong Province, 28–55, 198, 200, 231, 232, 247, 250, 266, 273; history, 29–31
Guangzhou, 20, 30–32, 33, 36, 45, 48, 54, 58, 59, 64, 108–09, 179, 207, 208, 212, 221, 225, 226, 228, 232, 234, 275, 294
Guangzhou–Shenzhen Expressway, 44–46, **47**, 228, 231–34, 262
Guangzhou–Yueyang Expressway, 49
Guiyang, 14, 226
Guizhou Province, 226
Guzhen, 52–54. *See also* Lamp King Tower

H

Han Dynasty, 30, 244
Hangzhou, 22, 29, 59, 219, 227, 260, 279, 290, 297
Hangzhou Automobile City, 219, **220**
Hebei Province, 33, 116, 225, 243, 247
Hefei, 14
Hengyang, 48, 49
heritage urbanism, 269–79; comparison to United States, 269, 272–73
Herzog, Jacques, 24, 132–33, 140
highways, 14, 16, 43–50, 76, 77, 108–09, **111**, 114, 123, 124, 136, 171, 217, **217**, 222–23, 225–27, 228–34, 247, 248, 282, 285; comparison to United States, 16, 45, 222–23, 229, 234; up Mt. Everest, 16; National Trunk Highway System, 16, 49, 222. *See*

also Guangzhou–Shenzhen Expressway, roads
historic preservation, 101–04, 111–14, 115, 130, 131, 151–56, 269, 271, 272, 275–76, 277. *See also* heritage urbanism
Ho Puay-peng, 300
Holiday Town estate (Shanghai), 201
holidays, 35, 105, 187, 242, 272
Home Depot, 18, 51, 214, 265
home improvement, 194, 214, 236, 238, 239, 265, 299
Hong Kong, 19, 29, 30, 31, 32, 34, 35, 36, 41, 42, 45–46, 47, 48, 49, 50, 54, 137, 139, 156, 227, 230–32, 242, 245, 250, 275; Hong Kong Disneyland, 46; Hong Kong International Airport (Chek Lap Kok), 46; Lantau Island, 45–46, 47–48; relationship with mainland China, 35, 50
Hong Xiuquan, 29–30
Hopewell Centre (Hong Kong), 36, 231
Hopewell Holdings/Construction, 48, 231. *See also* Gordon Wu
Household Responsibility System, 31–32, 182
housing, 15, 17, 21, 42, 63, 99, 146, 149–50, 154–55, 163, 167–69, **170**, 175, 179, 190–94, 196, 197, 199, 200, **204**, 275, 284, 286, **299**; affordable, 41, 149–50, 167–69, 194; estates, 14, 18, 91, 190, 195, 200, 202–08, 214, 215, 254, 284, 292–94; marketing of, 18, **21**, 203–04, 205–07, **206**, 209–10, **210**, 211, **212**, **213**, 248; villas, 158, 190, 200, 201, 202, **203**, 205, 207–14, **211**, 292. *See also* Old and Dilapidated Housing Renewal program, *specific estates*
Huangpu River (Shanghai), 59, 61, 65, 67, 70, 71, 76–79, 87, 89, 90, 91, 223; bridges and tunnels, 76–79, **78**, 80, 223
Huang Qiaoling, 22
Huang Rui, 159, **161**
hukou, 175–76, 178, 180, 182, 185–86
Hundred Flowers campaign, 160
hutong, 129, 130, 140, **140**, 143, 147–49, 151–54, 156, 169, 190, 293; destruction, 129, 147, **151**, 153, **168**, **170**, 190, 293, **298**; history, 147, 153, 156

I

IKEA, 18, 214, 236
infrastructure, 42, 43, 44, 47, 48, 63, 66, 80, 110, 123, 124, 154, 166, 179, 187, 195, 225, 231, 234, 285; celebration of, 25, 77–78, 82 222–23. *See also* *specific types*
International Foreign Trade Center (Shenzhen), 36–37, **38**, 281
Isozaki, Arata, 141, 142
Ito, Toyo, 73

J

Jacobs, Jane, 285

Japan, 19, 33, 141, 207, 209, 218, 295; Japanese
  aggression in China, 69, 87, 98, 104, 142, 227–28,
  270, 291

Jardine House, 139

Jardine, Matheson & Company, 58

Jen Lin–Liu, 276

Jiangmen, 31, 52

Jiang Shigao, **33, 38**

Jiangsu Province, 33, 108

Jiangwan (Shanghai), 66–70

Jiang Zemin, 28, 142, 277

Jia Zhangke, 184, 258. *See also The World*

Jinan, 14

Jin Mao Tower, 57, 84–87, **86**, 90, 139

Johnson Fain Partners, 137

Johnson, Hewlett, 109–10, 224

Ju'er Hutong, 150

K

Kohn Pedersen Fox Associates (KPF), **86**, 87–88

Koolhaas, Rem, 134–36, 286–87

Kuomintang, 64, 115

L

Lamp King Tower, 52–54, **53**

land conversion. *See* agricultural land

land leasing, 195–96, 287

Lanzhou, 15

Lee, Tunney, 48

Liang-Chen Plan, 100–01, 102–05

Liang Qichao, 101, 126

Liang Sicheng, 101–04, 106, 107, 108, 111–15, 126,
  162, 266, 268; persecution during the Cultural
  Revolution, 114–15

Lianyungang, 33

Li Conghua, 19

Lin Huiyin, 101, 115

Li Qinfu, 22

Li Shilin. *See* Grand Epoch City

Liulichang Culture Street, 130, 269–70

Logue, Edward, 285

Lotus (retail chain), 18, 234

Lo, Vincent H. S., 275–76, 279

Lujiazui (Shanghai), 71–73, **74**, 79–81, **82–83**, 84,
  85, 91

M

Macau, 30, 250, 262

MacCannell, Dean, 253

MacPherson, Kerrie, 59–60

manufacturing, 19, 22, 50–52, 54, 88, 99, 193, 218,
  300. *See also under* automobiles

Mao era, 18, 27, 93–94, 96–107, 112–16, 118, 149, 160,
  174–79, 182, 186, 191–94, 253

Maoism, 18, 27, 126, 174, 175, 176, 177, 178, 179, 186, 191,
  193, 268, 284, 293. *See also* Mao era

Mao Zedong, 27, 34, 35, 54, **92**, 93–94, 96, 98, 100,
  102, 104–05, 106, 107, 108, 111, 112, 113, 114–16, 117,
  151, 156, 159, 160, 174, 176, 177, 178, 179, 191, 255,
  265–66, 268, 293

Maple Park Motor Cinema (Beijing), 234, **235**

Marxism. *See* Karl Marx

Marx, Karl, 98, 141, 151, 174, 252–53, 269

May Fourth Movement, 62, 65, 101, 105

McDonald's, 18, 214, 235, 239, 271, 282, 285

McDonough, William, 300

McGrath, Charles, 245, 246

McMansions, 17, 202, 207, 213, 214, 215, 292

middle-class, 77, 241–42, 253, 286

migrant workers, 20–21, 22, 40, 41, 54, 127, 146, **173**,
  173–74, 178–87, **185**, 221, 265, 286, 294, 297;
  displaced by development, 128–29; remittances
  from, 187; social isolation of, 184–87, 294; working
  conditions for, 183–84, 294. *See also* economy:
  disparities

millionaires, 21–22, 245, 293

Ming City Wall Park 113, 118–19, **118**

Ming Dynasty, 85, 88, 94, 95, 96, 105, 107, 116, 118, 145,
  146, **147**, 158, 225, 262, 269, 270

Ministry of Construction, 141, 155

Mission Hills Golf Club, 245–46

Mori Corporation, 87

Moses, Robert, 16, 229, 285

Muschamp, Herbert, 252

N

Nanchizi neighborhood, 153–56, **157**, 163, 167

Nanhai, 54

Nanjing, 29, 44, 65, 67, 75, 87, 94, 98, 101, 107, 108,
  145–46, **147**, **172**, **206**, **216**, 227, 235, 236, 238,
  238, 239, **239**, 247, 255, 279, **283**, 284, 290, 295,
  299–300; "1912" shopping district, **277**, 279; city
  walls, 107–08, population, 270; suburbs, 207, 208,
  210, **210**, **212**. *See also* Fuzi Miao

Nanjing Road (Shanghai), 73

Nanjing University, 23

Nantong, 33

National Day (1999), 125–29

Nationalist era, 71, 208, 268, 272, 279; government,
  65, 68, 98, 111, 227 movement, 64, 65

New Jersey Turnpike, 45, 223, 229, 232, 234

new towns, 25, 55, 70–71, 88–91, 139, 178, 282. *See*

also "One City, Nine Towns"
New York, 15, 16, 24, 27, 35, 40, 49, 59, 81, 84, 102,
    115, 123, 124, 136, 178, 183, 190, 195, 198, 199, 206,
    222, 227, 229, 231, 272, 275, 279, 287; World's
    Fairs, 24, 124
Ningbo, 32, 33, 47, 59
Nixon, Richard, 34
Nouvel, Jean, 73
Novgorod, 103

O
Old and Dilapidated Housing Renewal program
    (ODHR), 149–50, 163, 167
Old Beijing Miniature Landscape Park, 145, **146**
Olds, Kris, 72
Olympic Games, Summer 2008, 16, 47, 54, 78, 119,
    121–24, 125, 127, 129–34, 141, 142, 292; compared
    to the Columbian exhibition, 292; compared to
    National Day, 1999, 125; Humanistic Olympic
    Cultural Relics Protection Program, 119, 130;
    National Aquatics Centre ("Water Cube"), 131, 132,
    133, 134; National Stadium ("Bird's Nest"), **120**,
    131, **132**, **133**, 132–34, 140, 142; Olympic Green,
    123, 129, 131–32, 134, 142; Olympic Village, 131;
    redevelopment as a result of, 123–24, 129–31;
    venues, 123, 131, 132–34
"One City, Nine Towns" (Shanghai), 88–90
Opium Wars, 29, 30, 33, 58, 261
Orange County, California, 212
Orange County housing estate, 212–13, 214
Oriental Plaza (Beijing), 128, 150, 286
Ove Arup & Partners, 134, 136

P
pagodas, 67, 85–86, 139, 227, 260, 267, 290
Pan Shiyi, 138–39, **138**, 293
Panyu, 52, 54
Pearl of the Orient (TV tower), 57, 73–75, **75**, **76**, 79,
    81, **82**, 84, 87
Pearl River (Zhu Jiang), 28, 45, 46, 47, 48
Pearl River Delta, 18, 28–32, **29**, 40, 43–55, 184,
    198, 208, 212, 227, 231–32, 233, 245, 247, 262,
    290; history, 30–32; population, 49–50. See also
    individual cities
Pedersen, William E., 87
People's Liberation Army, 27, 36, 39, 102, 116, 293
Perrault, Dominique, 73
Philadelphia, 14, 49, 153–54
Piano, Renzo, 73
Ping'an Avenue (Beijing), 126–27, 167
Pitch, Anthony, 93
Polo, Marco, 189–90

population statistics, China, 14, 20, 123, 174, 176, 179,
    180, 181–82, 185, 187, 191, 235, 241–42, 258, 286,
    294
Porteous, J. Douglas, 171
Portman, John, 139
property rights, 13, 43, 77, 167
Pudong (Shanghai), 24, 62, 65, 71–88, 90, 91, 137,
    195, 223; "Great Port of Pudong" plan, 65; "Head
    of the Dragon," 71, 81; depictions in film, 81. See
    also Shanghai
Pudong International Airport, 284

Q
Qianmen District (Beijing), 95, 130–31, 269–70
Qingdao, 33, **76**, 207, 208
Qing Dynasty, 30, 39, 59, 62, 101, 110, 130, 145, 146,
    147, 153, 156, 158, 208, 261, 269, 270
Qinhuangdao, 33
Quanzhou, 59

R
real estate market, 42–43, 149–50, 155, 163–64,
    174–75, 194–96, 204–14
recreation, 242, 243–47, 287
redevelopment, 13–14, 15, 71, 88, 98–101, 102–05, 108–
    09, 126–31, 143, 146–47, 149–156, 160, 162, 164–171,
    194–96, 269–70, 275–76, 279, 282–84, **283**, 286,
    293; comparison with American urban renewal, 15,
    163–166, 282; displacement of residents by, 15, 16,
    77, 126–31, 146–47, 149–50, 154–56, 166–71, 190,
    196, 222–23, 275–76, 284, 286, 293; psychological
    effects of, 162, 166–71. See also urban renewal
Red Guards, 21, 22, 114–15, 266, 268, 270
retail, large scale. See "big box" retail stores
roads, 16, 43–44, 48, 60, 64, 67, 100, 109, 190, 205,
    217, 219, 220–22, 224, 225–28, 231, 232, 234, 282;
    history, 225–28; replacing city walls, 63, 108–11,
    111, 114; ring roads, 16, 45, 49, 76–77, 78, 100,
    114, 123, 127, 137, 214 222, 223, 236, 284. See also
    corridor urbanization, highways, specific roads
Rogers, Richard, 73
rotating restaurants, 36–37
Rouse, James, 272–73, 276, 279

S
satellite imagery, 17, 44, 45, 70, 197–98
satellite new towns. See new towns
Scheeren, Ole, 134
Schell, Orville, 114
Schumpeter, Joseph, 151. See also creative destruction
Shanghai, 17, 18, 20, 24, 30, 33, 44, 46–47, 48, 49, 54,
    57–91, **61**, **82–83**, 140–41, 176, 179, 182, 183, 195,

202, 205, 207, 208, 218, 220–21, 223, 224, 226–27, 239, 243, 244, 245, 247, 269, 270, 275–77, 282, 292, 299; architecture, 57–58, 62, 73, 81, 84–86, 139; bridges and tunnels, 71, 76–79, **78**, 223; city walls, 63, 108–09; construction, 15–16, 183; depictions in film, 81; foreign settlements, 60–66; history, 58–70; new towns, 70–71, 88–90; population, 59, 71, 88, 146–47, 180–81, 275; redevelopment, 15, 71, 146–47, 284, 286; sprawl, 190, 198; suburbs, 44, 201, 210, 211; urban planning, 55, 63, 66–73, 79–81, 191–94, 202. *See also* Greater Shanghai Plan, Lujiazui, Pudong

Shanghai Urban Planning Exposition Center, **56**, 57–58, **90**, 90–91

Shanghai World Exposition 2010, 147, 292

Sheng Qi, 162

Shenzhen, 23, 24, 27, 31, 32, 34–43, **38**, 45, 46–47, 52, 54, 59, 77, 245, 248, 254, 255, 256, **257**, 258; construction, 27, **33**, 36–37, **38**, 281; economic growth, 20, 32, 34–35, 231–32; population, 35, 40–41; "Shenzhen tempo," 37, 281; suburbs, 207, 210; urbanization, 36, 40–43; urban planning, 41–43; urban villages, 41, 294

Shikumen, 275

Shinohara, Kazuo, 73

shopping malls, 14, 18, 20, 45, 54, 150,167, 183, 186, 190, 200, 219, **220**, 234, 236, **237**, 238, 248, 250, 252, 262–65, **263**, **264**, 273, 276, 284, 285, 293, 294; origins in Parisian arcades, 250–53. *See also specific malls*

Shunde, 54, 184, 250

Siheyuan, 96, 126, 143, 147–50, 152–54, 156–58, 159, 210, 275; history, 147–48; modern incarnations, 150, 156, **157**, 158, 210; restoration, 152, 156–58

Silk Road, 267

Singapore, 19

Sit, Victor, 100

Skidmore, Owings & Merrill, 84

skiing, 243, 244

skylines, 16, 36, 72, 73, 75, 79, 81, **82–83**, 84, 91, 98, 137, 207, 231, 263, 287

skyscrapers, 14, 20, 36–37, **38**, 57, 72, 73–75, 79, 81–88, **82–83**, **86**, 91, 134–36, **135**, 137, 281, 294; history, 24, 81–84; relationship to traditional Chinese architecture, 85–86; symbolism, 85–86. *See also specific buildings*

Smith, Adrian, 84, 85, 86

Smolenska, 103

socialism, 34, 104, 176, 192–93, 266, 293–94; socialist city, 98–100, 174–75, 191–94; "socialism with Chinese characteristics," 28, 31. *See also Danwei*

SOHO China, 138–39, 209, 293

Song Dynasty, 101, 152, 270

South China Mall, 54, 236, 262–65, **263**, **264**

South Korea, 19

Soviet Union, 28, 106, 113, 174, 175, 176–77, 178, 228, 248–49; influence on Chinese government, 98, 174, 175, 176, 177; influence on urban design, 75, 98–100, 107, 112, 114–15, 191, 194; relationship with China, 34, 98–100, **99**, 102–04, 114, 176–77, 178. *See also under* urban planners

Special Economic Zones (SEZs), 19, 32–36, 40, 42, 43, 47, 66, 71, 197, 245, 255. *See also* economy, Chinese

Speer, Albert, 131–32

Speer, Albert Jr., 88, 131–134

Splendid China, 254–56, 258, 267

sprawl, 17–18, 41, 43–45, 91, 136–37, 149, 164–65, 179, 190–91, 194–95, 197–98, 234, 238–39, 292–93; comparison to United States, 165, 190, 194, 195, 202, 292–93; factors of, 43, 191–97, 202, 217. *See also* corridor urbanization, suburbs

squares, public, 14, 54, 55, 67, 100, 105–06, 268, 279, 285, 287–90, **288–89**. *See also* Tiananmen Square

Starbucks, 18, 206, 235, 276

Stewart, Charles T., 164

Stilwell, Joseph, 98, 227

"Story of Springtime," 27

strip development. *See* corridor urbanization, sprawl

stubborn nail, **12**, 13, 155, 162, 284

suburbs, 17, 44, 45, 88–90, 147, 158, 164–65, 169, 189–215, 217, 234–39, 248, 253, 263, 292–93; characteristics, 200–05, 238, 292–93; comparison to United States, 198–202, 204–05, 238–39, 292–93; growth, 190, 292–93; history, 189–90, 207–08; in popular culture, 214–15. *See also* sprawl

Sudjic, Deyan, 123–24

Sun Yat-sen, 30, 47, 65, 67, 71, 126, 127, 224, 255, 279, 290

sustainability, 24–25, 207, 222, 281, 294–301. *See also* environment

Suzhou, 59, 158, 209–10, 227, 260, 261, 297

T

Taiping Rebellion, 29–30, 62

Taiwan, 19, 98, 235, 242, 250

Tang Dynasty, 30, 249, 267–68, 270, 290

Tang Paradise theme park (Xi'an), 267–68, **267**

Tao Ho, 80

theme parks, 14, 18, 116–17, **117**, 145, 214, 219, **240**, 246, 248–58, **249**, **251**, **252**, 252–58, **261**, 301; historical, 255, 265–69, **267**; miniature, 145, **146**, 254–56, 259, 260–61, 262; precursors to, 116,

250–52, 258–62; "world parks," 254–58, **257,** **259,** 262. See also shopping malls, specific parks

theme towns, 88–90, 209, 210–14, **211, 212, 213.** See also "One City, Nine Towns," new towns

Third Front (urban dispersal), 177–78

Three Gorges Dam, 14, 255–56

Tiananmen (Gate of Heavenly Peace), 94, 95, 96, 100, 101, 105, 111, 113, 116, 143, 156, 159, 162

Tiananmen Square, 98, 105–106, 113, 125–26, 127, 130, 131, 136, 140–41, 142, 155, 167, 193, 234, **235,** 285, 290; protests, 38, 39, 125, 126; renovation for National Day, 125–26, 243

Tianjin, 20, 33, 179, 198, 207, 243, 249, 258, 261

Timmerman, Kenneth, 256

Todd, Oliver J., 225–27

tourism, 16, 54, 73, 77, 123, 128, 130, 143, 152, 242–44, 254, 255, 256, 262, 266, 267, 269, 270, 271–72, 273, 285, 301

township and village enterprises, 32, 52

transportation, 48, 68, 99, 187 193–94, 197, 217–39, 282, 297; commuting, 17, 99, 169, 194, 201, 218; public transportation, 17, 169, 200, 201, 298, 301; transportation planning, 127, 221, 222. See also automobiles, bicycles

treaty ports, 33–34, 59, 63–64, 207–08, 224, 225

Tsinghua University, 23, 102, 115, 141, 150, 153, 154–55, 214, 244

Tsin, Michael, 63

tunnels, 14, 46, 71, 76–79, 114, 229

U

United States, comparison with China, 14–17, 19, 21, 24–25, 44, 49, 77, 165–66, 178, 180, 183, 186, 192, 194; migration of workers, 182–83, 198–205, 223, 235, 281–82, 284–85, 291, 292–93; suburbanization, 163–65, 198–201, 202, 204–05. See also urban renewal

University of Pennsylvania, 67, 101, 154

urbanization, 31–32, 41, 44. 50, 171, 174, 177, 180, 194, 195, 198, 281–84; comparison with United States, 180, 281–82, 286; scale, 15, 50, 90–91, 105, 123, 124, 165–68, 171, 178, 190, 197–98, 284–90; speed, 15–16, 35–37, 151, 190, 198, 281–84

urban planners, 80, 155, 222, 282; Chinese, 18. 22, 42, 63, 66–68, 76, 79–80, 100–04, 108, 113–14, 115, 116, 137, 154, 169, 273; foreign, 23, 72–73, 79, 88, 104, American, 23, 66, 67, 80, 96, 165, 208, 227, 276; Soviet, 98–100, 102–04, 107, 112, 113–14; See also Liang Sicheng, specific names

urban planning, 57, 63, 67, 90, 127; 128, 174, 179, 192, 193, 282–84, 285, 287; classical Chinese, 94, 116, 148; conservation, 151–54; exposition centers, **56,**
57–58, **90,** 90–91, **203;** Soviet principles, 98–100, 107, 191, 194. See also specific cities

urban renewal, 71, 129–31, 146–47, 155, 166–67, 171, 190, 293; American, 15, 24, 163–66, 272, 282. See also redevelopment

urban sprawl. See sprawl

urban villages, 41, 193, 294

V

vacation homes, 243

Vanke (China Vanke Company, Ltd.), 201, 204, 210, 293

Visser, Robin, 162

Vogel, Ezra, 34

Voronin, Nikolai N., 103

W

walls, city, 41, 63, 89, 95, **97,** 102, 107, **109,** 109–10, 111, **113,** 115, 116, 117–18, **118,** 130, 147, 189, 191, 224, 270; destruction of, 63, 106, 108–09, 111–14, 227, 266, 273; in Europe, 110–11; history of, 107–08, 116; reconstruction of, 118–19, **119;** reproduction of, 116–17, **117,** 260. See also under Beijing, Shanghai. See also Grand Epoch City, Great Wall, Ming City Wall Park

Wal-Mart, 18, 51, 214, 235–36

Wang Jinsong, 159–60

Wang Shi, 293

Wangfujing Street (Beijing), 128, 137, 155

Wedemeyer, Albert C., 98, 227–28

Wenzhou, 32, 236

Window of the World, 254, 256–58, **257;** in film, 258

Wong & Ouyang, 141

Wood, Benjamin, 275–79

Woodall, Pam, 19

Woo, Han-Veng, 108

World, The (Shi Jie), 184, 258

World Financial Center, 57, **86,** 87–88

Wu Hung, 96–98, 104–06, 161

Wu Liangyong, 94, 102, 104, 150, 152, 154

Wu Ping ("stubborn nail"), **12,** 13, 284

Wu, Sir Gordon Y. S., 36, 45–49, 228–34, **230,** 262

Wuxi, 14, 211, **211,** 249–50, **251, 252,** 260

X

Xiamen, 32, 33, 59; Xiamen University, 18, 245

Xi'an, 107, 224–25, **267,** 267–68, 290, 295, 297, **300.** See also Chang'an

Xidan (Beijing), 137

Xinghai, see Dalian

Xing Tong, 139

Xinhua News Agency, 128, 247–48

Xinjiang Province, 127, 128
Xinjiang Village (Beijing), 127–28, **129**
Xintiandi, 275–79; similar projects, **277**, 279

Y
Yangtze River (Chang Jiang), 14, 46, 49, 55, 59, 66,
    71, 89, 242, 255, 270, 294–95, 301; Yangtze Delta,
    46, 190, 242
Yantai, 33
yao dong (vernacular housing), 297, **299**
Yao Ming, 22
Yeh, Anthony G. O., 42, 43
Ying Zao Fa Shi, 101–02
Yuan Dynasty, 94, 95, 107, 147, 225, 269
Yuanming Yuan, 116, 260–62; housing estate, 209
Yueyang, 49

Z
Zengguang Street (Beijing). *See* Xinjiang Village
Zhang Bo (architect), 102
Zhang Bo (developer), 212–13
Zhang Dali, 161–62
Zhangjiang, 32
Zhang Jinqiu, 102, 267–68
Zhang Nian, 162
Zhang Xin, 138–39
Zhang Yuan, 162
Zhang Yuchen, 22, **23**
Zhao Liang, 162
Zhao Shen, *see Dong Dayou*
Zhejiang Province, 32, 46, 52, 127, 219, 243, 268
Zhejiang Village (Beijing), 127
Zhongshan, 18, 31, 46, 48, 52, 54, 268, 273–75, **274**
Zhongshan University, 266
Zhou Dynasty, 95, 225
Zhou Enlai, 98, 102, 141
Zhuhai, 32, 45, 46, 47, 48, **261**, 262
Zhu Rongji, 72, 79–80